Reform and Retrenchment

Reform and Retrenchment

A Century of Efforts to Fix Primary Elections

ROBERT G. BOATRIGHT

OXFORD
UNIVERSITY PRESS

Oxford University Press is a department of the University of Oxford. It furthers the University's objective of excellence in research, scholarship, and education by publishing worldwide. Oxford is a registered trade mark of Oxford University Press in the UK and certain other countries.

Published in the United States of America by Oxford University Press
198 Madison Avenue, New York, NY 10016, United States of America.

© Oxford University Press 2024

All rights reserved. No part of this publication may be reproduced, stored in a retrieval system, or transmitted, in any form or by any means, without the prior permission in writing of Oxford University Press, or as expressly permitted by law, by license, or under terms agreed with the appropriate reproduction rights organization. Inquiries concerning reproduction outside the scope of the above should be sent to the Rights Department, Oxford University Press, at the address above.

You must not circulate this work in any other form
and you must impose this same condition on any acquirer.

Library of Congress Cataloging-in-Publication Data
Names: Boatright, Robert G., author.
Title: Reform and retrenchment : a century of efforts to fix
primary elections / Robert G. Boatright.
Description: New York, NY : Oxford University Press, [2024] |
Includes bibliographical references and index.
Identifiers: LCCN 2023049368 (print) | LCCN 2023049369 (ebook) |
ISBN 9780197774083 (hardback) | ISBN 9780197774106 (epub) | ISBN 9780197774113
Subjects: LCSH: Primaries—United States—History—20th century. |
Election law—United States—History—20th century. | Elections—
United States—History—20th century. | Political parties—
United States—History—20th century. | United States—Politics and
government—History—20th century.
Classification: LCC JK2071.B64 2024 (print) | LCC JK2071 (ebook) |
DDC 324.273/0154—dc23/eng/20240110
LC record available at https://lccn.loc.gov/2023049368
LC ebook record available at https://lccn.loc.gov/2023049369

DOI: 10.1093/oso/9780197774083.001.0001

Printed by Integrated Books International, United States of America

Contents

List of Illustrations   vii
Acknowledgments   xi

1. Introduction   1

PART I. THE MIDDLE YEARS: PRIMARY ELECTION REFORMS, 1928–1970

2. Reform or Retrenchment?: An Overview of Changes in Primary Election Laws, 1928–1970   23
3. The Direct Primary and the Decline of the Progressive Movement   60
4. Hostile Takeover: Nonparty Group Capture of Primaries   83
5. Defective Primary Laws   108
6. Primaries and Partisan Advantage   143
7. Are Southern Primaries Different?   173

PART II. WHAT THE HISTORY OF PRIMARY ELECTIONS CAN TELL US ABOUT CONTEMPORARY REFORM IDEAS

8. Contemporary Primary Reform Efforts   203
9. Why Primary Reforms Rarely Work   227
10. The Future of the Direct Primary   279

Notes   293
Bibliography   299
Index   319

Illustrations

Figures

2.1.	Primary rule changes by year and direction, 1928–1970	44
2.2.	Primary rule changes by year and direction in Progressive states, 1928–1970	45
2.3.	Primary rule changes by year and direction in Nonpartisan League states, 1928–1970	49
2.4.	Primary rule changes by year and direction in states with defective primary laws, 1928–1970	52
5.1.	Percent of Democratic seats in the Michigan House and Senate, 1900–1970	127
5.2.	Percent of Democratic seats in the Alaska and Hawaii Lower Chambers, 1958–1970	131
5.3.	Percent of Democratic seats in the New Mexico House and Senate, 1900–1970	134
5.4.	Percent of Democratic seats in the Indiana House and Senate, 1900–1970	138
6.1.	Primary rule changes, selected states, by year and level of party competition, 1900–1970	149
6.2.	Changes in legislative competitiveness by region, 1900–1970	158
6.3.	Rule changes for a separate group of selected states, 1900–1970	164
7.1.	Primary rule changes by year and direction in Southern states, 1928–1970	185
8.1.	Types of legislative introductions by cycle, 2000–2020	214
8.2.	Direction of legislative introductions by cycle, 2000–2020	217
8.3.	Direction of legislative introductions by sponsor party and cycle, 2010–2020	223
9.1.	Open seat primary fractionalization by party, 1970–2018	264
9.2.	Challenger primary fractionalization by party, 1970–2018	265
9.3.	Primary challenges to incumbents and general election turnover, 1970–2020	267
9.4.	Primary challenges to incumbents by party, 1970–2020	268
9.5.	Ideological primary challenges to incumbents, 1970–2020	269

Tables

2.1.	Coding of Changes in Primary Laws	35
2.2.	Hypotheses Regarding Changes in Primary Laws and Variable Measurement	39
2.3.	States with Significant Nonpartisan League Activity	41
2.4.	States Described in Contemporary Literature as Having Defective Primary Laws	43
2.5.	Primary Law Changes in Progressive Reform States	46
2.6.	Primary Law Changes in Nonpartisan League States	50
2.7.	Primary Law Changes in States with Defective Primary Laws	53
5.1.	States Described in Literature of the Time as Having Defective Primary Laws	118
5.2.	Categorization of Responses to Defective Primary Laws	119
5.3.	Categorization of Defective State Primary Practices	122
6.1.	State Competitiveness and the Direction of Rule Changes, 1942–1970	156
6.2.	Direction of Rule Changes by Partisanship and Region, 1938–1970	157
6.3.	Decade-by-Decade Comparison of Reform and Non-Reform States, by Legislative Competitiveness, 1930–1970	159
7.1.	Primary Law Changes in Southern States, 1928–1968	184
7.2.	Adoption of the Direct Primary and the Primary Runoff in Southern States	196
8.1.	Subjects of Introduced Primary Legislation, 2001–2020	213
8.2.	Introduced Legislation by Party of Sponsor, 2011–2020	216
8.3.	Selected Legislative Introductions by State, 2001–2020	218
8.4.	Legislative Introductions by Direction, Party of Sponsor, and Majority Status of Sponsor, 2011–2020	221
8.5.	Legislative Introductions by Bill Type, Party of Sponsor, and Majority Status of Sponsor, 2011–2020	222
9.1.	Primary vs. General Election Voter Traits, 2010	238
9.2.	Primary vs. General Election Voters' Preferences, within Parties	239
9.3.	State Primary Electorate Ideology Variation Summarized	241
9.4.	Primary vs. General Election Voter Ideology, by State/Primary Type	244
9.5.	Primary vs. General Election Voter Traits, 2014 and 2018	246

9.6. Primary vs. General Election Voters' Preferences, within Parties,
     2014 and 2018   248
9.7. Primary vs. General Election Voter Ideology, by State/Primary Type,
     2014 and 2018   249
9.8. Correlations between Level of Primary Competition and General
     Election Results   262
9A.1. State-by-State Voter Ideology Means   272

Acknowledgments

I had the good fortune to get enough compliments about a paper I wrote about congressional primaries in 2007 that I have wound up making the study of congressional primaries—and in particular, the relationship between political polarization and primary competition—a major thing that I do as a political scientist. One of the hazards of studying contemporary elections, however, is that after every election I tend to be exhausted, and I tend to crave doing research that enables me to ignore the vitriol that characterizes contemporary American elections. This project began, therefore, as a way to do some research that did not require me to pay attention to the news. In other words, studying the things contemporary politicians say about each other is scary. Studying the things that politicians of the 1920s said about each other can be entertaining. This book is the culmination of over a decade of efforts to avoid contemporary politics.

Despite that escapist impulse, I am hopeful that this book can contribute to contemporary debates. During the time I have been working on this book I have taken part in many discussions of how to make American elections better—discussions sponsored by, among others, the National Institute for Civil Discourse, the Hewlett Foundation, the Skoll Foundation, Unite America, and other groups. Part of the lesson I hope readers will draw from this book is that many contemporary reform ideas have been tried in the past, with mixed results. I am optimistic that there are ways to improve American elections, but we can only do this if we know the history of elections and respect the diverse ways in which the American states have experimented with electoral politics.

An earlier version of the material in Chapter 2 was originally published in *Polity* (Boatright 2019), under the title "Retrenchment or Reform? Changes in Primary Election Laws, 1928–70." I thank *Polity* and the University of Chicago Press for permission to reprint this material, and I also thank the journal's anonymous reviewers for their comments on the original piece, in particular on the best way to present the figures used in Chapter 2.

Many of the sources in Chapter 4 are taken from four different collections: the Nonpartisan League Archives and the John Miller Baer Papers, both held at the North Dakota State University Institute for Regional Studies in Fargo; the National Nonpartisan League Files, held at the Minnesota Historical Society and available on microfiche; and the A. C. Townley Speeches and Related Materials Collection, held at the University of North Dakota, Grand Forks. In several instances, newspaper clippings and other correspondence in these files are not marked by date or are missing other identifying information. Research at these archives was supported by a grant from the Everett C. Dirksen Congressional Center. I thank the NDSU staff for assistance in using the archives.

Research for Chapter 6 at the Hiram Johnson Archives, Bancroft Library, University of California, Berkeley, was supported by Clark University's Francis Harrington Fund and the June Patron Fund. I thank the Bancroft Library for providing access to these materials. I also thank Kathy and Reed Rowan for hosting me while I did my research at Berkeley.

The deep dive into literature on contemporary state politics in Chapter 8 was made much easier by the feedback I received from National Institute for Civil Discourse colleagues Ted Celeste, Brent Hill, and Makayla Meacham about state legislative politics.

Chapter 9 draws in part on a research study on primary election timing, supported by the William and Flora Hewlett Foundation. A much earlier version of this research was published as part of the *Routledge Handbook of Primary Elections* (Boatright and Moscardelli 2018). I thank Routledge for permission to reprint this material, and I thank my coauthor Vin Moscardelli for his contribution to this project.

I have presented drafts of the chapters of this book at many different conferences, including meetings of the American Political Science Association, the Midwest Political Science Association, the Southern Political Science Association, and over a five-year stretch of meetings of the New England Political Science Association. I have lost track of all of the copanelists and panel discussants I have had at this meeting, but I have benefited greatly from the opportunity to discuss this work at so many venues. I received particularly helpful feedback on Chapter 7 from participants in the University of Connecticut American Politics Workshop and the Congress and History Conference. I also have had many instructive conversations with colleagues on the International Political Science Association's Research Council on Political Finance and Political Corruption, all of which helped me to understand the comparative literature on elections that I draw on in Chapter 5. I will certainly leave out some of the people who offered comments in these various venues, but I do recall particularly useful conversations about the book with Molly McGrath, Julia Azari, Ray La Raja, Chris Galdieri, Seth Masket, Daniel Klinghard, Caroline Tolbert, Ned Foley, and Richard Pildes.

I thank Angela Chnapko and the staff at Oxford University Press for shepherding this book to publication. I thank my Clark University colleagues, and in particular my occasional coauthor Valerie Sperling. I also received research help from Clark student research assistants Rebecca Hadik and Brittany Klug.

Most of all, I thank my family for their tolerance for this project, and in particular I thank Audrey for her love, support, and perseverance.

1
Introduction

In February 2021, during the first weeks of the 117th Congress, the member of Congress who arguably received the most media attention was newly elected Republican congresswoman Marjorie Taylor Greene. Greene had won an open seat primary in a solidly Republican district in rural Georgia, despite (or maybe because of) her support for the bizarre QAnon conspiracy theory. In January 2021, details had emerged regarding Greene's support for executing Democratic leaders; her belief that the Parkland, Florida, school shooting was a hoax; threats she had made against a survivor of that school shooting; and her claim that "Jewish space lasers" had caused wildfires in 2020 in California (DeBonis and Kane 2021). Greene's comments prompted calls for her expulsion and a tense, party-line vote in which Greene was stripped of her committee assignments.

Congress has always had its share of oddballs, and Greene is by no means representative of her party or of Congress in general. Yet the fact that someone with such odd beliefs could win an election may say something about the flaws in our method of selecting candidates. She is also not the only recently elected member of Congress who defeated other candidates who are more conventionally qualified; one could make similar arguments about some Democratic members of Congress and, of course, about the process that led to Donald Trump's election as president in 2016. It is perhaps natural to blame our system of primary elections for such results when one dislikes the nominees, just as it is natural to celebrate the system when it yields candidates to one's liking. Of course there are also some who would complain when primary elections merely reinforce the status quo—when relatively conventional, uncharismatic politicians win primaries characterized by low voter turnout and little competition. These complaints are nothing new; they have been with us since the advent of the direct primary in the early years of the twentieth century.

This, then, is the dilemma inherent in American primary elections: in theory they look appealing, and at times they produce candidates we like. However, it is also easy to blame them for outcomes we don't like, and when they do inevitably disappoint us, history tells us there is really not very much we can do about that. Many scholars have documented the excitement that surrounded the establishment of the direct primary during the 1900s and 1910s, and many others have explored the alleged failings of twenty-first-century primary elections. The task of this book is to explore the time in between those two moments, to provide a history of primary election reforms. What happened once the enthusiasm surrounding the adoption of primary elections wore off? How have political parties, politicians, and state governments sought to reform primaries? The most common historical narrative has been one of retrenchment; political parties, in this story, gained control over the primary process and worked to ensure that it mostly met their needs. As I will show, however, no such retrenchment occurred. The history of primary elections is in many ways a history of failure—not the failure of the direct primary, but the failure of efforts to change the primary. Although states have tinkered with the mechanics of their primary election systems for a century, primaries have neither lived up to the hopes of their early proponents nor reflected the fears of their detractors. This does not mean, however, that there is no history to be told. The study of primary elections can help us learn much about the enduring legacy of Progressive ideas, about regional political trends, and about the resilience of parties. Understanding this history of failure, furthermore, is a first step toward redirecting the attention of would-be reformers to more fruitful approaches to changing American politics.

Orphans of the Progressive Movement

It is difficult to overestimate the excitement that surrounded the establishment of primary elections. A national conference was convened in New York in 1898 for the purpose of discussing primaries. The conference featured the mayors of several major cities; religious leaders; the presidents and chancellors of the nation's best universities; and leaders of various labor unions, chambers of commerce, and municipal organizations. Special issues of the two leading political science journals of the day, the *Annals of the American Academy of Political and Social Sciences* and the *American Political Science Review*, were devoted to discussions of the merits and potential problems of primaries. In sum, thirty-three articles about primaries were published in these two journals between 1902 and 1931. And at least two compendia of articles on primary elections were published to serve as resources for debates among high school students (Fanning 1905; Beman 1926).

Not all that was written about primary elections was positive, but most of the material was at least cautiously optimistic. And some of what was written went beyond cautious optimism to promises of wholesale change in the nature of American politics. Political bosses would disappear, Americans would choose among candidates of high integrity, elections would feature vigorous debates about the issues that matter the most to voters, and voters would be newly empowered to make meaningful choices about the direction of the country. Years later, political scientist V. O. Key (1956, 92) would describe the movement advocating primaries as having an "evangelical tone" that made opposition virtually impossible. By the 1920s, all but three American states had introduced primaries for most elective offices.

This is a remarkable level of success for a reform that was expected by some to shake up the political status quo. It is also a suspicious level of success; it is rare to find other examples in American political history of political reforms that spread so rapidly. Certainly none of the other Progressive reforms of the era—the initiative and referendum, nonpartisan elections, recall elections, the city manager form of government, and merit selection of judges, to name a few—were so quickly or widely adopted. While Charles Merriam, the era's leading authority on primaries, attributed this success to the innate appeal of the idea (Merriam and Overacker 1928), British political scientist Alan Ware (2002) argued much later that primaries spread because the parties found that they did not object to them as much as they had expected: primaries gave parties the ability to avoid the often thankless task of placating rival factions, and parties quickly found that if they really wanted to ensure that their preferred candidate received the nomination, they could usually do so. While the logic of Ware's claim seems to fit better with late twentieth-century theories about political parties, some comparisons of the two perspectives have found that Merriam, in fact, may still have the stronger argument (Lawrence, Bowler, and Donovan 2013).

This is also a level of success that should have prompted some ruminations about what the negative consequences of primaries might be. Many observers simply asked whether voters were truly qualified to pass judgment on so many candidates. Others worried about the sorts of candidates and campaigns that would emerge. The 1898 conference featured several speakers who warned that the primary would create a different, and arguably inferior, sort of politician. Some participants argued that primaries would yield timid candidates who would never risk offending anyone or discussing substantive ideas, and others warned that primaries would reward divisive, demagogic politicians who would prey upon uneducated and largely apolitical voters. The visiting Russian political scientist Moisei Ostrogorski (1902, 265–269), an aspiring latter-day de Tocqueville, warned of the folly of allowing the state to define and regulate parties, arguing that this would render parties unable to adapt to changing political circumstances or to adopt new issues. The eminent scholar of political parties Henry Jones Ford (1909) warned that primaries would merely exchange one group of politicians for another, while at the same time increasing the size of the political class and confusing voters with a surfeit of choices. P. Orman Ray (1926) worried that primary elections would spawn a new class of political professionals. More elections would require more expertise in elections, and a whole new breed of campaign consultant would be born. William Bennett Munro (1926) claimed simply that primaries would promote insincerity in politics. After people had lost the nomination, they would be expected to turn around and endorse the person who had defeated them. Whatever harsh things they had said during the primary election would have to be taken back.

In the broadside *Repeal the Direct Primary*, Bernard Freyd (1926) combined all of these arguments, deriding the establishment of primaries as a meaningless experiment. Freyd characterized the advocates of primaries by quoting British novelist G. K. Chesterton's characterization (from *The Victorian Age*) of one who would seek reform for its own sake:

> As a philosopher he had only two thoughts, and neither of them are true. The first was that politics as an experimental science, must go on improving, along with clocks, pistols or penknives, by the mere accumulation of experiment and variety. (cited in Freyd 1926, 60)

Despite the eloquence of Chesterton's point, Freyd's argument often teetered into vitriol. Yet Freyd ultimately argued that the American people were better than the election system they had created and would come to their senses. It is natural among U.S. states, he claimed, to experiment with democratic procedures, but Americans also "idealize our hard-headed practicality" (Freyd 1926, 64). Now that the "swashbuckling melodrama performed by the Progressives" had subsided, it was time to have a more honest appraisal of what the direct primary had wrought.

Three features of the pro- and antiprimary arguments should be apparent to the modern reader. First, the rosiest predictions about the introduction of primary elections were certainly overblown. By the 1970s, some scholars had noted that primaries had weakened the parties. But there is little evidence that they significantly changed the composition of Congress, the engagement of voters, or the conduct of national politics. If Congress is different today, it seems like a stretch to blame this difference on century-old reforms.

Second, the arguments against primaries sound remarkably similar to complaints raised about primary elections today. These views are easily reconciled with a strain of British conservative thought shared by writers such as Edmund Burke and Michael Oakeshott—a wariness of change for its own sake—as well as with American appeals to the wisdom of the Founders. Yet at the same time, they can be connected to complaints made by many contemporary observers who would profess to have little in common with traditional conservatism. It is not uncommon today to find, for instance, arguments that the patchwork of state primary laws enables some candidates to "game the system," and that the proverbial "smoke-filled rooms" of the late nineteenth century tended to produce politicians who knew how to get results. In a contemporary Washington characterized by steadfast refusals to negotiate over almost anything, there are some on both the political left and right who recall with fondness the ability of lawmakers of prior decades to engage in "transactional politics," and who blame contemporary primary elections for doing away with those sorts of politicians (see, e.g., Rauch 2015; Walter 2015).

Third, however, it is hard to imagine a time when the subject of primary elections drew so much attention. Although (as we shall see in Chapter 8) in some states legislators have called for eliminating primaries for some offices, there is no movement to abolish them altogether. In the academy there are many on the left (Milkis and Mileur 1999) and the right (Marini and Masugi 2005; Watson 2009) who have argued that Progressive Era reforms were ultimately either contradictory or harmful, but in these accounts the primary has escaped the sort of criticism reserved for other, less widely adopted, changes. Primaries are here to stay, but they have no advocates. There is no longer a compelling theoretical argument in their favor, if there ever was one to begin with.

When the Excitement Wore Off

Primaries spread quickly during the 1900s and 1910s, but soon afterward the heated arguments on both sides disappeared. The proponents of the direct primary lost interest, and the opponents gave up. As we shall see, the primary laws of many states changed during the subsequent decades, but there was no national effort to adopt any particular primary model, let alone to do away with them entirely. Freyd's moment of "honest appraisal" never came. This is a loss for American democracy. The arguments for and against primaries are not merely arguments about corrupt political bosses. They are arguments about how capable voters are of making choices and how reasonable it is to give voters the task of deciding among candidates they know little about, who are running for offices the responsibilities of which voters do not really understand. They are arguments about what role partisan differences should play in elections. They are arguments about what function political parties should serve in a democracy. And they are arguments about the appropriate role of citizens in states or districts where one party dominates. These arguments remain a part of American political discourse, yet they take place without the option of substantially changing the partisan primary. In an era when many other Western democracies continue to have robust, expansive discussions about all manner of potential changes to candidate selection, these arguments serve as a potential warning: once the partisan primary has been established, it may be that there is no going back.

Stories can and have been told about the adoption of the direct primary. Yet states did not simply adopt one primary model, and the numerous different forms primaries took complicated any stories about who "won" the battle over the direct primary. Following is a brief summary of some of the most consequential differences in primary laws:

- States differed in their laws regarding who could vote in party primaries. While some states limited voting to previously registered party members or people who at least claimed that they had voted for the party's general election nominees in the previous elections, some states required that parties allow any registered voter to cast a ballot. Subsequent research on primaries would standardize references to such rules, categorizing primaries as closed or semiclosed, depending on whether party affiliation was required in advance of the primary or could be declared on the date of the primary.
- The primary ballots provided to voters also differed across states; in some instances, voters received a ballot listing only one party's nominees, while other states allowed voters to in different party primaries for different offices. Contemporary writers have, again, established shorthand means of describing these elections: open primaries are those in which voters do not need to declare party affiliation and can engage in "crossover voting," while semiopen primaries are those in which voters receive the ballot of one party or the other but do not need to register as a party member.
- The requirements for candidacy also varied across states; some states required candidates for a party's nomination to have a history of affiliation with that party, while others did not. In some instances, candidates could seek the nomination of more than one party at the same time.
- There were frequent debates about whether primaries should be mandatory, and in what circumstances they should be mandatory. Should primaries be required for minor parties? Should they be required in cases where there was only one declared candidate? In such instances, primary elections might impose substantial costs for state and local governments, but if primaries were optional in these instances, on what grounds should they be required for major parties?
- Concerned that multicandidate fields might result in unelectable candidates winning with pluralities, rather than majorities, of the vote, some states experimented with using primary runoffs. Some states set thresholds of 50 percent for avoiding a runoff, while others set the threshold lower.
- States experimented with rules regarding primary dates; some allowed parties some leeway in determining when to hold their primaries, while others established fixed dates. In some instances states allowed the parties to hold their primaries on different dates, while others did not. This was of particular concern at the time because the Supreme Court had held in *Newberry v. United States* (256 U.S. 232 (1921)) that Congress could restrict spending in general elections but not primaries, so there were many

concerns raised about the cost of primaries, the advantage that particular primary dates might provide to wealthy candidates, and the costs associated with two different election periods.

These are just some of the issues that were debated during the 1900s, 1910s, and 1920s; many other rules, often idiosyncratic in nature, were enacted. While many of these questions may seem arcane or overly technical to the contemporary reader, they are still occasionally debated, and in almost all instances they have to do with an enduring tension within Americans' political attitudes: on the one hand, we are willing to entertain the belief that political parties are, to a degree, private associations, yet the long tradition of American skepticism toward parties has prompted frequent calls to intervene in internal party affairs. We are wont to believe that parties are by their nature corrupt—perhaps more corrupt than individual politicians or governmental organizations—yet we feel no better about them when we have a greater role in their affairs.

How did Americans get from the heated debates about primary elections that characterized the first three decades of the twentieth century to the odd, occasionally unfair, but mostly obscure system we have today of nominating candidates for office? There has been no detailed study of the history of the direct primary during the mid-twentieth century. After the 1928 publication of Charles Merriam and Louise Overacker's *Primary Elections*, virtually everyone lost interest in the subject. The number of academic articles on primaries dwindled; by my count, there were five articles on primaries in the two major political science journals noted earlier between 1932 and 1960. When primaries did receive careful treatment, it was often because they had taken on a uniquely regional flavor. V. O. Key's classic *Southern Politics in State and Nation* (1949) went to great lengths to demonstrate that Southern primaries had taken on a distinctive character. Lesser known but equally magisterial works such as Duane Lockard's *New England Politics* (1959b) showed that other regions of the country had also adapted primaries to their own needs. Yet the big questions raised in the 1910s and 1920s by political scientists—and in particular, by opponents of the direct primary—went unanswered during this era.

When primaries again became a subject for political inquiry, in the 1970s and beyond, they looked different. The Democratic Party's McGovern Fraser Commission mandated sweeping changes to the party's delegate selection rules. Up until that point, presidential primaries had for the most part been meaningless affairs in which voters had the option of registering their preference among a wide variety of actual candidates and pseudo-candidates heading up "favorite son" lists. The Democratic Party's establishment of delegate selection rules led to the increased use of presidential primaries; this in turn led Republicans to follow suit, which in turn led many states to synchronize their nonpresidential primaries with their presidential primaries as a cost-saving measure. This is not to say that very much attention was given to the dynamics of nonpresidential primaries during this time, but at the least voters and reformers once again became concerned about who could vote in primaries, when primaries took place, and other concerns that had first been broached during the Progressive Era.

The pivotal years for understanding this change are those that passed when no one was really paying attention. What happened to primary elections in what I term the "middle years" between 1928 and 1970? Why did Americans—and in particular, those Americans who had been so instrumental in their creation—lose interest in them? And were the critics of primaries ultimately correct? Here is a sampling of what we know about primary elections during the middle years:

- Voter turnout in primaries peaked in the 1920s but fell precipitously over the subsequent twenty years (Ansolabehere et al. 2006, 2010).
- Similarly, competition in primary elections also fell during the 1930s and 1940s and has remained low since then (Ansolabehere et al. 2010).
- Political office became a career, rather than a temporary sinecure, for members of the U.S. Congress. Since World War II, there has only been one election in which fewer than 85 percent of House members sought re-election; the average re-election rate for those running has been 94 percent. Barely 1 percent of House members are defeated in primary elections (Jacobson 2013, 30–32). Although some state legislatures introduced term limits during the 1990s, overall the re-election rate for state legislators has been similarly high (Jewell and Breaux 1988).
- One reason the incumbency advantage grew was that the establishment of the direct primary ensured that individual candidates, not parties, decided when it was most advantageous to run for office. As Carson and Roberts (2013, 92–95) describe matters, before the direct primary political parties were able to reduce the risk of running for office by offering nominees a fallback position—a party job or the promise of support in a future election—if they ran. Without such assurances, prospective candidates were on their own to determine when it was most advantageous for them to run. As a result, the level of competition in races featuring an incumbent declined, and the level of competition in open seat races increased. Similarly, the quality of the candidates running in incumbent and challenger primaries declined. Strategic candidates were content to wait their turn. This was the case regardless of the type of primary laws in place.
- During much of this period the South was the great exception. With no functioning Republican Party there, primaries took on greater importance, and voting in primaries often exceeded general election turnout (Davidson 1990, 24). Southern primaries also had greater competition (Ewing 1953,

33), but Southern legislators were re-elected at rates similar to their Northern counterparts and used their seniority in the House and Senate to play a dominant role in congressional committee leadership. Southern distinctiveness was showing signs of declining by the 1970s, however.
- The decades following the introduction of the direct primary were marked by a growth in Democratic Party strength, an increase in general election competition between the two parties, and a marked increase in bipartisanship in Congress. By the 1970s, however, the parties had begun to drift apart from each other ideologically (Theriault 2008), a drift that has continued up to the present and has resulted, in the eyes of many observers, in increased governmental dysfunction.
- Perceiving a lack of substantive disagreements between the parties during the 1950s and 1960s, many political scientists wrote about a decline in party strength and a lack of meaningful alternatives for voters. This approach was best characterized by the American Political Science Association's (1950) report calling for more responsible parties.
- Candidates for federal office in the 1950s and 1960s began more aggressively using new media technologies to run highly individualized campaigns. It was not uncommon for candidates at all levels to air advertisements that neglected to note their party affiliation. The development of "candidate-centered elections" was noted in both primary and general elections (Menefee-Libbey 2000).
- Finally, the tail end of this era marked the beginning of an inexorable decline in Americans' confidence in government, trust in their political leaders, and engagement in the political process (Dalton 2004). Arguments about the reasons for this decline abound, but the decline shows, at a minimum, that by the 1970s it would appear odd to claim that primaries improved Americans' attitudes toward politics.

Few of these changes were caused by the introduction of the direct primary, but they cannot be understood without reference to it. A lot else went on during the middle years that explains changes in American elections and American political parties. The Great Depression and the New Deal (1929–41) focused the energies of social reformers on economic issues, not electoral reform. Cold War politics of the 1950s and the civil rights movement and social unrest of the 1960s transformed American parties, but these transformations would have occurred regardless of the mechanisms the parties used to choose their nominees. Changes in how politicians interacted with voters also were afoot; the increasing role of television advertising in political campaigns probably had more to do with the development of candidate-centered elections than did election laws. Even when particular features of electoral law came under scrutiny, these were mechanisms with more obvious ties to those larger issues. The decision in *Baker v. Carr* (369 U.S. 186 (1962)) and the subsequent "reapportionment revolution" that yielded contemporary congressional districting practices have much more obvious connections to changes in party ideology and partisan power than do primary laws.

These developments correspond to some of the fears, past and present, that critics of the primary system have voiced, but to the extent that they are not just consequences of primaries, they also complicate our efforts to measure the effects of the direct primary. It is difficult to consider American elections of the twentieth century and conclude that they were either a victory or a travesty for American democracy. If they had been, perhaps more people would have been paying attention to them at the time. There was simply too much else going on. But the lack of dramatic effects carries with it a story of its own. As I show in the next chapter of this book, states continued to tinker with their primary rules throughout this period. So if primaries did not matter to political reformers, they certainly did matter to parties and elected officials—the people who were, after all, most affected by the mechanics of primaries. There is a lost history here, but the absence of attention paid to primaries poses the possibility that all sorts of changes might have taken place.

With the Progressive movement largely spent, it is possible that parties worked to make primaries safer, more predictable affairs. There is certainly precedent for thinking that parties might have the will and the ways to do this; after all, we know that when the Democratic Party's new presidential primary system yielded, in its first two outings, two political outsiders as nominees, the party acted to change the role of primaries in delegate selection, ensuring that "superdelegates" who were not chosen in primaries would be present to aid establishment candidates. So we know that American political parties, despite allegations of weakness, do have the ability to impose order on candidate selection proceedings. On the other hand, the types of people who win election are changed when selection rules change. As early critics of the direct primary pointed out, the sort of people who win primaries will then work to ensure that the system protects them. Even a brief change in rules can create a new class of "insiders."

Does a similar logic apply in other types of primaries? Can that logic explain changes in other types of primary laws? When primary laws of the middle years are considered, this is often the shorthand that academics use. Key (1956, 121) argues that parties gradually achieved control of the primary system through a combination of formal rule changes and informal agreements. Ware (2006, 69) summarizes the period from the 1920s onward as a time when the Democratic Party sought to simultaneously placate reformers while maintaining or enhancing informal control over the primary process. State-specific studies provide numerous accounts of how party leaders paid lip service to reform while at the same time rigorously working to balance tickets, aid party loyalists, or entice prospective insurgents to stay out or bide their time (Zimmerman 2008, 65). Yet this story is often provided with relatively little supporting evidence. This book seeks to provide that evidence. As we shall see, that evidence is complicated, but it hardly points to a uniform reassertion of party power. Primary election laws changed during this era, but there is no single, overarching reason why they changed, and there is no clear direction in which these changes have gone. Nonetheless, we can tell a national story about changing primary laws, rather than relegating them to the domain of regional histories of the United States.

Where This Book Fits in the Contemporary Literature on Primaries

There has been more scholarship on the direct primary during the past two decades than there was during any other twenty-year period since the establishment of the primary. This book is intended in part as a response to some of the works on the primary of the past twenty years. The aforementioned Alan Ware book, *The American Direct Primary* (2002), and John Reynolds's *The Demise of the American Convention System* (2006) were the first major reconsiderations of the adoption of the direct primary since Merriam and Overacker's 1928 book. The Ware and Reynolds books, discussed in more detail in Chapter 2, were important efforts to clarify why parties went along with the adoption of the primary. Both accounts note that the direct primary was not as radical a break from prior nomination methods as it might appear to some, that parties benefited in some ways from the direct primary, and that the primary did not spread merely because it seemed a good idea. These books led the way for scholars of the 2010s to ask new questions about how primaries had worked and what a contemporary primary reform agenda might look like.

My previous work on primaries (Boatright 2013, 2014, 2018) falls into this literature. This book, however, is best seen as a response—not a correction as much as an extension—to three other scholars' recent major works on elections: Hans Hassell's *The Party's Primary* (2018), Shigeo Hirano and James M. Snyder Jr.'s *Primary Elections in the United States* (2019), and Erik Engstrom and Jason Roberts's *The Politics of Ballot Design* (2020).

In *The Party's Primary*, Hassell demonstrates the range of ways in which political parties have exerted informal control over primary elections. Political party organizations engage in a range of coordinated activities, including directing donations and endorsements toward preferred candidates and offering inducements to other candidates to get out of the race. In most cases, the party-preferred candidates are more moderate or more politically experienced than their opponents, and party interventions are designed to improve the party's chance of winning the general election. Although Hassell's examples are drawn from the 2000s, his argument can certainly be applied to prior years: regardless of nuances in primary election laws, political parties usually get the nominees they want. Furthermore, in elections in which party elites do not coalesce around a preferred candidate, there are often strategic reasons why parties do not wish to control the process. I address components of Hassell's argument in Chapters 2, 8, 9, and 10.

The story I present here is generally consistent with Hassell's argument. As I will show, reforms that appear designed to strengthen or weaken the parties often fail to have significant effects. In some cases, this is because parties have found a way to minimize the effects of these laws. In other cases, reforms that on their face might appear to be antiparty reforms can actually serve the short-term interests of the party in power or of an influential politician within the party. Neither my argument nor Hassell's suggests that parties always get what they want; rather, both books argue that formal rules do not structure the political process nearly as much as do informal methods of exerting political control.

Hirano and Snyder's *Primary Elections in the United States* is the culmination of a decade of work on primaries conducted by the authors, occasionally in collaboration with Stephen Ansolabehere and John Mark Hansen. I draw upon smaller points from this project in Chapters 2, 3, 7, 9, and 10 of this book; it is certainly the most detailed study of the history of primary elections published to date. The book is animated by a straightforward question: Has the direct primary worked? Or to narrow the question somewhat, is it an improvement on other methods of candidate selection? The authors show that the primary does provide a democratic means of resolving factional conflicts in one-party areas, and that contrary to fears of some early opponents of the direct primary, voters tend to support well-qualified candidates when confronted with candidates of similar ideological views.

Hirano and Snyder's principal concern is to defend the primary and develop ways to measure the consequences of the establishment of the direct primary. My intent in this book is not to dispute their assertion that the direct primary "works"; rather, it is to dispute the notion that there are reforms that will make the direct primary work better, or differently. Hirano and Snyder provide a table noting some of the major modifications to primary elections during the twentieth century (2019, 30–32), and they devote a section of their book to speculation about the potential effects of contemporary reform proposals (282–306). Like this book, they are skeptical that any of these reforms will have major effects. This book is a history not of primaries, but of primary reforms: it is an effort to explore the reasons that past reforms have had few major effects and why we should be cautious about future ones.

One lesson of the contemporary literature on primary elections is that we should be skeptical of unicausal narratives, or narratives that purport to show some sort of steady progress toward goals such as democracy, equality, or inclusivity. In this regard, my argument most closely resembles Engstrom and Roberts's (2020) account of changes in ballot design in U.S. elections. While their book is not directly about primaries, they take on an aspect of American elections that has consistently been manipulated by parties and politicians for short-term advantage. Engstrom and Roberts show that some principles of ballot design appear superior to others, but that it is impossible to develop any sort of argument about what the "best" way to design ballots is. They show that there are distinct historical eras and patterns in which ballots were systematically changed in different states for the purpose of achieving what appeared to be more democratic outcomes or for aiding particular candidates or movements. And perhaps most importantly, they show that ballots were often changed or manipulated in accordance with ideas or assumptions about what the results might be, even when there was little evidence to back up these assumptions. The history of primary election laws is, like Engstrom and Roberts's tale about ballot design, a history from which we can extract different narratives, but it is not necessarily a story of linear progress or enlightenment.

Plan of the Book

The first seven chapters of this book explore different theories about changes in direct primary laws. They draw upon data from 1928 through 1970, but they use some historical developments from before and after this period in order to contextualize these theories. In Chapter 2 I summarize the consequential changes in primary laws and categorize primary law changes according to their consequences for political parties. Some primary law changes, such as restricting voting to registered party members, are clearly efforts to enhance the control of parties, while others, such as allowing candidates to simultaneously pursue the nomination of more than one party, are aimed at reducing the power of parties. Summarizing which types of changes happened, in which regions of the country, and at which times, is a means of establishing whether, in fact, there was any sort of retrenchment—whether parties gained greater control of primaries during the middle years. As the chapter shows, the evidence is mixed; overall there is no clear evidence that there was retrenchment, but there definitely are regional variations of note.

Chapter 2 also presents four basic theoretical arguments about changes in primary laws and seeks to test each of these arguments. In this chapter I explore the possibility that the decline of the Progressive movement led to a reaction on the part of parties that had been threatened by the Progressives, that states where primaries were temporarily captured by nonparty movements such as the Nonpartisan League (NPL) responded by changing their laws, that changes were more common in states that had particularly odd or unworkable primary laws, and that changes in primary laws served as a tool in intraparty competition. None of these theories are mutually exclusive, but they require different analytical methods and inquiry into primary law changes in different types of states.

These theories cannot, however, be tested solely through the sort of categorization that I employ in Chapter 2. Exploring each requires a careful review of the histories of different states and different primary reform efforts. Accordingly, Chapters 3 through 6 explore each of these theories in greater detail. In Chapter 3 I explore the role the direct primary played in Progressive thought. I show that the primary, for all of its successes, had never been a major goal of the leading Progressive thinkers; as a consequence, when the Progressive movement declined there were few leading American intellectuals who wanted to fight for the primary. Those Progressives who did champion the primary, however, were ambivalent about the precise mechanisms of the primary itself, which meant that these thinkers tended to disengage themselves from arguments about whether primaries should be open or closed, whether ballot access limitations were warranted, or other such debates.

Chapter 4 considers the aftermath of the NPL's capture of the Republican Party in North Dakota from 1916 to 1920 and the threat that the NPL posed to political parties in neighboring states. Much like the contemporary Tea Party, the NPL presented itself as a movement that was independent of the parties, and it deliberately used Republican Party primaries as a means of replacing traditional Republicans with League members. Unlike the Tea Party, however, the NPL's interests (which centered upon aiding small farmers) really were not easily reconciled with the dominant ideas in either party, and its organizing methods were much more like those of European socialist parties than American parties' activities. Primary law changes throughout the Midwest can be seen as efforts to prevent such outside groups from gaining power. Individual NPL members did, however, gain elected office in many midwestern states, and these candidates also advocated for primary law changes that would further weaken parties. In short, changes to primary laws in many agrarian states show the legacy of both the NPL's successes and the successes of its opponents in containing the League's threat to the established two-party system.

In Chapter 5 I consider the possibility that some direct primary laws were simply not very good laws. Many states adopted laws that proved to be unwieldy, while others' primary laws contained unenforceable provisions. Some states required, for instance, that even extremely small fringe parties be required to hold primaries; others tacked onto their primary laws rules regarding candidate debates or the establishment and distribution of binding party platforms; and still others adopted provisions prohibiting candidates from lying in their campaigns. While such efforts may have stemmed from noble impulses, in some instances they yielded unforeseen consequences. As is apparent in many legislative conflicts, however, it can be difficult to separate sincere efforts to mend unworkable laws from malicious efforts to undermine them entirely. New York, for instance, certainly had complicated primaries when they were first introduced, yet the state's eventual decision to abolish primaries entirely was probably not the only solution available to the host of minor problems the state faced. For a contemporary example, one might look no further than congressional votes on the Affordable Care Act: How does one separate efforts to mend parts of the law that have had unforeseen consequences from efforts to do away with the law entirely? In this chapter I explore what literature from comparative politics tells us about "bad laws" and seek to determine which primary law changes were sincere efforts to fix legitimate problems.

Chapter 6 discusses the relationship between primary law changes and partisan competition. In comparative politics, it is common to explain election law changes as a tool in party conflict. In the case of campaign finance laws, for instance, there is ample evidence that ruling parties often seek to change the law so as to entrench themselves in power or to increase their fundraising advantage over their opponents. The same arguments have been made in the United States with regard to campaign finance, to voting rights, and to the drawing of congressional districts. These claims suggest that changes to primary laws should follow a similar logic, yet primary law changes have never been systematically explored as a tool for partisan advantage. I do this here, but I also note that one of the reasons primary law changes have not been as easy to study as the election law changes noted earlier is that their effects are not well understood. Theories abound, for instance, about the effects of holding early as opposed to late primaries, or about the advantages to parties of restricting voting to registered party members, but the evidence does not always support these conclusions. Parties, in other words, have often sought to change primaries to aid themselves and harm their opponents, but the changes they have enacted have not always aided them in the manner they expected.

When political scientists have tried to develop theories about primary laws, they have tended to exclude the South from their arguments. Because there was effectively no Republican Party in the South for much of the twentieth century, it makes sense to look at the South separately. Despite unique features of Southern primaries, such as the primary runoff and, of course, the elaborate means by which African Americans were excluded from primaries, some of the same problems emerged in Southern primaries as in Northern ones. The South, as I show here, was not entirely immune to the Progressive movement; it was touched by the organizing efforts of the NPL; Southern states dealt with the same sort of technical fixes to "bad laws" as did Northern states; and despite limited two-party competition, we can see some changes in the South as efforts to address the possibility of emergent general election conflict. Chapter 7 explores the extent to which the South fits some of the theoretical paradigms presented in Chapters 2 through 6.

The story told in Chapter 2 through 7 is largely historical. This part of the book seeks to bring order to the various reasons that states tinkered with their primary laws during the middle years of the twentieth century. It shows that parties did not gain control over the primary, but they did modify primaries substantially and repeatedly. By 1970, the primary had become a standard part of American state politics, but the effects of particular primary election mechanisms remained unclear. If primaries did not have the consequences that either proponents or opponents predicted, neither did smaller modifications to primaries always yield predictable effects.

Some of the early concerns about primaries are still with us today, despite the changes of the middle years, while other concerns have largely disappeared, to be replaced by new ones. To give just a few examples, states continue to experiment with opening or closing primaries, and there is still no strong consensus about the effects of such changes. States continue to move their primary dates around, without a clear understanding of what the "best" time for a primary to be held is. For these two issues, little has changed since the 1920s. Other early concerns have disappeared; for instance, early twentieth-century concerns about "balancing" state tickets—ensuring that parties nominate candidates who represent all of the different regions of the state—may still be of interest to some but play little role in discussions of primaries. But perhaps most consequentially, primaries are today blamed for a host of ills that have little correspondence to older debates. Primaries have been said to represent only ideological extremists, to exclude moderate voters, or to result in the nomination of unrepresentative or unelectable candidates. They have been blamed for the increased polarization of Congress and of national politics. While some contemporary authors (including this one) have argued that this claim is not accurate, it is also evident that such claims would have been puzzling to early twentieth-century politicians.

In some regards, we know a great deal more about the dynamics of primary elections since 1970 than we do about primaries in earlier years. Improvements in the data available to researchers on voter turnout, campaign spending, and other features of elections have shed light on matters that earlier researchers could only speculate about. But states continue tinkering with their primary laws, and while calls to abandon primaries are scarce, there is a widespread dissatisfaction with them. Accordingly, in Chapters 8 and 9 I take a look at the fit between contemporary primary rule change proposals, on the one hand, and on the other, what actually seems to matter in contemporary primary elections. I seek to make three points in these chapters. First, states continue to tinker with primary elections, in part due to unrealistic beliefs about what the consequences of primary reform will be. Second, contemporary research on primaries shows that no amount of tinkering is likely to bring about measurable change. And third, the two most consequential developments that make contemporary primaries different from primaries of past years—the ideological sorting of voters and candidates and the nationalization of primary elections—are largely immune to the sorts of reforms in the primary reformer's toolbox.

Undertaking this exploration of contemporary primaries requires a different methodological approach. In the first seven chapters of the book, the data of most relevance were primary law changes. Some authors have noted that many primary reform proposals were floated during this time but were never enacted. It is prohibitively difficult to explore all of the proposed changes across the American states over the forty-year period considered in these chapters. It is much easier, however, to identify all of the legislation introduced to change primaries over the past two decades. It is also much easier to explore the partisan logic of contemporary primary law changes (particularly given the greater ideological homogeneity of the parties) today than it would have been in the 1930s. Thus in Chapter 8 I begin by exploring the fate of various pieces of primary law change legislation introduced since 2000. Thus exploration shows that there is still no consensus about what primaries should look like, but that beliefs about partisan advantage still continue to influence thinking about primaries. In this chapter I also provide a survey of contemporary research showing the rather minimal consequences of most primary election law changes.

In Chapter 9 I explore reasons that most reforms will not work. The fault here may lie in part in mistaken beliefs about the mechanisms of these reforms, or in part in our inability to agree on what a measurable change brought about by reform would be. For the most part, however, primary reforms are problematic because of changes in the nature of political conflict in America. To put matters bluntly, the nature of party competition today is different than it has been for most of the history of the direct primary. In this chapter I consider two major changes in primary election competition. The first of these is the "nationalization" of primary elections. One problem in studying primary elections is that with the exception of some presidential primaries, nomination contests for multiple offices occur at the same time. Voters cannot be expected to know very much about very many primary candidates, so they often take their cues from broader political trends. As I show in this chapter, the same sorts of trends that influence general elections—partisan swings, anti-incumbent sentiments, dissatisfaction with the economy, and other such "macro" features—can influence primaries. The effects of these influences, furthermore, can swamp the effects of election rules.

The second change is the role of ideology in primary electorates. One common concern in contemporary studies of primaries is that the primary electorate is somehow more extreme than the general electorate. It stands to reason that ideologically distinct parties will yield ideologically distinct primary electorates. Yet I argue here that these claims are exaggerated; there is little evidence that Democratic primary voters, for instance, are any different from the types of people who vote for Democrats in the general election. Partisans choose nominees, but ideological extremists do not. And in cases where the primary electorate does look different from the general electorate, this is not the fault of primary rules. Rather, it is a consequence of particularly ideological candidates pulling voters into the primary, or in some cases, driving them away. These effects, again, would likely occur regardless of election rules.

Chapter 10 concludes with some thoughts on the century-long American experiment with primary elections. The past century has taught us to be suspicious of claims that electoral reforms will have noticeable results. This is a recurrent problem for reforms in other areas of electoral politics, such as campaign finance or the drawing of legislative districts. Promising measurable results may be necessary for building reform coalitions, yet when such results do not appear, those who have supported them may become disillusioned and disengage from politics. One solution, I argue, is to "go big": to explore much more fundamental reforms than those that have generally been attempted. In the case of primaries, "big" changes might include ranked choice voting, multimember districts and at large elections, or abandoning primaries entirely. Another solution—one ultimately endorsed by disillusioned Progressives of the 1920s—would be to turn away from process reforms toward the more fundamental social and economic changes that some electoral reform proponents might believe in. I have reservations about both approaches, but they would certainly yield bigger changes and more fruitful conversations than our century-long experiment with the primary has done.

This book is addressed to two audiences. It is aimed in part at those who wish to consider the role of the direct primary in American political history. There was much written about primaries during the 1910s and 1920s, and there is a growing literature on the subject today. This book is an effort to bridge these two eras, to explain how we got from there to here. Having done that, however, this book seeks to reorient discussions about what, if anything, to do about primary elections today. Studies of primary elections conducted since the 1970s have brought us to a point where the old questions have either been definitively answered or shown to be impossible to answer. If we are to have an intelligent debate in the upcoming years about this peculiar American institution, we need to rethink the terms of that debate. Too often, reform advocates in state legislatures, in the academy, and in the broader electorate have flailed about, introducing all manner of changes based on theories rather than evidence, or introducing changes that have already been adopted and discarded in the past. It is my hope that the combination of historical analysis here and empirical consideration of some features that are *not* generally considered in discussions of primaries can help us to avoid this situation. We should not assume that small fixes will change the way primaries work, but we should also be clear that although many of the problems that plague American politics today may be evident in primaries, they are the fault of our politicians and our parties, not of the election systems that bring them into office.

PART I
THE MIDDLE YEARS
Primary Election Reforms, 1928–1970

2

Reform or Retrenchment?

An Overview of Changes in Primary Election Laws, 1928–1970

Claims about American political history can often take root and become conventional wisdom even when they are not entirely accurate. As noted in Chapter 1, the dominant account of the spread of primary elections has been the contention by Merriam and Overacker (1928, 61–95) that the triumph of the primary election was an example of democracy in action: primaries were so overwhelmingly popular among voters that party bosses, who preferred control over nominations, were unable to stand in the way. This account persisted for a long time even though it may not actually have been true. Just as the Merriam and Overacker argument went unchallenged for nearly a century, however, so arguments about the alleged decline of primary elections between the 1920s and 1960s have been adopted without serious critical analysis. The conventional wisdom has been that following the spread of primaries in the first two decades of the twentieth century, political parties reasserted themselves, that restrictions were placed on primaries to make them more predictable and less open to insurgent candidates or to unaffiliated voters. There is compelling evidence that competition in primary elections declined between 1920 and 1970: fewer candidates sought party nominations for Congress or for governorships (Ansolabehere et al. 2010; Jewell and Olson 1988), incumbent renomination and re-election rates increased (Ansolabehere et al. 2007; Hirano and Snyder 2019), and voter participation declined (Key 1956, 135). Yet such findings are not necessarily evidence of a change in election laws; they may be consequences of such changes, but they are not on their face evidence that changes happened, nor do they provide any insight into why changes took place, if indeed they did.

The intent of this chapter is to provide a way to quantify changes in states' primary election laws between 1928 (when the Merriam and Overacker book was published) and 1970, the last election year before the enactment of the Democratic Party's McGovern-Fraser reforms and the increased prominence of presidential primary elections. On one level, this chapter simply seeks to catalog changes in primary election laws, with an eye toward the direction of these changes—that is, were the changes intended to expand the primary electorate or restrict it, expand the control of parties over primaries or reduce it, or expand

Reform and Retrenchment. Robert G. Boatright, Oxford University Press. © Oxford University Press 2024.
DOI: 10.1093/oso/9780197774083.003.0002

ballot access for candidates or restrict it? Primary elections were originally championed as a means of taking power away from party bosses and handing it to "the people." I seek to measure transfers of this power during the years after primaries had been almost universally adopted.

In addition to providing a catalog of changes during this era, in this chapter I also develop from the literature four distinct theories about why restrictions might have been placed on primaries during this era. One common claim is that with the decline of the Progressive movement, anti-Progressive forces reasserted themselves—the parties struck back. A second claim in literature on individual state or regions is essentially an expansion on the first: studies of insurgent politics in states such as Minnesota and the Dakotas have alleged that primaries were "taken over" by organized outside groups that sought to use the primary to advance the candidacies of individuals whose views were antithetical to those of party regulars. Such claims, reminiscent of contemporary assertions about the role of the Tea Party in Republican primaries, suggest again that primary laws were flawed but point to broader, more ideological consequences than in the second explanation. A third common claim is that primaries did not, in fact, work all that well; many explanations of declining voter turnout in primaries have noted that primary ballots were often too long, state primary laws were easily manipulated by candidates, and some of the most "democratic" primary laws contained provisions that were simply unworkable. Changes to primaries may, then, have been a result not of party leaders' antidemocratic tendencies but instead have been a democratic response to voter disillusionment. And fourth, some state or regional accounts of changing party laws have noted the coincidence of changes in primaries and the expansion of two-party competition: primaries may have made sense in states where one party was dominant but were of less value when voters had a clear choice between two electorally viable parties.

These four explanations all assume that primary laws did, in fact, become more restrictive, or less open, in the middle decades of the century, but they contain contrasting accounts of the causal motor behind these changes. Although there is substantial variation in the falsifiability of these claims and in the data one might use to test them, all of these claims suggest that the timing, the place, and the state of partisan competition in the states making changes to their laws are of consequence. Accordingly, this chapter proceeds in three parts. First, I lay out the arguments that have been made about the spread and alleged decline of primaries. Second, I present a method for matching a content-based coding of changes in primary elections with data on the characteristics of the times and places at which they were changed. In the third section I discuss the results of such tests. The analysis in this chapter sets the stage for the more nuanced historical treatment I provide in the subsequent chapters of how primaries have changed since the 1920s.

The results of this chapter do not clearly establish that one theory is the single correct one. They do, however, demonstrate that the alleged decline of primaries is not shown in changes to primary laws. There are distinctive eras of legislative change in the administration of primaries, and there are distinctive patterns evident in different types of states. Political parties did not enforce control over the primary process, but they did adapt primaries to their needs. In some circumstances these needs entailed increasing party control over the process, while in others they entailed relaxing party control.

The Rise and Fall of the Direct Primary Movement

It may be news to some readers that parties did increase their control over primary elections in the middle of the twentieth century; after all, all American states use primary elections in some form or other for most state and federal offices today, and while there are occasional proposals to change the way primary elections proceed, there is little public discussion today about abolishing primaries. It is helpful, then, to briefly summarize the spread of primary elections and arguments about why primaries were adopted before summarizing arguments about their decline.

The Adoption of Primary Elections

Primary elections were used sporadically during the late nineteenth and early twentieth centuries in individual cities or counties in states as varied as California, Pennsylvania, Minnesota, and South Carolina (Anderson 1902; Delmatier, McIntosh, and Waters 1970, 33; Meyer 1902; Ware 2002, 110–113). By 1900, however, the direct primary had become a favorite proposal of Progressive reformers, following a conference held on the subject in 1898 (Ware 2002, 81). Prominent Progressives such as Wisconsin's Robert La Follette and California's Hiram Johnson argued in favor of the direct primary in their campaigns for office, claiming that primary elections would take the power of choosing candidates away from unaccountable and corrupt party bosses and hand it to the people; this change would, in turn, enable candidates to be accountable to the people rather than to party leaders. Wisconsin passed the first mandatory statewide direct primary law by referendum in 1904. Within the next eleven years, forty-three states had followed Wisconsin's example.[1]

State primary laws differed dramatically in their content and scope, however. The most salient distinction, one that remains with us today, is in who can vote in primary elections. The Wisconsin law established what became known as an open primary, in which anyone can vote in any party's primary, regardless of his or her past voting history. While some states established similarly open systems, others established closed primaries of various sorts, requiring voters to register with a party before the primary, swear an oath of loyalty to the party and its eventual nominees, or state that they had supported the party's nominees in the past election. It was feared that in an open primary, voters hostile to the party might vote for a weaker general election nominee or at least for a nominee unrepresentative of the party. Closed primaries provided some level of control for party leaders.

State primary laws varied in other, more idiosyncratic ways as well. Under South Dakota's 1912 Richards primary law, for instance, parties were required to hold representative conventions before the primary in which they would choose a "majority" candidate and a "protesting" candidate.[2] Parties were also required to vote on what the themes of the campaign would be. In the case of presidential nominees, they chose these themes without the approval of the candidates themselves. While on its face an admirable effort to encourage deliberation on issues within the parties, the results were rather comical, as parties announced themes such as "true democracy" and "equitable adjustment, economy, progress, and prosperity," which hardly provided voters with a clear choice (Berdahl 1923). R. O. Richards, the law's namesake, was reportedly unhappy with the parties' cavalier treatment of his law and wondered whether the courts might require parties to adopt themes that actually said something concrete about their objectives. Despite efforts by legislators to repeal the law, it was overwhelmingly popular among South Dakota voters and remained in place until 1929 (see Merriam and Overacker 1928, 91; South Dakota Legislative Research Council 2005). South Dakota's law may have been one of the most elaborate, but it was not sui generis. Such laws illustrate the difficulties in simply using legislation establishing a direct primary as a binary variable.

On one level it is easy to extract a narrative from these changes, but doing so means that one must focus more on the decision to have primaries than on the specific nature of primary laws. Merriam and Overacker's *Primary Elections* (1928; see also Merriam 1908) served as a capstone for the period, firmly linking the primary to other Progressive goals and surveying the diversity of primary laws and their pros and cons. Merriam and Overacker's book was also arguably written at a high-water mark for primaries; voter turnout and electoral competition did surge in the 1910s and 1920s, but declined shortly thereafter. There is little analysis in that book (in part because such analyses were not a common tool of that era's political scientists) of why primaries were adopted, beyond the assertion that they were a good idea and were extremely popular. Other article-length studies of the time clearly frame the battle as one between Progressive reformers, with the public on their side, and reactionary party bosses.

Alan Ware's *The American Direct Primary*, published in 2002, contends that Merriam and Overacker's argument relies too much on the power of public opinion. The popularity of the idea of primaries does not explain the speed with which parties adopted them. According to Ware, some urban machines did what they could to sabotage the law, but for the most part the machines decided quickly that not only could they continue to nominate their preferred candidates through primary elections, but they could in fact benefit from having states assume the responsibility for regulating their nominations. Parties could use their organizational strength to help preferred candidates win their primaries and could abstain from elections in which they truly did not care which candidate won. The other major account of the development of the direct primary, John Reynolds's (2006) *The Demise of the American Convention System, 1880–1911*, also claims that the Progressives latched onto the idea of the direct primary some years after parties had begun to explore using it. In Reynolds's telling, the direct primary was a natural outgrowth of delegate selection primaries. Parties began as early as the 1860s using primaries at the county level, largely as a cost-cutting measure—it was less expensive to have party members in some areas cast votes on a particular day than to bring them all together. In both accounts, primaries spread because they were advantageous to parties.

Lawrence, Donovan, and Bowler (2013) operationalize the major differences between Merriam's and Ware's arguments about the timing of primary reforms, using independent variables that seek to capture a state's level of party organization, the existence of prior Progressive reforms, the strength of third parties, and the number of candidates seeking office. Although they note the difficulties inherent in seeking quantitative evidence that accords with Merriam's and Ware's claims, they contend that the available evidence provides more support for Merriam than for Ware. This is a noteworthy finding, given the persuasiveness of Ware's argument and the close fit between the Ware argument and contemporary, rational choice–oriented theories of party behavior. Lawrence and his coauthors caution, however, that their findings do not disprove Ware's contention that parties adapted to primaries quickly; the parties may, for instance, have found the direct primary was not as bad as they had feared, or they may have come to be dominated by individual politicians who had experience winning primaries.

The Decline of Primary Elections: Four Hypotheses

In this chapter I seek to provide a test similar to that of Lawrence, Donovan, and Bowler, but one that concerns conventional wisdom about changes in primary laws following the implementation of the direct primary. Unfortunately, the distinctions between arguments about the fate of the direct primary are nowhere near as precise, nor as tied to individual authors, as is the Merriam/Ware distinction about the origins of primaries.

Existing studies provide some evidence that state governments had second thoughts about primary elections. Merriam and Overacker (1928, 97–106) catalog efforts in numerous states to repeal primary laws. They clearly show that there were attempts to rein in primaries, but they also show that these attempts met with mixed results. Similarly, Ware (2002, 227–229) shows that over 70 percent of the states that had primary laws endured repeal efforts between 1919 and 1926; most of these efforts were, however, unsuccessful, and in many instances it is difficult to distinguish between sincere efforts to fix problems with primary laws and efforts to roll them back. There are some clear cases, such as New York, where states abandoned primaries entirely. In other instances, however, primary laws were modified and standardized. South Dakota, for instance, abandoned the Richards primary by the late 1920s but replaced it with a conventional closed primary. Davis (1980, 42–49) lists the twenty-five states that introduced presidential primary laws, then provides a list of eight states that repealed their presidential primary laws between 1917 and 1935. Many academics writing about primaries during the 1920s (see, e.g., Overacker 1928, 1930, 1932; Kettleborough 1923a, 1923b; Boots 1922; Ray 1919) seem to have been reluctant to categorize developments during that decade as part of a larger effort to do away with primaries. Merriam and Overacker (1928, 107) conclude their survey of repeal efforts in the 1920s by noting that "if the repeal movement has reached its height at the present time the supporters of the direct primary have little to fear. Whether or not that is the case only time can tell."

Nonetheless, as we shall see in the hypotheses discussed below, the consensus that developed among academics in subsequent years has been that the period from the 1920s through the 1960s was one of retrenchment; such is the attitude, for instance, adopted by Key (1956) and Jewell and Olson (1988). Although there has been little documentation of this retrenchment, more recent literature has at a minimum set out a metric for what retrenchment might entail, even if this literature has not directly engaged the question of whether or why such a retrenchment did in fact occur. It is to be noted that this is a metric that was not in place at the time. Kaufmann, Gimpel, and Hoffman (2003), for instance, note that since the McGovern-Fraser reforms, contemporary progressives have championed the open primary for its alleged results—the potential for the open primary to produce an electorate more representative of the population and to produce candidates more attuned to the views of the state's voters. Those who argue in favor of California's "top two" primary and for expanding the primary electorate to counter extremists on the left or right clearly see the degree of openness in primaries as being equivalent to the degree of party control in primaries. Such claims, however, equate party control with ideological extremity, a contention that may be tenable today but certainly was less so in the middle of the twentieth century. If, however, one wishes to equate openness with unpredictability, then it is easy to see how closed primaries were more likely to yield party-preferred nominees; the smaller electorate and the emphasis on past support for the party provided parties with a greater understanding of how to use the primary electorate to achieve their goals.

I propose that accounts of this period have offered four different hypotheses about why retrenchment took place. A first hypothesis is that it was a consequence of the decline of the Progressive movement. Scholars of Progressivism frequently refer to the decline of the movement in the 1920s and 1930s. Historians such as Richard Hofstadter (1955, 266–267) have alleged that Progressives split over World War I, or at least changed their focus from domestic reform to international politics; that the Great Depression sapped the energy of Progressives; that Progressives were co-opted by the Roosevelt administration and came to focus on economic matters; or simply that the Progressives, having achieved many of their goals, failed to unify around an agenda to expand or protect what they had achieved. In this account, the decline of the Progressive movement enabled political party leaders to step in to adjust primary laws so as to render primaries less of a threat. The public overwhelmingly supported the idea of primary elections, and many party leaders by this time had been elected in primaries and were satisfied that they could achieve their goals through primaries. Establishing preprimary conventions, raising the threshold for ballot access, or instituting party loyalty tests for voters were ways of taming primaries without doing away with them.

Hofstadter's *The Age of Reform* (1955) lays out perhaps the clearest critique of the limits of the direct primary. The Progressives, he argues,

> were trying to do something altogether impossible – to institutionalize a mood. When the mood passed, some of the more concrete reforms remained; but the formal gains for popular government, while still on the books, lost meaning because the ability of the public to use them effectively lapsed with the political revival that brought them in, and the bosses and the interests promptly filtered back. (266)

The direct primary, he goes on to explain, did not noticeably change the kinds of people nominated for office. It was also expensive and cumbersome for parties, government, and candidates, and placed a premium on campaigning while at the same time weakening party responsibility and party government. It also did not clearly make voters any better off. Given these problems, the abandonment of the direct primary by reformers left it with few advocates. This is a point on which

Merriam and Overacker (1928, 277; see also Geiser 1923) concur; they show, however, that when primary reform was placed on the ballot it was soundly rejected. The uninformed voter (of whom Progressives were so afraid) liked the primary despite its flaws. Restrictions short of repeal, then, might have a potential constituency among disappointed Progressives and might go unnoticed by the average voter.

While some theories about retrenchment suggest that primaries did not work very well, the converse of this is the allegation that primaries worked too well. The primary was clearly antiparty in nature, and as such it fit well with other Progressive goals such as nonpartisan elections, changes in judicial selection methods, and a shift from electing to appointing some state and municipal officers. While some opponents of primaries warned that they could have the unintended consequence of empowering organized groups to effectively hijack party nominations, such arguments were not taken seriously in the literature of the 1910s or 1920s, in part because the only organizations strong enough to do this had developed outside of the parties, not within them (see, e.g. Wiebe 1967, Argersinger 1995). For reformers, the worst potential consequence of primaries was that the occasional unqualified individual politician might make it through the primary, not that there would be any organized effort to manipulate primaries.

Hence, a second hypothesis is that the "hijacking" of party primaries by nonparty groups led to a reassertion of control by party organizations over the primary process. The rise of groups such as the Nonpartisan League (NPL) in the Dakotas and Minnesota, then, came as somewhat of a shock for many of those who had supported primaries. The NPL sought to establish a slate of candidates who would then run in the primary of whichever party was expected to be strongest in the state. The NPL's effective takeover of the North Dakota Republican Party, and subsequently of the state's governorship and legislature, created a situation in which party labels were useless to voters. Many observers from outside of North Dakota alleged that the NPL had ties to Germany or to communism, and the NPL's initial successes were often written off as a consequence of North Dakota's large immigrant population or other state-specific features. When NPL candidates started to gain ground in neighboring states, however, many midwestern politicians urged their states to change their primary laws in order to prevent the NPL from gaining power.

Many accounts of the NPL and of agrarian movements of the era show the rapid spread of NPL support, the success of the NPL's style of organizing, and the movement of political observers outside the Midwest from mild curiosity to concern (Morlan 1955, ch. 5; Gieske 1979, 37–44; Omdahl 1961, Smith 1981). In the broader literature, Ware (2002, 234) makes some reference to the problems of this region, noting that there was an increase in the 1930s in the number of prominent Northern candidates who established personal, as opposed to partisan, coalitions.[3] He makes few normative claims about this, but he does note that this phenomenon harmed the vitality of local party organizations, thus creating a potential constituency for more ordinary politicians who wished to reassert some control. Such changes might not affect well-established and popular senators such as Idaho's William Borah or North Dakota's William Langer, but more restrictive primary rules might prevent more such politicians from emerging.

This claim thus resembles the first hypothesis in that it suggests a desire on the part of party leaders to reassert power. In contrast to the first hypothesis, however, basing arguments on the strength of the NPL or other organized nonparty forces suggests one clear threat to parties, whereas pointing to the decline of the Progressives does not necessarily connect restrictive changes in primaries to a well-defined event. And in contrast to the third hypothesis, below, using the NPL as a catalyst for change suggests a much larger and more consequential defect than poorly written ballot access provisions or other technical details. For measurement purposes, this hypothesis calls our attention to the states where restrictions were enacted.

A third hypothesis is that some of the features of primary laws simply did not work. Feldman's (1917) study of the New York primary law of 1912 documented many of the comical consequences of implementing the law. New York required all parties to hold primaries, so in some legislative districts ballots needed to be created for minor parties' primaries, despite the fact that some of these parties received fewer than one hundred votes statewide. In New York City, so many candidates and so many offices were on the ballot that the ballots voters received were over fourteen feet long; unsurprisingly, counting votes was a disastrous process. Some tinkering with the law would seem to have been in order—and would not necessarily even count as the sort of step that Progressives would have opposed. Faced with an opposition that wanted to do away with primaries altogether, however, the initial advocates of primaries faced charges that the ballot problems in New York, far from being easily fixable glitches, were signs that the direct primary was unworkable and should be abolished. No changes could be made unless reformers had the will and stamina to fight off poison pill amendments, so the primary stayed as it was until it was abolished at the statewide level in 1921, ostensibly because of low voter turnout (Zimmerman 2008, 65).

New York's example is not unique, but it does serve to illustrate the possibility that many adjustments to primary laws in the middle of the twentieth century were made for technical or administrative reasons, rather than out of opposition to Progressive rhetoric about openness. The question is not only how to categorize adjustments but how to measure the results of adjustments. A 1937 piece on changes in Michigan's ballot access laws illustrates this point. Confronted with a long list of "frivolous" candidates on the ballot, Michigan implemented a filing fee for candidates. The number of candidates seeking office declined in some parts of the state but not others. As the author of the article (Dorr 1937) contends, the Depression may have increased political unrest and therefore increased the number of people inspired to seek office. This may be so, but in the absence of a legitimate control group (or perhaps a quantification of what "frivolous" means), we cannot know. We cannot, then, know if some adjustments were a means of re-establishing party dominance or of fixing legitimate problems in the primary itself.

A fourth and final hypothesis is that changes in primary laws coincided with an increase in two-party competition. In one-party states, primary laws might have usefully provided choices to voters in a way that the general election could not. Southern states, which adopted primary runoffs during the 1930s, provide a textbook example of the ways in which primaries effectively took the place of the general election; in states such as Louisiana and Texas, for instance, factions competed within the Democratic primary and subsequent runoff, but the eventual Democratic nominee was assured of victory in the general election (see Bullock and Johnson 1992). In many non-Southern states, Republican dominance ensured that the Republican primary effectively conferred victory even without the runoff. As the Democratic Party gained strength in the North, primaries became less useful for the Republican Party and could actually prove harmful if there was a possibility that the primary would produce a weak general election nominee. In histories of California politics (again, discussed below) most writers have argued that the state's unusual cross-filing provision—in which candidates could run simultaneously in more than one party's primary—caused few problems in the 1930s and 1940s, when Republicans dominated the state, but was abolished by Democrats once they had achieved parity and a narrow legislative majority in the 1950s. The causal order here is important: primary laws were changed after two-party competition developed; the rise of two party competition was not a consequence of changes in the primary laws.

This argument is well-established in literature on California (Bell 2012; Delmatier, McIntosh, and Waters 1970; Gaines and Tam Cho 2002). This argument gains the most academic support as a broader explanation in V. O. Key's *American State Politics* (1956, 111–121). Key claims that there is some evidence that the direct primary was most enthusiastically adopted in one-party states, as a response to one-partyism. There was, he claims, an "evangelical tone" to calls for the direct primary, and parties had little normative standing in arguing against it. Once primaries were established, however, parties needed to develop means of regularizing conflict. This need could be resolved informally in one-party states with factional conflict, but as the threat of victory for the minority party increased, so did the need to develop formal means of producing strong nominees. Key points, in fact, to the character of the laws of the last states to adopt the primary; in the 1940s the four laws newly establishing primary elections created systems that were closed (Connecticut and Rhode Island), had preprimary conventions that whittled down the candidates on the ballot (Utah and New Mexico), or had formal balancing provisions (New Mexico).[4] These are all states where general elections became more important at the time.

These different arguments are neither mutually exclusive nor specific to the time period under consideration here. They do, however, suggest that an analysis sensitive to developments in primary laws across different regions of the country and across different types of party systems is in order.

Data and Method

All of the above hypotheses concern the relationship between, on the one hand, the direction and timing of changes in primary laws, and on the other, the characteristics of the states in which these changes were made. In the following discussion of these changes, I catalog all major changes in primary laws between 1928 and 1970, drawing on two sources.[5] First, in the decade following the publication of Merriam and Overacker's *Primary Elections*, Louise Overacker published articles biennially in the *American Political Science Review* summarizing changes in state primary laws. I draw on Overacker's (1928, 1930, 1932, 1934, 1936, 1940) descriptions, omitting changes that she described as being minor. Second, I use descriptions from the *Book of States* (Council of State Governments, 1936–1970) of changes in primary laws between 1936 and 1970. Here, as in Overacker, the descriptions tend to distinguish between major and minor changes in the laws. I checked these sources against the list of primary election law modifications offered by Hirano and Snyder (2019, 30–32).

My analysis begins in 1928 not because it is the alleged beginning of retrenchment—most accounts of primary repeal efforts make reference to legislative changes in the early 1920s—but because it is the last year in which a comprehensive study of primary legislation was published. The analysis ends in 1970; following that election, the McGovern-Fraser reforms established rules encouraging states to hold presidential primaries and establishing rules for ballot access and voting in these primaries. For administrative reasons many states adjusted their primary election laws to fit the McGovern-Fraser rules. This ensured a substantial exogenous shock to states' primary systems, and it resulted in primary reforms that effectively ended the period of alleged retrenchment discussed here.[6]

A small number of technical details related to these sources are in order here. First, there is some overlap between these two sources; the period from 1936 to 1940 provides at least a small test of whether either source omits changes that are measured by the other. For this period, both Overacker and the *Book of States* list the same changes and describe them in the same manner. This comparison also suggests that there is no evidence of glaring omissions in one source that are included in the other. Second, I was forced to make distinctions between major and minor changes. Overacker's descriptions clearly note when she views some changes as being relatively inconsequential; in some cases she summarizes these changes briefly while in others she merely notes that some states made small changes without describing what these changes were. This also ensures some continuity between the two sources; my judgment in comparing the two is that all of the changes mentioned in the *Book of States* are significant enough that they resemble what Overacker would have considered to be major changes. Third, I include Southern states here, unlike Ware and Lawrence, Bowler, and Donovan. Given the nature of the analysis that follows, I see little reason to exclude the South, and Southern states are included in the Overacker and *Book of States* summaries. Because other studies exclude the South, however, I treat the South separately in some of the analyses that follow in order to identify differences in the passage and direction of reform laws.

For each change in state laws, I determined whether the changes represented a reduction or an expansion of party control of primaries For instance, I coded changes from open to closed primaries, the establishment of preprimary conventions, sore loser laws, or restrictions on voting or ballot access as a reduction of popular participation (and hence an enhancement of party control), while changes in the opposite direction were coded as expansive changes (and hence as reductions of party control). Table 2.1 summarizes all such changes. This coding method requires a certain amount of judgment in that it does not take into account the stated rationales for the changes.

In the final column of Table 2.1, I provide a brief justification for the coding decisions. Some of these are obvious—restricting voting or ballot access is considered by all students of elections to be an effort to reduce uncertainty in primaries and to increase party control. Others may be less obvious to the reader but are unanimously held by analysts to have a particular effect (restrictive or expansive) on primaries. In a few instances, the *Book of States* or Overacker's summaries merely list the intent of legislation (e.g., "stricter rules") without providing details of why these rules are stricter. These are generally minor modifications to the rules. In all cases in which studies of primary rules are not in agreement about the intent of particular changes (e.g., for runoffs and changes in campaign finance laws pertaining to primaries), I have consigned these changes to the "no effect" category.[7] In order to show both the number of changes in

Table 2.1 Coding of Changes in Primary Laws

	Effect on Popular Participation	Number of Cases	State (Year)	Justification for Coding and Other Notes
Abolishes cross-filing	Restrictive	1	CA (1960)	Prevents candidate from running in more than one party
Candidate must be party member	Restrictive	1	NJ (1928)	
Challenges frivolous candidates	Restrictive	1	OK (1928)	
Creates signature thresholds	Restrictive	2	CA (1946); OK (1946)	Limits ballot access
Higher signature thresholds	Restrictive	1	TX (1948)	Limits ballot access
Identifies incumbent on ballot	Restrictive	1	MS (1962)	
Miscellaneous stricter rules	Restrictive	1	OK (1962)	As described by *Book of States* without details
No write-ins	Restrictive	2	AL (1948); AR (1948)	Limits ballot access
From open to closed	Restrictive	4	CO (1928); ID (1960); HI (1962); AR (1968)	Limits ballot access
Party affiliation test	Restrictive	2	CO (1938); FL (1938)	Voter must show allegiance to party
Preprimary convention	Restrictive	3	MA (1934); ID (1962); NM (1962)	Allows party to winnow number of candidates
Reduces offices for primary	Restrictive	1	MD (1928)	

(*continued*)

Table 2.1 Continued

	Effect on Popular Participation	Number of Cases	State (Year)	Justification for Coding and Other Notes
Repeals direct primary	Restrictive	1	IN (1930)	
Repeals Richards primary	Restrictive	1	SD (1930)	Richards primary requires voters to approve party platforms and candidates to commit to those platforms
Requires party enrollment	Restrictive	1	KS (1928)	
Sore loser law	Restrictive	3	ND (1948); AZ (1962); MO (1968)	Prevents defeated candidates from running as independents
Stricter ballot access laws	Restrictive	2	AL (1932); MA (1966)	As described by *Book of States* without details
Stricter write-in law	Restrictive	1	MT (1948)	As described by *Book of States* without details
Changes runoff to plurality	No effect	1	UT (1950)	Possible effect, but literature not in agreement
Lists candidate occupation	No effect	2	CA (1932); MI (1932)	Provides information about candidates
Moves primary to later	No effect	3	MT (1964); ND (1964); UT (1964)	Possible effect, but literature not in agreement
Runoff	No effect	5	FL (1930); OK (1930); AR (1948); GA (1950); VA (1952)	Possible effect, but literature not in agreement

Table 2.1 Continued

	Effect on Popular Participation	Number of Cases	State (Year)	Justification for Coding and Other Notes
Spending limits for primaries	No effect	1	VA (1962)	Possible effect, but literature not in agreement
Abolishes preprimary convention	Expansive	3	MA (1938); NM (1956); NM (1968)	Reduces ability of party to endorse or winnow number of candidates
Creates blanket primary	Expansive	1	WA (1936)	
From closed to open	Expansive	5	ID (1940); MI (1940); MO (1946); AK (1968); UT (1968)	
Consolidated ballot	Expansive	1	ND (1962)	Limits potential for party-line voting
Expands primary	Expansive	2	MT (1928); NC (1928)	Raises number of offices with mandatory primary
Creates mandatory primary	Expansive	6	ID (1932); KY (1936); NM (1940); UT (1940); RI (1948); CT (1956)	
Creates more open primary	Expansive	1	MN (1934)	As described by Overacker without details
Eliminates party affiliation test	Expansive	4	ID (1938); MI (1938); ND (1938); UT (1938)	Increases ballot access
No preprimary endorsements	Expansive	1	CA (1962)	

(*continued*)

38 REFORM AND RETRENCHMENT

Table 2.1 Continued

	Effect on Popular Participation	Number of Cases	State (Year)	Justification for Coding and Other Notes
Establishes one primary date	Expansive	2	NY (1956); RI (1962)	Reduces "second mover advantage"
Reintroduces primary, with preprimary convention	Expansive	1	NY (1968)	
Repeals party enrollment	Expansive	1	ND (1932)	Increases ballot access
Total N	29 restrictive changes, 28 expansive changes, 12 no effect	69		

Sources: Author's data, drawn from *Book of States* and Overacker (1928, 1930, 1932, 1934, 1936, 1940).

primary laws and the overall trend in the direction of these changes, the figures that follow thus show the sum total of changes in primary laws, whatever the impact, and my measurement of the direction (restrictive or expansive) of the changes. The primary law changes included in this table are not all of the same magnitude, and a case could be made for scaling them to distinguish major and minor changes, as some recent studies seek to do.[8] To some extent, the exclusion of minor changes, as defined in the data sources, does this. While I do note instances of obviously very consequential changes in the narratives that follow (such as the implementation of the direct primary or the shift from closed to open primaries), I do not think there is an adequate method for quantitatively scaling all primary law changes. Hence, my focus is simply on the ability, or willingness, of states to enact changes that were consequential enough to be noted in the Overacker or *Book of States* summaries.

The coding method here may also miss some changes, in that I am relying on the research of others as opposed to conducting my own exhaustive summary of state legislative records. This method also ignores unsuccessful legislation: bills or referenda that were rejected, or proposals that were circulated but never voted upon. As noted earlier, Ware uses repeal attempts as an indicator of retrenchment regarding primaries. Such an argument might provide a fuller picture of a changing set of attitudes about primaries, but it also runs the risk of assuming that idiosyncratic behavior on the part of some legislators (in the U.S. Congress, for instance, any legislator can introduce a bill on any subject) constitutes a trend. There is, then, no perfect method to track changes, yet I contend that if there are patterns, they should be evident in analysis based on the coding here.

The hypotheses presented earlier suggest, however, different sets of independent variables, some of which are easy to quantify, others of which are not. Table 2.2 summarizes the independent variables of relevance here, with the caveat that not all are easily measurable. At a minimum, measurement strategies differ, so there is no single test one can undertake that would distinguish between competing explanations.

All measurements in Table 2.2 concern the characteristics of individual states; our main concern here is how to distinguish between states that changed their primary laws and states that did not. The state groupings are not mutually

Table 2.2 Hypotheses Regarding Changes in Primary Laws and Variable Measurement

Hypothesis	Independent Variable	Measurement	Sources	Discussion
States with strong Progressive movements are more likely to implement primary law changes	Strength of Progressives	Passage of Progressive legislation	Lawrence, Donovan, and Bowler (2013)	Preliminary evidence, Chapter 2; detailed discussion, Chapter 3
Primaries were taken over by nonparty groups	Strength of the Nonpartisan League	Presence and amount of Nonpartisan League organizing activity	Morlan (1955); Gaston (1920); Gieske (1979)	Preliminary evidence, Chapter 2; detailed discussion, Chapter 4
Primaries did not work well (for public or for parties)	Allegations of difficulty implementing primaries	Presence or absence of statements in academic articles making such allegations	Various; see Table 2.4	Preliminary evidence, Chapter 2; detailed discussion, Chapter 5
Level of two-party competition increased	Change in the amount of party competition	Democratic and Republican seat shares in state legislature	Dubin (2007)	Preliminary evidence and detailed discussion, Chapter 6

exclusive, and some readers might legitimately quarrel about the inclusion or exclusion of some states in the particular groups. The listings here are, again, intended to be a precursor for the historical account in the chapters to come.

One must of course be sensitive to the different state baselines for this analysis; states that had particularly open primary laws as of 1928 may have been unable to further liberalize their laws, while states that had no primary at all could not further restrict their primary laws. Primary laws are sufficiently complex that it is not possible to provide any sort of baseline measurement of the openness of primary laws, but the tables in this chapter list the pattern of changes in several of the more active states; readers with knowledge of these states can evaluate these patterns with reference to the state's overall political characteristics. My goal, however, is to examine aggregate trends in order to see if there were easily observable movements in the states toward more or less expansive primary rules.

For hypothesis 1, regarding change in Progressive states, I use as a starting point Lawrence, Donovan, and Bowler's (2009) list of states that adopted the citizen initiative between 1898 and 1918.[9] Given that direct democracy was one of the major Progressive reforms, and given that it was not adopted as widely as was the primary, this serves as a list not only of states with a successful Progressive movement, but of states whose political institutions were sufficiently malleable that Progressives were able to pass significant reforms. As the authors note, these two concerns are not the same. The list serves as only a partial measurement of our variable of concern; it tells us where Progressives exercised some degree of power. Progressives were more likely to be Republicans than Democrats, but there is no clear way to identify Progressive candidates. The Progressive Party, formed in 1912, was largely a vehicle for the presidential ambitions of Theodore Roosevelt and, later, Robert LaFollette; although it did run some candidates for other offices, the party was never inclusive of all candidates or politicians who identified in some way with the Progressive movement. Hence, there is to my knowledge no state-by-state measure of Progressive decline, but we can at a minimum see where there was a peak of Progressive influence from which there might be a decline. It is noteworthy, in addition, that the list here has substantial overlap with the list of NPL-influenced states in hypothesis 2.

Hypothesis 2 largely concerns regional problems with the primary. While it is certainly possible that nonparty groups were active in many regions of the country, the historical record regarding primaries has focused almost exclusively on one such group, the NPL, and the agrarian states of the northern Plains in which the NPL was most active. Studies of the NPL have listed states where the NPL maintained chapters (Gaston 1920) or prominent legislators who sought and/or received the endorsement of the NPL (Morlan 1955), so it is not difficult to identify the states with an NPL presence using this measurement. Table 2.3

Table 2.3 States with Significant Nonpartisan League Activity

State	Description	Source
North Dakota	Birthplace of the Nonpartisan League	Morlan (1955); Gaston (1920)
Minnesota	Extensive organizing activity	Morlan (1955); Gieske (1979)
Idaho	Endorses Senator William Borah	Morlan (1955)
Nebraska	Endorses referendum to reinstate direct primary	Morlan (1955)
South Dakota	Moderate amount of organizing activity	Gaston (1920)
Montana	Endorses Representative Jeanette Rankin	Morlan (1955)
Colorado	Small amount of organizing activity	Gaston (1920)
Iowa	Small amount of organizing activity	Gaston (1920)
Kansas	Small amount of organizing activity	Gaston (1920)
Oklahoma	Small amount of organizing activity	Gaston (1920)
Texas	Small amount of organizing activity	Gaston (1920)
Wisconsin	Small amount of organizing activity	Gaston (1920)

lists the states in this category, in roughly descending order of the level of NPL activity.

The measurement of hypothesis 3 is perhaps the least precise of the four tests we can undertake here. Many of the descriptions of state primary laws clearly indicate that relatively nonpartisan observers had noted defects in the primary law. As noted in Chapter 1, primary elections received enough scholarly attention in the 1910s and 1920s that the major political science journals of the day (the *American Political Science Review* and the *Annals of the American Academy of Political and Social Sciences*) published many studies of primary laws. These included critiques of particular methods, broad summaries of patterns, and several case studies of individual states. Many of these studies focused on particular defects in state laws. Given that these articles were written by academic observers, not partisan activists, I assume that such criticisms were at least somewhat merited and identified the states subject to these critiques as states where changes were appropriate as a means of remedying particular problems. Table 2.4 lists these states, along with the source of the critique and a brief description of the problem in question. Here there is certainly the possibility of bias; some states may have received the attention of scholars while other states with similar problems were ignored, and some of the authors of these works may have overstated the magnitude of the problems. This list does, however, at least provide a starting point for considering remediable defects.

Finally, hypothesis 4 requires that we obtain an adequate measure of two-party competition over time. There are many potential indicators of party competition—one might use vote share in presidential or gubernatorial races, representation in various offices, or party registration. Here I use the balance of party power in the state lower and upper chambers over the period from 1928 to 1970. This is a measure that one can obtain for forty-six states over most of this period, and it is arguably superior to voting in that it is not specific to individual candidacies.[10] The data for this variable are taken from Dubin's (2007) *Party Affiliation in the State Legislatures* and converted to percentages. Because it is more difficult to separate the quantitative measurement from the historical discussion of changes in partisan competition, I defer most of the analysis of this claim to Chapter 6, but I outline the basic argument here so that readers can keep it in mind while considering the other hypotheses. Because some of the claims about defective laws described in Chapter 5 also may have been made for partisan gain, I also use the state legislative seat share data in that chapter to illustrate the relationship between party support and the timing of claims about problematic laws.

The tests here are not necessarily conclusive, but they do aim to separate out different groups of states in order to infer the reasons behind legislative changes. This allows one to make more nuanced arguments about legislative changes than if one follows Key, Lockard, and others by analyzing changes according to geographic region of the country. To the extent that the groupings are not mutually exclusive, there may be multiple causes of legislative changes in some states.

A Preliminary Test of the Hypotheses

Figure 2.1 shows changes in primary laws by year and by the intent of the laws (as described in Table 2.1). The black bars show the total number of states changing their primary laws in any given year, and the gray bars show the direction of such changes, subtracting the laws that increase party control over the process from those that open up the process. A gray bar above the x axis indicates that the majority of laws passed in a given year were aimed at opening up the primary process (reducing party control), while one that falls below the x axis indicates that the majority of a given year's laws aimed to increase party control—that is, to render primaries less open.

The figure shows that states tinkered with their primary laws almost constantly between the 1930s and late 1960s, with the exception of the World War II years. There is, however, no consistent overall direction to these changes; there

Table 2.4 States Described in Contemporary Literature as Having Defective Primary Laws

State	Description	Source
Alaska	Crossover voting	McBeath and Morehouse (1994)
California	Plurality winners; cost of campaigning	West (1923)
Colorado	Poor quality candidates	Wallace (1923)
Hawaii	"Raiding": parties run candidates in opposition party primary	Pratt and Smith (2000)
Illinois	Poor quality candidates	Wallace (1923)
Indiana	Uninformed voters	Guild (1923)
Iowa	Bad timing of primary election dates for farmers	Horack (1923)
Maine	Heightened regional conflict	Hormell (1923)
Michigan	Frivolous candidacies; filing fee too low	Dorr (1937)
Missouri	Candidates take ballot spots, then withdraw	Loeb (1910)
New Mexico	Heightened regional conflict	Holmes (1967)
New York	Ballot too long; too many minor party primaries	Feldman (1917)
South Dakota	Richards primary (which requires voters to approve party platforms and candidates to commit to those platforms) is too complicated for voters to understand	Berdahl (1923)
Virginia	Primary held too late	Sabato (1977)

is no movement. One could, perhaps, infer that the restrictive laws passed in 1928 and 1930 were the end of the backlash noted by Merriam and Overacker, followed by an opening up of primaries during the 1930s. Following the 1930s, however, there is no period of more than four years when the majority of legislative changes appear to be going in the same direction; in other words, there is little evidence from the aggregate data that this is not a random process. The large number of changes in 1962 is noteworthy, perhaps, given that year's proximity to changes in congressional districting and voting rights—and it perhaps calls for giving some extra scrutiny to Southern primary laws. Again, however, the large

44 REFORM AND RETRENCHMENT

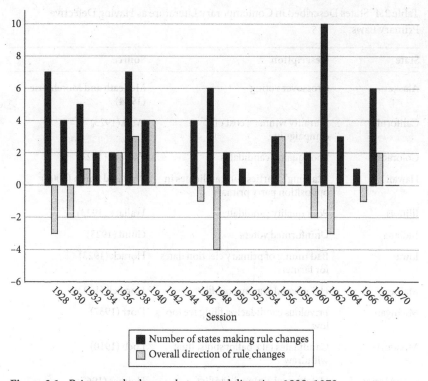

Figure 2.1. Primary rule changes by year and direction, 1928–1970

Notes: The figure on the y axis is the net number of changes in state primary laws for each session; the session date listed on the x axis is the final year of the two-year legislative session. The "number of states making rule changes" category includes changes that were neither expansive nor restrictive.
Source: Author's data.

number of legislative changes in that year renders the year only a slight outlier in relation to other years. Without focusing on where these changes are taking place, it is difficult to infer anything other than that there is no overwhelming evidence of a move against primaries during this period. This pattern alone may well confirm Merriam and Overacker's contention that the repeal movement had largely run its course by 1928.

In the following analyses, I distinguish between the hypotheses by comparing changes among different types of states. This approach does not necessarily prove any one hypothesis at the expense of the others, but it does illustrate patterns of change. It is important to note here that the unit of analysis is the rule change, not the state. There are a total of sixty-nine consequential rule changes, but these rule changes took place in only thirty-three states. Seventeen states thus had no changes at all; sixteen states changed their rules only once, and three states (Idaho, North Dakota, and Utah) changed their rules five times. Perhaps unsurprisingly, none of the states that changed their rules three times or more changed them consistently in the same direction. Almost all of the states that enacted reforms fall into one of the groupings in the first three hypotheses—although collectively the three groupings include thirty-four states, there are only eight states that enacted primary laws over this period and twelve law enactments that are *not* included among these states; four of these eight are Southern, and two are states that adopted the direct primary for the first time during this period.[11]

The Progressive States

Figure 2.2 compares primary reforms in states where the Progressive movement had been successful to reforms in those where the movement was not successful. Table 2.5 provides a list of these changes. Fifteen of these twenty-one

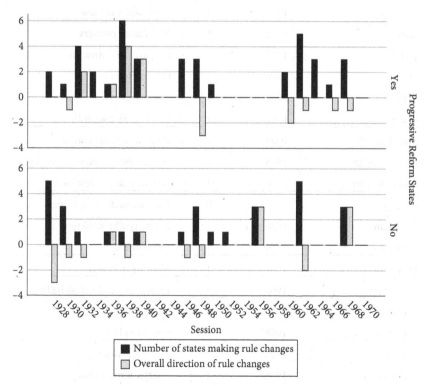

Figure 2.2. Primary rule changes by year and direction in Progressive states, 1928–1970

Notes: The figure on the y axis is the net number of changes in state primary laws for each session; the session date listed on the x axis is the final year of the two-year legislative session. The "number of states making rule changes" category includes changes that were neither expansive nor restrictive.

Source: Author's data.

Table 2.5 Primary Law Changes in Progressive Reform States

State	Year	Direction of Rule Change	Description
Arizona	1962	−1	Sore loser law
Arkansas	1946	0	Runoff
Arkansas	1948	−1	No write-ins
Arkansas	1968	−1	Open to closed
California	1932	0	List candidate occupation
California	1946	−1	Create signature thresholds
California	1960	−1	Abolish cross-filing
California	1962	1	No preprimary endorsements
Colorado	1928	−1	Open to closed
Colorado	1938	−1	Party affiliation test
Idaho	1932	1	Mandatory primary
Idaho	1938	1	No party affiliation test
Idaho	1940	1	Open primary
Idaho	1960	−1	Open to closed
Idaho	1962	−1	Preprimary convention
Massachusetts	1934	−1	Preprimary convention
Massachusetts	1938	1	Abolish preprimary convention
Massachusetts	1966	−1	Stricter ballot access laws
Michigan	1932	0	List candidate occupation
Michigan	1938	1	No party affiliation test
Michigan	1940	1	Open primary
Minnesota	1934	1	More open primary
Mississippi	1962	−1	Identify incumbent on ballot
Missouri	1946	1	Open primary
Missouri	1968	−1	Sore loser law
Montana	1928	1	Expand primary
Montana	1948	−1	Stricter write-in law
Montana	1964	0	Move primary later
North Dakota	1932	1	Repeal party enrollment
North Dakota	1938	1	No party affiliation test

Table 2.5 Continued

State	Year	Direction of Rule Change	Description
North Dakota	1948	−1	Sore loser law
North Dakota	1962	1	Consolidated ballot
North Dakota	1964	0	Move primary later
South Dakota	1930	−1	Repeal Richards primary
Utah	1938	1	No party affiliation test
Utah	1940	1	Mandatory primary
Utah	1950	0	Change runoff to plurality
Utah	1964	0	Move primary later
Utah	1968	1	Closed to open
Washington	1936	1	Blanket primary
15 of 21 states had changes		1	40 total rule changes
Maine, Nebraska, Nevada, Ohio, Oregon, Wyoming			No changes

Sources: Author's data, drawn from *Book of States* and Overacker (1928, 1930, 1932, 1934, 1936, 1940).

states changed their primary rules at least once, accounting for accounting for forty laws (58 percent of the total in all states). This suggests, first of all, that the Progressive states were slightly more likely to experiment with their primary laws than were other states; 71 percent of them made some sort of a change, as opposed to 62 percent of other states. They were also much more likely to experiment with their laws multiple times than were other states. Ten of the twenty-one Progressive states changed their primary laws more than once, while only four of the remaining twenty-nine states made more than one change.

In a way, these changes were unsurprising—one would expect that these would be the states that would have the capacity to innovate, and as such, to enact laws sufficiently complex or ambitious that they would need to be revisited. The top half of Figure 2.2 shows, however, that there was no clear era of retrenchment in these states; although the Progressive movement may have waned by the 1930s, the laws enacted in the that decade in Progressive states tended to be aimed at making primaries more open. Between 1928 and 1940, the Progressive states generally acted to make primaries mandatory (where they weren't already), to abolish party affiliation tests or enrollment requirements (five states did this), or to switch from closed to open primaries. The lone outlier to this pattern is Colorado, which closed its primary in 1928 and established a party affiliation test in 1938.[12] Massachusetts established a preprimary convention in 1934, only to abolish it four years later.[13] And South Dakota's Richards primary, perhaps the nation's most ambitious and unwieldy primary law, was finally repealed, after several failed or incomplete attempts, in 1928.

The period from 1950 onward shows some contraction, but the nature and locations of these changes did not result in a one-to-one rollback of all of the expansive laws enacted in the 1930s and earlier. For instance, states such as Idaho, Michigan, Minnesota, Utah, and Washington all established open or blanket primaries during the 1930s and 1940s; restrictive reforms in the subsequent decades tweaked these reforms by, for instance, limiting write-in candidacies or prohibiting "sore losers" from running but did not fully close the primaries. The scale of the contractions, then, was not sufficient to return these states to the level of party control that had existed before the 1930s.

In the postwar years, however, there were some states that had not had a strong Progressive movement that enacted laws aimed at opening up primaries, while some Progressive states passed laws increasing party control. This may be simply an instance of the rest of the country catching up to the Progressive states. Yet Progressive states were more active than others in establishing sore loser laws or limiting ballot access for write-in candidates in the late 1940s. Two Progressive states closed their primaries in the 1960s, and several states moved their primaries later, a reform that has no clear implications for party control. Again, some changes may have been simply matters of improving the primary—Mississippi's decision to identify incumbents on the ballot was driven by concern over the confusion caused by multiple candidates with the same name or similar names.

One can, of course, quarrel with the determination of which states are in fact Progressive states—most notably, Wisconsin does not appear on this list, and one might question whether some of the Southern states that do appear were actually all that progressive. The fact that these states include so many of those willing to experiment, however, indicates that Lawrence, Donovan, and Bowler's claim that these also were states where institutional changes were possible is worth considering. It also is worth noting that the states that did not enact reforms maintained some form of Progressive experimentation of relevance to primaries: Nebraska held nonpartisan primaries during most of this period, Oregon maintained some of the nation's strictest campaign finance regulations, and Nevada continued to permit voters to vote for "none of the above" on their general election ballots. Yet the findings here are substantial enough to not be affected by the addition or subtraction of one or two states.

The Nonpartisan League States

Figure 2.3 and Table 2.6 show changes in primary election laws for states where the NPL had done some organizing during the 1910s. While the immediate threat of the NPL had certainly receded by 1928, its success in some of these states indicates that concerns about primaries being hijacked by nonparty groups might resonate with local politicians and voters. The data here show, however, that states where the NPL had been most successful—namely, North Dakota and Minnesota—actually opened up their primaries further in the late 1920s and 1930s. It seems evident from the cases here that fears about open primaries played little role in rule changes in these states. The Southern states Oklahoma

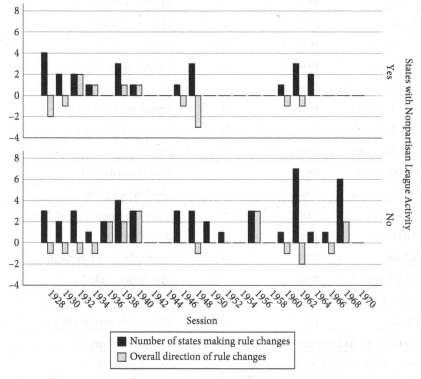

Figure 2.3. Primary rule changes by year and direction in Nonpartisan League States, 1928–1970

Notes: The figure on the y axis is the net number of changes in state primary laws for each session; the session date listed on the x axis is the final year of the two-year legislative session. The "number of states making rule changes" category includes changes that were neither expansive nor restrictive.

Source: Author's data.

Table 2.6 Primary Law Changes in Nonpartisan League States

State	Year	Direction of Rule Change	Description
Colorado	1928	−1	Open to closed
Colorado	1938	−1	Party affiliation test
Idaho	1932	1	Mandatory primary
Idaho	1938	1	No party affiliation test
Idaho	1940	1	Open primary
Idaho	1960	−1	Open to closed
Idaho	1962	−1	Preprimary convention
Kansas	1928	−1	Requires party enrollment
Minnesota	1934	1	More open primary
Montana	1928	1	Expands primary
Montana	1948	−1	Stricter write-in law
Montana	1964	0	Move primary later
North Dakota	1932	1	Repeal party enrollment
North Dakota	1938	1	No party affiliation test
North Dakota	1948	−1	Sore loser law
North Dakota	1962	1	Consolidated ballot
North Dakota	1964	0	Move primary later
Oklahoma	1928	−1	Challenge frivolous candidates
Oklahoma	1930	0	Runoff
Oklahoma	1946	−1	Create signature thresholds
Oklahoma	1962	−1	Misc. stricter rules
South Dakota	1930	−1	Repeal Richards primary
Texas	1948	−1	Higher signature thresholds
9 of 12 states had changes			23 total rule changes
Iowa, Nebraska, Wisconsin			No rule changes

Sources: Author's data, drawn from *Book of States* and Overacker (1928, 1930, 1932, 1934, 1936, 1940).

and Texas restricted primaries in roughly the same manner as other Southern states, and many other changes appear more likely to have been the consequence of defective rules (again, South Dakota) or other forces than of concern about NPL-like forces. Indeed, apart from the efforts in many of these states to institute sore loser laws in the late 1940s, the pattern here seems to be one of loosening party control.

Simply noting that the NPL organized in some of these states, however, does not demonstrate that it had any success. What the persistence of open primaries in states such as Minnesota and North Dakota may show, however, is that the individual politicians who reached office as part of the NPL effort—politicians such as North Dakota senators William Lemke and Lynn Frazier—benefited from it as individual politicians, whatever the consequences of the primary for their parties. By the late 1920s it had become apparent in some NPL states that further opening primaries might actually dilute NPL strength; the NPL's rival faction in North Dakota, the Independent Voters' Association, actually pushed for a top two primary out of the belief that it could rally voters of both parties against the NPL (Blackorby 1963, 129–130). Some students of agrarian politics of the era have also argued that primary elections in the individual states, whatever form they took, had relatively predictable results, so whichever groups had sufficient control to write primary laws had an incentive to maintain the status quo that put them in power (Goldberg 1955).

An alternate means of identifying potential support for nonparty movements might take into account third-party strength, either in the years preceding or following the establishment of the direct primary. The rationale for such an approach comes from the observation by, among others, Reynolds (2006), Crespin (2004), and Argersinger (1995, 137), that the introduction of the direct primary caused a decline in support for minor parties as those who championed those parties' issues sought to run in the major parties' primaries rather than as minor party nominees in the general election. Argersinger further notes the large number of antifusion laws passed in the late nineteenth and early twentieth centuries that reduced the vote share of minor parties. Looking at party seat share in the state legislature (as I will do in Chapter 6 when I consider the relationship between general election competition and primary reforms), however, fails to show any relationship between third-party strength and changes in primary laws. The two states with the highest level of third-party representation, Wisconsin and Vermont, did not change their primary laws at all over this period, and three other states that had strong but short-lived third-party surges (Idaho, Louisiana, and Massachusetts) did not change their laws in years proximate to the peaks of third-party representation. It may be that the seat share measure does not adequately capture third-party support, but at any rate there is little suggestion that primary law changes (as opposed to implementation of the primary in the first place) are related to third-party support.

States with Defective Primary Laws

Figure 2.4 compares the frequency and direction of primary reform in states with problematic primary laws to reforms in other states, and Table 2.7 lists the reforms in these states. Here, we have problems interpreting intent. It is not clear that changes to unworkable laws need to result in restricting the process, nor is it clear that changes in these states' primary laws were enacted as a means of remedying defects. For that matter, we have no absolute standard to measure

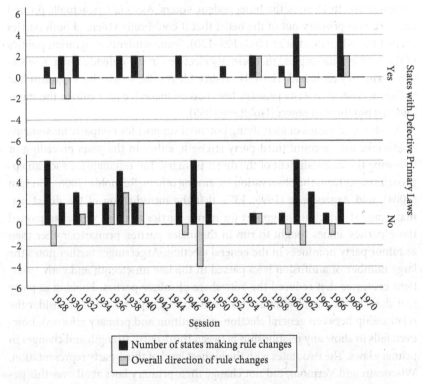

Figure 2.4. Primary rule changes by year and direction in states with defective primary laws, 1928–1970

Notes: The figure on the y axis is the net number of changes in state primary laws for each session; the session date listed on the x axis is the final year of the two-year legislative session. The "number of states making rule changes" category includes changes that were neither expansive nor restrictive.
Source: Author's data.

Table 2.7 Primary Law Changes in States with Defective Primary Laws

State	Year	Direction of Rule Change	Description
Alaska	1968	1	Closed to open
California	1946	−1	Create signature thresholds
California	1960	−1	Abolish cross-filing
California	1962	1	No preprimary endorsements
Colorado	1928	−1	Open to closed
Colorado	1938	−1	Party affiliation test
Hawaii	1962	−1	Open to closed
Indiana	1930	−1	Repeal direct primary
Michigan	1932	0	List candidate occupation
Michigan	1938	1	No party affiliation test
Michigan	1940	1	Open primary
Missouri	1946	1	Open primary
Missouri	1968	−1	Sore loser law
New Mexico	1940	1	Mandatory primary
New Mexico	1956	1	Abolish preprimary convention
New Mexico	1962	−1	Preprimary convention
New Mexico	1968	1	No preprimary convention
New York	1956	1	One primary date
New York	1968	1	Reintroduce primary, with preprimary convention
South Dakota	1930	−1	Repeal Richards primary
Virginia	1952	0	Runoff
Virginia	1962	0	Spending limits for primaries
11 of 14 states had changes			22 total rule changes
Illinois, Iowa, Maine			No changes

Sources: Author's data, drawn from Book of States and Overacker (1928, 1930, 1932, 1934, 1936, 1940).

whether, in fact, these states' laws really were that unworkable. In some cases, the problems are clear; as noted previously, there is ample anecdotal evidence that primaries in New York, Michigan, Missouri, and South Dakota were abused by candidates and resulted in confusion for voters. Some of the complaints included here, however, may either be subjective or may be matters that could be resolved without changing the law. If candidates in the primaries are chronically bad, perhaps that says more about the state's politicians than its laws. Perhaps this is why Illinois, Iowa, and Maine enacted no major laws to alter their primaries.

Hence, the data in Figure 2.4 show some unambiguous responses to problems in the law, along with several apparently unrelated changes. New York had responded to its primary problems by abolishing the mandatory primary entirely before the time period considered here; after the Progressive reform era had clearly passed and every other state in the country had adjusted to using primaries, New York reintroduced the mandatory primary in 1968. Indiana likewise repealed its direct primary in 1930 after facing administrative problems. South Dakota's abolition of the Richards primary was (as discussed further in Chapter 5) considered a response to the fact that the law never worked as intended.

There are, admittedly, other ways to resolve primary problems. The widely reported problems of "spot" or placeholder candidates, frivolous candidates, and the like may well have been resolved in some of these states by technical fixes that escaped the attention of those watching primaries from the vantage point of Overacker or the *Book of States* authors. Michigan and Missouri clearly made several changes to their laws over this period, enacting laws requiring that candidates' occupations be listed, preventing "sore losers" from appearing on the ballot, and changing the way in which filing fees were administered. Did these smaller changes solve the states' problems? It is difficult to prove that they did, but these states did choose not to do away with primaries.

There is some overlap between the states with alleged defects and the Progressive states—something to be expected, perhaps, given the greater level of experimentation in Progressive states. The more likely changes are to be made, the more likely it is that some of them will have problems. The California case—discussed in more detail later in the chapter—and the South Dakota case are two examples in which it is difficult to determine whether we are looking at defects, at a backlash against the Progressive movement, or both.

Finally, New Mexico presents an intriguing example of a state that sought to make larger changes to confront problems in its primaries. As discussed in Holmes (1967), New Mexico's early decades as a state were riven by regional conflicts, and the state's Democratic Party was reluctant to establish a direct primary in the first place because it felt that regional ticket balancing was necessary in order to avoid general election defeat. New Mexico was the next-to-last state to institute a direct primary (not including Alaska and Hawaii), and the original 1940 primary law also allowed for a preprimary convention (one was not actually used until 1950). Partisan opposition to having a primary in the first place was broken by the state's charismatic governor Clyde Tingley, who had sufficient personal clout to push it through the legislature. The state's subsequent abolition of the direct primary in 1956, re-establishment of it in 1962, and abolition of it in 1968 show not that the primary or the primary system was flawed, but that the state's regions and its large Latino population used primary laws as a means of factional battle, and they were evenly matched enough that slight changes in power in the state legislature—changes that, because they were factional and not partisan, are difficult to measure—resulted in changes in the law itself. Part of the conflict here also pits incumbent officeholders—who built personal followings and used the direct primary to their advantage—against local party officials. Following the period considered here, the state reintroduced the preprimary convention from 1976 to 1982 and abandoned it again in 1984 (Hain and Garcia 1994).

In sum, some of the states with problematic laws clearly sought to address them, and some of the reforms listed here are clearly efforts to deal with state-specific issues in administering the primary. There is, however, no clear direction to the efforts to amend primary laws—some states abandoned the primary because of problems while others took more measured steps and others appear to have been unable or unwilling to fix problems, and the nature of some of the problems appears to have been subject to debate.

The Rise of Two-Party Competition

There is substantial anecdotal evidence that some states' primary reforms coincided with an increase in general election competition (that is, two-party competition). Reforms in, to give a few instances, California, Connecticut, and North Dakota, have been attributed to a resurgence of Democratic Party support in these states. As with the cases discussed above, there is substantial overlap between cases—the states where general election competition is alleged to be the cause of reform are often states that had a strong Progressive movement. At the very least, using a shift in competitiveness is problematic for two reasons: first, because it calls our attention to states that were uncompetitive at the outset of the time period considered here, and second, because competition increased in most non-Southern states over this time period, so there is some risk of selecting on the dependent variable.

While it may seem logical to conclude that rule changes may come about because of an increase in general election competition, it is also difficult to come up with a compelling argument about what sorts of changes should take place. As I discuss in greater detail in Chapter 6, there is compelling evidence that primary election law changes do have a strong relationship to changes in the level of two-party competition, but the direction of change depends in part on which party is dominant in the state, whether it is seeking to preserve an eroding advantage or to reinforce a newly found one, and whether the party believes that the existing primary laws are advantageous or not.

There are, however, several techniques one might use to look for relationships. I first sought to develop a hazard model, of the sort used in Lawrence, Donovan, and Bowler's (2009, 2013) work on the adoption of Progressive proposals. I experimented with doing so using controls for the state types discussed above, using various measures of partisanship or party change—in party control of one or both houses, or in the percentage of Democrats or Republicans in the legislature—as independent variables. Regardless of how one specifies the model, and of whether the dependent variable is the incidence of rule change or the incidence of a restrictive or expansive rule change, there are no significant results for the partisanship variables. Such models merely confirm trends evident in the data—that, for instance, the states with a legacy of Progressivism were more likely to tinker with their rules than were others.

Overall, however, two-party competition increased in non-Southern states over this period, and the increase for the full period is evident in states that changed their primary laws and in those that did not. It did not increase in lockstep over the period, but this increase is substantial enough that it may suggest that forces much stronger than electoral rules were afoot. I explore this relationship more fully in Chapter 6. State-specific accounts of changes in primary laws often discuss partisan motives, but there is no single model that synthesizes the competing narratives outlined earlier. There is some evidence that states acting to restrict or expand their primaries look different from each other in their level of partisan competition; our ability to measure this is complicated, however, by the difficulty of passing legislation and by the fact that many states that made no changes to their primary laws went through changes that resemble those in states that did change their laws.

Discussion and Conclusions

The hypotheses explored in this chapter all have some degree of support, but none provides a conclusive explanation for changes in primary laws. Given, on the one hand, the diverse state political cultures captured here, and on the other, the overlap between the groups described in these theories, this is no surprise. It is clear, however, that any alleged retrenchment by parties—any organized effort to restrict primaries—was short-lived and local in nature.

Literature on primary elections during the middle decades of the twentieth century is very fragmented. One can glean an explanation of the effects of primaries in the South, the Northeast, the Plains states, and the far West from the major works on these states (e.g., Key 1949; Lockard 1959a). Yet to date there has been no larger assessment of the development of primary elections nationwide. This is striking because the major works on the establishment of primaries point to patterns and mechanisms that are not regional. The Merriam argument points to the popular appeal of primaries, while the Ware argument discusses the ability of parties to adapt to the primary. Whatever the merits of these claims, they are arguments that indicate that there is a national story to be told about changes in primary laws.

Comparing the Hypotheses

The hypotheses explored here all suggest that changes in primary laws can be explained by using institutional features of the states and the laws themselves. In the case of the Progressive states, what matters may not be the ideas of the Progressives themselves but the precedent of adapting state election laws—if state laws can be easily modified, and if there is a tradition of doing so, then continued experimentation with primaries may be predictable. In the case of states with defective laws, it stands to reason that an ability to compare one's state with neighboring states—to consider the options and the consequences of different technical changes to the laws—will ultimately yield repairs to the law. The notion of using partisan advantage to explain changes has, of course, a long history in research on various aspects of election law, including campaign finance laws, voting and ballot restrictions, and the like. It is hardly controversial to note that parties might have sought to change primary laws to give themselves an advantage. The relevant question in any instance of change is whether we are looking at a change brought about by legitimate problems in the law, by bipartisan consensus, or by partisan maneuvering. In many of these cases, the "correct" answer is debatable.

The hypothesis here that garners the least support is that the parties feared what amounted to a hostile takeover of the primary process at the hands of groups such as the NPL. This may ultimately speak to failures on the part of the NPL; by the late 1920s it was a spent force everywhere but North Dakota. North Dakota may have been an idiosyncratic enough state that this was inevitable, and in any case former NPL leaders had sufficiently embedded themselves in the Republican Party there that they may have prevented changes to the laws that got them into office. Many of the states where the NPL was active fit into the other hypotheses' categories, and much of the change in these states may well have had to do with other factors.

Finally, none of the hypotheses here should be taken to contradict larger arguments about the behavior of voters and candidates in the primaries of this era. Many accounts of primary elections during this period simply note that they were not used very much. Lockard (1959a), for instance, notes that in the years after primaries were adopted in New England there was an increase in voter turnout and in electoral competition, but without fail this subsided after a decade or so. Hirano and Snyder (2019) also note the decline in primary competition during these decades. Legal changes may have played a role in this decline, but it seems unlikely that they come anywhere near fully explaining it. In short, some changes in primary competition came about not because of changes in the law, but for entirely different reasons.

Conclusions

There are at least three ways in which the story told in this chapter is not conclusive, however; we cannot understand the trajectory of primaries in the twentieth century merely by relying on a look at which changes happened. First, it should be noted that the measurement techniques here are somewhat limited. There is no conclusive way to group the states discussed in the different hypotheses, and the groupings of states are thus sensitive to errors on my part or on the part of other researchers. In the discussion of defective laws, for instance, I rely on my own reasonably comprehensive survey of literature on primary laws and their problems. It is possible that I missed some compelling arguments about defective laws, that there were some problems that simply were not written about, or that some of the alleged "problems" were not in fact problems or were not different from practices in other states. Similar criticisms could be made about the other groupings, the accuracy of the data on changes in primary laws themselves (that is, the completeness of the Overacker and *Book of States* reviews), or the accuracy of state legislative partisanship in capturing the level of party competition. I have used the sources here in an effort to avoid bias, so I suspect that nothing has been left out that would change the basic patterns, but there may well be room for change in some of the measurements. The evidence here is intended to be suggestive, not conclusive, and to establish a theoretical framework for different historical inquiries.

Second, this chapter has synthesized a large number of state-specific works. There is no reason to doubt the accuracy of these works, but there is of course an ad hoc quality inherent in noting that some of the findings here do or do not accord with the accepted histories of some of these states. I argue that grouping states together to look for common themes—to ask, for instance, whether the logic of reform in the 1930s and beyond looked similar in states where there had been a viable Progressive movement—has its merits, but there is no way to prove that legislators in these states all were thinking the same things when they passed similar primary laws at similar times. Similarly, the groupings here have identified a few anomalous states, which that did not pursue reforms at the times that similar states did, or vice versa.

Third, the period considered here was chosen in part because of data availability and in part because it has, in my opinion, received too little attention. One could push the analysis here further back in time, in order to conduct further investigations into the merits of work that focuses on the adoption of primary laws in the 1910s and 1920s or to disentangle reforms from the 1970s to the present. In the case of the former, there is already substantial research, but this research is focused on the adoption of primary laws, which seems to have a different logic than the adaptation of states to primaries in later years. Claims about retrenchment, however, often include repeal efforts that predate the beginning of the period here. In the case of the latter, I have noted that the Democratic Party's establishment of a presidential primary system gave states a strong push to adapt to the national party's needs. Some work on primaries in the 1970s (see, e.g., Wekkin 1984) has described efforts by the national party organizations to do away with open primaries. At a minimum, another hypothesis would be necessary to account for this era. States have continued to tinker with their primary laws; Hassell (2013) lists thirteen states where legislation to close or open primaries had been introduced in 2011, and the more consequential reforms of recent years, such as California's top two primary, might be explainable using the same concepts considered here.[14] In the chapters that follow, I am most interested in understanding the 1928–1970 time frame, but in order to fully understand it, we will need to look a bit at events immediately before and after it.

At a minimum, the data here do fill the missing link between stories of the adoption of the primary and more recent arguments about changes in primary laws. They show that there are theoretical stories that can be told about changes in primary laws after 1928, and the conventional argument about retrenchment is not one of these. It is true that the nearly universal acceptance of primary elections in the century's first decades made primaries a fixture of American politics; as these data show, however, there has still been much room for adjustment in the nature of primary laws, and party conflict, existing election laws, and states' experiences with the primary caused distinctive patterns of change long after primaries had been established. We now turn to a detailed discussion of each of the theories proposed in this chapter.

3
The Direct Primary and the Decline of the Progressive Movement

Perhaps the most convenient story to tell about changes in primary laws has to do with the decline of the Progressive movement. In its simplest version, the story goes somewhat like this: the direct primary was a reform championed by Progressives. The Progressive movement dominated American politics during the early twentieth century but declined during the 1920s. Once Progressivism had faded, it was easy for political parties to reassert control over elections—either through repeal of Progressive legislation or through modifications that may have left these laws on the books but diminished their antiparty effects. Accordingly, parties became able to use primaries as a means of conferring the nomination upon their chosen candidates.

This chapter explores whether this claim is true. Embedded within the claim are five basic assertions that are common in the literature on primaries:

(a) The direct primary was a Progressive reform.
(b) The direct primary was *only* a Progressive reform; that is, there weren't other advocates for direct primaries at the time, or there weren't other justifications for the establishment of the direct primary save for those offered by Progressives.
(c) The strength of Progressives to defend their reforms diminished after 1920.
(d) Progressive support for the direct primary did not change over time.
(e) The Progressive case was not merely for the direct primary, but for a direct primary that specifically limited the power of parties altogether. In other words, restrictions on the direct primary, such as closed primaries, preprimary conventions, and the like, are inherently anti-Progressive.

As we shall see throughout this chapter, not all of these assertions are strictly true. Most consequentially, it is difficult to find a sustained argument in favor of the direct primary among the most theoretically informed explanations by Progressives of what their philosophy entailed. It may well be true that the direct primary was among the most successful political initiatives enacted during the

Progressive Era, but that does not mean that Progressives were unanimous in their support of it.

This chapter thus begins with a detailed account of how leading Progressives discussed the direct primary, with a particular focus on the work of Herbert Croly, Walter Weyl, and William Allen White. Second, I turn to the question of what Progressive decline was, how one might measure it across the states, and how one might measure Progressivism. Following this, I explore the politics surrounding the expansion and restriction of primary election laws, with particular attention to the states of Massachusetts, Ohio, and Wisconsin. I have chosen these states because of their different experiences with Progressivism; Progressives scored major early victories in each of these states, but the movement lost influence at a different pace, and for different reasons, in each. Collectively, however, these examples show that the decline of Progressivism did not result in an abandonment of the direct primary. Instead, these states' experiences show that the direct primary could easily be detached from other Progressive reforms—in part because it never really was a Progressive reform in the first place.

The Progressive Case for (and Sometimes against) the Direct Primary

There are many ways to categorize Progressive political reforms. Rosenblum (2008, 189–202) divides the chronology of reform efforts into four stages: civil service reforms, which mostly involved reducing the number of patronage and elected positions in government; changes to municipal governance, such as the establishment of nonpartisan or off-cycle elections; the establishment of primary elections; and direct democracy reforms such as the initiative, referendum, and recall. Rosenblum's list accommodates much of the institutional reform agenda but does not include the economic reform agenda. Robert La Follette, the architect of the Progressive movement in Wisconsin, presented a broader view of the Progressive agenda, describing it as a "shift from pure individualism to social control." This shift included expansion of government power to regulate business practices, increased trust in popular majorities, and an expansion of government functions to meet social needs (Nye 1951, 199–200). La Follette's vision emphasized the importance of insulating the administration of policies from the process of creating them. This expansive agenda included all of the mechanisms cited by Rosenblum, but it framed them as much as an economic or social tool as a political one.

These categorizations are somewhat vague, however, in that there was no clearly articulated hierarchy or agenda to the Progressive movement. Many of the ideas of reformers were not new; the direct primary, for instance, was framed as a response to the corruption of party bosses, but some political scientists and historians at the time (e.g., Dallinger 1897; Merriam 1908) and since (Reynolds 2006) have noted that things that looked like primary elections developed gradually over the course of the nineteenth century, and many political party leaders supported them even though they were not sympathetic to the rest of the Progressive agenda. The same can be said for the direct democracy proposals.

There were also important distinctions between types of Progressives. Eastern urban Progressives, such as Robert Luce and Butler Ames in Massachusetts or Tom Johnson in Cleveland, initially focused on municipal reform and avoided class-based or religious rhetoric (Abrams 1964; Warner 1964). Midwestern Progressives such as La Follette, on the other hand, often drew inspiration from the Populist movement and inequalities between farmers and the business elites who controlled commodity grading and pricing. While these two groups found common cause in their advocacy for direct democracy and other such political reforms, they differed in the particular policy outcomes they believed would follow those reforms.

The unifying thread among all of these efforts was the claim that steps must be taken to combat corruption. A focus on political corruption allowed different types of Progressives to present their own explanations of who was corrupt or of what a less corrupt polity would look like. Where there was agreement on first steps, as was the case for the direct primary or the initiative and referendum, Progressive reforms were highly successful. As long as the frame was corruption, opponents were put in the unenviable position of having to make a case in favor of practices that had been defined as being corrupt. Those who were skeptical of Progressivism might question the ability of citizens to use the tools Progressives offered, and many empirical studies of these electoral reforms have borne out the contention that after a period of public enthusiasm, the system adapted and little of substance changed. One way to think about this is that, as Cain (2015, 40; see also Hofstadter 1955, 265) notes, the proponents of any governmental reform always overpromise about the results (and the opponents tend to exaggerate the negative consequences), and in the end supporters are either disillusioned or call for further reforms.

The direct primary was thus discussed by Progressives as one of many reforms. Buenker (1973, 161) notes that the direct primary was an easier sell than many other process reforms. Because it was already in place in some states and municipalities, and because parties had grudgingly accepted it in these places, it was arguably less threatening than untried reforms. It was not as explicitly antiparty as municipal reforms such as the short ballot, the establishment of the city manager position, or civil service reform. It was also easy to understand, and hence the mass public was more unambiguously supportive of the concept.

Progressive Intellectuals and the Direct Primary

The most theoretically sophisticated Progressives, then, were often skeptical that primaries would lead to substantial change and thus spent less time discussing them, while writers with a more pragmatic interest in government reform showed more enthusiasm. As evidence of this, let us consider four foundational works from the Progressive Era: Herbert Croly's Herbert Croly's *The Promise of American Life* (1909) and *Progressive Democracy* (1915), Walter Weyl's *The New Democracy* (1912), and William Allen White's *The Old Order Changeth* (1910). Croly and Weyl hailed from a more academic background, while White spent much of his career as a reporter and newspaper editor. While all three of these writers sought to develop coherent analyses of the Progressive political program, and all three framed Progressivism as a response to corruption and party control of politics, they varied in their advocacy for different types of reforms and in their expectations of how the public, and the policies government produced, would be shaped by electoral reform.

Herbert Croly is widely considered today to be the most influential Progressive writer, and while no Progressive writer can truly be said to have articulated all of the goals of the movement, Croly perhaps came closest to doing so. His major concern in *Progressive Democracy* was the corruption of state governments. Croly focused on the states because he believed that the U.S. Constitution provided an adequate structure for government. The difficulty of amending the U.S. Constitution also meant that federal reform would simply be more difficult than state-level reform. State constitutions were, according to Croly, less coherent than the federal constitution, and the frequency of changes to state government institutions had made them prone to corruption or to inept governance. While Croly contended that there was a role for federal politicians such as Theodore Roosevelt in articulating a moral case for reform, he saw greater opportunity for technical change at the state level. State governments had, he argued, "abandoned themselves to legalism" (1915, 252); they tended to pass more laws and to pass them in a haphazard way that undermined direct citizen control of government.

What was needed, therefore, was a grand vision of how Progressive reforms might fit together at the state level so as to transfer more power to the people. Croly spoke favorably of states such as Oregon and Wisconsin that had enacted primaries as part of such a plan, but in *Progressive Democracy* he did not single out individual electoral reforms for scrutiny. The direct primary, he argued, had been taken up by politicians in response to public demand, but it had not been taken up as part of a general reform plan (334). In practice, it had limited the power of party bosses, but at the expense of emphasizing partisanship. Although the direct primary limited party discipline and the loyalty of elected officials, it also prevented the development of any sort of shared spirit or purpose among the voters (343–344). This sort of frustration might lead to the enactment of other sorts of Progressive reforms; the frustration engendered by the gap created between party politicians and the people would possibly prompt the people to be more sympathetic to more clearly antiparty reforms such as the initiative and referendum, but the direct primary would thus be a cause of antiparty reforms, not a part of them.

This argument built upon criticisms of the direct primary that Croly had made in *The Promise of American Life*. In that book, Croly did not worry as much as other Progressives (such as Walter Lippmann) about the ability of the public to understand politics, but he did see public education and knowledge about politics as a necessary second-stage goal for Progressives. Many of the Progressive reforms he championed, such as the short ballot, the elimination of some elected offices, and changes to judicial election procedures, sought to reduce the number of elections so as to increase the ability of citizens to make informed choices. The direct primary, he wrote, would increase the number of elections, diluting the ability of citizens to make informed choices (1909, 342–343). Lower citizen interest in elections would have the effect of strengthening parties, enabling them to control the flow of information in low-salience races.

Walter Weyl, Croly's partner in establishing the *New Republic*, presented a more sympathetic view of primaries in his major work, *The New Democracy*. Like Croly, Weyl believed that the corruption of party bosses was the major reason for Progressive reforms. Corruption stemmed, he contended, from the belief that parties were "extra-legal, and therefore, irresponsible" (58). Americans had a relatively optimistic view of political and economic change, and they were therefore willing to tolerate some corruption in politics. Yet the economic developments of the late nineteenth century had cemented the ties between political party leaders and business leaders, resulting in a "plutocratic" politics. Corruption was more prevalent and easier to identify at the local and state level than at the federal level, but the two levels of politics were not as separate from each other as Croly believed. Corruption spread from one level to the next, and thus state-level reform might be a precursor to a broader reform agenda. The enemy for Weyl was not just party control of politics, but business control of the parties.

Weyl therefore took Croly's argument a step back. A first response to this problem was not popular control of politics (although that remained a necessary goal) but popular control of the parties themselves. Parties must be seen not as private entities but as public entities, clearly distinct from business. They must be legally regulated. The direct primary was thus both a practical and symbolic step toward doing this. As the direct primary extended from local to state to national elections, it became understood that the people have, and should have, a role in selecting candidates: "When direct nominations are reinforced by laws against corrupt practices, the power of the majority over the making of nominations is correspondingly augmented" (299).

Hence, the direct primary was not a cure in itself for corruption; Weyl cautioned that wealth would still have "ineradicable" influence on politics in many ways, but it was impossible to legislate against this sort of influence (300). Weyl also did not give higher priority to the direct primary than to other reforms; he argued that recall elections had much greater promise in limiting corruption than did the direct primary (311). All of the Progressive direct democracy reforms, however, were symbolic. Even when they were not successful, and even in instances where they were threatened but not actually introduced, they held the possibility for compelling "the plutocracy" to govern in a more efficient, less overtly corrupt fashion (311).

The strongest intellectual argument on behalf of the direct primary comes from William Allen White's *The Old Order Changeth*. White, a Kansas-based journalist and writer, styled himself as a spokesman for middle America and was active in Republican Party politics throughout the late nineteenth and early twentieth centuries. Although *The Old Order Changeth* is one of many books written by White, it stands out for its effort to explain the economic changes that led to Progressivism, in much the same style as Croly's and Weyl's books. White, like these other writers, saw Progressivism as a response to the intertwining of business and government. This intertwining had brought about the emergence of an extraconstitutional form of aristocratic rule, in which political parties had corrupted American institutions precisely because they had removed the ability of the people to hold politicians accountable.

The direct primary was far more pivotal to White's argument than to those of Croly and Weyl because White was more concerned with mechanisms of accountability than the other two and less concerned with putting forward an all-or-nothing Progressive agenda. He spoke highly of the effect the introduction of the secret ballot had on citizens' beliefs about accountability (37), while noting that in practice it did not solve the accountability problem. The direct primary had similar, perhaps even greater, potential to increase accountability, but in order to do so it must be mandatory, not optional (39). White distinguished between use of the direct primary in the North and in the South, and he noted that many state-level introductions of it had been halfhearted accommodations by politicians to public sentiment. This suggests that White cared a great deal about the openness of primary laws, but he noted as well that the gradual and partial introductions of it had whetted the public appetite for greater openness and that ultimately most states were on a path toward open, mandatory primaries.

As with the secret ballot, however, White's main concern was that the direct primary must show results. Throughout the book he sought to tie the introduction of the direct primary to state-level legislation, such as the regulation of railroads, improvements in civic education, and a wide range of restrictions on political spending and interest group influence (50–66, 78). One can quarrel with the argument here that the direct primary led to all of these reforms, but even so, White showed an awareness that for the direct primary to be successful, its advocates must be able to claim credit for substantive changes. The goal of any electoral reform, he argued, must be "defining the rights of the owner and the user of private property according to the dictates of an enlightened public consciousness" (71).

Like Weyl, White saw the symbolic value of the direct primary. Yet a major difference between White, on the one hand, and Croly and Weyl on the other, is that White believed that the direct primary and other electoral reforms, coupled with the sort of educational enlightenment that the other two recommended, would ultimately produce further reform. Measuring the effects of the primary, or of any similar electoral reforms, would be harmed, he argued, by placing them in the context of any agenda or platform. That platform would emerge organically.

White began his book with two broad discussions of the roots of Progressivism: one was the dislocation caused by rapid economic change and technological development, while the other was the massive wave of immigration at the turn of the century. The first of these had caused a demand for policy change, while the second had created a mass public that did not necessarily think of itself as American (246–248). Immigration provided an opportunity for major change in that immigrants did not necessarily think of their allegiance as being to their states or to a political party, and democratic reform could lead them to think of themselves first as Americans. The symbolic value of Progressive election laws was thus far more important to White than to other Progressives, and it could lead to substantial change in public policy, a blending of mass sentiment and elite control.

The Context of Progressivism

The preceding summaries suggest that there was substantial variation in how valuable Progressives found the direct primary to be. There were certainly other Progressive writers who wrote about the direct primary, and indeed the author of the foremost study of primaries at the time, Charles Merriam (1908), made clear his sympathies for the Progressive agenda. Even Merriam, however, worried by the time he updated his book (Merriam and Overacker 1928, 344–350) that the direct primary would fail to live up to reformers' ambitions. Both Croly and Weyl recognized that the primary had existed before the Progressive movement developed, and that there were many self-interested reasons why party leaders might wish to experiment with it. Retrospective works by authors such as Alan Ware (2002) and John Reynolds (2006) have noted that parties were able to use primaries to divest themselves of financial commitments to the candidates and to avoid the messy process of balancing the party ticket. It is easy to argue in hindsight that the introduction of optional primaries put states on a path toward having mandatory primaries that could not easily be taken away (Jacobs 2022).

Each of the Progressive writers, however, retained a skepticism that political parties could be relied upon to pursue Progressive aims sincerely. This was an enduring feature of these authors' worries about federal-level policy; all of the leading Progressive fretted, for instance, about whether Woodrow Wilson was sincerely committed to Progressive goals or was merely seeking to win the votes of disenchanted Progressives (see, e.g., Croly 1915, 15). Even White, of the three the most supportive of the primary, emphasized that it was preferable to have the direct primary introduced through voter initiative (as had been the case in Texas) because this removed parties from any claims to own the primary or to determine the mechanisms of it (50).

At the same time, however, none of these three provided a wholehearted defense of the primary for its own sake. The direct primary might produce positive results; Croly and Weyl were skeptical of this, while White was optimistic. It is difficult when reading these books to conclude that the Progressives really thought that the direct primary was a Progressive reform—it existed before the Progressives, but it gave parties more of a role than did other electoral reforms. Just as Weyl and White thought that the direct primary had symbolic value for voters, so it had symbolic value to Progressives in that they could point to it and its rapid spread as evidence that the public was hungry for reform. But the reservations that Croly and Weyl had about its effects on voters suggest that Progressives would not necessarily be willing to defend the primary if it came under attack, and that they were open to rethinking even their tepid endorsements of it should it ultimately fail to bring about the changes that White forecast.

Retrospective accounts of primary laws suggest that even by the 1920s Progressives were becoming skeptical of what the direct primary had wrought. Buenker (1973, 134–140) notes that the direct primary created a range of unforeseen problems. He focuses on the development of an urban/rural split in support for the primary: parties quickly discovered that primary candidates with an existing organization had substantial advantages, and such candidates tended to be found in major cities, within existing political machines. Hence, lawmakers from cities such as Cleveland, Boston, and Chicago were enthusiastic about allying themselves with Progressives in championing the primary because it benefited them and put rural politicians in these states at a disadvantage. The natural policy concerns of these legislators might also be reason to ally themselves with some parts of the Progressive agenda, but there was an element of self-preservation here. Paula Baker (2012, 110–122) suggests that the introduction of primaries was the principal cause for the development of campaign finance regulation, as high-profile, state-level primaries attracted wealthy businessmen and prompted an explosion in campaign spending. MacNeil and Baker (2013, 24) contend that the cost of primaries deterred many potentially qualified candidates from running, and that the quality of the U.S. Senate was harmed not only by the direct election of senators but also by the fact that the establishment of direct election coincided with the establishment of primaries.

The preceding discussion suggests that there was no strong commitment among Progressive intellectuals to the direct primary. It by no means suggests that a small number of Progressive intellectuals represented the full scope of the Progressive movement, or that Progressive politicians necessarily took their orders from a largely eastern elite coterie of thinkers such as Croly and Weyl. Some Progressives did succeed in framing the direct primary as an integral piece of a coherent reform agenda; Robert La Follette's "Wisconsin idea" is perhaps the best case of this and is perhaps one reason that the direct primary in Wisconsin remained largely untampered with long after the Progressive Era (see Lovejoy 1941; Nye 1951, ch. 5; Unger 2000; Jacobs 2022). But the discussion does suggest that the direct primary was at best a somewhat problematic means toward a larger end. Progressive arguments about the place of the direct primary in the movement suggest three things: that the direct primary itself was not necessarily worth fighting for if challenged; that advocacy for the direct primary was based on a set of expectations about human behavior and voters' actions that might not ultimately be proven accurate; and that with the possible exception of White, there was little concern among Progressives about variations in primary laws. As we shall see in the next section, then, the decline of Progressivism meant that there was no longer a compelling case to be made about how the direct primary, or its components, fit within larger discussions of popular control of government—but it is not at all clear that there ever was such a case.

The Decline of Progressivism

There are many accounts of why Progressivism faded. Hofstadter (1955, 268–289) claims that Progressives were divided over World War I, and that after the war ended the alliance of urban reformers and agrarians could not be repaired—urban writers retreated to stereotypes about the ignorance of rural Americans, and the moral impulse that had always been latent in Progressivism found new outlets in Prohibition, restrictions on immigration, and even support for the Ku Klux Klan. Wiebe (1967, 292) notes further that the prosperity of the 1920s led wealthier Progressives to conclude that the movement had gone far enough.

Many studies of Progressive politicians have noted that the movement failed to produce a charismatic national leader. Progressives were suspicious about whether Theodore Roosevelt and Woodrow Wilson truly shared their vision; even if one sets these presidents aside, however, it is evident that there was no politician after 1920 capable of rallying support. Robert La Follette's presidential campaigns did not necessarily unite the movement, and the academic consensus is that after La Follette, politicians who sought to present themselves as "Progressives" (with Henry Wallace, the 1948 Progressive Party candidate for president, being the obvious example) were using the term without any clear meaning at all (see Nye 1951, ch. 7).

Although some Progressives did accommodate themselves to Franklin Delano Roosevelt, FDR had such a large Democratic majority to work with in Congress that he did not necessarily need to reach out to Republican Progressives. According to Graham's (1967) account, some Republicans at the state level, such as Oregon Progressive leader William U'Ren, linked their Progressive agenda to aspects of the New Deal, but their articulations of that agenda were more conservative than what Roosevelt was proposing. In this account, the moral underpinnings of the Progressive movement, its focus on the states rather than on federal politics, and its belief that gradual electoral and economic change could ward off more radical social change were ill-suited to the politics of the 1930s and 1940s (Graham 1967, 129; Link 1959). An alternate argument, presented by, among others, Nye (1951, 329–330) and Hofstadter (1955, 360), contends that part of the decline of Progressivism lay in the nationalization of the movement; politicians such as La Follette sought to connect Progressivism to issues of national, not state or local, concern, and as a consequence the movement itself turned its back on its state-level successes.

These developments may well have been consequences of the nature of the Progressive movement. Progressives did not focus on developing organizations, raising money, or working to take control of the party machines themselves. The Progressives who were successful were, as Mowry (1958) describes them, masters of personal politics, and the consequence of such politics over time is to diminish the role of issues and ideology in campaigns. The ultimate result of this, writes Mileur (1999, 268), was to foster the creation of the "party in service," which would work on behalf of self-styled Progressives when they had a chance of winning, but without a deep connection to their policy agendas.

Partisanship was also an impediment to keeping the Progressive movement unified after World War I. While it was clear to Progressives that Presidents Warren G. Harding and Calvin Coolidge did not share their interests, many Progressives were nonetheless loyal Republicans and were very suspicious of FDR. Some of this suspicion had to do with genuine intellectual commitments: reservations about the proper use of federal power, for instance, or a suspicion that the Democratic Party remained too ideologically diverse and too beholden to its Southern wing (Nye 1951, ch. 7). La Follette, in particular, was also unhappy that Roosevelt had prioritized economic reform over political reform (Nye 1951, 371). The Progressive movement had always stood somewhat aloof from the parties, and in states with a strong mainstream Republican organization, Progressives had taken refuge in the Democratic Party largely because it had been easier to gain a foothold there (Wiebe 1967, 216). Yet Progressives in such states found it difficult to create alliances with sympathetic Republicans when seeking to legislate.

There are also many accounts of what became of the various writers profiled earlier (see, e.g., Forcey 1961; Moore 1974; Levy 1985). Many of the East Coast intellectuals who had spearheaded the movement died in the 1920s or grew skeptical of the movement's goals. Walter Weyl died in 1919, and Herbert Croly turned his attention away from politics during the 1920s. Walter Lippmann, often considered (along with Croly and Weyl) to be among the three leading intellectual voices for Progressivism during the 1910s, became sharply critical of some of the Progressives' assumptions by the 1920s. He rejected the notion that citizens were well-equipped to handle the sorts of responsibilities Progressives expected of them or that there was such a thing as "public opinion" independent of elite efforts to shape policy alternatives (Lippmann 1921, 1925). The major Progressive theorists tended to end their books with a general caution that Progressive electoral reform must be accompanied by expanded civic education; by the 1930s, Lippmann at least had been disabused of the notion that this was possible.

Attitudes such as Lippmann's were symptomatic of a general exhaustion with Progressive politics, but few of the broader critiques of Progressivism touched upon the direct primary or its relationship to this vision of popular control of politics. One exception was the work of John Chamberlain. In *Farewell to Reform: The Rise, Life, and Decay of the Progressive Mind in America* (1932), Chamberlain, a writer who had once been sympathetic to some Progressive goals, contended that the direct primary had proven to be a failure because it created the "illusion" of popular control—it assumed that the "spasmodic" articulations of public opinion captured in elections and mobilized by party machines represented something real (Chamberlain 1932, 148; see also Rosenblum 2008, 201). The direct primary had helped to elect Progressives. Yet it had just as often provided the public a choice among politicians who did not reflect their interests but made powerful appeals on the stump (McCraw 1974). Even Charles Merriam, who was more steadfast than most Progressives in his optimism about reform, admitted in the closing chapter of his *Primary Elections* revision (Merriam and Overacker 1928, 277, 344) that some limitations on the openness of the primary might actually be improvements.

These descriptions of the decline of Progressivism suggest that it would have been possible for opponents of the direct primary to pursue repeal because the Progressive case for the direct primary was already rather halfhearted, the leaders of the movement had largely exited politics by the 1930s, and Progressives were also somewhat disenchanted with the results of the direct primary. Had direct democracy provisions more dear to the Progressives' hearts come under attack, they might have put up more of a fight, but there was little Progressive advocacy for the direct primary by the 1920s and 1930s. This possibility does not necessarily indicate, however, that there was a threat to the direct primary. As we saw in Chapter 2, it is not clear that there was an assault on the direct primary in places where Progressives had been dominant. If the direct primary had failed to live up to Progressives' expectations, this may merely mean that parties could live with it. But to understand more about what happened to this (sort of) Progressive reform in the places where Progressives had placed it on the agenda, we turn now to an exploration of how one might use individual states' experiences to consider Progressivism, Progressive decline, and the relationship between these two things and changes in primary laws.

Progressivism and Progressive Decline in the States

It is difficult to draw a line between Progressive intellectual support for the direct primary, such as it was, and implementation of the direct primary in the states. In Chapter 2 I used one measure of Progressivism—Lawrence, Donovan, and Bowler's (2013) list of states that implemented direct democracy reforms—to define Progressives states. This is not necessarily a definitive list; as I noted in that chapter, it excludes obvious Progressive states such as Wisconsin and includes some states, such as Mississippi, that were not known as being particularly Progressive.[1] The reason I have used this list is that it shows places where one obvious Progressive reform did gain some traction. Other metrics—such as vote share for Theodore Roosevelt in his 1912 presidential campaign or vote share for avowed Progressive Robert La Follette in his 1924 campaign—might lead us to use a different list. There are drawbacks to these measures as well; as noted previously, the Progressive movement changed its focus during the 1920s from an emphasis on state laws to one on national policies, and hence one might expect the nature of Progressive support to change as well.

Using a defined list of states such as this also does not demonstrate that the direct primary was implemented because of the influence of Progressives. The direct primary was, after all, established nearly everywhere during the first two decades of the century, and it was established so quickly that it is difficult to determine who was responsible. The Progressive movement also cannot be neatly connected to one party or the other. While there is some evidence that the Progressives were most successful in states that had weak parties to begin with, there is again no correlation between party strength and establishment of the direct primary.

The measures in Chapter 2 do show, however, that there was no obvious retrenchment in states that had a history of implementing Progressive reforms. States that were receptive to Progressivism continued to experiment with the direct primary in the 1930s and beyond, to a greater degree than was the case in states where Progressives were weaker. This may be a sign that the success of Progressives had more to do with the willingness of legislators to change election laws than with the influence of Progressives themselves.

In this section I explore the role Progressive arguments played in experimentation with the direct primary during the 1930s, 1940s, and 1950s. I examine the decision to establish, and then abandon, the preprimary convention in one state, Massachusetts, where Progressive intellectuals had played a role in policy making during the Progressive Era. I discuss the acceptance of the direct primary in Wisconsin, a state where Progressive reforms were particularly successful, and in Ohio, a state where Progressives had initially had some success in the early twentieth century but were soundly defeated in subsequent years. I describe the role Progressive arguments played in the establishment of the direct primary in Rhode Island and Connecticut, two late adopters with little history of Progressivism in state politics. And I note the difficulty in separating Progressive influence from other motives for accepting and expanding the direct primary in two other states, North Dakota and California, which receive more careful treatment in subsequent chapters. Although these states do not show all of the possibilities for Progressive influence, they do show that Progressive arguments were accepted and incorporated into party strategy in all of these places, but that these arguments themselves were insufficient to counter the more immediate electoral needs of election-seeking politicians.

Massachusetts

Massachusetts was the home state of many of the foremost Progressive intellectuals, and it was an early adopter of many Progressive reforms, including the initiative and referendum, nonpartisan elections for city officeholders, the weak mayor/city manager system, and off-year elections for municipal offices. Simply because Massachusetts adopted Progressive reforms, however, did not make it a Progressive state. Self-styled Progressives never occupied positions of power in the state. In 1912 Theodore Roosevelt declared that Massachusetts had "a progressive temperament," implying that voters were sympathetic to

Progressivism but perhaps did not realize it. Richard Abrams (1964) argues that Massachusetts adopted many Progressive reforms in an incremental fashion, in order to stave off Progressive or socialist activism. This may be the case for the primary; in 1902, well before the direct primary had been adopted on a statewide level anywhere, Governor Murray Crane argued for the adoption of the direct primary at the municipal level as a means of heading off a statewide direct primary (Abrams 1964, 82).

Although Massachusetts did adopt the statewide direct primary in 1911, state leaders were arguably successful in slowing down the momentum of Progressivism and limiting the ability of Progressives to connect governmental reform to economic reform. The fact that governmental reform was taken up by industrialists (Crane, for instance, was part of the family that owned one of the nation's largest paper factories) meant that Massachusetts Progressives remained members in good standing of the Republican Party and never forged ties with labor unions, farming organizations, or opponents of the railroads. Massachusetts was a locus for immigration during the late nineteenth and early twentieth centuries as well, so some of the Progressive reforms, especially at the municipal level, were appealing to small-town Protestant Yankees seeking to limit the political power of the Irish and other immigrant groups.

The focus on incrementalism can be seen in the statements of Robert Luce, perhaps the most prominent politician of the time to present himself as a Progressive. Luce, the president of the Republican State Convention, told the 1910 convention delegates that "there is no insurgency in Massachusetts worth the name because there is no reason for insurgency. . . . Most of the measures that divide our brothers in other states are already part of Massachusetts law" (quoted in Frier and Overton 1992, 72). Luce was an advocate for the direct primary and for a "public opinion law," a sort of nonbinding referendum. Senator Henry Cabot Lodge worked to counter both proposals, but in doing so argued that he was sympathetic to many Progressive goals.

Massachusetts appears at first glance to have been a state where the Progressive political agenda—that is, the slate of reforms having to do with elections and government, rather than economics or social policy—was more fully realized than virtually anywhere else. But it was not because of the power of Progressives that it was realized. As a consequence, Progressives had little stake in governmental reform, and in particular, in the direct primary. Huthmacher (1959, 59) notes that Massachusetts Progressives raised few objections to steps taken to reduce primary competition—the so-called return to normalcy—in the 1950s largely because their reforms had not yielded striking results. As Progressives split along economic and ethnic lines, some liberals began to note that Democrats, such as Governor David Walsh, were pursuing economic policies that they appreciated. Conflicts over Prohibition and economic policy played out within the party primaries, heightening different factions' need to exert control over nominations. The major legislative changes that affected primaries during this period—the establishment of the preprimary convention in 1934, and the subsequent repeal of the preprimary convention in 1938—thus have more to do with efforts by the dominant factions of each party to select strong general election candidates than with efforts to counter Progressive influence.

The notion that there was a factional interest at play here is supported by a second set of changes in the 1950s. In 1952, Republicans introduced an "informal grassroots" convention, and the Democrats soon followed suit. This change would, by 1954, result in a decrease in candidates of both parties, but more so among Republicans (Lockard 1959b, 133). By this time the Democrats were the dominant party in the state but had less ability than Republicans to control nominations, while Republicans had the sense that they could only win statewide if they were able to ensure that they got the right candidate. Although it is beyond the scope of this book, it is of relevance that the parties would again change their preprimary convention rules in the 1980s; for statewide elections, Democrats introduced a rule by which candidates were required to receive 15 percent of the votes at the preprimary convention in order to appear on the ballot, while Republicans adopted a 10 percent threshold and added a line to the ballot noting which candidate had been endorsed by the convention (Natsios 1990). These rules were challenged in court, but the Massachusetts Supreme Court ruled that parties did have the ability to restrict ballot access. In both instances, arguments about the primary had more to do with effectively resolving intraparty conflicts than with norms about citizen voice in candidate selection.

Progressivism in Massachusetts thus had something to do with the establishment of primary rules, but because Progressives never "owned" the direct primary or many of the other electoral reforms of the early twentieth century, they had little stake in efforts to reshape them. To the extent that Progressives had sorted themselves into more clearly partisan and ideological factions by the late 1920s, they had more of a stake in winning nomination battles (and had the ability to do so) than in standing back and protecting their reforms. We can see this not only in the legislative changes that did happen, but also in decisions of the parties that are not captured in Chapter 2's list of legislation.

Wisconsin

In Wisconsin, in contrast, clear Progressive ownership of the direct primary (and at that, the open primary) created a sense of exceptionalism and what Wekkin (1984) calls "progressive mythology." While Massachusetts established primary laws gradually, as a form of defense, the direct primary was an integral part of La

Follette's "Wisconsin idea," along with second-choice voting, corrupt practices acts, the voter initiative, and voter recalls (Nye 1951, 217). By packaging all of these reforms together and positioning Wisconsin as an innovator and a national leader, Progressives were able to heighten the symbolic importance of the direct primary. La Follette, who served as governor from 1901 to 1906, packaged all of these reforms as a means of enabling popular control of politics. His erstwhile ally and eventual successor, Emmanuel Phillip, elected governor in 1914, argued in 1910 that the direct primary would ultimately fail to bring about the sorts of changes advocated for by La Follette, and he called for the establishment of regional caucuses to choose electors instead (Phillip 1973). Yet when Phillip was in office he did little to try to repeal the direct primary.

As time wore on, Phillip's concerns were borne out. As Masket (2016, ch. 7) has shown, voting in the state legislature became more polarized along partisan lines. Anecdotal reports (e.g., Hall 1923; Margulies 1968) argue that it became more acrimonious as well. However, it is difficult to prove that any of these changes were related to primaries or to the specific characteristics of primary laws themselves. For instance, a number of studies of crossover voting in the state's open primary were undertaken during the 1950s, 1960s, and 1970s, but none found any clear indication that openness made a difference or that voters meddled in the other party's affairs (Ranney and Epstein 1966; Ranney 1968, 1972). The connection of the open primary to Wisconsin and Progressivism was kept alive into the 1940s, furthermore, as La Follette's son (Robert Jr.) remained a fixture of state politics until he lost his 1946 renomination primary to Joseph McCarthy. The "Wisconsin idea" thus could be linked to specific political personalities, which may have helped it to endure.

During this time (and especially in the wake of McCarthy's upset victory), both parties experimented with endorsement procedures (Epstein 1958, 25). The Republican Party endorsed candidates occasionally, and in 1949 it passed a rule requiring a party endorsement (although it did not always follow this rule during the next decade). Democrats did not require an endorsement, but the party often did endorse. As in Massachusetts, parties sought to control or limit primaries episodically and without resorting to legislation. According to Hansen, Hirano, and Snyder's (2017) work on party factions, Wisconsin was one of four states that were consistently successful throughout the twentieth century in slating primary candidates. The coda to Wisconsin's experience with the direct primary came in 1976, when the Democratic National Committee sought to force Wisconsin and three other open primary states (Michigan, Montana, and Idaho) to close their primaries, to adopt party registration, and to take other means to prevent Republicans from voting in the state's Democratic primary. Michigan quickly capitulated, but Wisconsin did not. Wekkin (1984) reports that 80 percent of Wisconsin residents said in surveys that they opposed closing the primary. The state's newspapers, as well, weighed in against closing it, and ultimately the party relented.

While Wisconsin did very little experimenting with its primary after establishing it, its experience shows perhaps the purest example of the endurance of Progressive ideals. Not all Progressives were enthusiastic about the direct primary, as noted previously, and Wisconsin, like Massachusetts, had several prominent politicians who were sympathetic to some aspects of the Progressive agenda but not the direct primary. Wisconsin's version of the direct primary went substantially beyond what Progressives had called for elsewhere. Unlike Massachusetts, however, in Wisconsin Progressives clearly owned the direct primary; furthermore, they were able to point to their early success as a matter of state pride. The lack of experimentation during the mid-twentieth century suggests that Wisconsin politicians felt they had gotten it right the first time or that any experimentation would not be worth the potential conflict that would develop.

Ohio

Ohio is another state where Progressives won enough of a victory in the establishment of the direct primary and other reforms at the beginning of the century that they were able to push back against retrenchment but were not able to pursue any future reforms. The major champion of Progressivism in Ohio during the early part of the twentieth century was Cleveland mayor Tom Johnson, in office from 1901 to 1909. Johnson had an early interest in implementing a version of the Crawford County primary system in Cleveland, and he made common cause with western Progressives on a host of Progressive economic reforms. Cleveland adopted a variant of the Crawford County system in 1898, well before the statewide primary laws had been enacted.[2] The city's lawmakers rallied behind Johnson, and they were successful in pushing for a closed primary at the state level in 1906 (Warner 1964, 197). As part of this package, Senate candidates would appear on the state ballot by petition, and contributions to candidates or the parties were prohibited. The statewide direct primary law took effect in 1912, but the state's early experience with it was disappointing. Urban/rural conflict became a feature of early primaries, and some critics argued that, as had been the case in Wisconsin, one set of machine-like political leaders was exchanged for another. At the municipal level, some also argued that the direct primary upset efforts to provide ethnic balance to party tickets in cities such as Cleveland that had long sought to provide representation for a variety of ethnic groups.

Nonetheless, one subsequent evaluation of the state's direct primary concluded that it "elevated the tone and stature of government, both city and state." It "weeded out the grafters" and "[drove] from power the amoral politicians who used political office to promote their own selfish interests" (Warner 1964, 483). Johnson's major reform goal, however, had been to increase home rule for cities and to limit so-called ripper bills, which allowed state legislators to play a role in city government (Knepper 1994, 6–7). With these goals largely achieved, Ohio Progressives lost interest in the direct primary by the mid-1910s and turned their attention to reform of the state constitution. Ohio was left with primary laws that did not seem to do very much to achieve Progressive goals but were largely unobjectionable either to Progressives or to their opponents. There was, as shown in the previous chapter in Table 2.5, no legislation that restricted the operation of the direct primary in Ohio during the middle years of the twentieth century, but this lack of change shows neither the enduring influence of Progressives nor an effort by legislators to restrict the primary; rather, it shows the limitations of the law's influence. Geiser (1923) lists Ohio as one of the states where repeal efforts were discussed, but ultimately there were no substantive changes. Galderisi and Ginsberg (1986) show that Ohio had no noteworthy third-party activity during the twentieth century and attribute this to the acceptance by both parties of the direct primary; although Ohio regularly experienced state-level competition between the two parties, there was little interparty competition at the regional level. Different parts of the state had strong party organizations, and primaries were effective at resolving such competition.

The urban/rural split in initial support for the direct primary in Ohio was not unique; Buenker (1973) describes the split between Cleveland and the rest of the state as being analogous to the split in Massachusetts between Boston and the state's smaller towns. What is different about Ohio, however, is that each side in this conflict got something it wanted: Cleveland got greater home rule without impairing the functioning of parties at the state level, and the initial primary law was tempered from the beginning, through ballot access restrictions, so that it was acceptable to all sides. Johnson's legacy was much more limited than that of La Follette, however, so there was no statewide attachment to Progressive reforms. When both major parties in Ohio went on to experience heated factional conflict in the primaries in the 1950s and 1960s, reformers focused their ire not on the primary itself but on the drawing of the state's districts or the role that outside groups played in primaries (Diemer 1994; Thayer 1973, 106). The particular features of the state's primary were simply not consequential enough, or not malleable enough, to become a focus of attention.

One common thread in all of these states' experiences has to do with the rhetoric that was employed in talking about the direct primary. In Wisconsin, Progressive rhetoric was used to justify the maintenance of the direct primary long after the Progressives had departed from the political scene. In Massachusetts and Ohio, arguments about the primary tended to be framed with reference to partisanship, to which parties or party factions benefited from different types of laws. There is certainly a valid argument to be made about the function of political parties that can be abstracted from simple matters of party advantage. One might argue, for instance, that elections should reflect the will of the voters, and if primaries make it easier or harder for candidates with popular support to make it to the general election, such matters are normatively acceptable regardless of which party benefits. At the same time, however, it would be difficult to argue that a strictly partisan argument shows evidence that the Progressive movement, or a response to it, was the sole catalyst for reform. The ambiguous legacy of Progressives regarding types of primary laws—by which I mean the lack of clarity in the work of Merriam and others about whether a more open primary was necessarily better—also makes it difficult to determine whether subsequent modifications of the primary have been a matter of correction or an anti-Progressive retrenchment.

Progressivism and Late Adopters

To illustrate this, consider the case of two of the late adopters of the primary. Rhode Island adopted the primary in 1948, as a consequence of efforts by Democratic governor John Pastore. The progress of the state in adopting the primary is relatively easy to track by looking at the public pronouncements of the governors. Howard McGrath, governor from 1941 to 1945 and also a Democrat, argued for a closed primary with a party-endorsed slate; when Pastore took office, the new governor made a much more simplified call for a closed primary. Pastore packaged the direct primary as part of a relatively ambitious agenda that included expanded unemployment insurance and other redistributive measures. As had been the case in other states during the Progressive Era, the primary proved to be more popular and easier to push through the legislature than more comprehensive political or economic reforms, and the desire of the new Democratic legislative majority to show results led to quick passage of the direct primary law.[3] Pastore invoked vaguely Progressive rhetoric in his addresses in 1945, 1946, and 1947, referring to making "citizens feel that they have a direct responsibility in the selection of party candidates for higher office" (Pastore 1945, 10), but couching this in affirmations of the importance of parties: "The two party system is a vital force in the effectiveness of our democratic processes of government" (Pastore 1946, 8; Pastore 1947, 10–11). Following the initial adoption of the direct primary in 1948, Pastore noted in his 1949 address that the direct primary "is not perfect, but it is sound in principle" (Pastore 1949, 13). The 1948 law had allowed parties to hold their primaries on different days, a practice Pastore suggested should be changed. He contended as well that the primary had been sufficiently successful and popular that the provision in the law that called for resubmission of the law to the public for approval every four years should be removed. With these two emendations, Rhode Island moved on.

Connecticut presents another case in which Progressive rhetoric intersected with partisanship. The primary was not implemented until 1958, largely because Republican Party leader J. Henry Roraback effectively controlled the party from 1912 until his death in 1937. Afterward, the machine that he created maintained Republican control of the legislature not only through controlling nominations but also through gerrymandering that overrepresented rural areas of the state at the expense of the more Democratic and more reformist cities. The primary Connecticut established is to this day among the nation's most restrictive. It is a so-called challenge primary, in which the challenger to an incumbent must win at least 20 percent of delegates at the convention in order to appear on the ballot. Otherwise, no one else but the incumbent can enter the race; the prospective challenger also must meet a signature threshold of 2 percent of the party's enrolled voters in the jurisdiction in which he or she seeks to run and pay a filing fee (which is refunded if the challenger receives 10 percent of the primary vote). The primary was originally closed, although later the Supreme Court's decision in *Republican Party of Connecticut v. Tashjian* (479 U.S. 208 (1986)) established the right of parties to decide whether to make their primaries open or closed.

The primary was supported by a variety of good government groups; a diverse lot, including the Congress of Industrial Organizations (CIO), the League of Women Voters, the Communist Party of Connecticut, and the Minute Women of Connecticut (a conservative group) all spoke on behalf of the direct primary to the legislature, and most of these groups played a part in forming a group called Citizens for a Direct Primary (Lockard 1959a, 4, 6). A number of state legislators made strong enough rhetorical commitments to the primary that they found it untenable to back off these claims when the state's governor (Democrat Abraham Ribicoff) called a special session of the legislature for a vote on the bill (Lockard 1959a). This was particularly the case for Democrats; Republicans still maintained control of the legislature, and the legislators most sympathetic to the primary were Republicans who had chafed at the control exerted by Roraback over the party. As in Rhode Island, a popular governor led the charge for a primary law and sought to use his popularity to influence a reluctant legislature.

In both states, then, Progressive sentiment—or more broadly, a more generalized sort of reformist sentiment—played a role in the establishment of rather limited primary election laws. Yet this rhetoric was effective only when party control of the legislature or the governorship was disrupted. In Chapter 6, which considers the role of partisan gain more directly, we shall see that the same holds true even in states with a strong Progressive history, such as California. It is difficult to evaluate the experiences of these states in terms of Progressive influence; a simplified Progressive impulse—direct primaries are good—was part of the push for primary laws, but it was a sentiment divorced from the remainder of the Progressive agenda. This may be sort of a "half a loaf" scenario; advocates for the direct primary may have taken what they could get and walked away. Lockard (1959a) reported that in Connecticut there was no subsequent move to further open the state's primary after the initial law was passed.

Progressivism also intersected with other types of movements. The list of Progressive reform states in Chapter 2 includes many that were influenced by the Nonpartisan League (discussed in Chapter 4) and some Southern states (discussed in Chapter 7). In such cases, it is difficult to determine what role Progressives and their antagonists played either in the establishment of the direct primary or in subsequent modifications of it. The two states on this list that do not fall into those two categories, Michigan and Utah, also present complications. From the outset, the Michigan primary was dogged by claims that the law had not worked out very well in practice (Dorr 1937), so yet another impulse, the desire to modify the law to prevent unexpected results, was of concern. Utah, which only became a state in 1896, experimented extensively with its primary. Utah had adopted an optional primary in 1889, before statehood, but the parties rarely used it. In 1947 Utah established a convention system that winnowed down the number of candidates on the ballot to no more than two. Originally, it was required that candidates must receive 70 percent of the convention vote in order to avoid a primary; the limit was lowered to 60 percent in 2000 (Frei et al. 2012). One ostensible virtue of this system is that it enables candidates to avoid having to raise large sums of money for primary battles (something that is not entirely inconsistent with Progressive ambitions), but in practice the Utah primary system has also enabled factions with limited public support to place candidates on the primary ballot and, in some extreme cases, to block popular incumbents from appearing on the ballot at all.[4] As early as the 1950s, some authors (e.g., Key 1956, 125) argued that the Utah system exacerbated factional conflict. It is difficult to see the hand of the Progressives in all of this; while Progressives were not averse to factional conflict, the overwhelmingly negative response to it in the literature suggests that such conflict bears little resemblance to Progressive ambitions for openness and public voice.

Conclusions

There is little evidence that primary laws of the 1930s and beyond showed signs of either a backlash against Progressivism or a concerted push to perfect or expand what Progressives had achieved during the early years of the twentieth century. It is easy to simply note that Progressivism had ended—that concerns about electoral reform had been replaced by concerns for party advantage, or by concerns unrelated to electoral laws at all. Yet it bears emphasis, as well, that Progressives were not unalloyed advocates for the direct primary to begin with. Recall that William Allen White had emphasized that primaries would be judged based on their results. This was perhaps an unrealistic scenario; primaries produced victories for some candidates with Progressive sympathies, and they may have played a role in the establishment of some broader social and economic policies championed by Progressives. Yet there is simply no way to draw this sort of causal arrow, let alone to expect that parties or voters would draw such connections. Even in states where Progressivism had indisputably triumphed, such as Wisconsin, the primary produced some salutary results as well as some setbacks for Progressives, and there is no way to rerun, for instance, the Wisconsin elections of the 1950s under different rules in order to evaluate the law's effectiveness.

Recall also that the direct primary was seen by writers such as Herbert Croly and Walter Lippmann as something that would work only if accompanied by changes in voting behavior and a more generalized sort of enlightenment and public spiritedness on the part of voters. Only Lippmann lived long enough to pass judgment on this, and his judgment was a harshly negative one. Measuring something like enlightenment is also a rather hopeless sort of endeavor, yet it is here that the notion of Progressive decline is perhaps of more relevance. Absent a public discourse about election laws and the public good, it is difficult to argue that primaries could fulfill the function for which the Progressives had advocated. "Good government" groups persisted well past the Progressive Era—and they had occasional victories, as the Connecticut case shows—but to an extent the Progressive argument here required that the movement itself be an enduring feature of public life: that Progressives could not advocate for electoral changes and expect those changes, by themselves, to bring about enduring social and economic reforms. Lippmann perhaps saw this most clearly. As early as the 1930s, he was arguing that the Progressive argument for more democracy—the assertion that the choices available will compel citizens to learn more and to exercise their rights wisely—had been disproven by the facts. Party machines still existed in some form, and the economic dislocation of the 1930s, and perhaps of modern political life more generally, left people even more bewildered and subdued than before (Lippmann 1993, 25–27). He framed this in a broader account of the modern state: sovereignty was sufficiently diffused that people have no ability to see a public interest (1931, 267). By the 1930s, what was left of the Progressive response to this, he wrote, was advocacy for a greater role for the federal government, at the expense of direct popular control and voice (1936, 5). For Lippmann, then, Progressivism came off as a sort of backward-looking movement; its reforms might have worked in nineteenth-century America but were inadequate to the task of twentieth-century life. It was not just parties that would reassert control; private interests and demagoguery would also prevail.

On a more pedestrian level, however, it is worth revisiting a smaller point in the Progressive literature. White (1910, 50) argued that it was important that the people establish the direct primary through the initiative; that way, there would be a sense of ownership of the direct primary on the part of the people, not the parties. This suggests that the primary itself was not as important as were other direct democracy laws. While the early twentieth-century showed some examples of this happening, or of instances in which the legislature sought to abolish the primary and the people reestablished it through the initiative, all of the changes we have explored here have been cases in which legislators or political parties sought to modify the primary. There are no doubt instances where legislators considered limiting the primary but yielded out of concern about public opinion. Yet White's point suggests that we should never expect politicians to safeguard the primary. This poses a dilemma: it may be feasible for citizens to enact sweeping changes to election laws through the initiative and referendum process. In contemporary politics, we see this in ballot initiatives to limit gerrymandering or to radically change the primary, as in California. But the finer details of such laws, or technical modifications of them, will likely always be in the hands of the politicians. In this regard, it may be fortunate for Progressives that, to the extent that they cared about the direct primary at all, the primary did not suffer even greater limitations in the post-Progressive years.

4
Hostile Takeover
Nonparty Group Capture of Primaries

The establishment of direct primaries entailed a sacrifice of power on the part of political parties; this much was clear to everyone involved in American politics in the first decades of the twentieth century. Opinions diverged, however, on the question of who would take up the power that had been stripped from party bosses. For early Progressives, as we saw in Chapter 3, the answer to this question was clear: the people would gain power. Other observers, however, were skeptical of this claim. For antiprimary polemicist Bernard Freyd (1926), primaries would be dominated by "grafters," individuals who would game the new rules to their own private advantage. Others believed demagogic, individual politicians would establish personal followings (e.g., Mechem 1905). And still others, such as New Orleans mayor Walter Flower, spoke of so-called leagues, of temporary organizations that would use primaries to take over the parties for the sake of immediate goals, goals that might be shared by the public but did not have the sort of staying power that animated party coalitions (Flower 1898).

This final concern, the fear of a "hostile takeover" of the parties, is the subject of this chapter. This is a subject that has particular resonance in contemporary politics. Literature of the early 2010s on the Tea Party, for instance, emphasized its role as a faction within the Republican Party, but a faction that worked at cross-purposes with Republican leaders and that in some instances deliberately sabotaged the efforts of Republican Party politicians to govern or to win elections. The Tea Party is not a party per se, but its appropriation of the word "party" begs the question of what a party is and how one might distinguish between parties and what I, following Flower, shall refer to as "leagues," insurgent organizations devoted to gaining power through the primary process. As I shall show here, primary elections have always been at risk of being taken over by such organizations, but such groups have not had the sort of success that some writers of the early twentieth century feared.

This chapter focuses largely on the most successful league, or organized nonparty electoral movement, of the early twentieth century, the Nonpartisan League (NPL). The NPL controlled North Dakota politics from 1916 into the early 1920s, and after gaining control of North Dakota it aspired to elect candidates in at least twelve midwestern states, if not nationwide. The NPL was the first nonparty organization to fully exploit the direct primary for its own purposes, but its ultimate failure says much about the limitations nonparty groups face in seeking to use primaries to their advantage. As we shall see, politicians of the time fought back fiercely against the NPL, and this effort, combined perhaps with some unforced errors by NPL leaders, caused the NPL to rapidly recede from politics. Yet the experience of individual NPL politicians in the years following its 1920 loss of power, as well as the experiences of NPL politicians in other states, show that the NPL's decline would likely have been inevitable even without such events.

This chapter begins with a discussion of the NPL and its relationship to primary laws, both as a determinant of NPL success and as a means of limiting the spread of the NPL. I then discuss other leagues formed in subsequent years and the ways in which primary election laws constrained these groups as well. I close with some thoughts on the relevance of this history for contemporary primary elections.

The Nonpartisan League

The most successful effort at a "hostile takeover" of the primary process during the early decades of the twentieth century, and perhaps to date, was the NPL's brief tenure in charge of North Dakota politics between 1916 and the early 1920s. The NPL's story shows both why primaries were vulnerable to hostile takeover and why such takeovers have been rare and of short duration.

Origins

North Dakota must have struck early twentieth-century Americans as an odd place for a political revolution. The state was a follower, not a leader, in the late nineteenth and early twentieth-century rounds of reform campaigns. During the 1880s, 1890s, and 1900s several midwestern states experienced a substantial amount of unrest among farmers. Farming states such as Kansas, Iowa, and South Dakota had been receptive to third-party organizers during the late nineteenth century; according to some accounts, the withering of the Populist movement left residents of states such as Kansas and Nebraska suspicious of agitators from outside the two major parties (Argersinger 1995; Pickett 1918). North Dakota had not been particularly receptive to the Populists; in fact, during the 1890s both parties had supported the passage of antifusion laws as a means of rebuffing efforts by populists to gain a foothold in their organizations (Argersinger 1995, 137). Similarly, nearby Wisconsin experienced a pitched battle over the efforts by Robert LaFollette and the Progressives to enact an open primary law. In North

Dakota, Progressivism moved forward with less conflict, or at least with less national media attention. In 1906, following their 1902 failure to secure the nomination for the state's newly created second House seat, Progressives turned to the Democratic Party, rallying behind the gubernatorial candidacy of John Burke (Glaab 1981). Burke followed La Follette's lead, successfully pushing in 1911 for a direct primary, a presidential preference primary, and the establishment of initiative and referendum procedures. Charles Nelson Glaab argues, however, that his analysis of voting returns in 1904, 1906, and 1908 shows that Burke's support was strongest in urban areas, and that he did not incorporate the state's farmers in his coalition. As a result, although Burke's Republican successor, Louis Hanna, was sympathetic to much of the election reform work Burke had done, he antagonized farmers early in his tenure with his failure to pass a terminal elevator bill (the substantive import of which we shall explore in a moment).

In other ways, however, North Dakota was a highly unusual state. Unlike virtually every other state, North Dakota was almost entirely dependent on a neighboring state, Minnesota, for its economic well-being. North Dakota had no major cities and no organized labor movement to speak of. Seventy percent of the state's residents were employed in agriculture, yet farmers were not well organized by the Grange or other farming organizations. North Dakota's economy was highly susceptible to price fluctuations and to changes in the practices of Minnesota merchants. North Dakota was also, during the early years of the twentieth century, a state with a particularly large population of first-generation European immigrants; 27 percent of North Dakota residents were foreign born, and a majority were born outside of North Dakota (Morlan 1955, 3). Many North Dakota farmers were familiar with the political organizing techniques practiced by the more highly disciplined and ideological European political parties. Socialism and European socialist methods of organizing were arguably looked upon with more favor in North Dakota than in neighboring states, even including those where urban socialist movements flourished.

North Dakota farmers had many grievances about the high cost of transporting supplies into the state. As Robert Morlan (1955, 3–21) recounts in the most comprehensive historical account of the NPL, it was far less expensive for eastern and midwestern merchants to ship materials to neighboring states (and even to states farther away, such as Montana) than it was to send them to North Dakota. Meanwhile, there were no terminal markets in the state for its grain; farmers needed to sell wheat and other produce through exchanges based in Minnesota. This meant not only that much of the profit from North Dakota farming was realized outside of the state, but that there were frequent instances when farmers were not paid fairly for their produce. Estimates of the annual losses incurred by North Dakota farmers at the hands of the grading systems practiced in Minnesota during the first decades of the twentieth century ran into the tens of millions of dollars (Morlan 1955, 10). These losses fed the call by many North Dakotans for the establishment of a state-owned terminal elevator.

The NPL was formed in 1915 to capitalize on the discontent of North Dakota farmers, their interest in having a government that would play more of a role in directing the state's economy, and the perception that North Dakota politicians were not sufficiently responsive to the plight of the state's farmers. The architect of the NPL, Arthur C. Townley, sought to establish a highly regimented organization that stood outside of the party system but used the party primaries to elect candidates. As Herbert E. Gaston (1920, 6–7) described matters, the NPL was the only political organization (at the time) that used "commercial methods of salesmanship" to develop a membership base. Townley established the NPL as a dues-based organization. Organizers collected annual dues from farmers in the form of postdated checks; this ensured that the NPL could get a pledge of support from needy farmers, hedged against adequate crop sales. If the farmers failed to earn enough money when crops were harvested, or grew suspicious of the NPL, they could cancel their checks. Membership in the NPL entitled one to, among other things, a subscription to the *Nonpartisan Leader*, the NPL's newspaper. By 1916, the *Leader* had a readership of over thirty thousand.

Townley deliberately chose not to run for office himself during the NPL's heyday, so as to emphasize the purity of his motives. He learned his organizing techniques when the 1912 crop failure bankrupted him; after losing his farm, he became an organizer for the Socialist Party and ran unsuccessfully as a Socialist for the state legislature (Remele 1981, 71). His unsuccessful campaign convinced him, he was to later say, that there was more support for socialist ideas in North Dakota than there was for the Socialist Party, and that the route to success lay in disconnecting the two. Townley was by all accounts a particularly charismatic speaker, but he left behind little written material and in later life would adopt a variety of different ideological causes, eventually running for office in the 1950s as a staunch anticommunist (Remele 1988). His genius for organizing does not appear to have translated into a stable political agenda, although he did have the foresight to invest much of the NPL's dues in a sort of proto-think tank that would develop its policy (Remele 1981).

As the NPL grew in 1915 and 1916, Townley began to recruit candidates for state political offices. He insisted that all NPL candidates pledge themselves to its agenda. All candidates signed a pledge to advocate for state ownership of terminal elevators, mills, packing houses, and cold storage plants; state inspection of grain; state hail insurance; rural credit banks; and exemption of farm improvements from taxation (Gaston 1920, 60). Although this agenda could easily be reconciled with various existing political proposals, and although it was not inconsistent with the policies advocated by socialist or left-wing movements elsewhere in the country, initially Townley declined to pursue alliances with labor organizations or with Democratic or Republican politicians already in office in North Dakota. The result of this decision was a regimented political organization that addressed the needs of North Dakota farmers while avoiding entanglement in the national issues that divided the two major parties.

The Nonpartisan League's Capture of the Republican Party

Townley was always quite frank about his desire to use the primary to his advantage. In a 1956 interview with a Minnesota college student, he emphasized that he had played no role in the establishment of the direct primary, but that once it was instituted he sought to capture Republican nominations wherever possible: "That is where the voters were. They were Republican because that is their habit.... [Y]ou can't change their habits overnight" (Dobson 1956). Townley went on to argue that using the Republican nominating process does not make one a Republican, and that in some parts of North Dakota he had been willing to use the Democratic primary, or even Socialist primaries where they existed, if they presented the most viable means of winning the general election. The NPL did not endorse previously elected politicians, regardless of how supportive they were of the NPL agenda; the *Nonpartisan Leader* emphasized that only farmers could represent farmers (Morlan 1955, 64). This decision did not, however, prevent politicians from claiming that they had NPL support or from pointing out stances they had taken that resembled parts of the NPL platform. Some contemporary accounts alleged that Townley and his allies deliberately chose political nonentities to run; a mostly sympathetic article in the *Country Gentleman* (one of the nation's largest farming business magazines) noted that choosing unknown candidates ensured that voters would think about nothing beyond their support for the NPL agenda when voting (Pickett 1918).

All NPL members were entitled to a vote at its 1916 preprimary convention; for the most part, however, the slate was chosen by Townley and other NPL leaders beforehand. NPL candidates swept all of the primaries they entered. In the general election, NPL candidates won 81 of 113 seats in the state House, 68 as Republicans and 13 as Democrats. NPL candidates also won 18 of 49 state Senate seats—enough, with the aid of sympathetic holdovers, to establish a working majority (Morlan 1955, 89). The NPL also swept the governor's race and the other state races. The NPL wave was substantial enough that the opposition was split; some incumbent legislators acceded to much of the NPL program even though they themselves were not NPL members, while others dug in against the NPL. The NPL built upon this in 1918, going on to establish full control over the legislature.

If Townley was trying to create an organization composed of single-minded devotees to the cause, selecting political nonentities would have been a sensible way to do that. While few NPL candidates had long-standing ties to the parties, this allegation that the NPL chose "nobodies" for its candidates is not entirely accurate in regard to the NPL candidates for higher office. The 1916 NPL nominee for governor, Lynn Frazier, had held no prior office but had gained some notoriety for his advocacy of prohibition; while a modern piece on the NPL claims that Frazier was seen by many North Dakotans as "a prohibitionist crank" (Remele 1981), the connection of Frazier with a movement unaffiliated with the NPL (that is, prohibitionism)—and a popular movement at that— suggests that Frazier had the material to build his own following. The NPL chose not to focus on U.S. House or Senate races in 1916, however, perhaps out of a pragmatic belief that the state's incumbent representatives and senators were not beatable. This decision ensured that the best-known politicians in the state refrained from attacking the NPL (Wilkins 1981). When a U.S. House seat opened up in 1917, however, the NPL successfully rallied around the special election campaign of John Miller Baer, the *Nonpartisan Leader* editorial cartoonist. Baer's cartoons had won him a substantial following, and although they did not necessarily speak to his skills as a politician, they did give him a certain sort of fame.

Baer's tenure in the House was brief, although not uneventful. He sought to ally himself with progressives in both parties and to distance himself from socialists such as Wisconsin's Victor Berger (Reid 1977). As a federal officeholder with no NPL colleagues, he had a degree of freedom from following any NPL orthodoxy, and he won over some North Dakotans who were unhappy with the NPL's actions in North Dakota (*Courier-News* 1917). However, Baer was treated with suspicion by others; his German surname and NPL origins caused the *Boston Transcript* to refer to him as "the representative of a foreign influence in our Congress" (Reid 1977). Yet eastern news coverage of the NPL's 1916 sweep of state offices, coupled with the establishment of a foothold in Washington, D.C., piqued the interest of many Americans outside of North Dakota. NPL archives at North Dakota State University and the Minnesota Historical Society are replete with letters from individual citizens and various labor and socialist organizations asking for information on the league and encouraging it to seek to organize chapters in other states. Some of this correspondence was likely motivated by a concern about agricultural issues, while other letter writers from cities such as Cleveland and Chicago appear to have been viewing the NPL as representative of a sort of broader movement (Teigan 1917a, 1917b, 1917c; but see Selden 1920). As Usher Burdick (1944) notes in his history of the era, both friends and foes of socialism paid attention to anti-NPL propaganda, and they were drawn to pay attention to North Dakota politics because of their belief that something of consequence was happening. Both, Burdick (1944) argues, were disappointed by what they saw.

Although Townley had originally made a point of focusing only on North Dakota, some of the inquiries were attractive. Townley delivered a well-received speech at New York's Cooper Union in 1918, and East Coast newspapers and magazines such as the *Nation* responded enthusiastically (see Gaston 1920, 238; *Literary Digest* 1919). Although this speech received less coverage, Townley also spoke at the American Federation of Labor Annual Conference in 1917 (Townley 1917). The *Boston Herald* announced that the NPL was "the most interesting social movement in the United States" (*Literary Digest* 1919). NPL legal advisers Arthur LeSeuer and Ray McKaig spoke on behalf of the NPL at the 1919 Reconstruction Conference of the National Popular Government League (LeSeuer 1919). This conference included veteran Progressives (including many who had worked for Cleveland mayor Tom Johnson); women's suffrage advocates; and advocates of preferential voting, proportional voting, and other reforms. This was not a conference about reaching consensus; its overarching goal was to establish an agenda for postwar political and economic reform. It featured a lively debate about whether direct primaries were sufficient to achieve Progressive aims or whether they should be abandoned. But it was clear that the NPL was seen nationally as being about something broader than North Dakota; the archives of NPL secretary Henry Teigan are full of correspondence from the Popular Government League founder and director Judson King expressing his admiration for the NPL and encouraging it to take part in his convention (e.g., King 1917a, 1917b).

All of this attention naturally encouraged Townley and other NPL leaders to begin thinking about expansion. Teigan wrote back quite frank letters to everyone who asked him about expanding the NPL beyond North Dakota. As the NPL broadened its horizons, it did speculate about fielding a presidential ticket, but it clearly saw that its appeal would be limited to agricultural states. There were, however, very few states with as exclusive a focus on agriculture as North Dakota, so the NPL would have to seek alliances with other groups. Neighboring states also differed in their primary laws and in the receptivity of local politicians to the concerns of farmers. Gaston (1920, 242) listed eleven states besides North Dakota where the NPL sought to organize farmers; it also engaged in extensive organizing work in Saskatchewan and explored the possibility of fielding a presidential candidate.

The NPL's activities beyond North Dakota varied, as did its level of success. In Saskatchewan, the NPL laid the groundwork for creating a viable party of its own; the legacy of this party endured decades after, in the form of the Cooperative Commonwealth Federation (CCF), which governed the province during the early 1960s and mounted successful parliamentary campaigns between the 1930s and 1960s in Saskatchewan, Manitoba, and Alberta. The CCF was the direct forerunner of the New Democratic Party, which has for much of the past century been the third-largest party in the Canadian federal parliament. Although Canadian parties have at times used primaries to select candidates or leaders, there has never been a national equivalent to the U.S. primary system, so even in the early years of the twentieth century it made more sense for NPL activists to organize there as a party rather than as a faction within a party, as Mildred Schwartz (2006) has shown.[1]

The NPL had its greatest recruiting success in Minnesota; Gaston (1920, 239) reported that the Minnesota membership approached forty thousand people, nearly that of North Dakota, although Minnesota was a larger state. The NPL set up a national office in St. Paul. Although, as in North Dakota, many of the NPL ideas were popular, resistance in the state was particularly fierce. The NPL opted to focus its resources on a small number of high-profile races. It put most of its effort into the gubernatorial race there in 1918, supporting former congressman Charles A. Lindbergh in the Republican primary.[2] Following its failure in that race, the NPL sought to strengthen its alliance with organized labor, resulting in the creation of the Farmer-Labor Party, which would eventually elect several governors before merging with the Democratic Party in 1944.

In other midwestern states, the NPL had somewhat less success. Several states already had elected officials who were sympathetic to the NPL's agenda and welcomed its support. In Montana, the NPL endorsed the campaign of the nation's first female House member, Jeanette Rankin, who ran as an incumbent in the Republican primary, and then, following her defeat, as a third-party candidate. In Idaho the NPL organized itself following the North Dakota model, convening before the primaries and selecting a full slate to run in the state's Democratic primaries (Morlan 1955, 203). Idaho NPL members were largely satisfied with the state's two incumbent senators, Republican William Borah and Democrat John Nugent, so it opted to endorse these two rather than field its own candidates. Such practical decisions enabled the NPL to boast that it had won all of the races it entered in Idaho, an interest group tactic not uncommon in contemporary politics. Idaho parties responded, however, by temporarily abandoning the primary entirely and returning to a convention system in order to evict the NPL members from the legislature (Lansing 2018, 201). In South Dakota, Texas, and Iowa, NPL chapters deemed themselves too weak for the moment to field slates; in Iowa the emergence of rival (and slightly less radical) farmers' organizations had diminished the appeal of the NPL (Pickett 1918). This was a sign that the NPL might lose political clout at the same time that its agenda was accepted in other states (Dovre 1963). It was also, according to Lansing (2018, 199–204), a major weakness in the NPL strategy: it could use primaries to win legislative seats (even a majority), but it was not able to win control of the party organizations themselves.

These events show that although the NPL was looked upon with favor by some Progressives, it was quite different in its approach to elections. The NPL played no role in the establishment of primaries; rather, it seized upon them as a means for gaining power. The NPL's subsequent experience in power and its effort to expand beyond its North Dakota base show that the movement might well have spread even without the establishment of the direct primary. The NPL adapted its strategy in other states to better use different primary laws; in North Dakota, in contrast, the NPL was at least alleged by its critics to have used the laws in place to enhance its hold on government. There is little about the NPL that suggests an abiding interest in election reform. The NPL correspondence that has been preserved suggests that some of the better educated NPL members, such as William Lemke and Henry Teigan, were well-versed in the political science of the time. One enduring criticism of the NPL legislators, however, was that they did not know enough about politics to effectively run North Dakota, let alone to re-engineer government. NPL leaders understood the primary well enough to use it to their advantage, but they were also helped by the unusual circumstances in North Dakota.

Reactions to the Nonpartisan League

While NPL leaders were exploring expansion, however, they were running into increasing trouble at home. One emergent problem with the NPL's strategy of electing political novices was that its members had little understanding of the legislative process. Remele (1981, 81), in fact, argues that the NPL "think tank" was necessary in part simply to train NPL legislators in how to do their jobs. Although the NPL did pass many significant pieces of legislation, including changes in tax policy regarding farmers, transportation laws, and grain grading, in most instances NPL legislators voted as a bloc with little deliberation, following the lead of unelected leaders such as Townley and NPL attorney William Lemke. NPL members also had little ability to expand their coalition beyond farmers; former president Taft, observing the NPL's legislative difficulties, argued that the NPL would ultimately fail if it could not broaden its appeal, yet efforts to do this would, in turn, risk alienating the farmers who formed the organization's backbone (*Literary Digest* 1919).

By 1919 NPL legislators had embarked on an aggressive plan to reform the state's education system, consolidating several different school boards into one body with a state-appointed administrator. This created an intense backlash across the state, as many NPL opponents presumed that the state administrator would wield control over the curriculum and would, in effect, propagandize the state's children. The NPL's problems were compounded by a disputed school superintendent election; NPL attorney general William Langer ultimately had to rule on the seating of a superintendent, and his decision in the case (a decision to seat a non-NPL candidate, contra Townley's directive) led Langer to leave the NPL. Some NPL members, in addition, raised concern that state funds were being used for the purpose of promoting the NPL in neighboring states (Fossum 1925). As the Morlan book notes, it can be difficult to separate legitimate instances of corruption or overreach from allegations made by NPL foes. William Lemke, in particular, was dogged during his term as attorney general by criticisms over a home loan that he secured—criticisms that most modern histories of the NPL (e.g., Tweton 1981; Smith 1981) have concluded were unfair. What is indisputable, though, is that by 1919 NPL officeholders had staked out positions on a wide range of issues that went well beyond matters of agricultural policy; the NPL's official program on post–World War I reconstruction, for instance, included calls for women's suffrage, support for the League of Nations, and a graduated income tax (Morlan 1955, 216). Whatever the popularity or wisdom of such proposals, they clearly did go beyond the organization's original mission.

Economic prosperity also posed a risk for the NPL. Just as the NPL benefited in 1916 from the pairing of collapsing crop prices (which agitated farmers) and its use of postdated checks (which enabled these farmers to make a small investment in the NPL without immediate loss), so the NPL suffered when crop prices went up during the war years (Fossum 1925). Morlan (1955, 346) estimates that the NPL had as much as $2 million in canceled checks by 1923. Economic adversity ensured receptivity to the NPL message but no money to support the group, while prosperity increased farmers' ability to pay dues but reduced their level of concern.

As noted previously, many incumbent legislators were reluctant to stake out strong anti-NPL positions due to the organization's electoral success and the popularity of many of its proposals. In the 1916 cycle, few candidates were willing to criticize the NPL at all, given its close association with referenda that had passed overwhelmingly. As the NPL's tenure in office wore on, however, opposition to it in North Dakota took two forms. The NPL had risen to power in part due to its ability to use the *Nonpartisan Leader* to inform and entertain the public. An anti-NPL paper, the *Red Flame*, was published by an organization calling itself the Citizens Economy League and featured a variety of attacks on the NPL, some of which were policy critiques, but most of which were crude innuendo. In the *Red Flame*'s cartoons and in the sensationalistic writings of NPL opponent Jerry Bacon, editor of the *Grand Forks Herald*, Townley was presented as a political boss, every bit as corrupt as the party bosses of yore;

NPL officeholders were presented as opportunistic grafters, capitalizing on the ignorance of farmers in order to assume power; and the entire NPL enterprise was presented as an un-American, socialist project. Bacon published and distributed salvos with titles such as "Townleyism Unmasked! Now Stands before the World in Its True Light as Radical Socialism!" and "Carry the Truth to the People: A.fter C.ash Townley Smoked Out" (Bacon 1918, 1919). As World War I got underway, and as Americans became accustomed to anti-German propaganda, the German surnames of many NPL members (including Congressman Baer) were frequently invoked as part of the rhetorical attack. The occasional pacifist statement by an NPL member was often taken as a sign of covert sympathy for the Germans.

At the same time that the *Red Flame* was making its appeals, several rival "leagues" were formed, in part to confuse voters and in part to organize opposition. An entity calling itself the North Dakota Good Government League was formed in 1916; this organization purported to be composed of North Dakota farmers and alleged that the NPL was mainly organized by out-of-state activists (Morlan 1955, 68). In 1918, an anti-NPL group called the Anti-Socialist Union was formed by Republicans seeking to regain control of the party. The Anti-Socialist Union metamorphosized into the Lincoln Republican League, and then, in an effort to bring in Democrats as well, into the Independent Voters Association (IVA). The IVA made a point of welcoming disgruntled NPL voters and politicians, working to co-opt the more popular parts of the NPL platform (such as those having to do with grain prices) while emphasizing less popular instances of NPL overreach such as the school board decision and a variety of proposed constitutional amendments to establish several state-run banks and businesses (Tweton 1981, 95). Beyond this, the IVA's initial concerns had to do with process—the governor's appointment power, the NPL's bloc voting—rather than with specific policy results. The IVA, furthermore, took aim squarely at Townley and his control of the legislators, seeking to frame the NPL as a dictatorship and link it more directly with the emerging Soviet regime.

The IVA initially prevailed upon supporters in office to introduce legislation establishing a top two primary, the rationale being that the general election would then be certain to feature an anti-NPL candidate, and that in Republican districts Democrats could be persuaded to cross party lines in the general election to vote for such candidates (Tweton 1981, 98). The IVA also introduced legislation separating state and national primaries (Blackorby 1963, 129–130). When both bills were defeated, the IVA began selecting candidates using informal primaries, in which a gentleman's agreement among the candidates would result in the losers dropping out before the official primary. IVA efforts during the 1918 session were easily beaten back, as Governor Frazier and most NPL legislators were comfortably re-elected. By this time, however, schisms had emerged within the

NPL, and the IVA presented a ready-made power base for dissidents. Attorney General William Langer was by far the most prominent defector.

Langer was unusual because he had held elective office before the 1916 election. He was among the few NPL officeholders who were not swept into office by the NPL; accordingly, he had an independent streak and although he agreed with much of its economic program, he was very much an election-seeking politician in his own right. Langer ran as the IVA candidate against Frazier in the 1920 Republican primary, losing by merely five thousand votes out of one hundred thousand. The IVA also won one U.S. House seat (with a Republican) and, with a coalition of Republican and Democratic candidates, gained control of the state House. Party labels had become far less significant in elections than were the IVA and NPL labels, neither of which actually appeared on the ballot. Conflict between the IVA House and the NPL Senate severely disrupted the North Dakota economy, and the IVA sought to blame the NPL for this disruption. Frazier was successfully recalled in 1921 and replaced by an IVA candidate, and the NPL lost control of the state senate in 1922. Frazier would, however, go on to win the 1922 Senate election and serve three terms as an NPL Republican in the Senate. The IVA, having achieved its objective, quickly disintegrated.

In other states, the NPL also faced a mixture of crude but effective rhetorical attacks and calculated political maneuvering. In Minnesota, the NPL posed the greatest threat to the existing political power structure; much of its initial appeal in North Dakota had, in addition, been framed as a response to the alleged rapaciousness of Minnesota's merchants. In Minnesota, as well, there was a harsh rhetorical side to the battle with the NPL as well as legislative maneuvering by mainstream politicians. NPL recruiters were repeatedly harassed, beaten, and tarred and feathered; Townley himself was banned from visiting several Minnesota towns and was jailed for defying one such ban. Such overt hostility was trumpeted in the *Nonpartisan Leader* and used to stir up hostility toward Minnesota businessmen, but it took its toll on the NPL's efforts in Minnesota. At the same time, Minnesota Republicans were developing primary laws that would prevent the NPL from winning office. Both major parties began to hold preprimary endorsing (or "eliminating") conventions, in which a standard-bearer would be chosen. The Republican Party introduced this practice in 1920, with the expectation that those candidates who were not endorsed would drop out, leaving one candidate to confront the NPL candidate (Gieske 1979, 56). Although such informal methods remain common in other states, particularly in nonpartisan local elections, there was no way to force losers to drop out, and in practice many did not. In 1922 a state law was passed specifically allowing preprimary conventions and mandating that the candidate who received the party endorsement have that endorsement written on the ballot. After the NPL gubernatorial nominee won the preprimary endorsement, however, the legislature modified the law again to remove the endorsement from the ballot (Chrislock 1971, 187–188).

Montana, Idaho, Nebraska, and Kansas all saw their primaries abolished in 1918 or 1919 by state legislatures seeking to ward off the NPL (Morlan 1955, 239; Lansing 2018, 200–202). Repeal legislation was also introduced in Minnesota and Colorado, and South Dakota passed laws restricting primary voting to party members of long standing. These laws did not remain on the books for long; in Nebraska and Montana primaries were reinstated by referendum in the early 1920s (Morlan 1955, 301). For the pivotal elections in which it was seeking to expand beyond North Dakota, however, the NPL was compelled to run in these states as a third party or to issue endorsements of regular Democratic or Republican politicians. In Wisconsin, Progressives and NPLers reached a tacit agreement not to run against each other, while in Montana some defeated candidates issued cross-party endorsements as a means of combating the NPL. In Wisconsin the NPL also confronted other similar sounding "leagues" that had sprouted up, some in a legitimate effort to win over voters with Progressive inclinations, others aiming merely to sow confusion or capitalize on the NPL's name (Pickett 1918). As Morlan (1955, 295–296) notes, these circumstances were to some degree a consequence of the fact that parties outside of North Dakota had a few years to prepare for the NPL; they were not taken by surprise as were the North Dakota Republicans.

As V. O. Key (1956, 92) was to note decades later, it has always been difficult to argue against the direct primary. In the states that abandoned the primary, voters quickly reinstated it. The abolition of the primary was surely something the average voter could understand. Many of the more subtle changes in primaries, however, seem to have been noticed less by voters; at the least, movements to block the NPL while keeping the primary in place were successful in many states. Such changes may have been enacted to limit the spread of the NPL, but there were also legitimate policy arguments for them. The preprimary convention established in Minnesota, for instance, would be emulated in states as diverse as Massachusetts and Utah not as a means of blocking insurgents but simply as a means of simplifying voters' choices. As I have argued elsewhere in this book, changes in primary laws often are about short-term political battles, but this does not mean that the merits (or demerits) of such changes do not transcend these circumstances. Just as it is difficult, however, to blame the direct primary for the NPL's rise in North Dakota, so it is hard to blame the NPL's successes and (mostly) failures to extend its reach either on other states' primary laws or on the restrictions enacted by those states' legislators.

The Fate of the Nonpartisan League

Although it would not regain control of state government—at least in its original incarnation—the NPL did not disappear during the 1920s. It did, however, lose A. C. Townley. After a period of intense introspection, Townley decided that the NPL would be more effective if it were to operate more like a traditional interest group; he also decided to resign from the organization and to establish another one, the National Producers' Alliance.

The decision to reconstitute itself as more of a pressure group and to lift the authoritarian command over policy that Townley had practiced yielded three immediate results. First, it left a leadership vacuum; the NPL now stood for what a diverse assortment of members said it stood for. Second, this decision reduced some of the hostility directed at the NPL and diminished the effectiveness of claims about its authoritarianism. The decision redirected attention toward policy, but at the same time it allowed for some flexibility in the policy stances of candidates who claimed NPL support. And third, the NPL decision to endorse, rather than recruit, candidates meant that they vied for NPL support. NPL endorsees won most state offices in 1932, undoubtedly as a consequence of the Great Depression. In a sign that the NPL brand meant more than the party brands, William Langer became the only nonincumbent governor elected in that year (Smith 1981). Despite his earlier break with the NPL, Langer would go on to become its leader, serving two terms as governor (interrupted by a felony conviction in 1934) and then scoring a primary win over incumbent senator (and former NPL governor) Lynn Frazier in 1940.[3] Although Langer remained somewhat of an agrarian Progressive—and thus sympathetic, in a fashion, to the ideals the NPL had originally championed—during his tenure in office he was plagued by accusations of scandal, and the NPL was seen largely as a Langer campaign machine. During his time in office Langer became known as a formidable constituency service politician, and his own "brand" became far more important than that of the NPL. When the NPL decided at its 1956 convention to formally ally itself with the Democratic Party, Langer stayed behind in the Republican Party.

The twists and turns of Langer's career were not unique; Langer won all of his elections as a Republican, yet he ran in 1920 as the IVA candidate, and later as the NPL candidate. Frazier was the NPL candidate in every one of his elections save for the one he lost, in which Langer appropriated the NPL endorsement. By the 1920s, the NPL endorsement marked these politicians vaguely as agrarian Progressives, but with each subsequent election it conferred less and less information and constrained them in fewer ways. Olger Burtniss, the successful IVA candidate in 1920, would go on to receive the NPL endorsement in subsequent elections, serving six terms in the House and only being swept out by the

Democratic wave of 1932. William Lemke prided himself as being true to the original NPL ideals for much of his career, a commitment that caused him to break with the NPL as a response to Langer's activities as governor and run as a member of the Republican Organizing Committee, yet another factional group, this one formed in opposition to Langer (Rylance 1981). Lemke would go on to serve in the House from 1932 to his death in 1950. Following Huey Long's death, Lemke was persuaded to make an ill-fated bid for president in 1936 as the nominee of the Union Party, a party with ties to Father Charles Coughlin (Blackorby 1963).

The irony of the careers of these North Dakotans—not to mention the long tenures of NPL endorsees in other states, such as William Borah—is that these politicians' careers began from within an organization that prized discipline and disdained the politics of personality, yet each became a particularly idiosyncratic personality in his own right. Goldberg (1955) asserts that this is no accident—there was less organized opposition to these men because they were senate candidates, so legislative control was not an issue in their campaigns. Once Townley had turned his attention away from the NPL, there was also no one to give orders, even supposing anyone would obey them. The NPL brand was still immensely valuable, but individual politicians had the ability to use that brand, to explain away any of its liabilities, and to support only those NPL policies that were advantageous. This is precisely what candidate-centered elections in the United States are expected to do. According to Goldberg's count, NPL-endorsed senators won eight seats, in North Dakota, Minnesota, Nebraska, Wisconsin, Montana, Washington, and Iowa. These senators constituted a bloc of agrarian Progressives, and they worked during the 1940s and 1950s to forge alliances with senators from both parties on a range of issues. Many midwestern politicians also appropriated elements of the NPL's platform. Longtime North Dakota congressman Usher Burdick, for instance, ran unsuccessfully against Lynn Frazier for governor in 1916, yet was endorsed by the NPL when he ran for the U.S. House years later; Usher and his son Quentin (also an NPL member) held North Dakota's U.S. House seats with only a four-year interruption from 1935 to 1992, Usher as a Republican and Quentin as a Democrat. This streak in the politics of the region was arguably reflected as late as the 1990s and 2000s in the policy stances of many other politicians from the area, defining them in a way that their party labels did not.

The final act in the NPL's history, at least as an independent entity, was its move into the Democratic Party in 1956. As described by NPL activist Lloyd Omdahl (1961), the move was encouraged by Langer even though he did not join in it. Although the NPL was by this time little more than an extension of Langer's campaign team, Omdahl's account emphasizes Langer's role in recruiting younger members and working to develop a more active NPL that would persist after he left politics. These younger activists tended to be more liberal than other NPL members, particularly on social policy, and they were at odds with the increasingly conservative national Republican Party. It took eight years of negotiations for the NPL to join the North Dakota Democrats, and each body held its own nominating convention in 1958 before fully integrating. The original model for the move was the Democratic-Farmer-Labor Party in Minnesota, a merged party formed in 1944 in which the original factions at least had equal billing. The movement of the NPL to the Democratic Party posed the possibility of gains for both sides; the Democratic Party had historically been the weaker of the two major parties. If Democrats were to win elections following the merger, the NPL could claim credit. If Democrats lost, on the other hand, the NPL could not be blamed. The NPL had long since lost its ability to dictate policy to its members; it now functioned primarily as an extra bit of branding for Democrats. The merged party did score some victories in the following years, including those of Quentin Burdick, but the merger ensured that there was no way to prove who was responsible for these victories.

As we shall see in the next section North Dakota primary laws changed several times following the initial decline of the NPL. Some of these changes can be seen not as a response to the NPL as it originally stood but as a response to the new and different variant of the NPL captained by William Langer. The establishment of a "sore loser" law in 1938, for instance, was part of a national trend, but it was also an effort by anti-Langer forces to block him from running for the Senate (Vogel 2004). With the receding of the NPL threat, primary law changes in North Dakota became somewhat more about partisan advantage or about settling personal conflicts.

What the Nonpartisan League's History Tells Us about Primary Elections

Throughout the NPL's tenure as a political force, there was widespread consternation about its use of primaries; according to many NPL opponents, primaries might be about breaking the hold of party machines, but they were not about creating unaccountable "bosses" such as Townley (Bruce 1921). To the NPL's critics, there was something distinctly un-American about this approach to primaries, but it was not clear what could be done about it. The *Courier-News* of Fargo opined in early 1916 that primary laws should be amended so that only candidates who adhered to the "principles of the party" could run as its nominees (Morlan 1955, 74). This criticism, which echoed some original complaints about primaries, did not make it clear how such adherence would be demonstrated, although preprimary conventions or other ballot access restrictions might accomplish this, as would abandoning primaries entirely.

Neither the NPL nor the politicians who would go on to lead it played any role in the establishment of the direct primary. Rather, the NPL sought from its inception to take advantage of primary laws in North Dakota and to adapt its strategy to primary laws elsewhere. There is ample evidence of its decision to take the North Dakota laws as a starting point; Townley and others were never shy about pointing this out. There is, in addition, evidence that the NPL actively explored the ways in which other states' laws might force it to modify its tactics. The existing NPL collections contain few explicit examples of this, but there are some. In a 1918 letter to Minnesota state auditor O. J. Arness, Henry Teigan asked about Montana election law and noted the need to change tactics in different states in order to demonstrate effectiveness:

> No doubt it will be rather difficult to put Jeanette [Rankin, the NPL endorsee for the state's U.S. House seat] across on November 5. I am rather dubious about the possibility, but it isn't impossible, by any means. I was just wondering in that connection what sort of general election ballots are in use in Montana. Do you have the party column, or has the party column been abolished? You know we have no party column in this state....
>
> It is undoubtedly more important to put League candidates "over" in Minnesota and Idaho than it would be to do so in Montana this year. The fact that you do not elect any number of state officials there makes complete victory this year less necessary.

In this letter Teigan shows a willingness to learn enough about neighboring states' election laws to try to use them to NPL advantage, coupled with a surprising lack of such knowledge. The fact that the NPL hadn't acquired such information a month before the election shows that election laws and their nuances were not a major part of the project, even as it sought to adapt to them.

Similarly, the correspondence between Judson King and Teigan clearly shows that it is King, not Teigan, who is interested in how the NPL uses election laws or pursues reforms in those laws. In his letters King asks several questions about whether the NPL will enact referendum or recall laws, and he encourages the NPL to explore using proportional representation. These were ideas that even many Progressives did not support, but they are examples of the ways in which Progressives regarded the NPL as a fascinating, yet somewhat foreign, experiment. This would both help and hinder the NPL; this made the NPL a bit of a curiosity for some urbanites but also inspired a range of national politicians, including Theodore Roosevelt, William Howard Taft, and Warren Harding, to speak of the NPL as "alien," and the NPL's use of the direct primary was said by Taft to be "unfair and fraudulent" (Lansing 2018, 117–118).

The primary law changes in NPL states between 1916 and 1928 were largely reactionary in nature. They were efforts to block the NPL. These changes show, however, the limitations of considering reforms of any one type as inherently liberal (in the sense of opening up the process) or conservative in nature. The definition depended on who was in charge. Thus, doing away with primaries made sense in instances where regular Republicans were in power and wished to close off the ability for the NPL to gain strength within the party. In North Dakota, in contrast, the NPL triumph prompted others in the Republican Party to propose more open primary laws such as the nonpartisan top two primary law proposed by the IVA.

What are we to make of primary law changes in these states after the NPL lost power? One might argue for three possibilities. First, the NPL did not entirely go away; as the North Dakota case shows, midwestern farmers became more receptive to the economic aspects of the NPL message once the Great Depression had hit. The NPL's decision to become more of a pressure group proved to be successful in aiding the election of sympathetic Democrats and Republicans in 1932. Second, NPL power gradually receded even as individual senators who affiliated, or had previously affiliated, themselves with the NPL remained in office. No similar movement arose in subsequent years, in part because, as was the case for Progressives, the parties were to prove receptive to their ideas once they were separated from the sort of organization A. C. Townley had established. And third, it seems reasonable to expect that many states might fear the development of a similar movement and use the lack of organized opposition to pursue restrictive primary rules that would insulate the parties from competition.

In Chapter 2 I presented Table 2.3, summarizing the states where the NPL engaged in organizing work. As the Teigan letters demonstrate, the NPL had support in many different states, but in the late 1910s and early 1920s it sought to focus its attention on those states where it expected to do the best. The inclusion of twelve states in the list does not mean that these states were all equally receptive to the NPL or that the NPL had similar levels of success there—it certainly did not—but it does at least include all of the places where the NPL believed it had a chance to win elections. That is, these are at least states where we might look at any sign of an NPL legacy when we look at primary law reforms. There were memories of hostile takeover of the primary process.

In that chapter we also took a preliminary look (see Figure 2.3 and Table 2.6) at primary law changes in the NPL states in the decades following 1928. The states listed include four (North Dakota, Minnesota, Idaho, and Montana) where the NPL showed significant political strength, as well as some where there was documented concern about NPL activities, such as Wisconsin, Nebraska, and

Kansas, and some, such as Oklahoma and Texas, where the NPL made efforts but where there is little evidence that the NPL had very much success. The data in that chapter show that there was substantial change in primary laws in these states during the 1930s and 1940s—slightly more change, on average, than was the norm in other states. This is not necessarily a consequence of the NPL's legacy. By the 1960s, once the NPL had become a distant memory, these states were less likely to change their primary laws than were other states. The states that were more active in changing their primary laws were, as Table 2.6 indicates, states where the NPL had more of an impact. With minor, idiosyncratic, exceptions, the changes made before 1960 in the more NPL-friendly states of North Dakota, Minnesota, Montana, and Idaho were changes that expanded primaries, rendering it easier for activists from outside of the parties to win election. The lone restrictive change in North Dakota, the adoption in 1948 of a sore loser law, was, as we have seen, an effort to prevent William Langer from winning office. Michael Kang's (2011) work on sore loser laws shows that idiosyncratic state-specific reasons such as this appear to have played a greater role in the adoption of such laws than did any coordinated national or regional effort.

Before 1960, the more restrictive changes shown in Table 2.6 tend to be concentrated in states where the NPL was active but did not have any real influence. Oklahoma and Texas took several steps to restrict ballot access, but the NPL's poor track record in those states makes it an unlikely impetus for these changes. The Henry Teigan files contain many articles on the NPL from Colorado newspapers (e.g., *Denver Express* 1917), indicating, perhaps, that Coloradans were paying close attention to the NPL. However, references to Colorado primary laws in literature of the immediate post-NPL era (Freyd 1926), broader case study approaches (Reynolds 2006, 130–131, 175), and Colorado political histories (Cronin and Loevy 2012) say little about the NPL, focusing instead on partisan conflict, reactions to progressivism, or urban/rural conflict.

The NPL's rise and fall, then, suggests that primaries were vulnerable to hostile takeover, but that the sorts of organizations capable of such capture are simply not that common in American politics, and the U.S. system does not give them the ability to persist over more than a small number of election cycles. The NPL was in many ways the worst fear of early primary opponents, and it had many more advantages than any other nonparty electoral organization formed during the twentieth century. It succeeded because of the novelty of its organizing method, the unique circumstances of North Dakota, and its very focused and limited goals. It also could only have succeeded in a political era in which there was reflexive party-line voting yet parties did not provide a coherent ideological agenda to voters. In other words, the NPL was an ideological movement that took advantage of an antiparty innovation during an era when parties themselves were not overly ideological.

The facts that the NPL lost power and reconstituted as a more traditional pressure group, was not kept in office in North Dakota by changes in election law, was not driven from office by such changes, and was not kept out of office by such changes (barring, perhaps, the odd circumstances in Minnesota) suggest that there was no real need for the NPL states to revisit their primary election laws after the 1920s. The NPL agenda was, however, popular in many of these states when divorced from the NPL itself; although NPL leaders were not experts in election law, many of the election law changes made after the NPL's decline appear to have had the ability to help individual politicians with agrarian support (or at least with support outside the parties) gain office. The direct primary may provide an advantage to groups like the NPL, but such groups are rare and are eventually constrained not by primary law changes but by the inevitabilities built into the American two-party system.

Subsequent "Hostile Takeover" Attempts

The gradual rise of more programmatic parties in the post–World War II era meant that the prospects for any other hostile takeover attempt like the NPL became less and less likely. In contemporary politics, it is difficult to imagine an ideological movement that does not draw support mostly from one party or the other and hence amounts to more of a splinter faction within one of the major parties rather than an outside takeover attempt. Particularly with the decline of the Democratic Party in the South, it is also difficult to conceive of a regional issue that is truly as divorced from national partisan lines of cleavage as were the issues of concern to the NPL. In closing this chapter, let us consider first the plethora of smaller "takeover" attempts in various regions of the United States after the NPL, before turning to the most conspicuous contemporary attempt, that by the Tea Party.

Party Factions and Preprimary Endorsements

One distinguishing feature of the NPL was its selection of candidates in advance of the primary. This is a practice that was adopted in many states following the NPL's appearance; in many instances it was a tactic used to thwart the NPL. In some instances, this process was institutionalized in law; four states made changes to their preprimary convention laws between 1928 and 1968, and the four that adopted the primary for the first time during this period (Utah, Rhode Island, New Mexico, and Connecticut) all did so with a preprimary convention option attached. According to McNitt (1980), three other states adopted a preprimary convention after 1968; another two states allow for a final convention option if the primary fails to yield a candidate (in the South Dakota case) or fails to yield a candidate with at least 35 percent of the vote (Iowa); and four other states allow for informal preprimary endorsements by the parties. Minnesota's preprimary conventions, discussed earlier, were clear efforts to prevent the NPL from exploiting divisions among party regulars in an effort to reach office. Such conventions can be justified on other grounds, however. As discussed in Chapter 3, Massachusetts introduced a preprimary convention in 1934, abolished it in 1938, and readopted it much later, in 1982. The argument in Massachusetts in the 1980s had little to do with blocking outsiders; rather, the intention of the preprimary convention was to winnow the field in order to ensure that nuisance candidates did not determine the outcome when there were two or three equally competitive strong candidates. Only candidates who receive 15 percent of the convention vote can appear on the ballot. The actual winner at the convention may gain an advantage in the actual primary, but this is not necessarily the case; as in presidential primaries, if a candidate wins but fails to meet expectations, the losing candidate or candidates may gain momentum. The same has been found in recent Minnesota elections (Elazar 1999, 72–75).

The catalysts for establishing preprimary conventions have, however, generally been party factions, not outside groups. New Mexico (discussed in detail in Chapter 5) is an example of a state that also has used preprimary conventions as a means of brokering conflict between different factions; the state has used these to ensure that tickets are balanced or that other grievances are aired before the primary is underway (Holmes 1967). It is important to note that the lone NPL state that experimented with preprimary conventions after the NPL's decline was Idaho, a state where the NPL never controlled the Republican Party but in which an agrarian faction did find substantial support within the party.

The closest one can get to an instance where preprimary endorsements were used to deter outside groups from seizing power is the odd case of California. California had no formal preprimary convention, but in both parties informal associations began holding endorsing conventions in the 1930s, 1940s, and 1950s (Delmatier, McIntosh, and Waters 1970, 352). During this time California allowed candidates to cross-file: to run simultaneously in both parties' primaries. The formation of the California Democratic Council and the California Republican Assembly was undertaken in part to prevent candidates of the opposing party from winning the primary, and in part to prevent individuals with no background in either party from receiving the nomination, as journalist and author Upton Sinclair had done in the 1934 Democratic primary. I shall discuss the California case again in Chapter 6.

The California case shows that preprimary endorsements can be used by unofficial party organizations just as they have been used by official parties. The difference between unofficial and official parties can at times be blurred, as was the case for Southern "jaybird" primaries (discussed in Chapter 7). These primaries, declared unlawful by the Supreme Court in its *Terry v. Adams* (345 U.S. 461 (1953)) decision, were informal whites-only primaries held in parts of Texas. The losers of this primary would drop out, thus leaving a single Democratic candidate. The court's decision here has been said by some to be problematic as precedent, because even though the intent here was clearly to disenfranchise African Americans, the "jaybird" Democrats were an informal entity, and in practice their decision to endorse (and the subsequent nonbinding understanding that the losers would drop out) was no different than what went on in California. The Supreme Court was, then, declaring some views as impermissible grounds for an endorsing convention (Issacharoff and Pildes 1998).

These cases lack any sort of organized group that resembles the NPL. In some instances, the relevant conflict is between different groups within a party; in others the conflict is between party insiders and outsiders; in still others it is between a party and interlopers from the other party; and in yet others it is between the party and one individual. This may serve as testimony to the flexibility of American political parties—one distinguishing feature of the NPL was that it organized around an issue that it felt was receiving insufficient attention from the existing parties. Especially when one considers the ideological flexibility of American parties and the lack, during much of the twentieth century, of any need for state parties to adapt their positions to those of the national party, such issues are rare. In instances when regional issues put state parties at odds with the national parties—as was the case for civil rights in the South for much of this era—issue-based conflict played out in presidential primaries, not down-ballot races.

Interest Group Endorsements in Primaries

Thus, the responses the NPL generated in the 1920s do not have one clear analog in party efforts to block hostile takeovers. The NPL's own tactics, however, suggest another potential legacy: the NPL sought to winnow competition by settling on one candidate per race before the primary in a somewhat organized fashion. The NPL convention of 1916 had all of the trappings of a party organization, but it was a process that was not necessarily dramatically different from the processes organized interests have at times used to confer endorsements before the primary. Most such instances were not necessarily patterned on the NPL's actions, although some clearly were. For instance, Frank Packard, the leader of the Western Tax Council—an antitax group in the 1940s bankrolled by corporate leaders such as Pierre DuPont—proposed following Townley's model in establishing the group's clout in select states, using member dues to organize at the grass roots and then working, with these dues-paying members, to endorse promising candidates in select primaries (Martin 2013, 102). Packard had served a term in the 1910s as the North Dakota tax commissioner, and he openly praised A. C. Townley's model to Tax Council members, arguing that the NPL model was still applicable to groups with issue agendas fundamentally different from the NPL's agenda.

Although there is little evidence that Packard was particularly successful in his efforts, his proposal is little different from the sorts of grassroots mobilization efforts practiced by interest groups and pressure groups of all sorts in subsequent decades. One might connect the NPL easily to issue-oriented groups of the early and mid-twentieth century—be they Prohibitionists or the John Birch Society—except that the NPL was more organized and hierarchical than most of these organizations. With the decision to abandon the strict hierarchy and to behave more like a traditional group, the NPL cast its lot with organizations that might at times work for individual candidates but declined to pursue a takeover of any party or a single-minded focus on absolute fidelity on issues. The increased ability of labor, of single-issue advocacy groups, and of business groups to play a direct role in campaigns meant that national groups had the ability to endorse all manner of primary candidates by the late twentieth century, but again, these groups sought to work within one or both parties rather than to control them. No state or region had the peculiarities that led to the hostile takeover attempts of the NPL.

A Contemporary Analog: The Tea Party

The NPL case is instructive, as well, in considering contemporary "hostile takeover" efforts such as the Tea Party. During the early 2010s, Tea Party leaders made rhetorical claims that resembled those of the NPL, such as the claim that group members sought to use Republican primaries as a matter of convenience, that Tea Party voters could not be counted on to be Republican voters, or that elected Tea Party candidates could also not be counted on to follow the party's agenda in government (Zernike 2010, 85–86; Rasmussen and Schoen 2010, 11).

The structure of the Tea Party differed from the NPL in several consequential ways. There was no Tea Party hierarchy; there were instead many different Tea Party organizations at the local level (Berry, Portney, and Joseph 2014). A few local Tea Party groups used information from national groups or attended national gatherings, and some national groups assembled lists of Tea Party supporters for fundraising purposes (Mummolo 2013). Yet perhaps the nature of their issue concerns led Tea Party groups to be resistant to direction on specific issue stances. There was also no process by which the Tea Party might winnow primary fields or choose among competing candidates. In the absence of an endorsement process or a formal structure of any sort, it was possible either for professed Tea Party candidates to split the vote, allowing the election of a mainstream Republican, or for established politicians to rebrand themselves as Tea Party candidates.

The most consequential reason why it is inaccurate to speak of the Tea Party as a group that sought a "hostile takeover" of the Republican Party, however, was that almost all Tea Party supporters were already Republicans (Abramowitz 2012, 203; Cohen 2012, 229). While anti-elite rhetoric is a common feature of populist groups within both major parties today, usually these activists' political histories make it unrealistic to think of them as outside forces taking over the party's nominating process (Lo 2012). Most NPL candidates really were political neophytes who, at least initially, were expected to follow the directives of NPL leaders.

Such conclusions should not be taken as a suggestion that primary laws are not of importance in considering the successes and failures of modern groups such as the Tea Party. There is little evidence that Tea Party supporters gained control of the party machinery in the way that the NPL did, so efforts to open or close primaries (e.g., Winger 2013 on South Carolina; Moncrief 2012 on Idaho) in some states with strong Tea Party movements cannot be attributed either to the Tea Party or to efforts by mainstream politicians to defend against the Tea Party. They do suggest, however, one common thread. The NPL used primary laws to its advantage in North Dakota and then adjusted its strategy to reflect the different primary laws and different political circumstances of surrounding states. One can make the same claim about Tea Party efforts between 2010 and 2014; accounts of the 2010 Utah Republican party convention, where incumbent Robert Bennett was denied a ballot line and Tea Party–supported candidate Mike Lee went on to win the nomination, have suggested that Tea Party activists were overrepresented at the convention (Gardner 2010). Opponents of the Tea Party, like opponents of the NPL, experimented with changes to primary laws as a means of insulating primaries; for instance, some of those advocating for a top two primary in states such as Montana argued that Tea Party candidates might be deterred in this way (Eaves 2013). But in both cases there was little consensus on how to do so or on the effectiveness of doing so. The NPL would probably have existed in roughly the same form regardless of state election laws; it might even have been stronger in a different type of system, as the NPL's experience in Canada showed. So the Tea Party seems like a natural component of developments in American politics that are far larger and more consequential than American primary laws.

Conclusions

Were early critics of primary elections correct to be concerned about the possibility that primary elections might abet a "hostile takeover" of the parties? Contemporary political parties certainly have changed over the course of the century in ways that make organized takeovers difficult (but perhaps make less-organized incursions possible), and Freyd's claim that "parties" would replace parties is ultimately untestable. Yet our lengthy consideration here of the lone undisputed example of an outside group's takeover of the party machinery shows just how rare such circumstances are; how unique that lone instance was; and how even in that case, only a short-term takeover was possible. The NPL case speaks, more than anything else, to the resilience of the American party system.

The NPL case illustrates, in addition, the irrelevance of tinkering with primary laws in the face of an organized nonparty movement. It seems indisputable that there is a difference between having primaries and not having primaries; the NPL would not have organized within the Republican Party had there not been a primary system to begin with. The NPL—like other nonparty groups discussed later in the chapter, and like informal party factions—sought to use the tools it had at its disposal. Yet it is difficult to argue that some of the mechanisms explored here—preprimary conventions, top two primaries, or changes in the openness of primaries—would have mattered. Such changes, in addition, tend to be enacted in response to very immediate concerns, so it is difficult to make general statements about what works and what doesn't work. Here, perhaps, is the lesson the NPL provides to the study of primaries in other times and places: laws can channel the direction of such movements, but they are unlikely to play a noticeable role in defining their success or failure.

5
Defective Primary Laws

In the early years of the Missouri primary, it was common for people who shared the surnames of well-known political families to file for multiple offices, scare off competition, and then withdraw immediately before the election—after tipping off other potential candidates, who were able to step in at the last minute to file and then run without opposition (Loeb 1910). Some Michigan primary ballots included "spite" candidates, who had no real interest in winning the nomination but sought to pull votes away from candidates they did not like (Dorr 1937). Several Nebraska primaries in the late 1920s featured multiple candidates with the same name running against each other (Overacker 1932). And in the New York primaries of 1912, a law requiring primary elections for minor parties (even when these primaries were uncontested) resulted in a ballot that was fourteen feet long (Feldman 1917). Unsurprisingly, many New York polling places ran out of ballots.

There certainly was some bad behavior involved in these elections, but for the most part these seem like instances of bad laws, which did not take into account the ways people would try to game the system or simply failed to account for minor confusion that might arise on the part of voters. These problems are not necessarily indictments of the primary system per se; they just are instances of laws that required minor adjustment. Nebraska was one of many states that solved its problem by requiring candidates to list their occupation or their address, so that voters could distinguish between the incumbent and the opportunist who bore the same name without infringing on the opportunist's right to seek office. Michigan instituted a refundable filing fee, and other states raised their signature requirements in order to limit the number of frivolous candidates. These all seem like reasonable responses aimed at improving the primary, and they are enough of a staple of contemporary American elections that few voters or candidates see them as being particularly remarkable.

Many critics of the direct primary argued that the primary had failed to meet the high expectations that Progressives, and the general public, had for it. If this was the case, then it certainly seems possible that problems in the drafting of the laws themselves may have contributed to this failure, and that there was reason to fix these problems before public support for the direct primary declined further. On the other hand, how are we to know when a filing fee is too high? When does the specter of frivolous campaigns become an excuse for imposing all manner

Reform and Retrenchment. Robert G. Boatright, Oxford University Press. © Oxford University Press 2024.
DOI: 10.1093/oso/9780197774083.003.0005

of restrictions on candidates and voters? How should we distinguish between a minor irritant, such as the presence of two candidates with the same name on the ballot, and the much broader but harder-to-measure claim that primaries had lowered the quality of the legislature? Any claim that there were problems with the direct primary involved a certain amount of subjectivity, and any reform to fix these alleged problems risked making the primary less democratic, or less able to fulfill its creators' goals.

This was, of course, the point for some "reformers." In New York, the easiest response to the unwieldy and confusing ballot was simple: conclude that the primary did not work, and get rid of it. This is what the legislature eventually did in 1921. Many of the "problems" with the direct primary were spotted by those who had initially opposed the primary, and many of these closely resembled problems that these opponents had forecast well before the election. This is not to say that these problems were not real, but it does suggest that, as with any major law, it may become difficult for a legislature to enact minor fixes when a significant minority, or even a majority, in the legislature does not want the law to function well.

In Chapter 2, I proposed four reasons political parties were able, from the late 1920s onward, to pass laws restricting the openness of the primary and to reassert control over the electoral process: the decline of the Progressive movement, the threat posed by insurgent nonparty groups, public dissatisfaction with poorly written laws, and the increased importance of party control of nominations that accompanied rising two-party competition. In this chapter I address the third of these consequences: I explore the fate of allegedly "bad" primary laws. I do so by drawing upon contemporary literature that seeks to clarify some common features of bad electoral laws. I ask how we can understand responses to these laws, based on the motives of those who alleged problems in the laws and of those who controlled government. The results here show, I contend, that it is possible to develop a typology of bad primary laws, and that this typology has some utility in predicting whether the laws were repaired, left alone, or discarded altogether. Unsurprisingly, one major determinant of whether and how problems in primary laws were addressed was the nature of party conflict. States where there was bipartisan support for the primary were able to fix problems with their primaries, while states with partisan conflict over the primary were either saddled with ineffective laws or saw their primary laws be undermined altogether.

How to Study Bad Laws

There is to my knowledge no distinct academic specialty in the study of bad laws. Public policy literature generally concludes that there are predictable defects that can occur in the process of writing laws. Cohen, March, and Olson's (1972) "garbage can" theory of organizational choice posits that when confronted with a crisis, policy makers will generally select from a number of ready-to-hand options that will give the appearance of addressing the problem. This strategy almost ensures that there will be some lack of fit between laws and the problems they seek to solve; such problems will be more likely if the law enacted has not previously been implemented and evaluated elsewhere. In the cases described here, state governments that were aware of the popularity of primary laws in other states may have chosen to adopt another state's laws without reflecting on their fit to their own state or on the long-term effects the law might have, and the rapidity of these laws' implementation meant that there was little established knowledge on the laws' effects. This is consistent with David Mayhew's (1974) contention that legislators' major goals include position taking and credit claiming, both of which would emphasize the short-term value of being on the right side, as opposed to the long-term merits of the laws they are enacting.

While the concept of "bad laws" may be a bit too nebulous to have inspired its own literature, there is a substantial contemporary literature on what makes for a good or a bad election law. Schaffer (2008) contends that "clean election reform"—efforts to make laws more democratic—are prone to a variety of what he calls "iatrogenic" effects. Iatrogenic effects are a consequence of the treatment for an illness. They can appear even when the laws themselves are well-intentioned and there is widespread agreement about the nature of the problems the laws seek to address. Iatrogenic effects are inevitable given that many election reform laws have undergone limited testing before being implemented and their authors often fail to account for the responses of those affected by the laws. Schaffer considers a range of different reforms that have been implemented in democratic nations, focusing in particular on voter eligibility laws, voter insulation laws such as the secret ballot, and efforts to establish vote integrity. The most common negative or iatrogenic consequences of these laws include vote depression, the development of new means of cheating, and voter alienation. Such responses tend to result when laws are unduly complex, when they are overly restrictive, when the rhetoric that accompanies them fails to match the results, and when the establishment of the laws has immediate consequences that favor one party.

Schaffer's focus is mostly on contemporary elections, but he does draw lessons from late nineteenth- and early twentieth-century American reforms. He draws in particular on Argersinger's (1995; cited in Schaffer 2008, 60) work on fusion and antifusion laws in the Plains states during the Populist era. There, Argersinger shows that efforts to limit the power of third parties had unexpected destabilizing results for Democrats and Republicans. The lesson there, Schaffer argues, is that many election reforms are adopted as a response to a precipitating event or crisis and without careful consideration of their likely effects. This is a conclusion that can easily be used to understand contemporary American electoral reform efforts such as changes to the presidential nomination process or reform of election financing, as well as early efforts of the Progressive Era such as the direct primary. Schaffer contends that gradual reforms, modeled on similar efforts in similar places, are more likely to live up to their authors' expectations.

Schaffer's work was part of a substantial growth in work on the concept of "electoral integrity," most of which is associated with a project on that subject led by Pippa Norris. The literature that has grown out of Norris's work suggests three main questions to be asked about the allegedly failed, or at least problematic, primary laws. First, in what way is the law "bad"? There is, as we shall see in the next section, a rich and complicated literature regarding how elections can fail—essentially, how one defines a failure has much to do with how one understands the concept of democracy. Second, is the claim a sincere or an accurate one? A law may function exactly as intended yet still be held by its opponents to be flawed. Simply because some say that the law does not work should not be taken as prima facie evidence that it does not work. And third, is the claim generalizable? That is, are the problems brought about by this particular law those that would be present in any jurisdiction where the law is in place, or does the law fail in a particular jurisdiction because of that jurisdiction's characteristics?

Before elaborating upon each of these three questions, some qualification is in order. The determination that an election law does not work is ultimately a political one, so there is no pretense here that state legislators, let alone advocates for or against the direct primary, are political theorists. Yet a clear understanding of what about these laws had allegedly failed can provide an understanding of how easy it would be to fix the laws and what sorts of political alliances would be necessary to do so. It can also give us a better understanding of whether the direct primary, as a procedure, had inevitable shortcomings such as those cited by the direct primary's opponents, or whether it was simply not implemented well in some places.

How Should We Categorize Bad Election Laws?

Scholars of contemporary democratic elections have offered a variety of typologies for evaluating election laws. Most of these typologies have been developed for applied purposes in newer democracies—they are meant to compare "what works" across cultures or across different election systems, and they have served as fodder for a variety of techniques for rating the level of democracy or corruption in different places. All of these typologies share a concern for distinguishing between *norms* and *effects*—for considering whether a "better" or "more democratic" regime is one that fits a set of pre-established criteria, regardless of the voting outcome, or whether the measure of a system has to do with who votes, whom it elects, or what those it elects do with the power they have been granted (see Norris 2014, 10–11). These two concerns are difficult to disentangle.

The most complete argument about how one might identify bad election laws is that of Sarah Birch (2011). In her book *Electoral Malpractice*, Birch provides a four-part distinction between violations of electoral law, violations of norms, violation of internationally agreed-upon "best practices," and violations of the tenets of democratic theory. Birch distinguishes between *malpractice*, which is a deliberate effort to reduce the quality of elections, and *mispractice*, which is merely incompetence on the part of those administering the election. Birch's four categories are distinct in terms of how one would identify them and how one would measure them—in some instances they require familiarity with the stated purpose of the law, in others they require knowledge of the goals of the reformers and the rhetoric surrounding reform, and in others they require a knowledge of a nation's political culture and broader beliefs about matters such as equality or fairness. To wit, violations of electoral law may occur, but these violations say nothing about the law itself—that is, a government may enact laws that give it substantial leeway in manipulating results or in acting undemocratically. Norms are culturally specific, so a norm violation in one jurisdiction may be standard practice in another, and the judgment of when a norm has been violated can amount to the imposition of the culture of the person alleging the violation upon others who do not recognize it. Even international agreements about what "best practices" are may still be a matter of imposing norms; they are, in this case, norms shared by many people as opposed to norms prevalent in one culture. And the articulation of any particular theory of democracy can also be seen as subjective.

In Birch's framing, then, it is difficult to develop an airtight argument about what malpractice is, and correspondingly, any argument about what the "best" practices or laws are is likewise up for debate. Furthermore, to allege that there has been "malpractice" is to argue that governments have manipulated the election beyond some zone of acceptability. All governments seek to manipulate elections; for instance, the establishment of one particular voting system as opposed to another, the drawing of district lines, the establishment of suffrage criteria or candidate eligibility requirements, or even something as routine as the establishment of polling locations all are instances of manipulation. Birch argues, however, that we can still make arguments about the effects of malpractice: even if we cannot precisely define or sanction it, we can observe that certain sets of practices are correlated with suboptimal outcomes for the society. Malpractice, for Birch, ultimately can lead citizens to doubt whether they in fact reside in a democracy and to conclude that their votes do not in fact matter, which in turn can lead to greater malpractice and ultimately to corruption, inequality, and other political and economic conditions that are far removed from the electoral process itself.

We can, then, understand that democracy is ultimately about manipulation—for instance, about convincing voters of what their interests are or of using existing laws to seek short-term advantage—but still draw conclusions about when parties or government have gone too far. Birch concludes by considering the costs of different types of manipulation. Manipulating election rules tends to be the easiest way for parties or governments to seek advantage. A manipulation of the rules has a democratic element to it (that is, parties can claim a mandate for their efforts), and it is thus less likely than other types of manipulation to provoke backlash from voters. Manipulation of voters—essentially, campaigning—is expensive and can be contested by other forces. And manipulation of the vote itself, by, for instance, fraudulently counting the ballots, is more expensive still and tends to be the most likely to antagonize voters if discovered. There is, perhaps, an interplay between these types of manipulation—changing the law may allow for greater manipulation of voters or reduce the attention paid to oversight of the voting process itself.

Birch is not the only author who has sought to develop a schema for evaluating election malfeasance. In *Why Electoral Integrity Matters*, Pippa Norris (2014, 35–37) provides a three-part typology of how one might identify electoral fraud: as a violation of law, as maladministration, or as violation of democratic values and principles. Others who have been a part of Norris's project, such as Schedler (2002) and Davies-Robert and Carroll (2014) of the Carter Center, provide similar typologies. What all of these authors share is an understanding that normative evaluation of election laws will inherently have a degree of subjectivity, that one must determine whether effects matter or not, and that any evaluative standards must take into account the likelihood that candidates and parties will attempt to push the limits of the laws.

How Believable Are Allegations about Bad Laws?

Birch's argument about the relatively low cost of manipulating election laws suggests not only that laws can be written to fail, but that allegations that laws are not working should be inherently suspect. If voters can be convinced that a law is not effective, it will become easier for politicians to change the law in ways that benefit them.

Alberto Simpser's (2013) work on election manipulation suggests that this is not merely a "sour grapes" phenomenon, nor is it solely an argument made in order to gain immediate advantage. Simpser contends, in fact, that successful parties tend to manipulate elections and to question the fairness of election laws in order to increase citizens' cynicism about the electoral process and thus to diminish opposition to future manipulations. This framing certainly corresponds to the practices of contemporary parties in democracies that are struggling and to regimes that have practiced vote rigging and other schemes. Complaints about existing laws, then, can serve as a form of disinformation. They are, moreover, not even made merely to win elections—that is, just as we might expect complaints about voting laws to come from losers, we also might expect them from parties that have narrowly won or expect to have trouble winning in the near future. Dominant political parties may manipulate election laws in order to demonstrate their power to do so and thus to deter future opposition.

However, voters may not be easily fooled. One major conclusion of Norris's work is that public opinion is actually a reliable indicator of problems. Norris, Elklit, and Reynolds (2014, 37) contend that one can infer intent from the persistence of problems. Problems in one election are less significant than are patterns across elections or evidence in between election cycles of actions taken to influence the elections themselves. Publics, especially in established democracies, tend to assume that politicians will cheat, or that there will be problematic outcomes in individual elections. They will recognize problems (even deliberate fraud) in a single election as reflecting bad actors, as opposed to being a sign of a problem with the system. But if problems persist over time, this persistence is (rightly) taken as a systemic problem. To put matters simply, public perceptions that elections do not work are generally a good indicator that, in fact, elections do not work.

Hence, voters may be aware of manipulation, but those who manipulate elections themselves may also accuse others of doing so or argue that the laws themselves are unfair. It is difficult to know how to treat relatively minor instances of election rigging; Cheeseman and Klaas (2018), for instance, note that it is common practice for multiple candidates with the same name to run for the same office. Is this opportunism on the part of someone fortunate enough to share a name with an elected officeholder? A plot by opposition groups to confuse voters and defeat a nonpreferred candidate? When small infractions such as this occur, we cannot know whether they are a sign of systemic problems or an isolated instance of potentially problematic behavior.

Bad Laws or Bad People?

Third, a major conclusion in all of the electoral integrity literature is that it is difficult to identify laws that are bad across the board; an election law may work out well in one jurisdiction but fail in another. In such circumstances, it is hard to know whether the law itself is the problem or there are characteristics of the second jurisdiction that will always cause problems for democratic elections. This is, of course, a classic problem of constitutional design dating back at least to Montesquieu, if not further. In her study of "electoral engineering," Norris (2004) distinguishes between rational choice individualism (RCI) and cultural modernization theory. An RCI theory of elections assumes that politicians' incentives are shaped by formal rules, that in turn citizens' choices are made in response to politicians' strategies, and that electoral engineering can be modeled with accuracy across different jurisdictions. Cultural modernization theory, in contrast, holds that cultures adapt in an uneven fashion to modernization, and as a consequence, the effects of rules will vary across cultures.

Norris's concerns are specific to contemporary democracies; the "modernization" to which she refers has to do with recent developments: the rise of citizen politics, the changing importance of social identity, and the decline of parties and other political institutions. Yet the notion that culture might determine receptiveness to rule change is not by any means a distinctly modern concept. Schaffer (2008, xii), for instance, notes that the motives, knowledge, or capabilities of politicians are socially constructed and vary across cultures, time, and individuals. Research on political corruption often emphasizes historical or cultural traits. And the two aforementioned considerations of electoral manipulation both show substantial variations in the propensity of parties to manipulate. There are predictable patterns to this: Simpser (2013, 54, 57) shows that per capita GDP is negatively correlated with manipulation, and Birch (2011, 77, 161) shows that corruption and inequality are positively correlated with manipulation. Birch also shows that (perhaps contrary to conventional wisdom) urbanization is negatively correlated with manipulation.

There are many stereotypes about the relationship between political culture and the effectiveness of laws—for instance, that Southern European governments are corrupt or prone to cheat in elections. Not all of this can be entirely reduced to matters of geography or economics, although there are certainly some broad principles one can extract. Such cultural or economic distinctions are also present in discussions of political culture within the United States, as the state political culture typologies of authors such as Daniel Elazar (1972) indicate. At the extremes, we find examples in some poorly functioning democracies in which it is difficult to distinguish between the reformers and the alleged malefactors who have corrupted the electoral process. In Andrew Wilson's (2005) work on elections in the former Soviet republics, one common theme across countries is that elections themselves have become a sham, that Western calls for democratic reform are met with efforts to make elections appear democratic while still allowing for widespread fraud. In such contexts, it is often effective for ruling parties to encourage the formation of faux opposition parties or reform movements but to ensure that such parties or movements are either ineffective or duplicitous about their own goals.

Using Contemporary Electoral Integrity Literature to Study Early Twentieth-Century America

The electoral integrity agenda developed by Norris and her colleagues is one of several contemporary projects aimed at harnessing the knowledge of academics and practitioners in pursuit of reform. It is of a piece, for instance, with European anticorruption efforts, with efforts to develop systematic knowledge of election financing, and with other comparative election systems efforts. Although the contemporary effort has the support of many nongovernmental and other organizations, it is in some ways analogous to the large body of research on election reform that appeared in the United States during the early twentieth century. That effort was national, rather than international, in scope, and it did not have comparable financial and institutional resources. It also, perhaps more so than the international efforts described earlier, contained a diversity of opinion about the wisdom of changing elections. In other words, electoral integrity efforts generally do not include scholars who advocate for less-democratic elections, and anticorruption efforts do not include scholars who advocate for more corruption. The early twentieth-century American community of researchers on primaries, however, did include some prominent academics who argued that primaries were not a good idea at all, and even some of the most prominent members of the community developed some concerns about the long-term consequences of the experiment.

The principal source of claims that some primary laws were not working, then, is the collected scholarly treatments of state elections written by American political scientists. As documented in previous chapters, this is a relatively extensive yet also coherent literature. For this analysis, as in the prior chapters, I draw upon every article from the *American Political Science Review* and the *Annals of the American Academy of Political and Social Sciences* from 1920 onward on the subject of primary elections, as well as several book-length studies of particular regions of the country. These books and articles include many state-specific works (most notably the University of Nebraska series on state politics and government, begun in the early 1990s and ongoing), annual retrospectives on notable changes in the law, and explorations of regional differences. This is a large enough body of work that we can assume that if a state had a notable problem with its primary, it is likely that at some point that problem was the subject of academic inquiry. I make no claim that this is a comprehensive list (or that such a list could exist), but it does provide us a large enough sample of problems that we can try to determine what went wrong with early primary laws and how such problems were addressed, or not. It also does not mean we should trust every claim that there is a problem, but that we should take such claims seriously and consider their context. The list of alleged defects was first presented in Table 2.4; in this chapter I regroup them in order of the date of adoption of the primary. The results are shown in Table 5.1.

Many of the considerations presented in the comparative literature are directly applicable to looking at reforms in the American states, albeit in somewhat narrower form. This has been done with reference to contemporary problems facing the United States (see Norris, Cameron, and Wynter 2018), but there have been few efforts to apply these concepts to reforms as long ago as those I consider here. In identifying instances of bad primary laws, we can distinguish a range of potential causes, from laws that were corruptly written (that is, designed not to work as advertised), to laws that contained contradictory provisions or other characteristics that were a matter of oversight or poor drafting rather than ill intent, to laws that failed to take into account particular features of the states where they were implemented. Such features might include other laws unique to the state, the strength of the state's parties or even of individual politicians, matters of geography or the state's economic development, or matters of the state's culture. These causes are related to the effects that might be posited for the laws: What does it mean to say that a law is bad? A law may produce results that violate democratic norms, it may create measurable results such as low voter turnout, or it may produce short-term problems that seem distinctive to the state. There are, of course, many intervening variables that could render measuring results complicated. Perhaps most consequentially, though, there may be dispute about whether some effects were intended, or even salutary parts of the law or defects. A finding, for instance, that politicians elected through the primary are "worse" than those chosen before the establishment of the primary may show to some that the law is defective, in that it produced worse candidates, while to others it may be a sign that the law has given a greater advantage to nontraditional politicians and is therefore working as intended.

All of the comparisons here may scale differently than is the case with the international literature. The difference in political culture and receptiveness to democratic reform may be less across American states than across different countries. The states that adopted the primary all started from a similar nomination system based on party conventions, so the range of experiences with prior democratic elections these states had was, of course, narrower than would be the case if one compared democratic and undemocratic nations. And the variants in primary laws themselves are perhaps of less consequence than the variants across electoral systems. The difference between a closed primary with a preprimary convention and an open primary may well be less than, for instance,

Table 5.1 States Described in Literature of the Time as Having Defective Primary Laws

State	Description	Year of Adoption of Primary	Progressive State	NPL State	Source
Virginia	Primary too late	1905			Sabato (1977)
Iowa	Bad timing for farmers	1907		Yes	Horack (1923)
Missouri	"Spot candidates" take ballot spots then withdraw	1907			Loeb (1910)
South Dakota	Richards primary—too complicated	1907	Yes	Yes	Berdahl (1923)
Illinois	Poor quality candidates	1908			Wallace (1923)
California	Plurality winners; cost of campaigning	1909	Yes		West (1923)
Michigan	Frivolous candidacies; filing fee too low	1909	Yes		Dorr (1937)
Colorado	Poor quality candidates	1910	Yes	Yes	Wallace (1923)
Maine	Heightened regional conflict	1911			Hormell (1923)
New York	Ballot too long; too many minor party primaries	1913			Feldman (1917)
Indiana	Uninformed voters	1915			Guild (1923)
New Mexico	Heightened regional conflict	1939			Holmes (1967)
Alaska	Crossover voting	1958			McBeath and Morehouse (1994)
Hawaii	Raiding	1959			Pratt and Smith (2000)

the difference between a Westminster-style democracy and a proportionally elected parliament.

In the remainder of this chapter I seek to apply the major concepts from the comparative electoral integrity literature to the problems alleged regarding American state primary laws. Table 5.2 shows a two-by-two classification scheme for these various claims. On the left-hand side, I assume the claims about problems come from someone with a sincere interest in improving the primary—that is, someone who to a degree subscribes to the basic Progressive goals of allowing voter choice, holding fair elections, and so forth. Benign claims can either point to fixable, technical problems with the primary or can highlight subversion of the law's intent itself. Which of these is the case depends in part, of course, on the specific problem alleged, but it also depends on the motives of the governing party or of those responsible for implementing the law. This roughly corresponds to Birch's distinction between mispractice and malpractice. Given the sources that we have, I assume at the outset here that most cases will fall in one of these two categories.

On the right-hand side are claims made by those who may be critics of the establishment of the direct primary. This does not necessarily mean they are claims made in bad faith; as documented in previous chapters, some prominent political scientists were critical of the direct primary from the outset. Criticisms shown in the upper right-hand box could well show conflicting normative views of what elections should be. Those in the lower right-hand box, in contrast, echo the sorts of scenarios described in the aforementioned Andrew Wilson book on post-Soviet politics: neither the government nor its critics are concerned with repairing the law. The critics would prefer to see it dismantled, while politicians in office might wish to see it subverted.

For each of the claims about the primary here, we can also observe what became of the primary. Was the law amended? Were the problems fixed? The options in Table 5.2 suggest four likely effects. In the case of mispractice, technical repairs to the law would seem the most likely response, and should not necessarily be difficult to achieve. In the case of malpractice, legitimate allegations will be harder to achieve without political conflict. In the case of conflicting

Table 5.2 Categorization of Responses to Defective Primary Laws

	Intention	Claimant Benign	Hostile
Governing Party	Benign	Mispractice	Conflicting norms
	Hostile	Malpractice	Corruption

norms, we might also see political conflict, but here it would be conflict over efforts to place restrictions on the primary. And in the case of hostile intentions on both sides, we would expect greater efforts to restrict the primary—for instance, as we shall see in our examples in the next section some states that established the primary wound up abandoning it entirely.

These distinctions provide some leverage in determining the reasons for backlash against the direct primary and for American scholars' gradual loss of interest in the primary and other Progressive reforms. Did the primary actually fail to realize its advocates' goals? And if so, was this because the reform itself could not match up to their expectations; was it because of defects that were, or at least should have been, correctable; or was it because primary laws were manipulated in such a way that it could not actually succeed? Some of the defects of the direct primary were apparent to political scientists of the time. However, these political scientists were not able to draw upon a large body of knowledge about voting systems and elections. Using contemporary work on that subject is vital to determining how inevitable some of the direct primary's problems were and what some efforts to address them might have looked like.

Categorizing Bad Primary Laws

The states listed in Table 5.1 are grouped by the era in which they adopted the primary. The eleven states listed at the top all adopted the direct primary during the first two decades of the twentieth century. Hence, it is unsurprising that, with two exceptions, the articles alleging flaws in the primary were also written within a decade or two after the law's adoption. The 1920s were also, as noted earlier, a time when there was simply much more research published on the direct primary. Of these states, only four (Michigan, Missouri, New York, and South Dakota) exhibited primary problems that seem on their face to have been a matter of mispractice or malpractice. For each of these, redrafting the law—adjusting filing fees, clarifying how to treat minor party nominations, or adding lines identifying candidates more clearly—might have been feasible without abandoning the primary itself. Virginia, the first state listed here and the only Southern state, adopted the primary early but rarely used it, a subject taken up in Chapter 7.

The remaining six early adopters drew complaints that seem to have been more a matter of hostility toward or skepticism about the direct primary. Allegations of poor-quality candidates or heightened regional conflict do not suggest obvious technical fixes; implicit in such claims is the argument that party leaders are better able than voters to vet candidate qualifications or ensure geographic diversity among nominees. Efforts to strengthen the role of parties in primaries, such as allowing party endorsements or holding preprimary conventions, might be half steps toward resolving such problems. Problems with plurality winners might be addressed either through winnowing the number of candidates (as some states' preprimary conventions do) or by adopting a runoff provision. And the argument that voters were not sufficiently knowledgeable to vote seems to be a clear argument against the direct primary.

Some of the arguments made during this era are particularly difficult to evaluate because they are not clearly about the primary itself: they suggest that the primary might work better if other laws that are not specific to primaries were introduced. Concerns about the cost of campaigning, for instance, could be addressed by doing away with the primary, but they could also be addressed through the adoption of stricter campaign finance regulations. And many of the objections to South Dakota's Richards primary (discussed in more detail later in the chapter) centered on provisions of the law not clearly related to the actual process of voting for party candidates.

There are no clear geographic patterns to the criticisms raised about early adopters, nor do the criticisms raised here seem to have obvious ties to partisan or ideological conflict. Some of these states had a strong Progressive or Nonpartisan League (NPL) movement, but the presence of these two movements does not seem to have been causally related to any particular type of problem or response to it. The criticisms here are not obviously related to major distinctions in primary laws such as whether the primary is open or closed.

What is noteworthy, however, is which states are present or absent among the late adopters of the primary. Five states (Alaska, Connecticut, Hawaii, New Mexico, and Rhode Island) adopted the direct primary in the 1930s or later. Utah, although it allowed for optional primaries as early as 1889, did not adopt the mandatory primary until 1937, and when it did adopt a mandatory primary, it did so with an unusual preprimary nominating convention in which the delegates could place at most two candidates on the primary election ballot for each party. Connecticut, Rhode Island, and Utah adopted much more restrictive primary laws than early adopters had done—for instance, Rhode Island's direct primary law, enacted in 1947, permitted the parties to endorse primary candidates and to note their endorsements on the ballot; Connecticut required primary challengers to incumbents to get 20 percent of the convention vote to appear on the ballot; and Utah also established a nominating convention to determine ballot access (see Lockard 1959a, b; Key 1956, 125). Alaska and Hawaii, on the other hand, did not. Alaska alternated between an open primary and a blanket primary from before statehood until 2022, when it adopted a top four nonpartisan primary, and it has generally allowed the parties to determine their own primary rules (McBeath and Morehouse 1994). Hawaii adopted an open primary at the time of statehood and closed the primary following complaints about raiding (Pratt and Smith 2000). And New Mexico, as discussed in further detail later, has experimented continuously with preprimary conventions in order to address regional tensions within the party. Histories of these states all describe conflict over defects in the primary (crossover voting and raiding in Alaska and Hawaii, regional conflicts in New Mexico) while there has been no academic literature suggesting problems in Connecticut or Rhode Island (apart from an overall lack of primary competition). New York and Indiana, two states that abandoned the direct primary for several decades, also established restrictive primary laws upon reintroduction.

A final category of criticisms of the direct primary has to do with the timing of the election. Such complaints do not easily fall into the categories we have considered here, in part because we cannot determine the motives for holding the primary on any particular date. One might allege that parties hold primaries at a particular time of year in order to secure some sort of advantage. As discussed in Chapter 9, however, there is no consensus about the relationship between primary timing and competition, and thus it is not easy to determine either the intent of those who set the primary date or the legitimacy of claims about why the date is a problem.

Table 5.3 presents an initial effort to distinguish between different types of allegations about the direct primary, to distinguish claims about defects that would lead to technical corrections from claims that cast suspicion upon the direct primary altogether. These distinctions say little, however, about the intent of the law and about whether the states had the desire and ability to make these corrections. In order to measure intent, two further steps are necessary: an inquiry into whether these alleged defects were addressed, and a state-by-state look at how valid these claims were to begin with. We look first at changes in state primary laws following the emergence of complaints.

Table 5.3 Categorization of Defective State Primary Practices

		Claimant	
	Intention	Benign	Hostile
Governing Party	Benign	**Mispractice** Michigan Missouri	**Conflicting norms** Colorado Illinois Maine New Mexico
	Hostile	**Malpractice** Alaska Hawaii	**Corruption** Indiana New York South Dakota

Fixing Bad Primary Laws

Just as it is important to understand the reasons some states' primary laws were problematic, so it is important to understand how the states responded. This can help us to understand the sincerity and intent of claims about these defects. In other words, if criticisms were made in order to improve the law, and the state ultimately acted upon these criticisms, we can conclude that the criticisms had some merit.

We considered aggregate data on states' responses to alleged primary law defects in Chapter 2; Table 2.7 showed significant primary law changes that occurred following claims about defects in the state's primary laws, and Figure 2.4 compared the number of major primary reform enactments in these states to enactments in the rest of the United States. As the table shows, eleven of the fourteen states where criticisms were raised ultimately changed their laws, although not all of the changes were intended to address the problems. The three states that did not change their primary laws to respond to these criticisms—Illinois, Iowa, and Maine—are all states for which I categorized the allegations as matters of conflicting norms. There is no obvious remedy for improving candidate quality (the source of complaint in Illinois) or soothing regional conflicts (as was alleged in Maine). In the following discussion, I comment on the establishment of preprimary conventions, which are perhaps the most commonly used tool to confront problems such as these. The preprimary convention was not an automatic panacea for these problems, however. And whether the complaints about its primary date were valid or not, Iowa continues to hold its state primary in early June.

Most of the states with problematic laws, then, did change their laws at some point. These fourteen states were not particularly likely to experiment with their primary laws; as we have seen in the prior chapters, states with a strong Progressive movement or NPL presence were slightly more likely to make changes to their primary laws over the 1928–1968 period. The typical Progressive state changed its primary laws 1.9 times, as did the typical NPL state, while states with allegedly defective laws changed their primary laws only 1.5 times over this period. Only three of the states in this category changed their laws more than twice (California, Michigan, and New Mexico), while eight of the Progressive states and four of the NPL states fell into this category. However, two of the changes made by states with alleged defects abolished the statewide primary altogether, which of course limited any further changes until the primary was reintroduced, and two of the states considered here (Alaska and Hawaii) were not admitted to the union until 1959.

It is easy to identify instances where the stated intent of the reforms appears to match up to the complaints made about the laws. Michigan, for instance, changed its primary law three times during the 1930s, and some of the changes the state made—listing the candidate's occupation, for instance, or abolishing the party affiliation test for voters—appear to be technical efforts to address the problems that were raised. Other states that did not face criticism also made similar changes, and it is entirely possible that some reforms made during this era, such as the listing of candidates' occupations, were made in other states without attracting the attention of the scholars who tracked primary law changes.

There are also clear instances here where observers concluded that the primary was being manipulated by the parties. Concerns were raised in both Alaska and Hawaii that the parties were encouraging crossover voting or raiding. Both states modified their primary laws during their first decade of statehood, albeit in opposite directions: Hawaii changed from an open to a closed primary in 1962, while Alaska switched from a semiclosed to a blanket primary in 1968. These were by no means the only states where crossover voting took place—or was alleged to be taking place—but the relative youth of these states' party systems may have made it easier to change the primary law than it was in other states, such as Wisconsin, where concerns about crossover voting have been raised.

Some states also seem to have tried to address normative concerns about what a primary should look like given their own unique factors. In the Maine case, issues of regional balance in the party ticket were of concern to many because of the state's population distribution; questions were raised about Portland, the state's largest city, producing all of the statewide nominees. Even when such cities do not necessarily comprise a large share of a state's population, politicians from the cities may have a larger base of support and be more visible. Other states certainly have similar types of population distributions; Massachusetts, Illinois, and New York are just some of the states with this problem, and each of these states has experienced tension over how to ensure statewide tickets that have geographic balance. The state on this list that seems to have had the most problems in this regard, however, is New Mexico, which spent much of the 1940s, 1950s, and 1960s exploring how to adopt a primary system that had support from different regions of the state and the different ethnic groups that supported the Democratic Party.

Finally, the two states that made the most substantial changes in response to primary law defects show a range of different problems. The primary problems in New York, such as the requirement that minor parties hold primaries, seem like a clear case of mispractice. The fact that New York abolished its statewide primary altogether appears to have been an overreaction or a response to something other than the technical problem at hand. Indiana's decision to abolish the primary for statewide offices in 1930 also seems like an extreme reaction to allegations that the voters were simply not equipped to make good primary choices.

The questions in all of these cases are whether the criticisms raised about the state's primary were legitimate, whether the reforms solved the problem, and whether the reforms were intended to solve the problem. In the following sections I address these questions in a series of case studies, not only of the states, but of the reforms implemented and their histories in other parts of the country. Since the intentions of the reform advocates are important in distinguishing between the different categories, I draw on the party state legislative seat share data described in Chapter 2. These data can help us determine the role of partisan gain in any primary law change—for instance, a party that is anticipating losing control of the legislature may have reasons to allege that there are problems with the state's election laws, a party that has just gained power may seek to change laws in order to lock in its advantage, and so forth. While I hold off here on trying to draw broad conclusions about the relationship between partisan gain and primary law changes—that is the subject of Chapter 6—I show patterns here in order to help us determine whether we should be suspicious that partisan motives have some relationship to claims about defects in the laws.

Mispractice: The Case of Michigan

A pair of academic studies of Michigan primary elections of the 1930s draw attention to the problem of frivolous candidates (Dorr 1937; Pollock 1943). This problem was not unique to Michigan, but it did become more acute in Michigan during the 1930s. Michigan had a history of "spot" candidates or "dummy" candidates. Such candidacies take a number of different forms. Candidates would declare early for multiple different offices but drop out of some or all of these races before the filing deadline. This could have the effect of scaring off serious candidates by making it appear as if there was already a crowded race. Many such candidates bore well-known political names; in some cases, they had the same names as the incumbent or as other well-known politicians. This was a common tactic in early Michigan primaries (Millspaugh 1916) as well as primaries in Missouri (Loeb 1910) and New York (Feldman 1917).

It is of course difficult to develop metrics to determine what a frivolous candidacy is; for instance, candidates with the Kennedy surname but unrelated to the Massachusetts Kennedys have won elections not just in Massachusetts but (as recently as the past decade) in House or Senate elections in Louisiana and Minnesota. There is no way in which one might determine whether such campaigns were frivolous. However, the potential for voter confusion can certainly be heightened when the ballot is cluttered with unknown candidates. Many American states experienced a surge in Democratic candidates during the early 1930s, a surge that many analysts attributed to economic problems and to the increased competitiveness of the Democratic Party. Although certainly not all of these candidacies were frivolous, articles from the time suggest that many were regarded as such.

Michigan took several steps, at both the statewide and the county levels, to address this problem. In 1932 a statewide law was passed requiring candidates to list their occupation on the ballot. In 1935 many Michigan counties passed laws establishing refundable filing fees for primary candidates. The rationale for these fees was to deter candidates unable to raise the money for these deposits. Furthermore, candidates who received a negligible share of the vote (discussed in more detail below) would forfeit their deposits. These changes aimed to reduce the number of candidates and to reduce the confusion that dummy candidates might present.

Why was Michigan able to enact these new laws regarding filing fees? A simple answer is that the proposed solution was not that big of a change. Laws raising (or lowering) filing fees were common in many states during the 1910s and 1920s. There is also, however, a political story to tell. As Figure 5.1 shows, the Republican Party had been the dominant party in Michigan for much of the twentieth century; while Democrats occasionally voted in Republican primaries, the literature suggests that these votes were usually believed to be sincere, not malicious, in intent. Democrats had captured both legislative chambers and the governorship in 1932, and there had been a surge in the number of Democratic candidates during the early years of the Great Depression. Thus, Democrats were grappling with a problem that Michigan Republicans had noticed for some time, but the problem had been exacerbated by the depression. So while both parties had now observed this problem, neither had used it against the other, and Michigan Republicans had not been so thoroughly defeated in 1932 that they could not anticipate returning to power in subsequent years and benefiting from the new law.

Michigan also had a history of slight modifications to its primary, and Michigan law gave counties the authority to modify their own primary laws. Progressive governor Hazen Pingree had been an advocate for the direct primary during his tenure from 1896 to 1900 (as well as during his tenure as mayor of Detroit during the early 1890s). As in Ohio, the movement for the direct primary began in the cities, and the primary was adopted gradually throughout the state and was not adopted statewide until 1909. The state and the various cities and counties experimented with the primary in subsequent years; Pollock tallies twenty-five state-level changes between 1909 and 1941, mostly minor and having to do with timing. The filing fees, while they received some scholarly attention, were thus not a major moment in the primary's history in Michigan.

It is not at all clear that the new filing fee provisions were successful. According to Pollock's analysis, the number of primary candidates throughout the state peaked in 1932, and according to Dorr's analysis, the number of candidates in

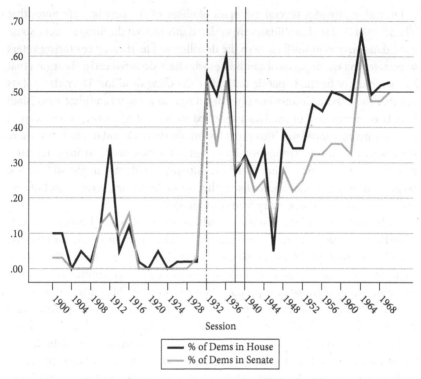

Figure 5.1. Percent of Democratic seats in the Michigan House and Senate, 1900–1970

Notes: Vertical lines signify years with primary election law changes, as described in Table 2.1. Solid lines represent expansive changes; lines with dots and dashes represent changes that were neither expansive nor restrictive.

Source: Seat share data from Dubin (2007) as described in Chapter 2.

the counties affected by the initial filing fee law peaked in 1934. The number of candidates for office declined throughout the state in subsequent years, but Dorr argues that in 1936 the number declined more sharply in counties that had instituted the filing fee. Pollock's 1943 book suggests that there was still an excessive number of candidates and that the state should explore further steps to simplify the primary ballot. He suggested a system that replaced petition signatures as a prerequisite for office with a system of sponsorships: a candidate's sponsors would not just sign forms, but would have their names listed on the ballot and perhaps write brief statements explaining why they were supporting the candidate. Pollock conducts two public opinion surveys showing overwhelming public support for the primary but indicating support for some proposals to simplify primary voting as well.

Dorr also provides several examples of abuse of the new law. He notes that when lists of declared candidates are updated throughout the filing process, some candidates may wait until close to the deadline to file, thereby confusing voters or threatening the deposits of candidates who have declared early. He argues that lists should not be made public until after the filing deadline. Dorr also points out that the Wayne County law provided a refund for any candidate who "shall have been nominated or shall have received 50 percent of the total vote received by the winning candidate." This provision might deter candidates in races where there were one or two strong candidates, but as the number of strong candidates grows, so does the possibility that lower-quality candidates might still receive 50 percent of the winner's vote share. This could, he argues, create a sort of cascade effect where large primary fields grow larger.

Both studies of the state's primary indicate that Michigan's history of minor experiments with primaries, as well as its hybrid system, in which county-level conventions took place and nominated some candidates for local office, made slight modification possible without the threat of partisan conflict or a movement to entirely eliminate the primary. Pollock contrasts Michigan's system with Ohio's: the direct primary movement in Ohio had been far more partisan and had resulted in conflict between Cleveland and the rural parts of the state. These conflicts made good-faith negotiations to resolve technical problems with the primary more difficult than was the case in Michigan, and they resulted in less statewide agreement about how parties might intervene to winnow the primary field.

To summarize, the Michigan reforms of the 1930s fit Birch's definition of *mispractice* in that the problems do not seem to be a systemic effort by one party to seek advantage over the other through mischief, and the solutions are bipartisan, technical in scope, and relatively minor in nature. Adjustments such as listing occupations and candidate addresses or adjusting filing requirements (as long as these adjustments are not too substantial) do not appear to have been a prelude to more radical changes, and they were in fact common adjustments in several other states whose primaries were not the subject of as much academic scrutiny during this period. While there is certainly some room to quarrel about which campaigns are "frivolous" and whether the term might be under- or overused, the belief that frivolous candidacies should be discouraged does not seem to be a matter of profound normative debate. Michigan would go on, in subsequent years, to enact more substantial changes, removing the party affiliation test in 1938 and establishing an open primary in 1940. Pollock's book is relatively silent on these changes, although the fact that Republicans retook the governorship and both chambers of the state legislature in 1938 suggests that, as was the case for regular North Dakota Republicans (as described in Chapter 4) and California Republicans (as described in Chapter 6), this was an effort to limit interparty, general election conflict by bringing dissenters into the dominant party.

Malpractice: Responses to Crossover Voting in Alaska and Hawaii

One commonly proposed change to primary rules has had to do with the qualifications for voting in a party's primary. There are many strong arguments to be made about the merits of allowing any interested voter to participate in a primary (that is, holding an open or semiopen primary), and about the merits of limiting primary voting to registered members of the party holding the primary (that is, having a closed or semiclosed primary). One frequent claim about primary voting, however, has been that some primary voters might take part in a primary in order to harm that party's chances in the general election.

Crossover voting—the act of voting in a party other than the one to which one belongs—can be either sincere or strategic. A Democratic voter in an overwhelmingly Republican district might decide to vote in the Republican primary because there is no competitive Democratic primary, or because she believes that a Republican is likely to win the general election and so wishes to help select the best Republican candidate. These are both instances of sincere crossover voting. However, a Democrat might also take part in a Republican primary in order to try to nominate the Republican candidate she thinks would be easiest to beat in the general election. This would be one instance of strategic crossover voting. Although calls for strategic crossover voting remain a feature of contemporary politics, there is no evidence that strategic crossover voting is particularly common or effective. It is a consensus in the literature that most crossover voters are sincere, that when they switch parties to vote for a candidate in the primary, they anticipate voting for that candidate in the general election (Alvarez and Nagler 1998; Hedlund 1977; Wekkin 1988, 1991; Wolf and Downs 2007).

Nonetheless, concerns about crossover voting prompted many changes in the openness of primaries during the 1932–1968 period. Three states opened their primaries in the 1940s, two opened them in the 1960s, and four closed their primaries between 1928 and 1968. Among these was Utah, which opened its primary in 1940 and closed it in 1960. Concerns about crossover voting assuredly prompted many unsuccessful rule change proposals as well.

Even when it occurs, it is difficult to determine whether crossover voting is advantageous to parties or not. When parties are ideologically distinct, crossover voters may pull parties and their nominees toward the political center, potentially making the nominees more electable, but at the cost of making the nominee less appealing to the party's more ideologically extreme voters. Crossover voters may, however, develop an enduring allegiance to the party to which they have crossed over. As a consequence, majority parties have at times sought to limit the ability of voters to cross over to their primaries, while minority parties have sought to encourage voters to join their primaries. As we saw in the case of the NPL in Chapter 4, opening primaries to nonmembers may also be a useful way of preventing factions from turning into third parties or of joining the minority party.

Claims about malicious intent were particularly common in Alaska and Hawaii during their first decade of statehood, but the two states responded differently. Before statehood, both states used a blanket primary. Alaska had used the blanket primary since 1947; McBeath and Thomas (1994, 214) quote editorials from the *Anchorage Times* speaking proudly of Alaska's use of it. Upon gaining statehood, Alaska adopted a semiclosed primary; voters were not required to register as members of any party, but they were not permitted to vote for more than one party's candidates on the same ballot. Alaska returned to a blanket primary in 1968 with the support of Republican governor Walter Hickel. As McBeath and Thomas recount matters, Democrats (traditionally the minority party) opposed the blanket primary because they believed Republicans were strategically crossing over to help nominate inferior Democratic candidates, while Republicans favored the blanket primary as a means of encouraging compromise among competing Republican factions. It was only after Republicans survived a short-lived surge in Democratic strength in the legislature that they were able to return to the blanket primary. Hickel ultimately failed to win primaries in the 1970s through the 1990s, losing to Republicans who may have benefited from Democratic crossover votes. Hickel ultimately won the 1990 general election running as an independent. As the Republican Party increased in strength over this period, Republican leaders became more skeptical of the blanket primary. McBeath and Thomas note, however, that by this time Alaska voters had become accustomed to, and supportive of, the blanket primary. Despite Republican efforts to close the primary, Alaska kept a blanket primary until the Supreme Court's decision in *California Democratic Party v. Jones* (530 U.S. 567 (2000)) declared the blanket primary unconstitutional.[1]

Hawaii's change in primary rules was accompanied by less partisan turnover. Prior to the 1950s, political conflict in the territory was not manifested in conflict between the two major U.S. parties. Hawaii used a blanket primary until 1949, when it adopted an open primary, allegedly as a means of encouraging stronger parties and showing Congress that it would be smoothly integrated into U.S. politics once it became a state. Democrats quickly became the dominant party, and in 1968 Democrats led the charge for closing the primary following allegations that Republicans had been crossing over to support weaker Democratic candidates (Pratt and Smith 2000, 118). Hawaii returned to an open primary in 1978, following factional conflict during that year's state Democratic Party convention.

Both of these states' histories show that allegations about malfeasance were an important part of calls for changing primary rules. In both circumstances, however, the claims appear neither to have clear support in fact nor to have resulted in changes that would have satisfied the accusers. As Figure 5.2 shows, one can make inferences about why Alaska changed its primary rules in 1968, but it is difficult to identify immediate consequences of the change. While electoral malpractice was alleged in both cases, ultimately distinctive features of state political culture—and how primary rules had played into them—shaped the attitudes of legislators and the public.

A contemporary reader can certainly find the claim of organized malfeasance here plausible, despite the scant evidence that voters actually do cross over strategically. What makes these allegations about malpractice, as opposed to mispractice, is the claim that there is an organized effort to interfere in the primaries. The mispractice cases above focused on the malicious, or at least unhelpful, efforts by individual candidates, but there were no claims that opposition parties were seeking to subvert the primary process. The Supreme Court's decision in *Tashjian v. Republican Party of Connecticut* (479 U.S. 208 (1986))

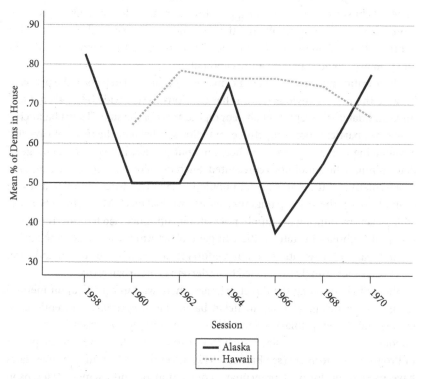

Figure 5.2. Percent of Democratic seats in the Alaska and Hawaii Lower Chambers, 1958–1970

Source: Seat share data from Dubin (2007) as described in Chapter 2.

allowed political parties to make their own primary rules independent of state laws about the primary, thus making rule changes easier and removing claims about primary manipulation from legislative decision-making.

The comparative politics literature provides many examples of malpractice in other nations' elections. While there were probably many opportunities for parties to engage in nefarious activities in the American states, there is little evidence that reform of the primary laws themselves—as opposed to legal actions or other such efforts—was an obvious response.

Conflicting Norms: The Case of New Mexico and the Preprimary Convention

The most prevalent normative complaint about primaries for much of the twentieth century was that they upset the ability of parties to balance their tickets. In Maine, the direct primary was criticized in the early twentieth century for giving the state's large cities an advantage over smaller towns and rural communities. In Massachusetts, Democrats struggled to ensure that Boston politicians—and more often than not, Catholic politicians—did not always lead the state ticket (Abrams 1964). And in New Mexico, leaders of both parties worried that the direct primary would shut out Latino candidates.

These criticisms are a matter of norms, not mechanical defects in the primary, because there is no obvious reason that elections to statewide office *should* feature candidates who represent all geographic areas of the state. Ticket balancing may make parties more competitive, but efforts to balance the ticket always risk advantaging one group over another; they put parties, not voters, in charge of determining who should be represented. Such decisions are not always, in fact, representative of the state's actual population characteristics. To offer just one example from the prior paragraph, efforts to "balance" Massachusetts statewide tickets by limiting the number of Catholic nominees led to underrepresentation of Catholics in state politics. In general, as American cities grew during the first half of the twentieth century, efforts to ensure a mix or urban and rural candidates increasingly threatened to underrepresent urban areas.

Short of abandoning the direct primary, there was an agreed-upon method for giving parties greater say in ticket balancing: preprimary conventions or endorsements. Preprimary conventions were initially proposed by primary opponents in progressive states such as Oregon as an effort to limit the power of Progressive reformers (see Barnett 1912). Over the past century, twelve states have used some form of preprimary convention or endorsement (Herrnson 1998; Green and Herrnson 2003; Elazar 1999). These procedures were not all designed solely to balance the ticket; they also often sought to prevent frivolous candidacies or to ensure that party nominees subscribed to the same general principles.

New Mexico's experience with the direct primary shows the importance politicians placed on ticket balancing as well as the limitations of using preprimary conventions to give the party some ticket balancing capability. New Mexico became a state in 1912, when the direct primary movement was in full swing. Despite frequent discussions about adopting the direct primary, however, New Mexico did not hold a statewide primary until the 1940 election. This was the case for several reasons. A case could be made that the state had more extreme internal political differences than many other states; in Holmes's (1967, 19) telling, the state's Anglo and Latino residents practiced very different styles of politics, and both of the state's political parties needed to appeal to both constituencies in order to win statewide elections. New Mexico did have a viable Progressive movement, led by Senator Bronson Cutting, but Cutting was able to wield power in both parties' conventions and thus did not need to push for a direct primary in order to achieve many of his goals. It is in fact striking how Cutting pursued many Progressive electoral reforms without giving consideration to establishing a direct primary (see Lowitt 1992, 33, 93, 145). However, strongly one-party regions of the state, such as the "Little Texas" region in the southeastern corner of the state, had a history of voluntary primaries, funded by the candidates; these regions did not have the political clout or desire to impose the primary on other parts of the state.

Through much of the early twentieth century, New Mexico Republicans wielded narrow majorities and opposed the direct primary, while the Democrats were split. After Democrats gained control of the governorship and the legislature in the late 1930s (see Figure 5.3), Governor Clyde Tingley led a drive for a direct primary in hopes of resolving factional conflicts within the party that had made recent conventions difficult. One major problem Democrats had faced was the movement of Cutting and his supporters, as a bloc, from the Republican Party to the Democratic Party. Cutting himself died in an airplane crash in 1935, but his endorsement of Franklin Delano Roosevelt in 1932 had prompted many Progressives to move into the party, thereby complicating efforts by longer-tenured Democrats to retain control of the party. The direct primary law passed in 1939 called for a closed primary with party registration, in order to make the movement of any such factions from one party to another more difficult. The New Mexico direct primary, then, was established in part to limit the power of erstwhile Progressives.

Ever since the establishment of the primary, the parties in New Mexico have vacillated over whether to use a preprimary convention. A preprimary nominating convention law was passed in 1950, and candidates were required to receive 25 percent of the convention vote in order to appear on the ballot.

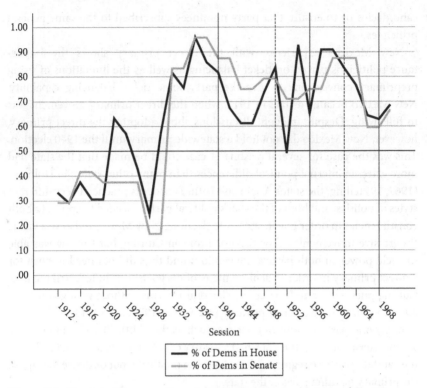

Figure 5.3. Percent of Democratic seats in the New Mexico House and Senate, 1900–1970

Notes: Vertical lines indicate years with primary election law changes, as described in Table 2.1. Solid lines represent expansive changes; dotted lines represent restrictive changes.

Source: Seat share data from Dubin (2007) as described in Chapter 2.

The convention was used in 1952 and 1954; following a brief resurgence of Republican power, the preprimary convention was abolished in 1956, only to be reintroduced following the 1962 election with a 20 percent threshold. The state used the preprimary convention in 1964 and 1966, abolished it in 1968, reinstated it in 1976, abolished it in 1984, and reinstated it again the following year. Currently, New Mexico parties use a preprimary convention with a 20 percent threshold for appearing on the primary ballot (Democratic Party of New Mexico 2018). The state has also adjusted rules about nominating petitions and signatures multiple times over this period.

Charles Judah (1957) attributes this conflict to racial tensions in New Mexico in the early primary years. Unqualified Anglo candidates would run in mixed areas in order to pull votes away from Latino candidates, upsetting parties' informal balancing efforts. Holmes does not go so far as to say that such mischief is an inevitable consequence of the direct primary, but he does note that changes in population patterns during the 1950s, such as the growing white population of Albuquerque and the growth of a highly educated scientific community around Los Alamos, changed the racial dynamics of the state in the years following the establishment of the direct primary. Holmes (1967, 185, 220–248, 273) lists many effects of the direct primary, including a decline in the number of seats the parties contested in the general election, longer-serving incumbents, fewer challenges to incumbents, a decline in both parties in the number of Latino nominees (particularly in places where the population was less than 40 percent Latino), a lack of stable factions, increasing independence of state legislators from the governor, and an emphasis during campaigns on apolitical characteristics of the candidates. While many of these claims are anecdotal, they correspond to the early primary opponents' concerns discussed in Chapter 1.

In New Mexico, as in other states, citizens' distrust of political elites may well have led voters to reject parties' efforts to improve elections. Holmes (1967, 243) notes that the major concern of the parties during the 1950s was to prevent racial conflict from spilling into the primary election. The ostensibly liberal émigrés to Los Alamos, many of whom had come from more racially progressive regions of the country, harbored a vision of the primary as a more democratic, progressive affair than the party convention and opposed any efforts by the parties to interfere with the primary (even when doing so might have increased their representation in state politics).

Holmes (1967, 220) concludes that the first decade of the primary put into office a different type of legislator, but that these legislators subsequently sought to use the preprimary convention to protect themselves from competition. This observation corresponds closely to the ways in which NPL incumbents sought to preserve their hold on office (Chapter 4). It suggests, as well, that Henry Jones Ford (who argued in 1909 that the primary would simply exchange one group of politicians for another) and William Howard Taft (arguing in 1912 that preprimary conventions would be just as corrupt as the nominations before the advent of primaries) had a point.

It is easy to see why the preprimary convention was of value to many different types of New Mexico politicians. New Mexico may well have posed an example of particularly different types of constituencies coexisting within the same parties—constituencies that needed some sort of balancing effort for the sake of harmony. The sorts of concerns raised in New Mexico do appear in other states, however. In a 1923 article on the Maine primary, Hormell describes the regional balancing efforts used by the Maine Republican Party before the primary and shows that urban candidates quickly came to dominate nominations. Lockard (1959b) shows a similar pattern in Massachusetts, as Boston-area politicians gradually came to dominate state politics. He shows, furthermore, that efforts there to use the preprimary convention to balance candidacies geographically were largely ineffective. Despite clear geographic divisions within the Democratic Party, Boston-area politicians gained control of the party relatively quickly and used the preprimary convention as a forum for personal combat. The result here, as in New Mexico, was a politics of shifting personal factions, not a brokering between stable ones.

Contemporary research (e.g., Herrnson 1998; McNitt 1980) shows that preprimary conventions and endorsements do winnow competition and so may be useful in preventing ideologically extreme plurality winners from emerging. Beyond this, however, they are not particularly effective in ensuring that party-preferred candidates win the nomination. In states such as Utah and Minnesota (Key 1956, 125; Frei et al. 2012; Elazar 1999; Gieske 1979), parties are at times ideologically distinct enough from the party's rank and file voters that a party endorsement has little effect. Nonetheless, preprimary conventions and endorsements have been supported in the past by the National Municipal League (1951) and the American Political Science Association Committee on Political Parties (1950; see also Green and Herrnson 2003). Moreover, parties today have the legal right to endorse, according to the Supreme Court's decision in *Eu v. San Francisco County Democratic Central Committee* (489 U.S. 214 (1989)), so it would be fruitless to argue against such activities.

The "defects" in ethnic or geographic balance brought about by the primary are thus a matter of normative preference; there are valid claims on both sides about what nomination slates should look like. These claims address questions about what role parties should play, what sorts of representation are valued, and how elections might be improved by reducing voters' choices. The tools for addressing these problems are often flawed and subject to contestation.

Corruption: The Cases of Indiana, New York, and (Maybe) South Dakota

What does it mean to talk about the corruption of a primary law? In much of the comparative politics literature described earlier in this chapter, the concept of "corruption" tends to be construed in a criminal or a moral sense, as a use of public resources for private gain or as a destruction of public institutions (see, e.g., Thompson 2013). A "corruption" of primary laws need not involve a criminal conspiracy or a private gain to be had by either side, but it does perhaps lead to cynicism or distrust of the arguments made in regard to the primary. Mark Warren (2006) contends that corruption of democratic processes entails "duplicitous exclusion": insincere arguments that purport to be taking place within legitimate democratic deliberations but are actually made with the goal of subverting those deliberations themselves. Warren emphasizes the importance of public trust that officeholders are making arguments in good faith. Warren's concept of duplicity would seem to include that arguments about "improving" the primary are made in order to hobble the primary itself, to reduce public support for it further, or to skew results in favor of one side or the other without admitting that this is being done.

It may well be common for opponents of the direct primary to have framed their arguments not as criticisms of the primary itself but as sincere concerns for particular consequences of the direct primary. It is not possible to conclusively judge the intent of criticisms of the direct primary, but in two major cases, those of Indiana and New York, states adopted the direct primary after the same sort of Progressive agitation that had prevailed in so many states, yet subsequently abolished the primary altogether as a result of complaints with no empirical support. South Dakota—where an ambitious and perhaps overly complicated primary was more gradually subverted—presents a case in which there was clearly corrupt intent on the part of those who would "reform" the primary, but where the reforms in question fell short of abolishing the primary altogether.

Indiana adopted the direct primary in 1915 for gubernatorial elections and U.S. House and Senate elections. Although the Progressive movement had not been particularly strong in Indiana, the direct primary had been championed by Senator Albert Beveridge, who served from 1899 to 1910 and continued to wield influence afterward, until his death in 1927 (see Gould 1974, 55–82). Beveridge soured somewhat on the direct primary during the 1920s, however. In the direct primary's first years it became apparent that, as in New Mexico, there would be substantial variation across the state in the way the primary was used. A 1923 study by Frederick Guild showed that, unsurprisingly, voter participation in the primary was highest among members of the Republican Party in strongly Republican areas. As in most states, primary turnout was quite high in the primary's first years but declined somewhat after that. In Guild's account, Republican politicians decried the "low" turnout of 50 percent, contrasting primary turnout to general election turnout. Guild showed that turnout was, in fact, as high as 70 percent in some regions of the state. Nonetheless, regular Republicans, concerned about Beveridge's 1922 primary victory over incumbent Senator Harry S. New (and Beveridge's subsequent general election loss to a Democrat) used claims about low turnout and a lack of voter interest as a reason to abolish the primary. Guild argued that the primary had had little effect in changing the people who held positions of power within the party, and thus there were few elected officials who supported it once the initial wave of public enthusiasm had worn off.

There is little written about Democratic Party views on the direct primary in Indiana. Democrats controlled both chambers of the legislature in 1915 when it was introduced, but lost both in 1920 (see Figure 5.4). The legislature abolished the primary for governor and senator for the 1930 election; it would not be reinstated until 1975. It is easy to regard this change as a method for Republicans to resolve factional conflict, but the arguments about lack of voter interest strike the modern reader as disingenuous, or as ones that might well have led to reforms other than doing away with the primary for major statewide races. Guild, in fact, argued that a preferential voting system would more effectively address factionalism within the party.

New York adopted the direct primary earlier than Indiana, and the direct primary there was championed initially by a more vibrant Progressive movement. President (and former New York governor) Theodore Roosevelt, along with Governor Charles Evans Hughes, advocated vigorously for the direct primary in 1907 and 1908 (Beard 1910). Leaders of both parties were strongly opposed, however. Several direct primary bills were introduced in the legislature between

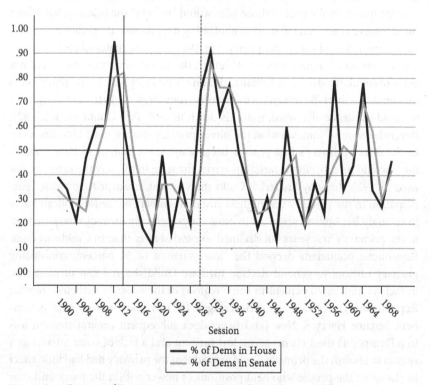

Figure 5.4. Percent of Democratic seats in the Indiana House and Senate, 1900–1970

Notes: Vertical lines indicate years with primary election law changes, as described in Table 2.1. Solid lines represent expansive changes; dotted lines represent restrictive changes.

Source: Seat share data from Dubin (2007) as described in Chapter 2.

1907 and 1910. The bill that finally passed in 1912 was, in the words of the reformist Legislative Voters Association (quoted in Feldman 1917), "scarcely to be recognized by the name of direct primary." It gave local parties substantial latitude in setting the hours for primary voting; separated party "enrollment" (which was required for voting in a primary) from party registration; allowed preprimary party "conferences" to agree upon their preferred nominees; and despite the limited primary franchise and substantial role for party organizations, set low thresholds for candidates' ballot access. The law also applied to minor parties. The result, in the 1912 election, was farcical. As Feldman (1917) reports, the New York City election board slated so many candidates that the 1912 ballot was fourteen feet long, and many precincts ran out of ballots. Despite the long ballots, almost no candidates not supported by the party organizations won nomination. Because all parties held primaries, the American Party held a primary whose victor received thirty-eight votes statewide, and the Socialist Party winner in one congressional district received two votes. This was all quite cumbersome and costly, and it was difficult to argue that the results were any different than they had been under the convention system.

Despite this preposterousness, and despite complaints about low voter turnout, Feldman and Louise Overacker (1923) show that voters did show up. Overacker demonstrates that voter turnout was higher in the rural parts of the state where party organization control was lower than in the city, and she shows that allegations of declining voter support were complicated by the enfranchisement of women in 1920. Both authors contend that the primary could have been fixed, but that party leaders in the legislature had no interest in doing so and that the state's governor from 1914 to 1918, Charles Seymour Whitman, was perhaps the only major politician in the state who did owe his election to the direct primary. New York abolished the direct primary for statewide candidates in 1921, following the ascension to the governorship of a more traditional Republican, Nathan Miller. The ostensible reason was low voter turnout (Zimmerman 2008, 65), but the primary was clearly designed to discourage voter turnout. New York would not re-establish a primary for statewide candidates until 1967, and the primary that was established at that time, which the state still uses, is one of the nation's most restrictive, a closed primary that requires candidates receive 25 percent of the vote at the state convention in order to appear on the ballot.

Without question the nation's most unusual direct primary law was the Richards primary, employed in South Dakota between 1912 and 1928. Richard O. Richards was an early Progressive activist and supporter of Robert LaFollette (Otto 1979; South Dakota Legislative Research Council 2005). Following LaFollette's success in establishing the direct primary in Wisconsin, Richards sought to create a more elaborate primary (modeled on a proposal Charles Evans Hughes had made in New York) that would give voters not only a role to play in selecting nominees but a role in choosing the issue platforms on which the candidates would run.[2] Before the actual primary, parties were required to hold conventions at which participants would debate what the party platform should be, and then to establish a majority and minority slate of candidates, pledged to two different platforms. These slates would then be subject to a popular vote in a closed primary, but without a ballot that indicated which of the two slates had received the most votes at the convention.[3] Only these two slates and candidate factions would be allowed on the ballot. Candidates of the "majority" and "protesting" slate were, furthermore, required to hold a series of debates about these issues—only one debate between representatives of the competing presidential candidates, but far more for other candidates. Competing gubernatorial candidates were to face off sixteen times before the primary and twelve times afterward. All parties were required to have two factional slates on the ballot (and thus even the most popular incumbents faced primary opposition), and minor parties or independent candidates were also required to pledge themselves to a platform and file that platform with the state.

A weaker variant of Richards's primary law was adopted by popular initiative, but most provisions were repealed by the legislature, leaving a relatively conventional closed primary in place. The closed primary was, in turn, repealed in 1915. In 1918, however, Richards managed to get his primary on the ballot again, in its full and complete form, and it was approved by a comfortable (58 percent to 42 percent) margin. The 1920 election was conducted according to Richards's specifications. In 1921 legislators again began repealing pieces of the law, and by 1929 the state had again returned to a standard closed primary, which it has maintained ever since.

A 1923 piece by Clarence Berdahl outlines many of the problems inherent in the Richards primary. The law's requirements for numerous debates were no doubt onerous, to the extent that Richards himself, as a candidate for governor in 1920, had trouble meeting them. The debates were popular, however, and they in fact brought surrogates for the presidential candidates to South Dakota to participate. The platform requirements wound up becoming farcical, as did the requirement that each party must have a "majority" issue and a "protesting" issue. The different factions adopted slogans such as "Patriotism, Progress, Prosperity, Honesty, Economy, Law and Order"; "Economy, Efficiency, Protection, Peace, Agriculture"; or simply "Americanness." These slogans were, as Berdahl notes, not particularly helpful for voters who wanted to make an informed choice between platforms. Richards argued that such platforms were illegal, but it was not clear how one might determine what a sufficiently precise platform would be. Furthermore, even if any clear policy commitments were to make their way into these platforms, there was no mechanism to obligate candidates to address these issues or to compel successful candidates to pursue them once in office. The law contained a number of other rules regarding campaign finance, the election of candidates for lower office, and the organization of party committees, but again, these do not appear to have been enforceable.

Why did South Dakota adopt such a complicated law? And why was it "corrupted"? Richards's vision was particularly idiosyncratic, but it did have an idealistic charm that appealed to voters; it required politicians to stand for something. In his history of the NPL, Michael Lansing (2015, 200–201) notes that the major paradox of the Richards primary was the role it gave to parties. In an era when most Progressives were skeptical of the power of parties and advocated for open primaries and other means of diluting party bosses' power, Richards's primary had the perverse effect of strengthening parties. Parties would decide what issues appeared on the ballot, and they would ensure that voters had only two alternatives. There was no possibility, for instance, for NPL activists to triumph over fractured opposition in a Republican primary. In Lansing's telling, Richards did not realize this; when his first foray into establishing a primary was dismantled in 1915, he reached out to the NPL for support, but when the full Richards primary was approved by voters in 1918, he had the support of Republican stalwarts who saw his primary as a vehicle for preventing the NPL from capturing the Republican Party. Once the NPL threat had receded, these Republicans could point to the absurdities of some of the Richards primary's provisions and again begin to dismantle it.

The Richards primary was corrupted, then, because its supporters championed it for insincere reasons: not because they thought it would work, but because they thought that its implementation would preserve their hold on government long enough for them to use it against Richards and his potential allies. Richards did not necessarily help to create a workable primary; throughout his career he remained an all-or-nothing advocate for the law he had developed rather than settling for a compromise version. As was the case in Overacker's postmortem on the New York primary, Berdahl concludes that despite its flaws the South Dakota law had some salutary features, and South Dakota did end the 1920s with a more comprehensive primary in place than New York did. But in the South Dakota case the fixing of problems went far beyond what reformers sympathetic to Richards's goals yet wanting to rein in his excesses might have done.

What can we make of these various case studies? One clear takeaway has to do with the role of party conflict in creating, identifying, and addressing problems. In all but the case of mispractice, the hostility toward the primary or toward primary reform came either from the party that expected to be at a disadvantage under the primary law or from a faction within the dominant party. And in cases where solutions were introduced, as in New Mexico and Michigan, the introduction of the solution often coincided with a significant shift in party control of the legislature. This may suggest that new majority parties were able to address problems in ways that their predecessors could not; such claims have been made about shifts in control of the U.S. Congress (e.g., Rohde 1991). Given that many of these changes took place during the 1930s, it may also be that, as discussed in Chapters 2 and 3, primary law reforms wound up on the back burner as the nation turned to confront more pressing problems. And it may be that the politics of the general election became more important as the Democratic Party became stronger in many of these states; this is a topic that will be discussed in Chapter 6.

Conclusions

Finally, what benefits do we get from placing early twentieth-century American reforms in the context of the contemporary literature on elections? The comparative elections literature begins from a point of view that often stands outside of mainstream American politics. In that literature, it is assumed that all political parties seek to manipulate elections to their advantage, and that claims about "democracy" are often merely a façade for the exercise of power. American parties, of course, do this as well, but, as I noted at the start of this chapter, the range of possible outcomes is somewhat more limited than in the comparative literature. No American state political party can (or at least has) taken serious steps toward abandoning the basic form of two-party, first-past-the-post, three-branch democracy that has characterized the nation since its founding. Whatever steps have been taken to disenfranchise particular groups or to tilt the political playing field have been accompanied by rhetoric about enhancing democracy. This can lead to a failure to understand categories, to understand that all arguments about restricting who can vote in a primary election, who can appear on the ballot, or how parties might meaningfully improve the choices voters have are not the same. This category failure may be one reason it has been so hard to get voters to think intelligently about primary reforms. Even the most obvious cases of violation of democratic rules and norms, as we shall see in our discussion of Southern elections in Chapter 7, are more about racism or partisan conflict than they are about the legitimacy of democratic election laws.

The comparative categories here, then, show that intentions matter. When states have had primary problems, due either to poorly written laws or to idiosyncratic features of the states themselves, it is important to identify cases in which both parties have something to gain from an improved primary process. In most of the states profiled here, this was not the case. Yet borrowing the distinctions between types of election law reforms from the comparative literature can help us to be more critical consumers of the stories about reform that appear in this literature and to bring some order to the frequent primary law changes that characterized many of these states' elections for much of the twentieth century.

6
Primaries and Partisan Advantage

In January 1909, San Francisco attorney Hiram Johnson spoke to the California legislature in favor of adopting the direct primary. Later that year, the state legislature considered Johnson's proposal, along with a host of other Progressive reforms. Recalcitrant Republican conservatives blocked most of the Progressive proposals, but they did adopt direct primaries for statewide offices (Lower 1993, 18). In 1910, the Lincoln-Roosevelt League, a Progressive factional group within the Republican Party, endorsed Johnson as its gubernatorial candidate. Johnson campaigned vigorously in the primary, easily defeating two more seasoned and business-friendly candidates. Not only did Johnson go on to win the general election, but he brought with him a working majority of state legislators also endorsed by the Lincoln-Roosevelt League. Johnson and his allies proceeded to expand the primary, to adopt initiative and referendum provisions, and to restrict the political clout of the state's powerful railroad interests. Johnson also championed the direct election of senators, and in 1916, two years after winning re-election as governor, Johnson ran for the Senate, where he would go on to work as an advocate for presidential primaries, the regulation of campaign spending, and other election reforms.

Johnson's brief tenure as California governor contributed to a radical remaking of the state's Republican Party. Johnson himself had little interest in party politics. In 1912 he ran as the vice presidential nominee of Theodore Roosevelt's Bull Moose Party, and he deliberately avoided referring to his party label in his Senate bids (McWilliams 1949, 181). Without explicitly endorsing Democrat Woodrow Wilson in 1916, Johnson ran a campaign on similar themes and did little to aid Republican Party nominee Charles Evans Hughes in California. Yet the Republican Party would dominate California politics for four decades after Johnson's initial election, and Democrats were often left in the embarrassing position of failing to have their own nominee in statewide races or of fielding nominees who were clearly not the choice of party leaders. These changes were arguably a result of the adoption of the direct primary and the movement of issue-based competition from the general election to the Republican primary.

Histories of the Progressive Era often present Johnson as one of the most influential Progressive leaders. Yet his successes are difficult to disentangle either from the trajectory of his own career or from the fortunes of the California parties. Was there an element of self-interest to Johnson's activities? Most accounts emphasize that when Johnson became active in the Progressive movement, he did not necessarily see himself as the major beneficiary, and he was not the first choice of the Lincoln-Roosevelt League in the 1910 gubernatorial election (Lower 1993, 30–31). It is also easy to find instances of actions taken by Johnson that seem entirely removed from calculations of his own political advancement. On the other hand, California did not just adopt Progressive reforms; it adopted Progressive reforms that seem uniquely tailored to the advantage of Republicans and of the Progressive Republican faction that Johnson led.

In his well-known work on the state's political culture, Carey McWilliams describes California as a state that one cannot easily fit into "the American scheme of things" and as "a state that lacks a political gyroscope, a state that swings and sways, spins and turns in accordance with its own peculiar dynamics" (McWilliams 1949, 6, 192). In 1913, two years after California adopted the direct primary for all offices, the state enacted a law allowing for cross-filing: for candidates to simultaneously seek the nomination of more than one party. Throughout the upcoming decades, California often had five or more parties with ballot access, thus ensuring that candidates had multiple ways to run for office. This led to some instances in which veteran politicians lost the nomination of their own party but won the nomination of another. More commonly, however, well-known candidates were able to win the nominations of multiple parties, occasionally winning the general election "at primary." The cross-filing system is credited by many historians with erasing programmatic distinctions between parties and creating a politics of personality (Bell 2012, 12; Mowry 1951, 151). Other historians have noted that rapid population growth in the state made it inevitable that partisanship would be particularly unstable in the California electorate (Delmatier, McIntosh, and Waters 1970, 210).

The partisan dynamics of cross-filing are clear. By the 1950s, the dominant Republican Party included movement conservatives and liberals. The Democratic Party, although temporarily aided by the Roosevelt campaigns of the 1930s and 1940s, occasionally saw its primaries captured by Republicans. Most candidates cross-filed during this era; by the 1950s over 80 percent of candidates were cross-filing and over 40 percent were winning at primary (Delmatier, McIntosh, and Waters 1970, 374–382). Republicans had initially been apprehensive about this; when the original cross-filing law was introduced, party regulars first sought to require candidates to affirm that they had supported the party whose nomination they sought in the last election. This law was subsequently amended to require candidates to pledge to support a majority of the party's candidates in the next election, and it was then dropped entirely. In 1952, once Democratic voter registration numbers had risen to the point that the party was competitive, legislators amended the cross-filing law to require that candidates state a partisan preference and run as the nominee of that party, even if they were also listed as another party's nominee. Following their capture of the state legislature in 1958, Democrats did away with cross-filing entirely.

Informal party groups similar to the Lincoln-Roosevelt League had existed in both parties during the 1930s, 1940s, and 1950s. Such groups had endorsed candidates or slates of candidates. Before the 1962 election, the Democratically led legislature abolished the practice of listing preprimary endorsements on the ballot. Both parties endured a decade of ideological conflict, but by the late 1960s, the Republican Party was firmly in the control of conservatives, and by the 1970s the Democratic Party had also largely aligned with the national party. Political parties in California are arguably still weaker today than in other parts of the country, and (as its recent adoption of the top two primary suggests) California is still a state willing to consider unorthodox changes to its nomination laws. But by the 1960s partisan politics in California had become more recognizable to observers from other states.

Winners and Losers in Primary Reforms

This brief account of changes in California's primary laws shows the complicated relationship between Progressive reforms and political advantage. Moreover, it shows the problems in determining *whose* advantage is at stake under any reform proposal. Is this a story of an antiparty movement? A good idea successfully sold to voters? A quest for personal gain? An effort by the Republicans or the Democrats to entrench themselves or ward off competition? Or an effort by a faction to secure control of one of the parties? A case can easily be made that all of these stories play a role.

In Chapter 2 I briefly argued for the merits of considering the relationship between partisan advantage and changes to primary laws. Although state-by-state analyses show that there is a plausible story to be told here, this story is complicated by the fact that any change in party strength might prompt a rethinking of the primary process, but conversely, any change in primary laws may forestall changes in partisan strength. There are clear causality problems here. There are, in addition, exogenous events that might substantially overshadow the effects of any change in primary laws. To take just two examples, the Democratic gains everywhere in the country during the 1930s certainly would have happened with or without any changes to primary laws. The California case study shows that Democrats might plausibly have sought to capitalize on their gains in the 1950s by adapting the state's primary laws, but it is difficult to argue that changes to California primary laws had an easily measurable impact on subsequent elections. In other words, changes to primary laws are simply not important enough to explain very much of the variation in two-party competition during the period considered here.

Despite the lack of major effects, however, partisan advantage remains an intuitive explanation for why primary laws would be changed. Even if the effects are not great, there is an elaborate and theoretically rich literature in American and comparative political science about how political parties seek to structure election rules to their advantage. If we think about primary election laws as rule changes akin to ballot access rules, voting restrictions, or campaign finance laws, we have a firm body of evidence that suggests that parties should try to structure primary laws to their advantage, even if their assumptions are faulty or they do not ultimately succeed in securing advantage. This literature stands in contrast to the less-developed or more historically contingent literatures discussed in the previous three chapters of this book.

Accordingly, in this chapter I explore the relevance of the widely used "cartel party" thesis and its alternatives to American primary elections. I use this to present a series of propositions about primary law changes between 1928 and 1970, and I then evaluate evidence about these changes both quantitatively and qualitatively. I show that there is suggestive evidence that partisan competition plays a role in changes to primary election laws. It is difficult, however, to attribute changes to parties, as opposed to attributing them to factions within the parties. I conclude the chapter by returning to the California example to show that it can be difficult to disentangle factions, parties, and individuals; primary laws have historically been a tool for political gain, but it is not always easy in the American context to determine how large and durable the coalitions behind primary law changes have been.

Theories of Partisan Advantage

It is common among contemporary students of comparative politics to view changes in electoral institutions as tools of partisan combat. Such combat can entail efforts by a majority party to seek advantage over its nearest competitors, but it can also entail efforts by two or more parties to shut out smaller competitors or potential competitors. This perspective is common, for instance, in literature on European party systems (Powell 2000; Farrell 2011). The contemporary comparative literature on such changes often is situated with reference to declining public support for political parties themselves as institutions. In the United States, such claims often underpin histories of voting restrictions (Hasen 2012), legislative districting practices (Bullock 2010), and campaign finance laws (La Raja 2008). As we shall see in Chapter 7, Southern primaries—and in particular, the runoff provisions in these primaries—have often been understood as a tool for perpetuating one-party Democratic dominance, as well as being something to be manipulated for individual or factional advantage (Jewell and Cunningham 1968; Parent 2004). Primaries have generally been exempt from such considerations, but one might simply chalk this up to an overall lack of scholarly interest in primary election law change.

One can certainly conclude that Ware's (2002) arguments about the adoption of primaries are consistent with claims of partisan advantage. Ware, as discussed earlier in this book, contends that primaries were adopted so quickly and in so many states during the 1900s and 1910s because parties realized that, despite the "antiparty" arguments employed by reformers, they could use them to their own advantage. In Ware's formulation, then, the adoption of primaries conferred an advantage on parties over antiparty forces. This claim, however, is complicated by the rarity of stable two-party systems in the American states and the need to specify which parties we are discussing: When we say parties benefited, are we talking about majority parties in competitive states? Majority parties in one-party states? Competitive minority parties? It is essential to gain some leverage on this question if we are to seek quantitative evidence of partisan interests in the adoption of, or change in, primary laws. And given that the focus of this book is on instances of change over time—that is, the potential for multiple changes in primary laws in the same places, rather than the initial implementation of primaries—we must explore both the anticipated and the actual effects of such changes.

One useful distinction in doing this comes from the comparative literature on party finance. The cartel thesis, as formulated by Richard Katz and Peter Mair (1995), posits that political parties seek to insulate themselves from the public by becoming quasi-governmental organizations. They do so by, among other things, establishing state subventions or public financing mechanisms to fund activities that were once paid for through "private" activities such as volunteer work or individual contributions. In a later article, Katz and Mair (2009) extend their consideration to include other types of state support for parties, such as the use of governmental resources to promote party activities or subsidized or free access to broadcast media. There may be normative justifications for such interventions, but in Katz and Mair's view, the impetus for these changes tends to come from political parties, and parties would not champion such efforts were it not in their electoral interest to do so. Given the need for bipartisan (or multipartisan) support for electoral policy changes in many democracies, Katz and Mair emphasize the collusion involved in making such changes; two or more parties that tend to compete for power but have relatively stable levels of support may find it in their interest to jointly advocate for state supports as a means of locking out potential upstart parties, or to ensure a relatively predictable level of state support. Schemes that, for instance, guarantee public funding according to a per-vote or per-seat formula fit this description: they reward parties based on past performance, making the formation of new parties difficult.

The cartel thesis has been highly influential in the comparative study of electoral systems. One major alternative or elaboration of the cartel theory, however, is Susan Scarrow's (2004, 2006) theory of partisan advantage. Whereas Katz and Mair emphasize collusion, Scarrow emphasizes the ways in which changes to party finance laws can be used by a majority party to disadvantage its competitors. The crucial difference, for Scarrow, is that parties may pursue laws that will deal them short-term harm, as long as the law will harm their opponents more.

Contemporary considerations of these theories have tended to be limited to analyses of recent history, and in particular of changes in party finance laws. There is no reason, however, why the insight here cannot be expanded to consider other time periods or other types of electoral change. Primary election laws are analogous to party finance laws in many relevant ways: the specific details of primary laws are of low salience to the public; they can be used to confer obvious advantages on parties of a certain size (e.g., they can be said to correspond to the cartel thesis); they can be used to confer advantage upon different types of parties or voters (that is, they can also be said to apply to fit Scarrow's framework); and many different types of changes can be justified to the interested public on ostensibly nonpartisan, normative grounds. Unlike party finance changes, however, the effects of changes to primary election laws are quite difficult to measure, either before or after the changes are made. As was the case in other chapters of this book, then, changes to primary election laws have often been based on conjecture about who the winners and losers will be. This means that we are in a position of positing expected effects of primary law changes and attaching these to the occurrence, or lack thereof, of changes rather than looking for the results of the changes.

Hypotheses and Method

Let us begin, then, by simply looking at a visual representation of the timing of some state primary law changes. Consider the state-specific graphs presented in Figure 6.1. Each graph shows the percentage of Democrats in the two chambers of the state legislature over time. Solid vertical lines represent changes categorized in Chapter 2 as enhancing the power of parties over primary elections, while dotted vertical lines represent changes that reduced party power. I elaborate on the categorization of such laws in greater detail below. For now, however, consider the relationship between election reforms and party competition in the following examples:

PRIMARIES AND PARTISAN ADVANTAGE 149

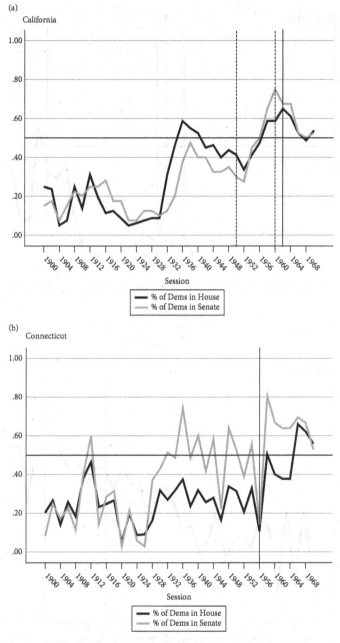

Figure 6.1. Primary rule changes, selected states, by year and level of party competition, 1900–1970

Notes: Vertical lines indicate years with primary election law changes, as described in Table 2.1. Solid lines represent expansive changes; dotted lines represent restrictive changes.

Source: Seat share data from Dubin (2007) as described in Chapter 2.

150 REFORM AND RETRENCHMENT

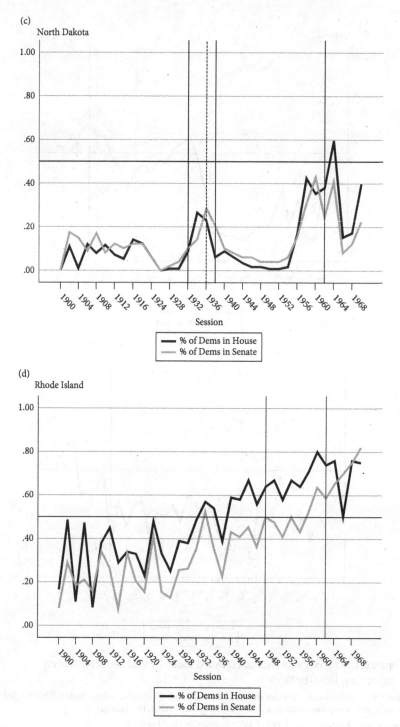

Figure 6.1. Continued

- In California, Republican politicians had filed for the Republican *and* Democratic nominations during the 1930s and 1940s. Given the heterogeneous nature of the Republican Party and its status as the dominant party in the state over this time period, cross-filing was widely held to be detrimental to the development of a strong Democratic Party organization. When the Democratic Party gained a majority in the state legislature in the late 1950s, it acted to abolish cross-filing, on the grounds that it confused voters.
- In Connecticut, Duane Lockard's (1959b) account of the establishment of the direct primary emphasizes that the state lagged behind others because of the strength of powerful Republican boss J. Henry Roraback. Following Roraback's death, divisions emerged within the Republican Party, and at the time the primary law was passed in 1955, the parties had split control of the legislature, something reformist factions in both parties used to their advantage, despite the obstinacy of both parties' leaders.
- In North Dakota, as we saw in Chapter 4, the legislative seat share of the Democratic Party increased during the 1930s, and again during the late 1950s. What was left of the Nonpartisan League switched its allegiance from the Republican Party to the Democratic Party in 1956 (Omdahl 1961). However, Democrats never reached majority status during either period. There were compelling reasons for Republican politicians to ensure that Democratic voters could be pulled into Republican primaries during this period, as their inclusion would aid the party's nominees. The Republican Party was also the more ideologically heterogeneous of the two parties in North Dakota, so individual Republican candidates might seek Democratic votes. The state's decision to repeal party enrollment and party affiliation tests, then, can be seen as a bid to increase voter support.
- In Rhode Island, the adoption of the direct primary coincided with the Democratic Party's attainment of majority status in the state House and of parity in the state Senate, and with the inauguration of a new governor who favored the primary (Moakley and Cornwell 2001).

These state examples suggest the following, more generalized claims.

A change in power may prompt new majority parties to enact legislation that enhances their advantage. In the case of California Democrats, cross-filing was seen as having worked to their disadvantage, so eliminating the practice and establishing party primaries was a means of solidifying Democratic gains that the party likely thought would have occurred earlier without the practice. In essence, California Democrats enacted more restrictive primary rules to compel candidates sympathetic to the broader ideological aims of the party to run as Democrats. In Rhode Island, Democratic gains led to the adoption of the primary, a move that opened up the candidate selection process to voters. While one might see these changes as moving in different directions—one gave voters fewer choices, another gave voters more choices—both coincided with a shift in power.

Anticipation of gains for the minority party might prompt the majority party to enact rules that could limit the likelihood that the minority party will make any further gains. In the North Dakota case, Democratic gains in the 1930s may well have prompted Republican efforts to lure Democratic voters into the Republican primary. In the California case, the repeated success of Republicans running in Democratic primaries prevented the Democratic Party from developing effective organizational support for statewide campaigns. Republicans, however, did act to ensure that their own party was not vulnerable by requiring candidates to divulge their actual party affiliation. As Figures 6.1 and 6.3 (shown later in the chapter) suggest, Democratic gains in California during the 1930s were far more limited than in many other states. In short, an increase in minority party strength may coincide with the enactment of rules by the majority party. These rules can, as in the case of change in party control, take a variety of forms.

Finally, the Connecticut case suggests that cross-party coalitions are possible. While changes in seat share may not capture the development of such coalitions, this case suggests that even an increase in majority party strength can relate to rule changes. That is, a majority party may be heterogeneous, but *the growth of one particular faction may prompt rule changes.*

These examples all posit some relationship between party strength and competitiveness, yet they are ambiguous about what will happen. Cumulatively, however, they suggest that reforms are *not* likely in states where partisan competition remains constant over time. Such stasis may mask shifting factionalism within the parties, but if one weighs this possibility against other potential scenarios, it simply seems less likely.

Measuring Changes in Party Strength

Here, as in Chapter 2, I have drawn upon the *Book of States* (Council of State Governments, 1936–1970) and Louise Overacker's (1928–1940) summaries of primary law enactments to compile a list of all changes to primary laws. I omit changes described by these two sources as minor. For each, I have noted the state and year of enactment. I follow the same method as in Chapter 2 to distinguish between expansive and restrictive laws.

The hypotheses presented here posit a relationship between primary rule changes and actual or expected changes in partisan competition. There are many potential measures of competition, and there are also different ways in which competition might be understood. One might understand it as a correlate of seat share—a legislature long held by Republicans but with an increasing number of Democratic seats might be understood to be becoming more competitive. This change may not be linear in nature; for instance, a change from 20 to 25 percent Democratic is potentially not as much of a problem for Republicans as a shift from 43 to 48 percent Democratic. One might, alternatively, understand changes in the competitiveness of elections as the primary variable of concern—a change in the number of competitive seats, or in the overall Democratic vote percentage (to continue the above hypothetical) for the legislature, or even in statewide races, might prompt defensive moves by the majority Republicans even if the two parties' legislative seat shares do not change. None of these measures is clearly superior to the others, but since in part we are trying to capture the anticipation by the majority party of future changes, each seems like a possible prompt for rule changes.

A much easier measure to use is change in party control, of the legislature or of the governorship. As the Rhode Island and California examples show, the change in seat share here is far less important than the change in majority status. Here, no assumptions about anticipating change are necessary; we have an actual change in power that prompts legislation designed to lock in or build open that change.

In the following section, I discuss the relationship between rule changes with reference to each of these variables. In measuring seat share, I use data on the composition of state legislatures (lower and upper chambers) from 1928 to 1970, drawn from Dubin (2007) and converted to percentages (for convenience, I refer to these throughout the chapters as House and Senate even though some states use other names). To assess competitiveness, I use two different variables used in Austin Ranney's (1965) various indexes of party competition at the state level: gubernatorial vote percentage and the folded Ranney index, beginning in 1938 and calculated on a four-year running average. The folded Ranney index averages state House and Senate composition and gubernatorial vote share, providing values from 0.5 to 1 measuring competitiveness, where higher values indicate greater competitiveness (for discussion and data see Klarner 2013). I also use measures of change in party control drawn from the Ranney data; here, Ranney uses values of 0 and 1 to show unified control and 0.5 to show split control; a change in either direction during the time immediately before a rule change would signify a change in the governing party's ability to enact such changes.

Such changes do not necessarily indicate that one party is doing something "right" or "wrong." For instance, an increase in Democratic strength in the 1930s in a state is likely evidence of a national trend toward Democrats, prompted by the Great Depression and the increase in Democratic strength at the federal level. Similarly, declines in Democratic strength in the South that began toward the end of the period under consideration here and have continued since are a broader reflection of changing Southern partisanship (again, likely prompted by changes at the federal level). These changes do not necessarily mean that rule changes should not occur in these circumstances; they do indicate, however, that we should not look to rule changes to forestall subsequent changes in legislative party strength. Rule changes may be an effort to prevent gains by the minority party, but none of the arguments presented above suggest that we should expect them to be particularly successful in this goal.

These data also do not necessarily address shifts in vote share for legislative races. Such measures do not exist at the state level for the period covered here. However, data collected by Holbrook and Van Dunk (1993) show that the Ranney index is correlated with district vote share measures (although Holbrooke and Van Dunk offer their own estimate, based on vote share, which they argue is superior).

More consequentially, these data also do not provide a measure of changes in factional strength within parties. The Connecticut example above, for instance, not only shows that the presence or absence of one powerful individual can affect the likelihood of rule changes; it is also reasonable to infer that the proportion of loyalists to the individual in question, J. Henry Roraback, also shifted over time. This might indicate that individual politicians changed their views or that the politicians in the legislature changed, in a manner potentially orthogonal to changes in partisanship. Legislator ideology measures (such as DW-NOMINATE scores at the federal level or the Shor-McCarty scores,[1] compiled for contemporary state legislatures) might be a means of addressing such matters, but again, such measures do not currently exist for the period in question, and we cannot in fact be certain that such measures would be an appropriate means of identifying party factions.

We have, then, a means of identifying primary law changes, with the caveat that the judgments used here (as to which changes increase or decrease party control) will not provide precise directives as to what governing parties might do if they are seeking to provide an electoral advantage for themselves. And we have a variety of party competition measures, each of which provides some means of identifying when changes are happening. The caveat here is that the measures do not exhaustively show all changes that would potentially be of concern to legislators, but they do provide a baseline estimate of changes in state politics.

Aggregate Patterns of Partisanship and Primary Law Change

Competitiveness and Rule Changes

As a first cut at investigating changes in primary rules, let us consider the relationship between the overall level of competition and the enactment of primary rule changes. Table 6.1 shows the level of competition in states passing restrictive laws or expansive laws and in those that either did not change their rules or enacted a change with no clear relevance to party strength. Each case in this table represents a state and year. The dependent variable here is the folded Ranney index, as described above. The vast majority of state/year cases, unsurprisingly, fall in the "no change or neutral rule change" category, which thus serves as a sort of control. The table clearly shows that restrictive rules are enacted in states that are less competitive than the norm, while expansive rule changes are implemented in states that are more competitive than the norm. This pattern does not appear to be driven by other factors; as the table shows, it holds for states with a strong Progressive movement and those without, and it also holds regardless of which party controls the various branches of government (although there are very few changes enacted in states with unified Republican control of the governorship and legislature).[2] Although Southern states comprise half of the restrictive changes, this pattern also holds across regions.

This table also shows the relationship between divided government and the enactment of primary rule changes. Expansive rule changes are far more likely in states with split control of government than they are in states where one party has unified control. Although only one-third of the cases here are instances of split control, these cases provide 47 percent of the rule changes and 69 percent of the instances of expansive rule enactments. States with unified party control are less likely to change their primary rules, and when they do so, they tend to enact restrictive rules. This suggests a relationship between shifts in party power and rule changes—if divided government is indicative of a recent or incipient change in party fortunes, then change in partisan competition prompts efforts to pass expansive rules, or in other words, to weaken parties.

Table 6.2 shows the relationship between partisanship and rule changes; here, two indexes of Democratic party strength—Democratic seat share in the state House and Senate and Democratic gubernatorial vote share—are provided for states enacting restrictive rules or expansive rules, and for states that either enacted neutral rules or did not enact primary rule changes. The top three lines of data show averages for all states. Then, given the overwhelming Democratic tilt in the South for much of this period, the table shows averages for non-Southern and Southern states.[3] The reader will note that there is a slightly larger number of cases here than in Table 6.1; given that Table 6.1 uses a four-year running average, beginning in 1942, it omits changes that happened between 1938 and 1940, while Table 6.2 includes these years.

This table corroborates much of what is shown in Table 6.1. In all states, as well as in just the non-Southern states, expansive rules are enacted in states where power is more evenly divided in both houses of the legislature. The

Table 6.1 State Competitiveness and the Direction of Rule Changes, 1942–1970

	Restrictive Rule Enacted	No Change or Neutral Rule Enacted	Expansive Rule Enacted	Total
All states	.74 (18)	.77 (711)	.88 (16)	.78 (745)
Progressive states	.77 (12)	.82 (289)	.88 (7)	.82 (308)
Not Progressive states	.68 (6)	.74 (422)	.87 (9)	.74 (437)
Unified Republican control	.82 (4)	.79 (208)	.95 (1)	.79 (213)
Split control	.80 (5)	.90 (235)	.91 (11)	.90 (251)
Unified Democratic control	.67 (9)	.65 (268)	.78 (4)	.66 (281)

Source: Seat share data from Dubin (2007) as described in Chapter 2. Ranney index measures from Klarner (2013).
Notes: Cell entries are Folded Ranney Index four-year moving averages. Each case represents a state and two-year legislative cycle. Scores range between 0.5 and 1; higher scores indicate greater levels of interparty competitiveness. Ns are provided in parentheses.
Differences across columns for all but the unified party control categories are significant at p <.05.

relationship between partisanship and gubernatorial vote share is somewhat less obvious. One might infer, however, that if there is an incumbency advantage for legislatures, then statewide vote shares, gubernatorial or otherwise, should be more sensitive to changes in voter attitudes than are seat shares. This would suggest that expansive rule changes are tied to Democratic gains across the board.

One should not, however, take the data in this table to suggest that Democrats had a greater propensity to champion expansive primary rules. Even when one leaves Southern Democrats aside, it must be remembered that the data in Table 6.1 show that rule changes are more likely when there is divided control than when there is unified control by either party. This presupposes that in these cases there must be factions in both parties that support the rule changes in question. Furthermore, the case studies considered earlier in this chapter suggested that expansive rule changes in many states were implemented by Republicans seeking to stave off further Democratic gains. It is difficult in many instances to determine which party "owns" the rule changes, but the fact that Republicans were more ideologically heterogeneous in many states than were Democrats suggests that in many instances expansive reforms were pursued with factional goals in mind, but not necessarily or exclusively with partisan goals in mind.

Table 6.2 Direction of Rule Changes by Partisanship and Region, 1938–1970

	Proportion of Democratic House Members	Proportion of Democratic Senate Members	Democratic Gubernatorial Vote	N
All States				
Restrictive rule enacted	.72	.70	.57	20
No change or neutral rule enacted	.58	.58	.57	794
Expansive rule enacted	.49	.51	.52	22
North/West				
Restrictive rule enacted	.56	.54	.44	11
No change or neutral rule enacted	.43	.45	.49	543
Expansive rule enacted	.50	.51	.53	21
South				
Restrictive rule enacted	.93	.91	.72	9
No change or neutral rule enacted	.90	.89	.75	251
Expansive rule enacted	.44	.35	.51	1

Source: Seat share data from Dubin (2007) as described in Chapter 2.

Changes in Competitiveness

The indexes discussed above can be used to show that different types of rule changes are related to the level of party competition. Yet they do not explain why changes took place at all. The hypotheses above suggest that changes in the level of competition (or the threat thereof) prompt rule changes. However, using a shift in competitiveness is problematic for two reasons: first, because it calls our attention to states that were uncompetitive at the outset of the time period considered here, and second, because competition increased in most non-Southern states over this period, so there is some risk of selecting on the dependent variable.

Overall, two-party competition increased in non-Southern states over this period, and the increase for the full time period is evident in states that changed their primary laws and in those that did not. It did not increase in lockstep over the period, but this increase (shown in Figure 6.2) is substantial enough that it may suggest that forces much stronger than electoral rules were afoot.

158 REFORM AND RETRENCHMENT

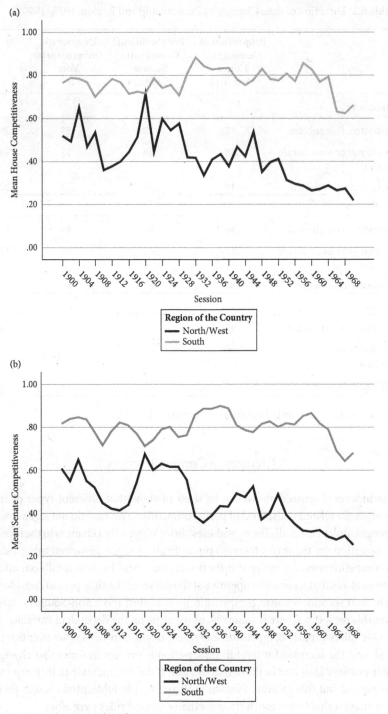

Figure 6.2. Changes in legislative competitiveness by region, 1900–1970
Note: Competitiveness is the absolute value of difference in percentage of seats held by each party.
Source: Seat share data from Dubin (2007) as described in Chapter 2.

Decade-by-decade measures, however, show a few interesting patterns among states according to their implementation of primary law changes. Table 6.3 shows changes in state House and state Senate balance, separating out states that passed restrictive (that is, party-enhancing) laws, states that passed expansive laws, and those that did not change their laws. The percentages here show how small the majority party's percentage of seats is and how this percentage has changed over the decade. I group the 1950s and 1960s together because of the small number of changes in the 1950s. A positive percentage indicates that on average the majority party's share of seats is smaller than it was at the outset of the decade,

Table 6.3 Decade-by-Decade Comparison of Reform and Non-Reform States, by Legislative Competitiveness, 1930–1970

	States Enacting Restrictive Rules	No Change	States Enacting Expansive Rules	All States
1930s				
Change in House competitiveness	4.6%	23.6%	25.5%	20.3%
Change in Senate competitiveness	5.6%	23.2%	19.3%	19.1%
N	6	19	6	31
1940s				
Change in House competitiveness	−9.8%	−3.2%	7.5%	−2.1%
Change in Senate competitiveness	−3.7%	4.8%	1.2%	3.4%
N	3	23	5	31
1950s–1960s				
Change in House competitiveness	6.1%	21.0%	18.5%	19.1%
Change in Senate competitiveness	21.1%	16.0%	5.2%	14.4%
N	3	23	6	32

Source: Seat share data from Dubin (2007).
Notes: Southern states excluded. Percentages show the average change in competitiveness for each state type. They do not sum to 100% across columns or rows.

Competitiveness = absolute value of difference in percentage of seats held by each party; change in competitiveness = difference between competitiveness at outset of decade and competitiveness in final election of decade.

"No Change" cases include states that passed rules that balanced each other out.

while a negative percentage indicates that the majority party's share of seats has increased. The percentages here do not specify which party holds the majority or whether the majority has changed hands. The simple comparison of means here also does not show causality – it does not show whether reforms were a result or a cause of changes in competitiveness. There is little evidence in the literature that primary reforms have the ability to substantially alter two-party competition, despite the fact that they are clearly intended to at least shape it somewhat.

Although the number of cases here is small, the differences are still intriguing. In five of the six cases here (all but the Senate competitiveness changes between 1950 and 1970) the states enacting restrictive rules saw either a smaller-than-average increase in competitiveness or a decline in competitiveness. There is little overlap between the states in each category from one decade to the next (that is, we are not just looking at the experience of the same three to six states over four decades), and the states in these categories are not obviously distinctive in other regards. States enacting expansive rules (rules reducing party influence) track close to the average for states that make no changes, again with the exception of changes in state Senate representation in the 1950s and 1960s.[4]

Is there a logic to these changes? Given that the 1930s and 1940s were a time of heightened competition outside of the South, as the Democratic Party gained seats in most state legislatures, one can read the passage of expansive primary laws as a response to this trend, as an effort by majority Republicans in some of these states to pull Democratic voters into their primaries (as in North Dakota) or by Democrats to capitalize on the successes of individual politicians (as in Rhode Island). One can read the passage of restrictive rules (as in Indiana or Colorado) as efforts by governing parties to impose more order on parties whose majorities were large enough that factional conflict had developed over nominations. The numbers here are, however, too small to draw conclusions with any certainty, and the national trends in these years clearly complicate our efforts to measure whether reformers were successful in their goals.

Table 6.3 excludes Southern states in part because there is virtually no change in partisan competition in these states' legislatures over the period considered here. Yet the logic outlined earlier is applicable to southern states as well. Efforts to increase party control over primaries, or to close primaries to other groups or factions, are more plausible when a party can afford to lose some voters or candidates, or when these voters or candidates have nowhere else to go. Such a description can certainly be applied to the predicament of African American voters in the South, and as we saw in Figure 6.2, rule changes in the South are almost all restrictive, even if the rule itself has no specific racial component. We will take address this issue further in Chapter 7.

In sum, state-specific accounts of changes in primary laws often discuss partisan motives, but there is no single model that synthesizes the competing narratives outlined above. There is some evidence that states acting to restrict or expand their primaries look different from each other in their level of partisan competition; our ability to measure this is complicated, however, by the difficulty of passing legislation and by the fact that many states that made no changes to their primary laws went through changes that resemble states that did change their laws.

State-Specific Accounts

It is appropriate, then, to take a more careful look at the sorts of time series shown earlier in the chapter. Figure 6.3 shows time series for all non-Southern states not shown in Figure 6.1 that had two or more primary law changes during the 1928–1970 period. As in Figure 6.1, expansive changes are represented using a solid line, restrictive changes are shown using a dotted line, and changes that fit neither category are shown with a line that has dots and dashes.

In many of these states, primary law changes coincide with a change in party control of one or both houses. In discussion of Figure 6.1, I noted that Rhode Island adopted the direct primary immediately after Democrats seized control of the legislature and the governorship, and that California Democrats abolished cross-filing immediately within two terms of gaining control of the legislature. Figure 6.3 shows similar developments: when Democrats gained control of both houses of the legislature in Idaho in 1932, they moved to adopt a mandatory statewide primary. When Democrats regained control of the legislature in 1940 after losing it for a cycle, they changed the primary from closed to open. And when Republicans won control of the legislature in 1960, they closed the primary and instituted a preprimary convention. Such changes are not necessarily reflective of any sort of ideological commitments on the part of the parties at the national level, however. In Michigan (see Figure 5.1), it was the Republican Party that repealed all party affiliation tests for voters and instituted an open primary in the two cycles following its acquisition of majority status in 1938. Partisan gain here was certainly not the sole motivation; as in many other states, there was a much more proximate normative cause: as Dorr (1937) notes, there was widespread unhappiness with candidates "gaming" the system by placing the names of "dummy candidates" on the partisan ballots to deter competition, and the open primary would likely have reduced the effectiveness of this practice.

In other instances, changes appear to be efforts to ward off minority party success, as we saw in our earlier discussion of North Dakota politics. Changes in the use of the preprimary convention in Massachusetts coincided with notable shifts in the fortunes of the parties; the preprimary convention—a tool that ensured greater party control over ballot access and, ultimately, the party loyalty of primary nominees—was implemented in 1934, following substantial Democratic gains, and was repealed in 1938, following a decline in Democratic fortunes. At no time did Democrats control the legislature, but the threat of Democratic victories prompted Republicans to increase the party's control over nominations. Similarly, Colorado Republicans changed the state's primary from an open to a closed one in 1928; following a decade of Democratic success, they then instituted a party affiliation test soon after regaining majority status in 1938. According to Cronin and Loevy (1993, 23, 70), these were efforts by a coalition of conservatives in both parties to insulate Colorado from the success Progressives had had in neighboring states.

The role of factions is also evident when one seeks to understand the relationship between reforms and partisanship in the states where legal changes coincided with peaks in support for one party or the other. In Connecticut, as noted above, Democratic gains in the 1950s enabled the establishment of a coalition of Democrats and renegade Republicans seeking to institute the primary. The coincidence between peaks of Democratic support and primary law changes in Utah and Montana, and of Republican support in Oklahoma, also suggest a role for factional conflict.

A change in factional conflict need not, however, be manifested in gains for one party. New Mexico (see Figure 5.3) presents an intriguing example of a state that sought to make larger changes to confront problems in its primaries. As discussed in Holmes (1967), New Mexico's early decades as a state were riven by regional conflicts, and the state's Democratic Party was reluctant to establish a direct primary in the first place because it felt that regional ticket balancing was necessary in order to avoid general election defeat. New Mexico was the next-to-last state to institute a direct primary (not including Alaska and Hawaii), and the original 1940 primary law also allowed for a preprimary convention (one was not actually used until 1950). Partisan opposition to having a primary in the first place was broken by the state's charismatic governor Clyde Tingley, who had sufficient personal clout to push it through the legislature. The state's subsequent abolition of the direct primary in 1956, reestablishment of it in 1962, and abolition of it in 1968 shows not that the primary or the primary system was flawed, but that the state's regions and its large Latino population used primary laws as a means of factional battle, and they were evenly matched enough that slight changes in power in the state legislature—changes that, because they were factional and not partisan, are difficult to measure—resulted in changes in the law itself. Part of the conflict here also pitted incumbent officeholders—who built personal followings and used the direct primary to their advantage—against local party officials. Following the period considered here, the state reintroduced the preprimary convention from 1976 to 1982, but abandoned it again in 1984 (Hain and Garcia 1994).

State patterns such as these provide strong suggestive evidence that partisan aims fuel the decision to enact primary rule changes. Each individual state's efforts may be contextualized with reference to matters other than partisanship: to the aims of individual politicians or movements, as in the case of California and other Progressive states, or to oddities of the state's political, cultural, or geographic makeup, as in the case of New Mexico. When coupled with the aggregate data shown earlier, however, these state patterns do suggest that the trajectory of partisan support in the period immediately before and after the enactment of primary rule changes is not accidental. The evidence may be circumstantial, but this may be the best we can hope for given that (a) rule changes will never be explicitly couched with reference to partisan advantage, and (b) rule changes are unlikely to be consequential enough to make a clear difference in representation. That is, we should not expect a change from an open to a closed primary to be an important enough change to ward off gains for the minority party, even if that was the reason for such a change.

The state patterns shown in Figure 6.3 should be considered, however, with reference to broader changes experienced in all states. To return to the Colorado example, it is of interest that Republicans moved to enact restrictive primary rules before and after the Democratic surge of the 1930s. However, virtually every state in the nation saw a Democratic surge during this period, and similar surges took place in states that did not change their primary rules. There were, in addition, more changes to primary rules in the 1930s than in subsequent decades—changes that may have had more to do with primaries being relatively new and perhaps more subject to tweaks by legislators. There were myriad factors influencing changes in partisanship in the state legislatures, just as there were myriad reasons for changes in primary rules.

One way to contextualize the relationship between partisan volatility and the instances of rule changes shown here is to consider the difference between thinking about what happens before a rule change and what happens afterward. To look at what takes place in a state before a change can provide one with clear evidence regarding the reasons a party was *able* to enact a change. If one looks at what happened after that law was changed, one might infer that legislators saw what was coming and sought to prepare for it, but such an inference would

164 REFORM AND RETRENCHMENT

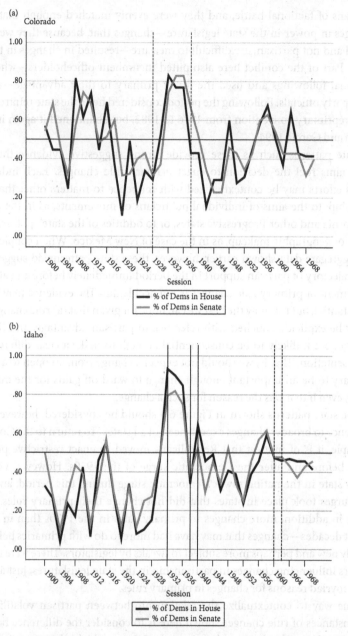

Figure 6.3. Rule changes for a separate group of selected states, 1900–1970

Notes: Vertical lines indicate years with primary election law changes, as described in Table 2.1. Solid lines represent expansive changes, dotted lines represent restrictive changes, and lines with dots and dashes represent changes that were neither expansive nor restrictive.

Source: Seat share data from Dubin (2007) as described in Chapter 2.

PRIMARIES AND PARTISAN ADVANTAGE 165

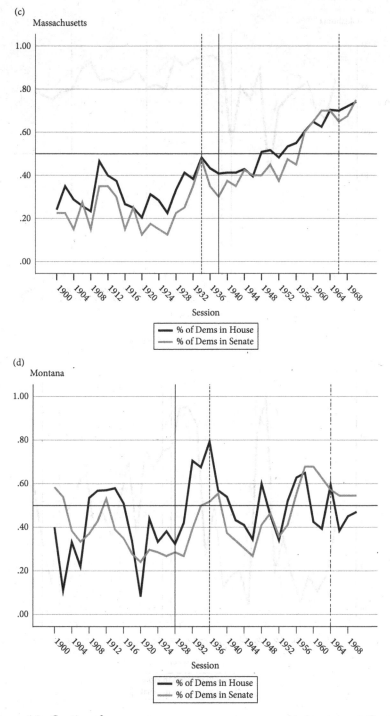

Figure 6.3. Continued

166 REFORM AND RETRENCHMENT

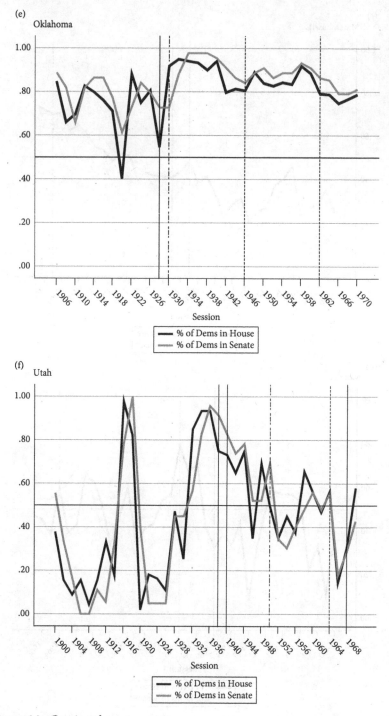

Figure 6.3. Continued

be a substantially weaker explanation for a change. This is not to say that such inferences are groundless; in the Colorado case, Republicans held onto power for longer than did Republicans in some neighboring states, so they likely both saw that they were having difficulties and had time to prepare. In the case of the restrictive changes enacted by states in the early 1960s, the cumulative impact of civil rights legislation and court decisions on redistricting may have signified to some states that primary results were likely to change, but the interval between these legislative changes and the next election cycle gave states time to enact additional primary laws.

The Politics of Personality

It would be naïve to assume that partisan goals would have nothing to do with primary reforms. It is taken as a given in comparative literature that any electoral reforms will be pursued either by majority parties seeking to cement their majority or through collusion of multiple parties, done with an eye toward preventing competition from minor party or antiparty sources. The American case poses a potentially different scenario in that primaries were a reform advocated by antiparty reformers, who did manage to gain legislative majorities in many states. Such reformers tended to espouse electoral reforms on normative, not partisan, grounds. Yet the data here provide strong suggestive evidence that, at a minimum, such reforms were enabled by recent or impending changes in the fortunes of the majority party. The nature of the reforms in question—whether they open up primaries to independents or members of the minority party or restrict voting or ballot access—is dictated by the nature of the coalition that is in power.

There are some important limitations to looking at the relationship between partisan gain and primary reform. First, the baselines here are elusive. Not all states were at the same place, in terms of the relative strength of the parties, at any given time, so we cannot necessarily link particular types of reforms to changes in party support across time or across states. Second (and this point is directly related to the first), many states did not change their primary rules at all during this time period. This list includes some states with quite restrictive primary rules, such as New York and Indiana, and others with very expansive ones, such as Wisconsin. And third, we have no systematic way of identifying the factions or individual politicians who instigated or benefited from primary rule changes. In the California example, for instance, a party faction, the Progressives, and an individual politician, Hiram Johnson, arguably had more to gain or lose from any particular rule change than did their parties as a whole. It is not at all uncommon to observe rule changes that aim to aid a single politician; sore loser laws, for instance, may be catalyzed by the campaign of one particularly consequential candidate.

To illustrate this problem, let us return to three developments that took place in California in the years following the implementation of primaries. As noted earlier, Hiram Johnson went on, after his tenure as governor, to serve for twenty-eight years as a senator, and during that time he continued to advocate for changes to primary laws in California and nationwide. While senators face obvious limitations in their efforts to direct the politics of their states, there is ample evidence in the biographical material on Johnson that he sought, as senator, to advocate for the maintenance and further development of some of the policies he had pursued as governor.

First, let us consider the maneuvering that took place in the state during the 1910s. California had established a nonpartisan direct primary in 1907. In Johnson's opinion, however, the law had gone too far. While Johnson advocated for the direct primary and made rhetorical use of calls for nonpartisanship, he believed that voters should be required to request a party ballot—that is, to state their party membership for the purpose of receiving the ballot of one party or another, but in such a fashion that they did not permanently register themselves as members of a party. In 1913, therefore, the legislature enacted a law allowing for cross-filing: candidates could run simultaneously for the nomination of more than one party. The law was amended in 1917, however, to require that candidates win the nomination of the party in which they were registered in order to appear on the general election ballot. In 1917 Johnson had commissioned a memo on the politics of the state's direct primary and on the importance of maintaining party enrollment for candidates (Memo to Governor Johnson 1916). The memo frames the abandonment of voters' party registration as a recognition that a sizable number of voters did not want to register as Democrats or Republicans, and that voters—especially newly enfranchised women—were being harmed by the requirement:

> Even under the heavy penalty imposed for failure to register party affiliation, namely, debarment for participating in partisan primaries, not all persons would so declare their affiliation. South of the Tehachapi alone, last year, more than 73,000 people refused to state their party affiliations, thus indicating their willingness to sacrifice their right to participate in partisan primaries in preference to registering their party affiliations. While in the whole state the numbers refusing exceeded 117,000.... Since the passage of the law in 1907, people have protested against such requirements as an invasion of their rights, as every registration clerk can testify, and now that women have the ballot it is more unpopular than ever. This large percentage of people have rights that are entitled to protection, especially when their rights can be protected without

jeopardizing or restricting the rights of others who feel differently about declaring themselves.

While Johnson wanted these people's rights to be protected, he felt that having a strictly nonpartisan primary would ultimately sow enough confusion that the voters would sour on the idea of the direct primary altogether. Opponents of the direct primary had relied heavily on the referendum results, and the referendum itself was misleading: the people had voted twice against the nonpartisan primary, and in 1907, when they voted for it, the language of the referendum was difficult to understand. Voters were in effect asked in the referendum to decide a number of unrelated issues with a single vote. The memo points out that within the legislature, those legislators who voted against the statement of party affiliation at the polls were the same ones who voted against the labor proposals of the Johnson administration, thus indicating that Johnson's opponents saw a nonpartisan primary as a means of weakening him. A party affiliation statement, presumably, would enable the governing party to better understand where its voters were and to use this information to organize voters and confer an advantage upon itself in elections.

Thus, the politics surrounding the particular features of California's primary laws were, if Johnson's analysis was correct, all about the incumbent governor and his intention to build a coalition within the Republican Party. Reforms that might seem on their face to be a means of advantaging the voters, of addressing Progressive plans for increasing the role of voters within the parties, were manipulated for precisely the opposite purpose. And public sentiment—as embodied in controversies over what voter intent was in the referendum—was also used as a rhetorical tool by both sides.

Second, primary politics in California became particularly confusing—and particularly susceptible to partisan or factional gamesmanship—once Johnson had moved on to the Senate. In the 1918 election, the top cumulative vote getter, San Francisco mayor James Rolph Jr., was excluded from the general election ballot. Rolph, a Republican, received the most votes in the Democratic primary but finished second in the Republican primary. Because Rolph had lost his own party's primary, he was blocked from the ballot, and hence there would be no Democratic candidate on the November ballot. Although Rolph presented himself as a Johnson supporter, Johnson made no endorsement in the race, either during the primary or afterward (Melendy 1964). The Republican primary victor, William Dennison Stephens, ran as a Progressive but kept his distance from Johnson. Democrats appealed to the California Supreme Court, arguing that their rights had been violated, but the court ruled against them. The end result of the 1918 election, in historian H. Brett Melendy's (1964, 330) accounting, was to sever Johnson from the Progressives. He continued to win Senate elections for the remainder of his career, but he now spoke for himself and for his own faction, not for Progressives. Meanwhile, the Progressive case for nonpartisanship was undermined, and California primaries became, for the next four decades, exercises in intra-Republican factional gamesmanship, not the sincere efforts to overcome partisanship to which some Progressives had aspired.

And third, consider Johnson's own activities after reaching the Senate. As a senator, Johnson was freed of the ability to police the finer features of California law, but he continued to make a rhetorical case for the direct primary and for his preferred variant of it. In his most noteworthy disquisition on the topic, on December 20, 1926, Johnson spoke on the floor of the Senate advocating for the use of the direct primary. While primaries were, by and large, a matter of state law, he sought to use his position in the Senate to defend California's primary and to present it as a model for other states. A defense of the direct primary was necessary, in his view, because many prominent Republican leaders, including former president William Howard Taft and the current vice president, Charles Dawes, had launched a sustained assault on the direct primary. In his 1922 "Liberty under Law" speech at the University of Rochester, Taft had reflected on the use of primaries and argued that they had been a disappointment: primaries were too expensive, they advantaged the independently wealthy, and they had failed to mobilize voters in the numbers that primary advocates had forecast. While Taft conceded that the people had good reason to be hostile to parties and partisanship, the solution was not to place politics in the hands of people who had no responsibility to the party agenda, but to push parties to separate themselves from their factions: to abet the formation of "great" parties that would offer strong, responsible, and patriotic candidates.

Dawes had taken this argument one step further. In a December 18, 1926, speech (Dawes 1926), he seconded a number of Taft's points, but went on to argue that because voters knew little about the candidates appearing on the party ballot, they were voting on the basis of personality, not on the basis of issues. This had decreased the quality of the people elected to the Senate and the House, and it had led both to the election of corrupt legislators who were beholden to particular interests and factions and to a certain unpredictability in Congress: small groups of legislators, no longer beholden to the party agenda, had the ability to obstruct the parties' goals. The result, he argued, was a "bloc" system in which the compromises had little to do with the aims of the public or the parties, what we today refer to as gridlock. Giving the people a greater role in selecting legislators had, in the end, made the legislature less beholden to the people.

Dawes took this argument even one step further. Making note of Italy's chaotic elections and Benito Mussolini's populist appeals, he argued that a failure of party politics played into the hands of aspiring dictators. The stakes were too high to entrust the responsibility of warding off such candidates to the public; instead, party conventions must be used to ensure that legislatures could legislate, and that the public would be able to judge party agendas, not individual candidates. Dawes did note that parties at times had failed in this and had nominated corrupt candidates, but he believed parties were better able to diagnose corruption than were the voters.

In his response, Johnson (1926a, 1926b) rejected a number of Dawes's empirical claims about party performance but also sought to reframe the question: the primary was not about the candidates, but about the voters, about ensuring that voters have a choice. The question had to do with who has the right to choose candidates for office. Candidates might organize voters, which would lead to the risk of wealth being a decisive factor, but there were plenty of examples of politicians who did not have great wealth—such as, one might infer, Johnson himself—who had organized voters successfully. The real danger posed by partisanship was that parties would reflexively support their own, thus increasing the possibility that a corrupt leader or a demagogue might consolidate power in office because there were no individuals or blocs that would stand up to party leaders. Congress must contain some people who could exercise independent judgment. Even a single individual, if not beholden to the party, could serve as the moral conscience of the legislature and stand up for the judgment and rights of the people. Johnson referred to himself here; he was, he argued, a "bloc of one."

While Johnson's rhetorical battles took place before his home state would embark upon the two decades of tinkering with primary laws that have been chronicled here, they all suggest the fungibility of the categories used here: When is a party, a faction, or a bloc truly distinguishable from one individual? While Johnson was hardly a proto-dictator, he sought to direct the California Republican Party, and perhaps the national Republican Party, as a means of advancing his political goals. Where this was not possible, he set himself in opposition to the party. Individual politicians will always stand to gain from any change in election laws, and it is difficult to be certain about the extent to which individual self-interest leads to the framing of laws that are reputedly in the public interest or in the interest of particular factions, ideas, or partisan aims. Johnson may have been the most noteworthy example of a politician who gained from his advocacy of particular primary law changes, but several other such reforms are identifiable in the mid-twentieth-century primary reforms. Other examples include descriptions of the machinations around Thomas Dodd's Senate candidacy in the Connecticut challenge primary in the 1960s (White 1983); the efforts of Democratic New York governors Al Smith and Herbert Lehman to weaken the state's Republican Party (Berdahl 1942); the disagreements between the Kentucky legislature and Governor Happy Chandler in the 1930s (Jewell and Cunningham 1968); similar conflicts between the New Mexico legislature and Governor Clyde Tingley in the 1930s (Hain and Garcia 1994); the evolution of

Nonpartisan League politicians in North Dakota, as discussed in Chapter 3; the efforts of Louisiana governor Edwin Edwards to secure re-election (Parent 2004); and Wisconsin Republicans' efforts to replace Senator Joe McCarthy (Epstein 1958). In all of these accounts, personal ambition for office appears to have had something to do with efforts to change primary laws. It is rarely the case that ambitious politicians admit that they are trying to change the law to advantage themselves; there is always a normative, good government argument available. But we cannot easily separate the two things.

Conclusions

Primary reforms have historically been described using normative "good government" language. They are presented as means of opening up the political process to more voters, of breaking the stranglehold of party bosses, or of preventing hostile voters from "raiding" a party's primaries. That there tends to be a normative rationale here is no surprise, just as it is no surprise that these arguments will be adopted and presented by politicians who have more self-interested goals. Much of the research on primaries has downplayed the actual effects of rule changes. Yet as this chapter shows, it is still possible to disentangle partisan interest from the public interest when considering the timing of primary reforms. The aggregate data, the state time series, and the state narratives here all suggest that primary reforms are taken up by party leaders or factional leaders with an eye toward cementing their own electoral advantage. These reforms all boil down, however, to complex and not always answerable questions of what the intent was, how sincere the claims were, and who the expected winners and losers really were.

7
Are Southern Primaries Different?

Histories of Southern elections feature many demagogic characters whose campaigns were dependent on racist appeals and on outrageous, crude, ad hominem attacks on their opponents. If Northern party politics was often deemed corrupt, histories of the South make it clear that the alternative was no better.

Southern states tend to be left out of many histories of primary elections or to be treated separately. As early as 1928, Charles Merriam listed Southern primaries separately from Northern ones (83). In his broader work on American elections, V. O. Key (1956) considered Northern and Southern primaries separately but argued that sectionalism would eventually decline to the point that one could more easily make comparisons. In studies published at the same time as Key's major works, Julius Turner (1953) and Cortez Ewing (1953) showed that competition worked quite differently in Southern primaries than it did in the North. Havard's (1972, 11–12) volume on Southern elections begins from the premise that the South was in "semi-quarantine" from the North from Reconstruction (1865–1877) until the New Deal Era of the 1930s, and that events during that time which have similar counterparts in the North should not be understood in the same way. In more recent work on the development of primaries, Alan Ware (2002, 17) agrees with Havard. Shorter works contemporaneous to Ware, such as Crespin (2004) and the studies in the Galderisi and Ezra (2001) edited volume, consider Northern and Southern primaries separately, and when Southern primaries are included in any quantitative analysis in these works, a control variable is included.

There are clear empirical reasons for this separate consideration. Yet it may lead us to ignore some of the shared history of Northern and Southern primaries. Many Southern states used primary elections before they had become widely adopted in the North, and the major Southern innovation in the conduct of primaries—the runoff election, also known as the "double primary" or "second primary"—can be justified on grounds other than racial exclusion. Runoff elections in America today are rarely used outside of the South, but they have been used in a variety of other electoral systems, most notably in French presidential elections. Now that we have reviewed the major arguments about the fate of the direct primary over the course of the twentieth century, it is necessary to consider where the South fits. To what extent did the development of Southern primaries follow an entirely different logic than primaries elsewhere? Can we see traces of the four theories about retrenchment and reform in the South, or does the politics of race so overwhelm concerns about the mechanics of elections as to make the South entirely irrelevant to the story we have considered thus far?

One premise of this book is that we can see state experimentation with primaries as a test of how well primary election laws have been adapted to accommodate the political circumstances of the different states. As such, externally imposed rules—or external shocks—may force states to choose rules that do not really fit. The post-1968 push by the Democratic Party to standardize primary rules is one reason the bulk of the historical consideration here ends in the late 1960s. The South, as we shall see, experienced two external shocks during the mid-twentieth century: the Supreme Court's decision in *Smith v. Allwright* (321 U.S. 649 (1944)) to prohibit states from establishing primary rules that prevent African Americans from voting, and the 1965 Voting Rights Act, which prohibited poll taxes, literacy tests, and other means of limiting African American participation in elections. These two steps taken by the federal government to intervene in state primaries prompted responses throughout the South. For much of this period, however, Southern states tended to treat primary elections as private affairs, and the various states' Democratic Parties were given substantial latitude to adapt primary rules as they saw fit. As a consequence, when reforms were made in the South, changes that would have been legislated in other states were adopted informally.

The South did, however, have some of the same experiences with primaries that have been explored in the previous chapters. The South did have a Progressive movement of sorts, and this is reflected in some Southern primary laws. Some Southern states' primaries were shaped by nonparty movements, and the Nonpartisan League (NPL), the subject of Chapter 4, did influence politics in some parts of the South. Southern states had some of the same technical problems as Northern states. And although two-party competition in the South was rare, it is also possible to see some Southern primary laws as efforts to prevent threats from the minority party. In short, the same theories that have been explored in the previous four chapters have some relevance to the South, but we must first account for the one-partyism of the South, the efforts to limit or prohibit Black voting, and the responses to federal government decisions.

In this chapter I provide a history of changes to Southern primary laws. I then summarize the bearing each of the theories of this book has on Southern primaries—that is, how we can understand Southern primaries and primary law changes as being about anything other than efforts to limit the political power of Black voters. Following this, I address the question of whether primary election laws that are uniquely Southern, such as the runoff election, can be understood as being about anything other than race. The discussion here suggests that we should not necessarily treat Southern primaries as being sui generis on account of their racial dynamics. Whether because of the lack of two-party competition or because of the racial history of the South, however, it is difficult to draw lessons from Southern primary law changes that might provide insight into other states' efforts to reform primaries.

Southern Primary Elections in Theory

Political Scientists' Theories about Southern Elections

The major political science works on Southern elections have tended to view primary elections through the prism of one-party politics and as one of many ways in which Southern state governments sought to prevent African Americans (as well as some whites) from playing a role in political decision-making. There are two major foci in these studies: the effects of the direct primary and the origins of the direct primary. While it might make sense chronologically to consider the origins of the direct primary first and then its effects, the course political scientists have taken is actually the reverse. The most influential studies of the mid-twentieth century sought first to understand how the direct primary fared in practice during the near-century of one-party rule in the South. In the best-known account, *Southern Politics in State and Nation*, V. O. Key (1949) considered the question of whether it is in fact appropriate to apply theories of party behavior to one-party systems. In other words, his concern was whether a one-party system is really a party system at all. He showed that the use of the primary to resolve conflicts created a politics of shifting, often unstable, factions. Individual politicians could construct primary coalitions organized around sectional interests or simply around a charismatic personality. There was, however, no way to ensure that these coalitions would persist or outlive the politicians who created them. There was variation across Southern states in the level of atomization, or the number of factions one might identify. Yet there was no enduring role in the politics of any of these states for ideology or policy divisions, and in most states demagoguery became a necessity for politicians looking to distinguish themselves. Key's emphasis, then, was on how primary election conflicts vary across states, but he provides few reasons why politicians might seek to change the primary.

The typologies developed by Key provided fertile soil for political scientists in the decades to follow, but for the most part these subsequent studies have sought to extend Key's story, to explore changes in Southern politics, and to consider the continuing relevance (or lack thereof) of Key's book during the civil rights era and the return of two-party politics in the South in the years to follow.[1] Some authors, however, did seek to amend Key's story about the effects of the primary. David Lublin (2004), for instance, notes in his account of Southern politics after Key that Democratic primaries remained dispositive long after African Americans had regained the right to vote in them. He discusses the ability of legislators to change their policy positions substantially without repercussion. This prevented the formation of any sort of enduring liberal movement in the South. Skillful white Democratic politicians realized that they could modulate the way they talked about race, depending on their audience, without facing any consequences. For the most part, one-partyism advantaged elites, although it was at times exploited by individual liberal candidates with a populist, anti-elite message such as Ralph Yarborough in Texas. The Southern primary, Lublin argues, thus succeeded in containing conflict long after it had lost its explicitly racial rationale for doing so.

While Key focuses principally on the consequences of the primary, some subsequent studies of Southern elections have made claims about the rationale for the primary. It is easy to take for granted the contention that the direct primary was instituted in order to prevent African Americans from voting. Yet some authors from the 1970s on have sought to complicate this story. In his study of Southern politics from 1880 to 1910, J. Morgan Kousser (1974) shows that suffrage restrictions preceded primaries by a decade or more. African American disfranchisement had already happened by the time primaries were established, so the impetus for adopting the primary must have been about something else. The establishment of the direct primary gave Democrats the ability to control the electoral machinery: to count votes and to determine whether Black votes are cast or are counted. At the same time, the veneer of democracy established by the primary was a means of bringing renegade white voters, most notably the populists, into the party. The rationale for the primary was to encourage the sort of factionalism and demagoguery that Key documented.

Aldrich and Griffin (2018) provide a history of Southern elections that largely corroborates Kousser's approach. Primaries established parties as private associations; this made it harder for new parties to form and for issue differences to prompt politicians to exit the party. By establishing and defending the Democratic Party in this way, Southern politicians were able to establish an internal politics that corresponded more closely to the practices of authoritarian regimes than to the norms of democratic politics. Dissenting arguments were resolved well before the electorate had a chance to seriously consider them, elections were a foregone conclusion, and politicians were rarely held to account when they abandoned the policies that they had advocated during their campaigns. The association between Progressive electoral reform ideas outside of the South and the Republican Party meant that there was little external pressure on these politicians. Aldrich and Griffin, along with Robert Mickey (2015), argue that this type of authoritarianism gradually broke down over the course of the twentieth century, and that whatever one might say about contemporary Republican dominance in the South, it is more democratic than what preceded it. Their comparison with authoritarian politics also, however, brings to mind the problems noted in Chapter 5 in separating the stated rationale for any sort of political reforms from the interests at stake. That is, just as observers from democratic countries do not trust contemporary authoritarian governments' stories about how their elections are conducted, we should perhaps look with suspicion on the reasons offered by Southerners about why they conducted their elections as they did during the first half of the twentieth century.

Collectively, these accounts make a persuasive case for treating Southern primaries differently. To the extent that they were about race, the incentive structure would seem entirely different than it is for other politicians. In other states, politicians might find reason to encourage or discourage some of their opponents' supporters from voting, but the establishment of a voting system premised on the disfranchisement of a sizable percentage of the potential electorate would seem categorically different from the practice elsewhere in the United States. Similarly, while there were many enclaves in the North where one party, usually the Republicans, prevailed, there were few Northern states where there was no possibility of two-party politics. According to these accounts, differences between North and South in the nature of party conflict and in the ability of one party to control the electoral machinery might make us suspicious that any of the drivers of election reform that we have documented in the North would be of relevance in the South.

Historians' Theories about Southern Elections

While political scientists' accounts of Southern primaries have emphasized the primary's role in structuring (or failing to structure) one-party politics, the major Southern historians have tended to discuss the primary as a feature of Southern political discourse or culture. Dewey Grantham, for instance, argues (1983, 10–13) that the Southern direct primary had the same intellectual roots as the Northern primary: it was the result of dissatisfaction with political machines and of a desire to reduce the power of the conservative elites who ruled the parties. Like other Southern historians, Grantham emphasizes that Southern states adopted the primary before most Northern states; although in many cases (as I discuss more below) these primaries were not mandatory or paid for by the state, they show, says Grantham, more of an openness to political reform in the South than the political science literature would suggest.

There are two related qualifications to this argument, however. First, Southern arguments about electoral reform, reducing corruption, or increasing the number of voices in elections were all predicated on excluding Black voters. C. Vann Woodward (1971, 347) contends that there is some evidence that the primary was successful in achieving these goals; overt corruption and cheating, he argues, declined with the adoption of disfranchisement and the direct primary because politicians found cheating to be less necessary. Grantham (1988) disputes claims that the Southern Democratic Party was not a "real" party during the first half of the twentieth century. It was, he says, able to perform all of the functions that a party does precisely because Black voters were excluded, and internal debates thus could be resolved democratically without the fear that whites would lose power.

Second, as Grantham discusses at length in *The South in Modern America* (1994), the elites that Northern reformers railed against tended to be the bosses within their own states, or in some instances, of business from their own states or neighboring states. For Southerners, the elites whose corrupting influence reformers worried about were often Northerners. This meant that any change to elections must be designed to insulate the state from outside influence. And here, again, one characteristic of the perceived intrusions of Northerners had to do with race—calls to allow Blacks to vote, to reduce segregation, and so forth were all seen as external impositions by the federal courts or by Northern political leaders. Over time, this led to a cultural attachment to the Southern electoral system: the institution of the white primary, the runoff system, and the style of campaigning practiced by Southern politicians.

The historians' approach is incorporated into contemporary political scientists' accounts as well. There is a vast political science literature on the realignment of the South and on the rise of the Republican Party in the South in the latter decades of the twentieth century. While many of these studies are framed as responses to Key—as efforts to ask whether the typologies of intraparty competition in *Southern Politics in State and Nation* are still relevant—they tend to treat midcentury Democratic primaries as cultural institutions, or as instances in which one candidate presents an account of Southern exceptionalism in a way that transcends party and wins over voters who choose Republicans in presidential elections. Lamis (1984a, 225) concludes that from the 1960s into the 1980s, individual Southern politicians chose either to clarify party conflict (as Senator Strom Thurmond did in South Carolina) or to blur party divisions (as Senators Herman Talmadge of Georgia and John Stennis of Mississippi did). Earl Black and Merle Black (2002, 46–39) similarly discuss the prevailing view that Southern senators and representatives were "long-term investments" and emphasized their seniority, committee chairmanships, and ability to procure district benefits in their re-election campaigns. For each of these authors, the primary thus has a cultural significance in preserving the Southern way of life and insulating the South from Northern elites.

The historians' arguments, then, do not necessarily dispute the arguments Key and other political scientists have made, but they do suggest that there is a rationale for cataloging changes to primary laws in the South, for exploring why they happened, and for seeing whether we can see these reforms as a matter of anything other than race and one-partyism. As we shall see, the story about changes in Southern primary elections is relatively simple. There were relatively few reforms to Southern primaries during the period from the 1920s to the 1970s, yet it is possible to see some of the same stories elaborated upon in the prior chapters in play. However, Democratic dominance meant that some changes may be difficult to detect because parties had the latitude to make changes without legislating them. Grantham's account, furthermore, suggests that we can seek to understand the history of the Southern primary with reference to the main theoretical frames of this book: we can explore the relationship between the Southern primary and Progressivism, group capture, poorly drafted laws, and party advantage. This sectionalism, or the sense of grievance against outsiders, gave Southerners powerful reasons not to change their election laws with the frequency that Northern states changed their primaries. And the possibility (and in two instances described below, the reality) of exogenous influence on the primary—in the form of federal court decisions—adds a source of primary election reform in the South that did not exist elsewhere.

A Brief History of Southern Primary Election Reforms

The story of the adoption of the Southern primary bears some resemblance to the story in the North. South Carolina is generally considered to be the first state to establish a direct primary; it did so in 1896. Grantham (1983, 10) describes the reasons for adopting the direct primary there as being similar to the reasons in the North: dissatisfaction with machine politics and a desire to weaken the political power of conservatives. At the same time, other states were experimenting with electoral mechanisms that were somewhat like the direct primary. Alabama and Georgia both developed delegate selection primaries for the state party convention; these created a county unit system for state offices that resembled the Electoral College. In the years preceding passage of the Seventeenth Amendment, Alabama also held a "pall-bearer's primary" to choose senators-in-waiting for the governor to appoint should there be a vacancy during his term (Hackney 1969, 270).

The Mississippi Constitution of 1890 gave the legislature the power to enact primary election laws, and calls for establishing a primary grew in Mississippi during the 1890s, but the legislature did not respond until 1902. Some counties had used a primary during the 1890s, a practice that was widely seen as being prone to manipulation by party leaders. The mandatory direct primary law of 1902 established a uniform primary date, but the law still allowed counties to control ballot access and permitted local officeholders to sit on the party committees, in effect allowing them to select their opponents (Kirwan 1951, 123–127).

Some southern states did not adopt the direct primary until after it had become common in the North. North Carolina, for instance, did not establish a primary until 1915; according to Grantham (1983, 361) this was a response to President Woodrow Wilson's advocacy for primaries. What all of the early adopters in the South have in common, however, is an informal primary process that gave the Democratic Party far more latitude than Northern parties had in establishing ballot access, choosing primary dates, or determining voter eligibility. Parties and candidates could manipulate primary laws according to temporary circumstances. For instance, after a vacancy arose for one of Mississippi's Senate seats in 1910, LeRoy Percy challenged former governor James Vardaman to a voluntary primary, which would not necessarily have had any bearing on the state legislature's decision about who to appoint but would have allowed the candidates to take steps to show how popular they were among voters (Vardaman declined, Percy was chosen by the legislature, and Vardaman won the 1912 election; see Kirwan 1951, 211).

Southern states also generally required parties to finance their own primaries, a practice that insulated the Democratic Party from general election competition. According to Mickey (2015, 56), seven Southern states had mandatory primaries during the 1930s and 1940s, but four of them required the parties to pay the costs of holding the primary, and in three others the state paid the cost of the Democratic primary but not those of other parties. Parties often passed these costs on to candidates. This practice reduced competition and insulated incumbents and other well-off candidates, but it also led to some bargaining among candidates; Key (1949, 423) reported that in states with a runoff it was common for minor candidates to run in the first primary and then give their support in the runoff to whichever candidate was willing to cover their primary expenses. This practice persisted in much of the South until 1972, when the Supreme Court's decision in *Bullock v. Carter* (405 U.S. 134 (1972)) held that Texas's assessment of large filing fees violated the equal protection clause of the Fourteenth Amendment.

This informality and party control facilitated Democratic hegemony in the South. The establishment of the direct primary in Mississippi and Texas had enabled Democrats to incorporate populists or other nonparty groups into the party. As the direct primary matured, matters that were legislated in other states and applied across all parties could be applied temporarily and selectively in Southern states. Many American states, for instance, passed laws requiring a loyalty oath for primary candidates and voters, or required some other demonstration of willingness to support the party nominee in the general election. Democratic Parties in some Southern states also employed loyalty oaths, but then changed the text of these oaths in 1948, following the Dixiecrat rebellion in the presidential race, from requiring candidates to affirm that they supported all party nominees in the past election to requiring them only to affirm that they had supported party nominees for state, county, and district offices (Heard 1952, 138).

This brings us to the subject of race and disfranchisement. Most Southern states passed disfranchisement laws during the 1890s and 1900s, at the same time that primary elections were becoming the norm. It is easy to link the two, to see the primary as a means of establishing white dominance. On the one hand, one can read Southerners' wariness of the Northern movement for the direct primary as a manifestation of a Southern concern for ensuring that Black voters be kept out of the primary. Valelly's (2004, 156–158) account of Reconstruction Era politics notes that Southerners valued the role of parties in making their own election laws and sought to avoid drawing national attention to their primaries lest they become vulnerable to the idea that the government might have a role in regulating primaries. On the other hand, some Southerners with sympathies for the Progressive movement told national audiences that the exclusion of Blacks from the primary was only temporary, until Black citizens could be properly educated, and that one day they would welcome them back into the Democratic Party.

Rather than being a uniform movement with clear links to the primary, disfranchisement moved in fits and starts and was also often driven by temporary concerns. Southern states introduced suffrage restrictions gradually between the mid-1880s and the early 1900s.[2] Many Northern states did so as well.[3] These restrictions were not exclusively targeted at African Americans; poll taxes and literacy tests, to give the two most obvious examples, disfranchised many white voters as well. They were also not specifically about the primary. Some politicians were quite explicit about this; North Carolina governor Charles B. Aycock, for instance, at one point stated (approvingly) that the white voters of western North Carolina had given up their right to self-government for the sake of disfranchising Black voters (Woodward 1971, 346), and at another point expressed his hope that disfranchisement would in the long run bring about "a larger political freedom and a greater toleration of opinion. . . . The Republican Party will be freed from the stigma of being called the 'Negro party'" (quoted in Kousser 1974, 72).

The most important feature of suffrage restrictions was that they could be used flexibly, according to the needs of the parties and the decisions of local party officials. Hence, poll workers could decide whether to administer any sort of test if the voter in question, whether white or Black, could be expected to vote against the interest of local leaders. In Mississippi, poll taxes were occasionally paid for large numbers of voters if they were expected to be compliant. In 1940, Ralph Bunche of the National Association for the Advancement of Colored People (NAACP) estimated that there were approximately 250,000 Black voters in the South—not a large number, to be certain, but indicative of leniency in some states, for some voters (Lawson 1976, 53).

Many of the exclusions of voters were predicated, then, on the status of political parties as private entities, or at least as entities with substantial latitude in enforcing voting rules. Most of the legal challenges of the 1930s, 1940s, and 1950s focused on these practices and the efforts to formally and informally establish a "white primary" in the South. The white primary is best seen as an outgrowth of episodic efforts by politicians to engineer a favorable electorate. Some Southern states had connected removing Blacks and poor whites from the electorate with the establishment of the primary itself; in Alabama, for instance, competing Democratic factions agreed that they needed to do this as early as the 1890s in order to prevent some politicians from reaching out to these groups, and the governor advocated for a direct primary on these grounds (Hackney 1969, 148). Laws explicitly restricting party membership to whites, however, came later. In Texas, for instance, the establishment in state law of a white primary stemmed from the efforts of an unsuccessful 1918 gubernatorial candidate, D. A. McAskill, who believed Black voters had contributed to his defeat. Prior to 1918, candidates had competed for Black votes in many parts of the state, and candidates promised patronage to Black voters just as they did to other groups (Lawson 1976, 24). Similarly, in the 1944 South Carolina gubernatorial primary the poll tax limited Black voting, but the candidates still competed for the support of eligible Black voters; establishing a white primary was intended to remove this temptation (Mickey 2015, 103).

Although by the 1940s many Southern states did have primaries restricted mostly or entirely to white voters, then, restricting the primary to white voters was one suffrage restriction among many. It was an effort by politicians and parties to make the primary electorate more predictable. It was distinctive to the South in that it was explicitly about race and in that it was more predicated on articulating a degree of private autonomy for parties that was different from what Northern parties had done. In other regards, however, the trajectory of Southern primaries followed that of Northern primaries: there was an initial surge in voter turnout following the establishment of the direct primary, and afterward primary turnout declined. In competitive primaries, however, it remained approximately as high as it was in competitive races in one-party parts of the northern and western United States.[4]

In sum, for much of the first half of the twentieth century, Southern states' changes to the direct primary took a different form from those of Northern states, for two reasons. First, the primary was established earlier than in many Northern states, although it was often less formal and thus less subject to legislative changes. Second, the dominance of the Democratic Party in the South ensured that concerns about the relationship between primary laws and general election success for the parties were different. It is certainly true that the primary was used to perpetuate white dominance, but it is even more the case that the primary was used to perpetuate Democratic Party dominance.

These features can help us explain what appears to be a relatively placid history of experimentation with primary laws when one uses the *Book of States* and Overacker data. Table 7.1 lists all legislation regarding primary election law changes over the period from 1928 to 1968 in the South. The table follows the example of the major works on the South of the mid-twentieth century in using the thirteen-state definition of the South, including the eleven states of the Confederacy plus Kentucky and Oklahoma.[5] Although the two added states had slightly different histories of using the direct primary than did the Confederate states, I consider these states together because of their shared history of discriminatory laws and one-party Democratic dominance. Figure 7.1 shows the timing and direction of Southern primary law changes, following the same format as in Chapters 2 through 6.

Figure 7.1 shows that Southern states moved in a uniform direction in the middle decades of the century, establishing runoff elections to bring order to the Democratic Party's dominance and imposing ballot access tests and other measures that one might associate with the Southern Democratic Party's racial politics during this time. This by no means suggests that we cannot understand some southern states' primary reforms as a consequence of factors identified in the various hypotheses considered earlier in this book. However, it does suggest that the direction of primary reform in the South was more consistent than in the North.

Not only is the number of primary election law changes smaller than is the case for the other state groupings considered in the previous chapters, the types of changes are also different, as befits the one-party, white-dominated Southern system. There are only seven primary law changes before 1944 that were consequential enough to be noted by Overacker or the *Book of States*. Oklahoma had only become a state in 1907, and its 1906 Constitution was an elaborate document heavily indebted to Progressive Era ideas. The reforms in Oklahoma over this period (and for that matter, into the 1960s) gradually rendered Oklahoma primaries more like those of other Southern states. Another peripheral state, Kentucky, had enacted a mandatory primary in 1912, made it optional in 1920,

Table 7.1 Primary Law Changes in Southern States, 1928–1968

State	Year	Direction of Rule Change	Description
Oklahoma	1928	Restrictive	Challenge frivolous candidates
North Carolina	1928	Expansive	Expand primary
Florida	1930	Neutral	Runoff
Oklahoma	1930	Neutral	Runoff
Alabama	1932	Restrictive	Stricter ballot access
Kentucky	1936	Restrictive	Mandatory primary
Florida	1938	Restrictive	Party affiliation test
(*Smith v. Allwright*)	1944		
Arkansas	1946	Neutral	Runoff expanded
Oklahoma	1946	Restrictive	Thresholds
Texas	1948	Restrictive	Higher thresholds
Alabama	1948	Restrictive	No write-ins
Arkansas	1948	Restrictive	No write-ins
Georgia	1950	Neutral	Runoff expanded
Virginia	1952	Neutral	Runoff
Mississippi	1962	Restrictive	Identify incumbent on ballot
Oklahoma	1962	Restrictive	Misc. stricter rules
Virginia	1962	Neutral	Spending limits for primaries
(Voting Rights Act)	1965		
Arkansas	1968	Restrictive	Open to closed

Source: Author's data, drawn from *Book of States* and Overacker (1928, 1930, 1932, 1934, 1936, 1940), as described in Chapter 2.
Note: Louisiana, South Carolina, and Tennessee had no primary law changes during this time.

but then returned to a mandatory primary in 1936. The reintroduction of the mandatory primary in 1936 was the result of factional conflict between the state legislature and the governor (Jewell and Cunningham 1968), and its reintroduction stabilized the competition between the two party factions.

Apart from these sets of changes, all that one observes on this list before 1944 is a small number of efforts to tighten restrictions for voters and candidates and a pair of late introductions of the runoff. Why is there so little change? Apart from the fact that some changes were matters of internal party rules, as opposed

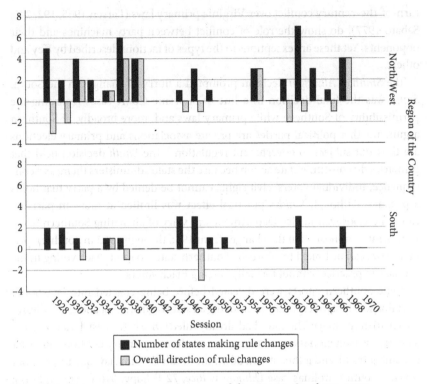

Figure 7.1. Primary rule changes by year and direction in Southern states, 1928–1970

Notes: The figure on the y axis is the net number of changes in state primary laws for each session; the session date listed on the x axis is the final year of the two-year legislative session. The "number of states making rule changes" category includes changes that were neither expansive nor restrictive.

Source: Author's data.

to state legislation, and thus escaped cataloging by our sources, three reasons stand out, all of which have to do with one-party dominance. First, one of the most common concerns among Northerners was the possibility of raiding or defections. There was little need in the South to modify primary voting rules, to change from open to closed primaries or vice versa, because there was nowhere else for voters to go. Second, there was no reason to believe that competition in the primary had any influence on the general election, so there was no reason to reduce competition on that ground. And third, because Southern politics was characterized by weak parties, a lack of party machinery, and shifting, personalized factions, there was no motivation to change the primary in order to advantage any one side. Some of the small number of changes we do see here, as in Kentucky, and some changes too early to include in the data, such as the turn-of-the-century conflict over Virginia primary laws (Larsen 1965, 192, 245; Sabato 1977), do show the role of conflict between party machines and their opponents. Yet these are exceptions to the types of factions described by Key and others.

The *Smith v. Allwright* decision prompted a flurry of changes in the South. *Smith* was the final decision in a line of Supreme Court cases regarding the permissibility of Southern white primary laws and, more broadly, of Southern arguments that political parties are private associations and primary elections are thus not subject to government regulation.[6] The *Smith* decision held that primaries do constitute state action because the state administers them; as a consequence, individual voters' civil rights cannot be denied by a party that holds a primary. Although *Smith*'s practical effect was limited at first—in part because the Roosevelt Justice Department was wary of alienating Southern white Democrats—almost all of the changes from 1946 through 1952 in Southern primary laws can be linked to efforts by Southern states to limit Black voting in the primary in practice without formally barring Black voters.

Some Southern efforts were defeated before being enacted into law. South Carolina was first to respond, by removing all state regulation of and expenditures related to the primary. The court had already ruled twice in the past decade that the federal government has an interest in the conduct of primary elections, in order to combat fraud, and it thus struck down the South Carolina law quickly, without hearing South Carolina's case (*Elmore v. Rice*, 72 F. Supp. 516 (E.D.S.C. 1947); Lawson 1976, 45–53). Following South Carolina's failure, other states moved quickly to exert greater control over nominations. The three remaining holdouts established runoff provisions, Oklahoma and Texas raised the thresholds for ballot access—thereby making it easier for the state to remove candidates—and Alabama and Arkansas moved to prohibit write-in candidacies. All of these laws were not explicitly about race, but they did reduce the risk for white Democrats that multicandidate primary races would empower Black voters.

This era also featured a number of other attempts to bring greater order to the primary process. Arkansas separated state and federal primaries and established campaign spending limits for candidates, but not for parties, in order to give the party a greater role in selecting nominees (Key 1949, 482, 637). Texas Democrats established an informal white primary, known as the "Jaybird primary," in which white candidates would compete before the actual primary and after which the losers would drop out. While it is difficult for the government to police such informal agreements, the court did strike down the Jaybird primary in *Terry v. Adams* (345 U.S. 461 (1953)). The ruling observed that the Democratic Party was so dominant in Texas that there was no plausible way for the loser in such a race to successfully contest the outcome in the actual primary or general election (Issacharoff and Pildes 1998).

Another string of improvised attempts to respond to *Smith* took place in Georgia. In 1946, the Georgia legislature followed South Carolina's model and repealed all primary laws, but the governor vetoed this legislation on the grounds that it was a wasted effort because it would be struck down by the Supreme Court (Key 1949, 636). Georgia legislators responded not only by expanding the use of the runoff election but by tightening voter registration rules, requiring regular reregistration (Mickey 2015, 119–128), and establishing segregated voting places (Weeks 1948). Georgia was one of several Southern states that required all candidates, not just Democrats, to be chosen through a primary in order to appear on the general election ballot.

Cumulatively, these changes show the intersection of suffrage laws and primary election laws—many Southern states took steps to make it difficult for Black voters to vote in the primary election and the general election. It is therefore difficult to precisely categorize what is and is not a primary election law in some instances. What is clear is that this set of primary law changes represents a uniquely Southern circumstance: the need to respond to an external influence in the form of the *Smith v. Allwright* decision. *Smith* had limited effects in terms of actually allowing Black voters to participate in primaries; the NAACP's Bunche estimated in 1947 that the number of Southern Black voters had tripled, from 250,000 to 775,000 (Lawson 1976, 53). Yet detailed accounts of the *Smith* decision contend that it forced Southern states to explore more and more convoluted and legally questionable means of disfranchisement, which ultimately contributed to sparking the civil rights movement (Zeldin 2004, 132; Klarman 2014, 231–248).

Table 7.1 also shows a small number of primary law changes enacted at the time that the civil rights movement was gaining force. These are mostly minor in nature and took place in peripheral Southern states, so it would be a stretch to call them a response to the Voting Rights Act or other federal interventions into Southern elections of the 1960s. Some Southern primary rules designed to enhance party control were struck down at this time, however. The Voting Rights Act did explicitly apply to primaries, so literacy tests, poll taxes, and other restrictions were removed. Just as consequentially for some Southern states, the three major redistricting decisions of the era (*Baker v. Carr*, 369 U.S. 186 (1962); *Wesberry v. Sanders* 376 U.S. 1 (1964); and *Reynolds v. Sims* 377 U.S. 533 (1964)) brought an end to the Electoral College-like means by which Georgia had chosen primary winners and ensured that Southern primaries would all be direct primaries (Mickey 2015, 318). Mickey reports that one result of this was that in the state's 1966 gubernatorial primary runoff in Georgia, two avowed segregationists reached the runoff but then realized it would be to their advantage to compete for Black votes.

Evaluating the Applicability of the Theories to the South

It is easy to tell a story a story about Southern primaries that emphasizes the South's distinctive concern with segregation and with combatting attempts by the North and the federal government to change its electoral laws. The South was, however, influenced by developments in Northern elections. And as we saw earlier, some Southerners did take pride in the South's early adoption of the direct primary. With the basic history of Southern primaries established, let us consider the relevance of broader theories of primary election law change to the South.

Progressivism and Its Aftermath

As is the case with the direct primary, so the Progressive movement in the South tends to be treated entirely differently than does the movement in the North. Some scholars of Progressivism have been willing to grant that municipal government reforms in the South had something to do with the movement (Kirby 1972, 3–4, 43–49). Many of these same observers go on to caution that the term "Progressivism" was often just used opportunistically, by Southerners and by Northern Progressives, to signify opposition to the status quo. William Link (1992) and Dewey Grantham (1983, 1994), however, both have emphasized that there was a vibrant Progressive movement in the South, but that this movement took on a different form than in the North because the South was more agrarian and because of the matter of race. Link (68, 95) notes that Progressivism could easily be paired with a belief in white supremacy; the Progressive contention that expanded democracy must be supplemented by expertise and education led, in the South, to an emphasis on excluding Blacks from politics until they could be properly educated to participate intelligently. Similarly, Progressive concerns about reducing corruption became, in the South, arguments that Black voters had been tools for corruption and fraud in elections. Disfranchisement was presented by some Southerners as a part of Progressive reform, and some Northern Progressives who held racist views of their own accepted this argument (Grantham 1983, 112; Bateman, Katznelson, and Lapinski 2018, 16–25). Whereas Northern Progressives decried the role of businesses or political bosses in elections, Southern criticisms of meddling in elections were directed at Northerners or the federal government. Hence, Progressivism emphasized regionalism to a greater degree in the South than in the North.

There is some debate about how this mutation of the Progressive movement influenced the history of the direct primary. Some Southern historians have argued that the South's early adoption of the primary enabled democratic efforts to achieve Progressive goals, particularly in Mississippi. There, the establishment in 1902 of a direct primary had produced a white electorate supportive of Progressive electoral reforms such as the initiative and referendum, but also of Progressive economic reforms in public health and the workplace (Ranney 2019, 106-113). These achievements may not have been recognized by Northerners because of the demagoguery of politicians such as Theodore Bilbo, James Vardaman, and Arkansas governor Jeff Davis, but if one considers their policies there is little doubt that they pursued reforms similar to those championed by Northern Progressives (Sanders 1999, 166; Woodward 1971, 372-394).

The fact that the direct primary was adopted in many Southern states before the Progressive movement, however, means that any efforts by Southerners to connect the two appear more as rhetorical ploys than as descriptions of what transpired. It is plausible to make the case, as Hackney (1969, 247, 324) and Kirwan (1951) do, that the direct primary was a response to populism. But even at the height of the Progressive Era, some Progressives had low regard for the Southern primary because it was often not mandatory and still gave such a major role to parties in paying for it and organizing it. W. A. White (1910, 50) singled out the Texas primary as a Progressive invention, because it had been enacted through a referendum, but dismissed the others. Woodward (1971, 372-394) responds to White, however, by alleging that most of the Southern Progressive reforms took place very soon after enactment of direct primary laws, indicating that by White's own test (see Chapter 3), the South actually outperformed the North in pairing electoral and social reform.

The complicated links between Southern and Northern Progressivism make it difficult to speak of a "decline" of Southern Progressivism. Many accounts of the decline of Progressivism in the North emphasize the particular issues at stake—increased immigration, changes in manufacturing, or concentration of wealth—all of which had less relevance to the South than to the North. While it is true that some Progressive reforms were overturned in the South, some these changes took place somewhat earlier than was the case in the North—for instance, the Mississippi Supreme Court struck down the initiative and referendum in 1922 (Ranney 2019, 112). Southerners were broadly supportive of Progressivism at the national level, as long as much of the enforcement was left to the states. Yet the South's recognition after 1928 that it could no longer play a role in selecting the Democratic nominee reduced Southern interest in supporting what was left of national Progressivism (Grantham 1994, 111). The absence of a credible Republican Party in the South, in addition, meant that Southerners had few reasons to make common cause with Progressive Republicans (Aldrich and Griffin 2018, 109). And the few Southern Republicans that there were tended to focus more on patronage than on political advocacy (Casdorph 1981, 175). Altogether, the separation of Southerners from national politics by the mid-twentieth century meant that Southern political institutions became more insulated from national trends by then than they had been at the beginning of the Progressive Era.

Hence, despite the potential links between the Progressive movement and the early years of the Southern direct primary, there is little evidence of an organized backlash on the part of political elites to the Progressive Era in the South once Progressivism had receded. There is one possible exception to this rule, however: the peripheral Southern state of Oklahoma. As Goble (1980, 214–215) reports, the constitution Oklahoma adopted in 1906, upon admission to the union as a state, was a long and complicated document, heavily indebted to the Progressive movement and packed with new proposals for governmental innovation. Among these was a requirement that both parties hold a direct primary for all offices. The retrenchments listed in Table 7.1 for Oklahoma do clearly indicate that the Democratic Party had given up a substantial amount of flexibility, which it gradually took back. This is not a linear path, however. For instance, in 1937 Oklahoma still had enough of a reform movement that it successfully suspended for a time the use of the primary runoff out of concern that doing so would place an undue fundraising burden on candidates (Ewing 1953, 14). Oklahoma's more complicated history of changes in its primary places it more in the company of the NPL states or Progressive reform states described in earlier chapters than is the case for any other Southern state.

Preventing Group Capture

In Chapter 4 we explored the effects of nonparty movements on primary election laws. The direct primary, as we saw there, was both a means of preventing nonparty groups from influencing elections and a way of incorporating the demands of such groups into the two-party system. While the most consequential group of this nature, the NPL, focused its efforts on the northern Plains states, its influence was felt in some Southern states as well. In addition, other movements that appealed to rural voters also gained a foothold in the South.

The NPL was the most consequential organized nonparty movement to come along after the adoption of the direct primary, but for the most part Southern states were not sufficiently threatened by it to pass laws designed to contain it. As a consequence, some candidates endorsed by the NPL were able to succeed running as Democrats. The most successful candidate was Oklahoma's Jack Walton, who won the 1922 gubernatorial race by putting together a coalition of NPL supporters, socialists, and union activists. Although Walton won the general election overwhelmingly, his was very much an individual victory. He had few supporters in the legislature from either the Democratic or Republican Parties, and following a tempestuous eighteen months in office he was impeached and unanimously removed from office by the Oklahoma Senate (Tindall 1967, 222–234). Walton's fate is illustrative of the individualistic nature of Southern campaigns and the difficulty Key reported that organized factions had in playing a role in Southern elections.

Just as Progressive influence in the South was diluted by the fact that Southern primaries were established earlier and with greater party control than those in the North, so group influence in Southern primaries was tested earlier than in the North. Many accounts of the Mississippi primary law of 1902 indicate that one goal in its establishment was to encourage populists to run as Democrats instead of forming their own party (Kirwan 1951, 56). Populists did not necessarily support this plan, believing that fraud was as likely to be deployed against them in primaries as in general elections. Yet the trajectory of Mississippi politics over the subsequent decades looks similar to that of the NPL, in that candidates with substantial support from people outside of the party mainstream were able to win office but ultimately only established personal followings that did not challenge the party or create any sort of enduring movement.

Other states had similar, albeit less dramatic, experiences. The Southern Farmers' Alliance, formed in the 1870s in Texas, held a series of nominating conventions of its own during the 1890s in order to choose slates for candidates to run in both parties' primaries. The Alliance was active in several other states as well, but in those states it often functioned more like an interest group than a party; it supported successful candidates in Tennessee, North Carolina, Kentucky, Mississippi, and Georgia, and it put its support behind the populist presidential ticket in 1892 (Woodward 1971, 202–238; Saloutos 1964). Early primary laws were manipulated in some states to combat Alliance influence; for instance, Texas enacted a poll tax in 1902 for the purpose of limiting Alliance strength and then promptly abandoned it once the threat from the Alliance had receded (Key 1949, 535).

The lessons of groups such as these were not lost on those who would champion voting rights for African Americans. African Americans in South Carolina established their own party, the Progressive Democratic Party, and held their own primary. This primary had many different functions: it served as an endorsement, as a statement of support for the Democratic Party, as a way to show the preferences of voters who might not be able to vote in the actual primary, and as a way to educate African Americans on political issues (Heard 1952, 192–200). The South Carolina effort drew support from the NAACP, which was interested in showing that black voters were capable of casting informed votes and in combating the perception that Black voters had in the past tended to be "bought" through corrupt means.

In the decades following *Smith*, groups representing Black voters also adopted a sort of hybrid group/party model in some states. During the 1960s the Tennessee Voters Council organized on behalf of gubernatorial candidates sympathetic to Black voters' interests (Greene and Holmes 1972, 183). A group calling itself the National Democratic Party of Alabama ran African American candidates against individual state politicians (such as Governor George Wallace and Senator John Sparkman) that it deemed particularly hostile toward Black voters (Lamis 1984a, 80). And three members of the Black delegate slate to the 1964 Democratic Convention from Mississippi, the "Freedom Democrats," ran for Congress in the 1966 general election as independents, using the Freedom Democrat moniker (Fortenberry and Abney 1972).

This history suggests that the Southern party system was not particularly hospitable to organized insurgency. By the time the populist threat had receded, there was little reason to fear such movements, but the Democratic Party had the tools to counter threats if necessary. None of the primary law changes documented in Table 7.1 appear to be direct responses to such efforts, except perhaps (again) for Oklahoma's changes. The adoption of runoff elections in the few remaining Southern states that did not already have them made it more difficult for insurgent candidates to succeed, but the timing of these changes makes it clear that they were more about race than about other types of insurgencies. As Havard (1972, 9) claims, the absence of any sort of mediating institutions prevented sustained collective action in the South.

Bad Primary Laws

In Chapter 5 we explored means of categorizing different types of bad or defective primary laws. Some primary laws, I showed there, truly had drafting errors or other problems that caused them to be unworkable, while in other instances allegations that laws were "bad" were raised for disingenuous reasons, by those who were opposed to the primary itself or to the party that benefited from it. Given the one-party nature of the South and the disfranchisement of Black voters, there certainly are grounds to criticize many aspects of Southern primaries or of the suffrage restrictions that accompanied the introduction of the primary. Yet as we have seen, many of the changes to Southern primaries that led to expansion of the franchise were imposed from without, through U.S. Supreme Court decisions, not through states' changes to their primary laws. Southern governments, in other words, had no reason to respond to sincere allegations from outsiders that the primary did not work. Furthermore, the widespread equation by Southern whites between Black voting and corruption and fraud means that we should treat with suspicion any allegation on the part of Southern state governments that they were changing the primary to reduce corruption. To put this in the language used in Chapter 5, the evidence regarding Southern primary law reforms for much of the twentieth century strongly suggests that reforms are a function of malpractice, of efforts by the governing party to render elections less democratic, at least as far as matters of race go.

It is possible, on the margins, to find some race-neutral instances of ways that Southern primaries were modified. In the early years of the direct primary, the conflict in Mississippi over whether to establish a uniform primary date is one example of this: reformers there argued that fraud could be reduced if all candidates ran on the same day (Kirwan 1951, 127). Later, Ewing (1953, 19) argued that Southern states, like Northern ones, experienced problems with "spot" candidates during the 1920s and 1930s: candidates with no chance of winning the primary, who chose to run (or were encouraged to run) in order to reduce other candidates' vote share. Spot candidates might share a last name with a more popular candidate, for instance, or they might simply clutter the ballot. Several of the changes shown in Table 7.1 might serve to limit such candidacies; Ewing suggested, however, that the establishment of the runoff primary made such candidacies less effective because no such candidates were likely to make it past the first round. This perspective is not shared by all students of Southern politics; others have alleged that strong candidates would seek to manipulate the first primary by strategically diminishing the vote share of others in order to get their preferred opponent in the second round (Kirwan 1951, 229).

One can raise similar claims that, in the abstract, some Southern reforms might be good ideas. For instance, deliberations in several states about the merits of having the state government pay the costs of holding the primary, as opposed to financing them through candidate filing fees or party expenditures, might involve legitimate claims about what is the most democratic choice. In Arkansas, a 1948 change in campaign finance laws for primaries was framed as a matter of preventing wealthy candidates from buying elections (Key 1949, 482). The law allowed, however, for unlimited party spending in primaries, leading some to suspect that the real intention here was to limit the spending ability of insurgent candidates, candidates supported by the Ku Klux Klan, or Republicans.[7] In other words, reforms that might have had the effect of improving problematic laws might have been adopted even if this was not the sole motivation behind their adoption.

Party Advantage

In Chapter 6 I showed that changes in primary rules often coincided with changes in partisan control of state legislatures. Parties looking to maintain the status quo act to exert greater control over the primary process, while parties at a disadvantage seek to expand the electorate and loosen restrictions on primary election voting and candidacy. Changes in party control of the state legislature also bring about changes in primary laws, particularly when the state has not historically been competitive in the general election.

The Democratic Party maintained large majorities in almost all Southern states throughout the period considered in this book. It is possible to find short-lived Republican Party gains in some peripheral Southern states, as I noted in the discussion of Oklahoma in Chapter 6. For the most part, though, there are no obvious moments we can point to when Republican gains coincided with changes in Southern primary laws.

This does not mean, however, that primary election law changes were not a means of securing an advantage for Democrats. Most Southern histories stress that the very establishment of the primary was a means of ensuring Democratic dominance. Some early accounts of the direct primary predicted that in the long run the primary, along with restrictions on Black voting, might help the Republican Party. North Carolina governor Charles B. Aycock predicted, for instance, that Republicans would no longer be seen as the "Black party" and could compete with Democrats on the issues of the day (Kousser 1974, 72). Decades later, however, historians are unanimous that such claims were wrong or disingenuous. Sabato's (1977) history of Virginia elections concludes by noting that the direct primary was deliberately employed by Democrats to contain conflict within the party and to limit the growth of the Republican Party even as Republicans gained Southern support in presidential races. Several of the accounts discussed earlier of the development of the direct primary—particularly of the Mississippi direct primary—also show that third-party movements of the late nineteenth century were harmed by establishment of the primary.

The most obvious way Democratic dominance in the South was secured was through the establishment of the runoff or second primary. The effect of the runoff was to prioritize intraparty competition over interparty competition, to ensure that ideological or issue-based cleavages were contained within the Democratic Party. As Key showed, it was impossible for durable factions to form within the party. Even voters who were perennial losers in Democratic elections—most obviously African Americans, but others as well—had an incentive to remain Democrats.

Rules regarding the financing of primaries also were a means of cementing Democratic dominance. In the four states where primaries were for most of the twentieth century paid for by the parties, Republicans were often unable to conduct primaries (Heard 1952, 105). Some states, in turn, required that only candidates who had won a primary were eligible to run in the general election. As a consequence, in Arkansas there were far more polling places for Democratic primaries, and Republican candidates were simply unable to mount campaigns that voters would notice (Blair and Barth 2005). While higher ballot eligibility thresholds or filing fees in Democratic primaries might seem not to be a means of penalizing Republicans, the lower barriers to entry into Republican primaries could in practice lead to more extreme or lower quality Republican candidates. More often than not, however, the requirement that parties hold primaries, and pay for them, in order to nominate general election candidates resulted in uncontested general elections (Casdorph 1981, 68–69; Mickey 2015, 244).

Some of the rules designed to restrain Republican influence could be manipulated as needed. The loyalty oath, as discussed earlier in the chapter, was a means of punishing Democratic candidates or voters who strayed from the party, but it could be suspended or changed in order to bring back defectors when necessary. Democrats were also sensitive to the value of maintaining the appearance of two-party competition. In Georgia in the 1920s, a group of Republicans in Fannin County (a rural area on the state's northern border) asked the state party to help it finance a primary. The resulting primary, restricted to white voters, produced candidates who posed no serious threat to the Democratic nominees, but they also led to increased conflict among Republicans, which ultimately worked to the advantage of Democrats (Holland 1949). Alexander Heard (1952, 107) also recounts instances in which Republicans reached out to Democrats, looking to field a candidate who would not actively campaign or pose any sort of threat to Democrats but would appear on the ballot. Many Democrats were sensitive to the interest on the part of local Republicans in holding patronage positions under Republican presidents and were willing to help out quiescent state and local Republican organizations in order to maintain amicable relationships with them (see, e.g., Heersink and Jenkins 2020).

Southern primary rules, then, had the effect of maintaining Democratic dominance, as did a wide range of informal practices undertaken by the various state Democratic Parties. There are few instances in the South in which a Republican threat seems consequential enough to have precipitated any of the changes shown in Table 7.1, but many changes intended to secure white dominance in Southern elections had the effect of securing Democratic dominance as well. Some of the more prescient accounts of Southern elections of the midcentury (e.g., Heard 1952) forecast that Republicans would eventually be able to mount a more serious challenge, but this challenge did not actually arise until the late 1960s or later.

Unique Features of Southern Primaries

Any observer of Southern primary elections today can find evidence that some laws intended to restrain Black voting continue to shape elections, even in an era when Black voter turnout routinely approaches or exceeds white turnout in Southern primary and general elections.[8] We are able, then, to think about the effects of Southern primary innovations today in a way that does not just focus on the effort to exclude African Americans from the process.

The Runoff

The principal Southern primary election law innovation was the runoff election, also referred to as the "second primary." Although the Democratic Party was firmly in control of the South at the time the direct primary was adopted, the runoff was not adopted at the same time as the primary in most states. Table 7.2 shows the pattern of adoption of the runoff. Only Mississippi and Texas adopted runoff elections before 1915; other states adopted it much later, for a variety of reasons and with different thresholds for when a runoff would be required. Arkansas, Georgia,

Table 7.2 Adoption of the Direct Primary and the Primary Runoff in Southern States

State	Direct Primary	Primary Runoff	Changes to Runoff	Notes
Mississippi	1902	1902		
Texas	1905	1905		
North Carolina	1915	1915		
South Carolina	1898	1915		Adoption of runoff coincided with mandatory primary law
Georgia	1898	1917	1950	
Louisiana	1906	1922		
Florida	1902	1930		
Oklahoma	1908	1930		
Alabama	1902	1931		
Arkansas	1900	1933	1946	
Kentucky	1912	1935	1936	Runoff abandoned after one cycle
Tennessee	1917	1937		Runoff optional, limited use
Virginia	1905	1952		Runoff optional, limited use

Source: Column 2, Hirano and Snyder (2019, 30–32); column 3, Bullock and Johnson (1992, 3); and columns 4 and 5, author's data from *Book of States* and Overacker (1928, 1930, 1932, 1934, 1936, 1940), as described in Chapter 2.
Note: States in **bold** adopted direct primary at the same time as the runoff.

and Virginia either adopted it or expanded the use of it in the years immediately following the *Smith* decision, although it was never widely used in Virginia and was abandoned entirely in 1969. Kentucky used a runoff for one election cycle during the 1930s. Four nonsouthern states—Maryland, Utah, Arizona, and South Dakota—have used the runoff at various times. The blanket, top two, or jungle primary systems used today in Washington, California, and Louisiana also function similarly to the Southern primary, with a nonpartisan primary followed by a runoff between the top two finishers in place of the general election.[9]

The runoff was therefore not an inevitable feature of the Southern direct primary or of the effort to prevent Black voters from playing a decisive role in the primary. Southern states did not necessarily have the data to test theories about the effect of the runoff on elections; hence, historical accounts suggest that the runoff was seen as establishing a "psychological white primary"—as a means of providing an extra insurance measure limiting the influence of Black voters (Kousser 1984). In a system in which few African Americans could vote, it ultimately appeared unlikely that their votes would matter for either of the candidates in the runoff, however. Instead, the existence of a second primary encouraged candidates running in competitive, multicandidate fields in the first primary to try to distinguish themselves through demagogic language regarding race. In primaries featuring an incumbent, the runoff provision encouraged a personalized politics in which issues did not matter (Key 1949, 204) and incumbents faced the possibility of a coalition of the "outs" from either the left or the right (Lamis 1984a, 202). Although not noted at the time, a contemporary finding that candidates are more likely to attack each other in the runoff than in the first primary seems likely to be generally applicable to all primaries with a runoff (Bullock et al. 2019, 78).

There have been two major efforts to catalog the consequences of the runoff system. In a 1953 book, Cortez Ewing synthesized several anecdotal accounts along with some state data, to show that double primary Southern states had more unopposed candidates than did other Southern states. Although incumbents were more likely to run unopposed, when they did face strong enough competition to be forced into a runoff they won less than half of the time. Ewing did not provide an unambiguous answer to why the existence of the double primary might lead to less competition, although he suggested some of the variation may be explained by differences in the political culture of double primary states. He also noted, however, that some candidates might also be deterred by the costs associated with running in two primaries. The fact that the double primary was introduced the earliest in Mississippi and Texas, two states with strong nonparty movements, suggests that the runoff was intended to clarify competition, not deter it. And Oklahoma's short-lived abandonment of the double primary in 1937 was, according to Ewing (1953, 14), undertaken out of concern for limiting candidate expenditures.

Four decades later, Bullock and Johnson (1992) tested four theories about the effects of runoffs: that they disadvantage the frontrunner, that they disadvantage incumbents, that they disadvantage women, and that they disadvantage Black candidates. They conclude that Ewing actually overstated the success rate of incumbents in primaries, but by the 1990s there was no support for any of the other three claims. They conclude that the runoff had the effect of limiting support for Republicans or for nonparty or third-party movements, but that there was no evidence that either the design or the intent of the runoff was to prevent Black candidates from winning or Black voters (who, again, already faced many barriers to voting for much of the twentieth century) from voting.[10] While one major effect of the runoff provision might have to do with turnout—compelling voters to vote a second time might benefit candidates with more extreme and dedicated supporters, or might benefit candidates whose supporters were more reliable voters—neither study found strong turnout effects.[11]

The runoff thus became an integral part of Southern elections, and it likely made sense there because of one-partyism, not racial discrimination. It is entirely plausible to consider that in a runoff today, one candidate might be penalized on account of his or her race or views about race, but this purported effect is only possible because enough barriers to Black voting have been dismantled that it is possible for Black candidates to mount competitive campaigns in the South. It is perhaps possible to envision runoffs between two white candidates where one candidate was called to account for racial liberalism, but such events say more about the attitudes of voters than about the design of primaries.[12] There have also been some recent Republican Party runoffs in which candidates sought the support of Black Democrats.[13]

In the analyses in the earlier chapters of this book of the relationship between different reforms and the role of parties in the primaries, I categorized the runoff as a neutral reform: one that neither helps nor hurts parties' efforts to control the primary process. It might be more accurate to say that the effects are mixed. On the one hand, the runoff ensured continued Democratic dominance in Southern elections. On the other hand, however, there are numerous instances in which the runoff failed to ensure the election of incumbents or other party-preferred candidates. Recall that Key and others disputed the notion that the Southern Democratic Party was organizationally coherent or did the things a "strong" party does. A candidate preferred by party leaders might have greater opportunity to make it into a runoff, but opposition forces had an opportunity to coalesce around an alternative. Southern elections show frequent instances in which candidates corralled forces hostile to the status quo into winning primary coalitions, and the de-emphasis on issues and the shifting nature of primary factions also undermine whatever power party leaders might have wielded.

To further assess the effects of the runoff on party control, one might consider the effect a runoff would have in a system unlike that which prevailed in the South at the time. Primary runoffs in the contemporary South can be evaluated based on their effects on the general election—that is, one might compare states to determine whether candidates who face runoffs do worse in the general election than candidates in similar states that do not have them.[14] One could also measure the effects of the presence of general election runoffs on the parties; in the small number of instances in which minor party candidates play a significant role, do runoffs enable more moderate candidates of either party to get elected? These are concerns that might factor into any decision about whether runoff provisions strengthen or weaken parties, but such concerns were not relevant in the South until after the Republican Party's return to relevance.

Suffrage Restrictions

While the runoff is certainly the most distinctive feature of Southern primary laws, it is not the only one. Several of the states discussed here had idiosyncratic rules, adopted to address fleeting circumstances or short-lived political movements. The South was also distinctive, of course, in its efforts to limit suffrage. Because the primary election was more dispositive for choosing officeholders than the general election, it is challenging to separate primary election laws from suffrage restrictions. As noted earlier, it is not evident that the direct primary and the disfranchisement of Black voters were undertaken at exactly the same time, although the two sets of laws did frequently interact.

Several analyses of Southern politics have presented histories of suffrage restrictions, data regarding the major laws on the subject, and accounts of Supreme Court jurisprudence on the subject.[15] Each of these studies has noted the steady diet of changing suffrage laws throughout the period from the close of the Civil War in 1865 until the 1960s (and even beyond). Klarman (2004, 135), furthermore, notes that suffrage restrictions could be implemented by norm, by party rule, or by law; these various paths make it difficult to provide a complete and accurate catalog of restrictions. Many of the regional studies considered here, especially those of Mississippi, Alabama, and Georgia, note further that individual counties were given wide discretion in whether to use or impose their own restrictions.

To be certain, the South was not the only part of the country to impose suffrage restrictions; Indiana, to give just one example, adopted in 1917 a detailed set of questions that functioned the same way the Southern "understanding clause" did (Kousser 1974, 48). One might also contend that many nonsouthern states used loyalty oaths or other tests designed to prevent raiding or crossover voting. Yet again, it is possible to trace Northern laws of this nature to partisan competition. Bateman, Katznelson, and Lapinski (2018, 55–56) argue that Southern politics throughout the twentieth century was characterized by distinctive periods of high and low anxiety about race and about Southern influence in U.S. politics. The primary was adopted at a period of low Southern anxiety; Southerners did not feel that their methods of conducting elections were under threat, and hence they could speak of the primary as part of a national movement toward greater democracy while at the same time empowering the Democratic Party to limit Black voting. Legal conflicts over suffrage and over the primary both increased during three "high anxiety" periods during the middle of the century (1935–1941, 1949–1951, and 1961–1967). This explanation suggests that suffrage law changes, like primary law changes, respond to the same external stimuli.

Conclusion

The purpose of this chapter has been to show how theories about the evolution of primary elections apply to the South. Many researchers have treated the South as a separate case when looking at twentieth-century American political development, as a region in "semi-quarantine." As I have sought to document here, formal changes to Southern election laws were often driven by outside (that is, Northern or federal) influences. Southern politicians could often achieve their goals through less formal modifications to primaries. In addition, it is difficult at times to separate the imperatives for white Southern politicians of maintaining dominance from the rhetorical need to describe Southern elections in terms that would resemble the normative beliefs of election reform advocates outside the region. The South shared with the rest of the United States an enthusiasm for primary elections and for the notion of democratizing candidate selection. The lack of any alternative to the Southern Democratic Party, and the relatively unstructured politics within the Democratic Party, meant that even when Southern states adopted laws that looked like Northern laws, the results were often different.

PART II
WHAT THE HISTORY OF PRIMARY ELECTIONS CAN TELL US ABOUT CONTEMPORARY REFORM IDEAS

8
Contemporary Primary Reform Efforts

What is the contemporary relevance of the history of state primary laws that we have considered so far? While there is, as I have sought to show, a logic to many of these reforms, the trajectory of reforms defies a simple narrative. It does not show that parties asserted control over the primary process, nor that in practice primaries failed to live up to the promises of Progressive Era reformers. Instead, primary election law changes have just as often been motivated by efforts to secure partisan or factional advantage as they have been driven by efforts to strengthen democracy. There has been no path toward more democracy, nor are primary elections, regardless of the form they take, a vehicle toward greater democracy. This lesson is every bit as relevant in today's politics as it was during the early twentieth century.

It would be tempting for modern scholars to look back on the history of primary elections, however, and fault reformers of all types for being guided by folk theories. As I shall document in this chapter, we know today that changes in primary election laws are often guided by such theories—the belief, for instance, that making primaries more open to candidates and voters will weaken parties, benefit candidates with agendas that do not fit neatly into the prevailing party ideologies, or increase voter turnout. Similarly, advocates of restrictive primary laws have contended that closed primaries will give parties a greater role in selecting nominees who can win general elections, will ensure more moderate nominees, or will enable party leaders to broker intraparty conflicts. Contemporary research has shown, however, that primary election reforms are blunt tools that do not necessarily yield any of these results. Or, to put matters more directly, there is little evidence that the reforms discussed in this book make much of a difference in election outcomes.

We might look charitably on past reformers by acknowledging that they did not know their reforms would be ineffective. There is a logic to these folk theorems, and the data were simply not there to disprove these arguments. Today, however, we do have copious evidence that beliefs such as these are mistaken. Yet as I shall document in this chapter, states continue to tinker with their primaries, and primary reform efforts continue, guided by these same beliefs.

The previous chapters of this book considered successful efforts to change state primary laws. One problem with that analysis of primary law changes during the 1930s, 1940s, 1950s, and 1960s is that it is prohibitively difficult to gather information on legislative proposals during this period. One can identify successful efforts to change laws, but it simply is not feasible to assess claims about what parties, or individual legislators, tried to do. Claims such as Alan Ware's (2002, 227) observation that more than 70 percent of states with direct primaries experienced repeal efforts in the 1920s may serve as evidence of an organized movement to alter primaries (especially since these efforts appear to have been coordinated by the same people), but beyond this period one can neither assess whether these legislative proposals were idiosyncrasies nor systematize this claim across multiple states and multiple years.

It is possible, however, to identify all legislative proposals to change primary laws in recent years. This is an important endeavor for three reasons. First, it enables us to draw conclusions about what parties try to do. We cannot necessarily use proposed legislation to understand parties' motives in the past, but we can seek to understand how majority and minority parties seek to use primary election laws strategically, how contemporary liberals and conservatives think about primaries, or how recent or impending changes in party control of the legislature influence decisions about whether to open or close primaries. Second, we can use contemporary proposed primary election laws to determine whether beliefs about the effects of these laws continue to influence legislators. And third, the preceding chapters have shown that there are distinctive regional or state-specific patterns in willingness to experiment with the primary; we can see whether contemporary primary law legislation still conforms to these patterns.

The National Conference of State Legislatures (NCSL) has since 2000 maintained a searchable database of introduced legislation for all states. The NCSL data provide the ability to analyze efforts to change primary laws. In this chapter I draw upon the NCSL data to describe primary election legislation introduced over the past fourteen years, compare it to past legislation in the states, and assess the likely partisan aims behind the legislation. I look for patterns in legislative introductions according to region of the country, past history with reform efforts, party, and majority or minority status. I conclude that partisanship is the major determinant of efforts to introduce primary law reforms, with Democrats exhibiting a preference for loosening restrictions on primaries and Republicans exhibiting a preference for enhancing party control. Republicans, however, are more concerned with party control in legislatures where they are in the majority; Democratic proposals seem driven more by ideology and less by a quest for partisan advantage. The chapter provides a summary of literature on the reasons for the introduction of particular laws and the limited evidence of the effectiveness of these laws. I then provide a general description of what has been proposed since 2000. Following this, I break down the data according to the partisan goals behind the proposed changes and the history of primary reform in the states where legislation has been introduced. This analysis serves both as an extension of this book's historical account into contemporary politics and as a prelude to considering why primary reforms rarely yield effects and how we might use our knowledge of primary laws to think more constructively about changing American elections.

The (Limited) Consequences of Primary Election Law Reforms

In the previous chapters I explored four arguments about why reform laws were enacted: the decline of Progressivism, reactions to insurgent movements such as the Nonpartisan League, the growing evidence that some primary laws simply were poorly written, and the rise of two-party competition. Although these hypotheses are neither mutually exclusive nor always borne out by the evidence, they can also easily be generalized to account for contemporary electoral phenomena. To wit:

- Certain characteristics of primaries may have a left/right dimension. Open primaries and nonpartisan primaries, for instance, have been championed by contemporary progressives and opposed by conservatives.
- Nonparty movements continue to occur within American politics; in recent years, to take an obvious example, the Tea Party movement has substantially changed the nature of many state Republican Parties. Competition between the Republican establishment and insurgent factions may still be reflected in efforts to alter primary rules.
- Many states still experience basic problems in their electoral systems, particularly when new and untested laws have been introduced.
- Finally, changes in party competition may still lead to efforts by majority parties to seek to use electoral law to lock in their advantage or to disadvantage opponents. This is likely to be less consequential when one party has a very large and stable advantage.

These possibilities suggest that we should be sensitive not only to the circumstances under which primary laws are enacted, but to those under which they are proposed. Unlike our focus in Chapters 2 through 7 on successful primary law implementation, however, looking at bill introductions enables us to look at the losers: Do minority parties introduce legislation designed to help them win elections? Do contemporary progressive ideas that succeed in progressive states also get introduced in other places? In short, what can we infer about the goals not only of those who succeed in changing the law but about those who fail?

Asking questions such as these, however, requires that we have a basic sense of what legislators think they will accomplish by introducing legislation. There are several literatures on the results (or lack thereof) of particular types of changes in primary laws. For most of these literatures, general election competition, candidate ideology, primary competition, voter turnout, and the success of party-preferred candidates are dependent variables. Summarizing these literatures does not presume that legislators know exactly what will happen as a consequence of their ideas, and in some cases, legislators may think they will get results that political science tells us are not that likely. Nonetheless, it is sensible to briefly summarize findings on what particular reforms accomplish.

Open and Closed Primaries

The most substantial literature on this subject concerns the differences between open and closed primaries. In closed primary systems, only voters who have previously registered as party members can vote in primaries; open primaries allow any registered voter to vote in any party's primary; and semiclosed and semiopen primaries allow some flexibility for voters to choose which primary ballot they will take on primary day. One common presumption about such laws is that closed primaries will advantage party-preferred candidates. The voters excluded from such primaries are believed to be more moderate, or less committed to the party, than registered party members. Open primaries, in contrast, have been said to advantage either insurgent candidates or more centrist candidates; they have also been said to be more subject to mischief-making on the part of nonmembers who may deliberately vote for the weakest general election candidate.

Research on this matter, however, has been mixed. Closed primaries do have lower turnout than open primaries (Geras and Crespin 2018), but there is little consensus on how this slightly reduced turnout influences other matters of concern. Some studies have also contended that open primaries lead to greater general election turnout (Calcagno and Westley 2008); Gerber and Morton (2003), however, argue that this is only the case for Republicans. Many state-specific studies, such as McBeath and Morehouse's (1994) study of Alaska politics, have documented claims by individual politicians that crossover voting is occurring and that a shift from open to closed primaries has been advocated by politicians aiming to prevent members of the opposing party from interfering in their primaries or to prevent their party from being pulled toward the political center.

Studies that seek to connect candidate ideology to primary systems have found very small differences and have noted that state culture is a more likely cause of variation than primary rules (Norrander and Stephens 2012). Nonetheless,

Gerber and Morton (1998), Kanthak and Morton (2001), and Kanthak and Loepp (2018) find that semiclosed and semiopen primaries produce more moderate congressional nominees than pure closed or pure open primaries. Bagashka and Clark (2016) argue that candidates elected through closed primaries show a greater level of particularism in their legislative activities. Other recent articles (McGhee et al 2014; Rogowski and Langella 2015) find no significant ideological differences by primary type for state legislators. And studies of "crossover voters" in open primary states have concluded that voters who cross party lines tend to be weak partisans who are voting sincerely, as opposed to voters meddling in the opposition party's primary in order to deliberately choose a weak nominee (Norrander 2018; Hedlund 1977). Norrander and Wendland (2016) conclude that given the complexities of individual elections and of party coalitions in each state, there is little evidence that the simplistic arguments about which party would benefit from open or closed primaries would be borne out by changes.

Nonpartisan, Blanket, or Top Two Primaries

Over the past two decades, electoral reform advocates, often on the political left, have advocated for the blanket or top two primary. In a blanket primary, voters are given a unified ballot and are permitted to vote for candidates of either party, with the top Democrat and top Republican proceeding to the general election. In a top two primary, the top two finishers, regardless of party, proceed to the general election. In either system, it is presumed that moderate candidates would be advantaged, particularly those running in districts that are safe for one party or the other. We have limited evidence, however, about whether this is the case. California adopted a blanket primary for the 1998 election, but the blanket primary law was struck down by the Supreme Court (in *California Democratic Party v. Jones*, 530 U.S. 567 (2000)) before the 2000 primary took place. California has used a top two primary since 2012, and Washington and Louisiana have also employed variations on the top two.

In a volume on California's experience with the blanket primary, Gerber (2001) concludes that the blanket primary did not have a noticeable effect on turnout, competition, or candidate ideology, but she cautions that it would be premature to draw firm conclusions based on a single election cycle. To date, however, research on the top two primary (Alvarez and Sinclair 2014; Kousser, Phillips, and Shor 2018; Masket 2013, 2019) has found few significant effects. A recent article by Grose (2020), however, argues that top two primaries in California have begun to yield more moderate legislators. Even were one to ultimately discover that California politics has changed, though, it would still be easy to argue that this is a reflection of California political culture or of the difficulties of disentangling the top two primary from the state's citizen redistricting law, which took effect at the same time (McGhee and Shor 2017). Studies of the primary in Louisiana (Parent 2004) and Washington (Donovan 2012) have also entertained claims that nonpartisan primaries advantage moderates but have cautioned that their states' distinctive political cultures make it difficult to draw firm conclusions.

Election Timing

The consequences of election timing are less well understood than most other primary reforms. Many early studies of primary elections posed plausible arguments about the optimal time for primaries. Merriam (1908, 137) posed the basic problem: if primary elections are too early, voters are less likely to focus upon them, and the general election will be too long—perhaps sufficiently long that voters will come to regret their primary choice. If they are held in the summer, no one will pay attention. If they take place in the fall, lesser candidates may be disadvantaged in the general election, and intraparty wounds may not heal. Geiser (1923) contended that early primaries would yield more costly general elections for candidates. More recent research has largely echoed these claims: Galderisi and Ezra (2001) contend that late primaries are more divisive for the party, while also observing that states with traditionally strong political parties tend to hold their primaries earlier. They also note that the dynamics of primaries can be changed by separating presidential primaries from nonpresidential ones, although they do not specify which is better for parties. High turnout in contested primaries can add an element of unpredictability to down ballot primaries. Elazar's (1999) study of Minnesota politics contends that Minnesota had the worst of both worlds: its February party-endorsing caucus was too early, prompting challenges to the party-endorsed candidates, but its September primary was too late, giving nominees too little time to run a general election campaign.

More recently, several studies have considered primary timing in the context of larger models of primary election turnout or competition, but results have been mixed. Johnson, Petersheim, and Wasson (2010; see also Lazarus 2005) investigate the relationship between primary election timing and general election divisiveness, concluding that early, divisive primaries can be harmful to incumbents. Galderisi and Ezra (2001), in contrast, contend that late primaries are more divisive for the party, while also observing that states with traditionally strong political parties tend to hold their primaries earlier. Kaufmann, Gimpel, and Hoffman (2003) contend that early presidential primaries can advantage more ideologically extreme candidates. Two dissertations on primary election rules (Sabella 2009; Kurlowski 2014) use primary election timing as a variable in models predicting turnout or competition; both conclude that it has little effect. Another recent dissertation uses primary dates to determine whether members of Congress change their voting habits or other legislative activities at the time of their primaries (Schmitt 2013). In a study of Spanish primary elections, Ramiro (2016) contends that early primaries can boost a party's general election vote share, while later primaries reduce it.

Despite the fact that legislation to change primary dates has been common since the inception of the primary, and despite the logic inherent in so many arguments about the merits of different primary dates, my own work on primary timing, which draws on data for congressional primaries from 1984 through 2014, shows no effect of primary timing on candidate competition or candidate spending (Boatright, Moscardelli, and Vickrey 2017). We did find that turnout decreases slightly in later primaries (Boatright, Moscardelli, and Vickrey 2020). It is difficult, however, to separate the effects of primary timing from the effects that concurrent presidential and subpresidential primaries have on turnout, and it is also difficult to control for state political culture. While there may be some normative arguments for holding primaries later, the evidence we have found on election results does not seem to justify making moving primaries around as much of a priority as it has been in many states.

Preprimary Endorsements and Conventions

Claims about party interests regarding openness and timing are thus somewhat complicated. The implications for parties of preprimary endorsement procedures are not. Any provision for parties to endorse candidates—including preprimary conventions, endorsing caucuses, or noting party endorsements on the primary ballot—is to the advantage of party organizations. Conventions almost by definition do winnow the number of candidates competing in the primary. The effects of endorsements, however, are not entirely clear. In one of the first studies of endorsements, Wallace (1923) argued that preprimary conventions tended to merely remove long shot or frivolous candidates from the ballot.

Much later, Herrnson (1998) reviewed the twelve states that allowed preprimary endorsements and concluded that endorsements were ineffective. Sabella (2009) found that turnout is lower in states with endorsement procedures, and Elazar (1999, 72–75) argued that in the case of Minnesota, party endorsements can actually harm candidates, depending on the mood of the electorate and the representativeness of the endorsing convention. Party endorsements today are rare (Dominguez 2013). Nonetheless, it has been found that endorsements from party leaders can be beneficial to candidates, regardless of the laws governing the primary (Hassell 2018), and parties in states such as California with nonpartisan primaries have fought to have party endorsement, or at least party affiliation, included on the ballot.

Runoff Elections

Primary runoff elections, traditionally used in the South, are also a means for parties to enforce order upon the primary process. The logic behind them, as discussed in Chapter 7, is that they prevent factional candidates from emerging victorious in multicandidate primaries; they provide parties with an opportunity to influence elections once the field has been winnowed to two finalists. Some studies have alleged that runoffs give an advantage to more conservative candidates (Gerber and Morton 1998). Others have explored whether they disadvantage African American candidates, although they have found no evidence that this is the case (Lamis 1984b; Bullock and Smith 1990). These can be seen as party-enhancing results, given the nature of the Southern Democratic Party for much of the twentieth century, but it should be noted that Southern party organizations have been weaker than their Northern counterparts, so it is not clear that these results are necessarily preferred by the parties. Runoffs can also be unpredictable because they tend to have extremely low turnout, so they may be more to the advantage of politicians (particularly those with loyal followings) than of party organizations. Some early studies debated what the threshold should be to trigger a runoff; there are many plausible reasons why a threshold of less than 50 percent might be appropriate, but it is not always certain what the interest of party organizations would be in such cases.

Alternative Voting Methods

A small number of primary reform proposals during the 2010s have sought to introduce alternative voting methods into party primaries. The most common such proposal is ranked choice voting (RCV), also sometimes referred to as instant runoff voting. In a ranked choice election, voters list the candidates in order of preference; if no candidate receives a majority of first-choice votes, the candidate with the fewest first-choice votes is eliminated, and that candidates' supporters' second-choice votes are applied to the remaining candidates. The process continues until one candidate has a majority of the votes. As Kathleen Barber (2000) notes in her history of proportional representation systems in the United States, the idea of using systems such as these was popular among some Progressives, was used in nonpartisan municipal elections in many American cities during the mid-twentieth century, and has recently been introduced again in some cities.

There is little literature on the use of RCV in primaries because proponents of the system tended to see it as an antiparty reform; in a partisan general election RCV could increase the vote share of third-party candidates without making them spoilers in races where neither major party candidate received a majority of the vote. In states where RCV has been introduced in general elections, such as Maine (in 2016) and Alaska (in 2022), the adoption of RCV has been by referendum not legislation, but these states' referendums have also contained language regarding primaries. State and federal primaries in Maine now use RCV, and the Alaska referendum established a top four primary with RCV in the general election. These changes have prompted some proposals to use RCV in primaries even in states that do not use it in the general election. There is no applied evidence about the effectiveness of these laws, but the experience so far in Maine has been that there were only a small number of elections in which one candidate did not win a majority on the first ballot. There is substantial ongoing research about the effectiveness of RCV, but much of this research frames RCV as an alternative to primaries; one of the most prominent recent arguments in favor of RCV, Lee Drutman's *Breaking the Two-Party Doom Loop* (2019, 196–199), contains an explicit call for abandoning primary elections.[1]

The pattern in all of these literatures is relatively clear: as the early twentieth-century literature suggests, there is a plausible logic to what party organizations might want if they wish to impose order upon primaries. A party looking to maintain control over the nomination process will have an incentive to hold closed primaries or otherwise to restrict voting and candidate entry to reliable party members. A party or faction looking to gain support in the electorate will, in turn, have an incentive to entice new voters and candidates into its primaries, to explore unpredictable changes such as nonpartisan primaries, or to change election dates. These incentives may not necessarily have had a consistent partisan dimension across the country for the bulk of the twentieth century, but to contemporary ears they can certainly sound like they correspond in some ways to liberal and conservative ideas about democratizing the political process. In practice, as the summary of recent literature has shown, these reforms do not always work as they are expected to. This does not mean, however, that legislators will be swayed by, or aware of, empirical evidence, and it does not even mean that they should be. This is, at a minimum, a question we can explore: Where are party-enhancing or party-weakening reforms introduced? Which parties introduce them? And what patterns can we see in the introduction of reform legislation across time?

Baselines: Reform Proposals since 2000

The NCSL maintains a searchable database of introduced legislation in all state legislatures since 2000. For the period from 2001 to 2010, it provides a summary of each bill, the state legislature in which it was introduced, and the bill's ultimate disposition. From 2011 to the present, the database has listed the bill's author, the party of the bill's author, and the bill's full legislative history. It is thus relatively simple to measure the number of introduced bills regarding various types of primary laws and to look at patterns in which types of topics are of interest over time. Several recent articles have summarized successful reform proposals of the past two decades (McGhee et al 2014; Hill 2022). Other recent studies (Anzia 2014, 91; Hassell 2018) have made anecdotal use of the NCSL data; here, however, I seek to provide a more comprehensive picture of activity regarding primaries.

For bills introduced after 2011, I assume that the party affiliation of the bill's author indicates that some advantage may accrue to that party should the bill pass. In other words, I assume that a legislator will not introduce a bill designed to harm his or her own party. This may not always be accurate; some changes in law may benefit factions within a party but not the party as a whole, while some pieces of legislation may have bipartisan support. It should, however, explain changes at least some of the time; a finding that members of one party are more likely to introduce a particular type of bill is far more likely to indicate expected partisan advantage than it would be to predict the converse. The degree of power that party has in the legislature (whether it is the majority party or not) also can relate to the assumed consequences of the legislation. I have not coded the partisanship of the authors of bills introduced before 2011, although I do look at topics and patterns across time for these. In the discussion that follows I consider the motivations of Democrats and Republicans and of members of the legislative majority and minority. Some primary reform legislation during this time was also introduced by Independent officeholders; while in some instances these Independents caucused with one party or the other, I consider them separately.

The following discussion concerns all pieces of legislation regarding primaries, with the exception of bills specifically about presidential primaries or that were principally concerned with voter qualifications or registration procedures. Within individual legislative sessions, I consolidated some introduced bills that had identical summaries; for instance, in the 2013 session, fourteen different bills were introduced in Illinois on the same day with identical language describing "technical changes" in state administration of elections. Likewise, in many states lower and upper chamber companion bills are introduced at the same time. However, I do count separate instances of identical legislation being introduced in different legislative sessions—there are many instances in the data, for example, of individual legislators consistently introducing the same bill for three or four different legislative sessions. Such actions would count as three or four different tallies in my count of introduced bills. I also exclude proposed primary law changes that were intended to be temporary responses to the COVID-19 pandemic.

This winnowing left a total of 501 separate introduced bills regarding primaries. I sorted these into five categories, chosen to reflect the five areas of research inquiry discussed above: primary type, primary timing, endorsement procedures, runoff provisions, and alternative voting methods. To these categories I added two other frequent subjects of legislation, the establishment of ballot access thresholds and the decision about whether to hold a primary if there is no candidate or only one candidate. I consign all other introduced legislation to a "miscellaneous" category. I refer at the end of this chapter to some of the more interesting pieces of miscellaneous legislation, but the bulk of the inquiry regards the above categories.

Table 8.1 shows the distribution of different types of primary legislation, and Figure 8.1 shows changes in the number of introductions for selected subjects across the ten election cycles since 2000.[2] It is evident here that few reform

Table 8.1 Subjects of Introduced Primary Legislation, 2001–2020

Topic	Number of Introduced Bills	Percentage	Number of States	Bills Passed
Primary type	272	54.4	45*	10
Closed	48	9.6	19	2
Semiclosed	26	5.2	18	1
Semiopen	27	5.4	20	3
Open	104	20.8	34	3
Blanket	11	2.2	6	0
Top 2	43	8.6	22	0
RCV	13	2.6	12	1
Endorsements	2	0.4	1	0
Runoffs	37	7.4	14	3
Move primary date	107	21.4	34	8
Threshold	6	1.2	4	0
Uncontested primaries	11	2.2	5	2
Miscellaneous	66	13.2	28	10
Total	501	100.0	49*	33

Source: Author's data, from National Conference of State Legislatures.

* Because multiple pieces of primary legislation were introduced in some states, totals in this column represent the number of states in which legislation was introduced, not a sum of the row totals in this column.

Note: Percentages total to over 100 percent due to rounding.

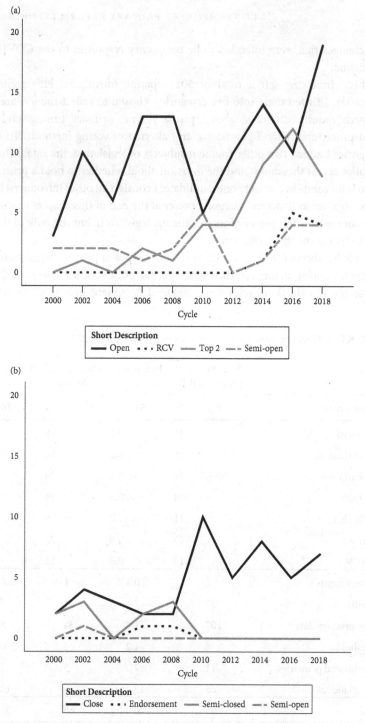

Figure 8.1. Types of legislative introductions by cycle, 2000–2020
Note: The first graph shows expansive legislation, and the second shows restrictive legislation. Numbers on the y-axis represent the number of legislative introductions.
Source: Author's data, from National Conference of State Legislatures.

proposals become law; most of those that do are minor or technical in nature. States have consistently considered moving their primary dates, sometimes by only a week or two, sometimes by several months. The type of primary is also continually up for debate; in the latter years of the 2000s, the number of proposals for open primaries surged, while after 2010 legislation seeking to establish closed primaries was more frequent. Reform ideas also spread across states over short periods of time. For instance, bills establishing blanket primaries were frequent in the 2002 and 2004 legislative sessions but subsequently disappeared. The 2000 *California Democratic Party v. Jones* decision had made the blanket primary unconstitutional, but perhaps it took time for legislators to set aside such efforts. Since California's introduction of the top two primary in 2012, however, twenty-one other states have seen legislation introduced to establish a similar type of election. Proposals for RCV, in addition, were uncommon before 2016 but have appeared in twelve states since that time. And there have been numerous proposals to change runoff procedures; in most instances these proposals have been in Southern states, where legislators have proposed doing away with the runoff or changing the threshold for holding a runoff. Legislation establishing runoffs has, however, been proposed in some Northern states as well. Overall, Figure 8.1 shows that there was an increase in reform proposals during the 2010s; the number of legislative introductions that would reduce party control of primaries has gone up, as the trend lines for open primaries and top two primaries shows. The number of pieces of legislation aimed at closing primaries has also increased during that time, however.

Table 8.2 shows the party affiliation of the legislators introducing various types of bills from 2011 onward. As this table shows, there are few primary law changes that are conclusively owned by one party or the other, a finding that runs counter to what one might expect. It does appear evident that Democrats are fond of the top two primary, while Republicans exhibit a greater interest in closing primaries. It is not possible to determine from this table whether such preferences have to do with ideology, partisan advantage, or some combination of the two. Yet some of the differences here do not have an obvious ideological component, as is the case for moving primaries or establishing ballot access thresholds, and legislators from both parties have introduced legislation establishing open primaries. Partisanship by itself is not a compelling explanation for the introduction of particular types of primary law changes.

The research discussion above indicates that certain types of primary laws can generally be seen as enhancing the power of parties or decreasing party power. For instance, closed primaries tend to increase the power of party organizations, as do restrictions on ballot access or allowing parties to endorse candidates. The extent to which a particular change advantages parties depends, of course, on the status quo ante; for instance, a bill proposing a semiclosed primary may be

Table 8.2 Introduced Legislation by Party of Sponsor, 2011–2020

Topic	Democrat	Republican	Nonpartisan, Independent, or Bipartisan	N
Primary Type	88	65	9	162
Closed	9	26	0	35
Semiclosed	1	0	0	1
Semiopen	10	3	2	15
Open	33	20	5	58
Top 2	27	13	0	40
RCV	8	3	2	13
Runoffs	13	9	0	22
Move primary date	28	27	0	55
Threshold	0	4	0	4
Uncontested primaries	1	3	0	4
Miscellaneous	19	16	3	38
Total	149	124	12	285

Source: Author's data, from National Conference of State Legislatures.

construed as reducing party power if the state currently has a pure closed system, but it would enhance party control if the state currently has a pure open or a top two system. I coded each law in this manner; thus, in Figure 8.2 measures that strengthen parties are shown as "restrictive," while those that weaken parties are termed "expansive." Although the figure shows that there is a steady amount of attention given to primary laws, there are three patterns: there are more efforts to enact expansive primary laws than to enact restrictive ones; the overall number of proposals regarding primaries increased following the 2010 election; and in particular, the number of bills aiming to enhance party control over primaries increased notably after 2010. We shall explore the partisan ramifications of this in the next section.

A final broad question one might ask here has to do with where legislatures are particularly preoccupied with changes to primary laws. Table 8.3 lists the states where there has been the most legislative activity. In the "topics" column I have listed the subjects of the introduced bills, omitting miscellaneous or minor proposed changes. There are no obvious common threads among the states with the most activity here. Some states listed here have a history of unusual

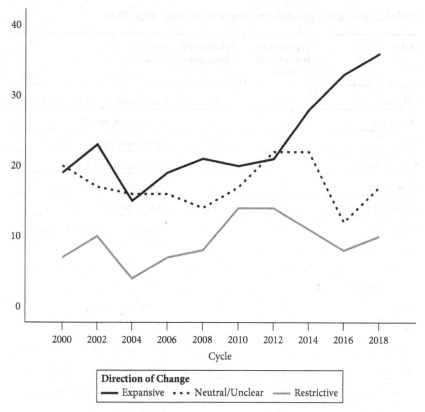

Figure 8.2. Direction of legislative introductions by cycle, 2000–2020
Note: Numbers on the y-axis represent the number of legislative introductions.
Source: Author's data, from National Conference of State Legislatures.

primary laws and of tinkering with their laws (e.g., California, Minnesota, and Washington), while others have a history of skepticism about holding primaries at all (New York, Virginia). Others, such as New Jersey, have made few changes to their primaries over time. There is also no pattern in terms of geography, partisanship, or level of party organization. In a few cases, the interest in primaries appears to stem from one or two persistent legislators; this is the case for Massachusetts and Mississippi. The states with the most activity have also had consistent activity over time; it is not the case that there was an obvious burst of interest in one or two cycles. The median state had eight proposed primary law changes; every state had at least three proposals, except for Nevada (only two proposed changes) and North Dakota (none).

These historical state tendencies are borne out when one considers the miscellaneous reform laws as well. States with a history of discontent with the direct

Table 8.3 Selected Legislative Introductions by State, 2001–2020

State	Number of Introduced Bills	Number of Sessions	Topics
Virginia	31	10	Move, semiclosed, runoff, Top 2
New York	24	9	Move, open, runoff
Illinois	22	9	Move, open, top 2
Massachusetts	22	8	Move, open, top 2, RCV
New Jersey	22	9	Open, uncontested, top 2
Mississippi	19	10	Move, open, top 2, RCV
Washington	18	7	Move, close, open, semiopen, top 2
Hawaii	17	8	Move, open, close, top 2
New Hampshire	17	9	Close, move
Oregon	17	8	Move, open, top 2
South Carolina	16	9	Close, move
California	14	7	Move, semiopen, top 2, threshold
Minnesota	13	8	Move, endorsement, top 2
Pennsylvania	12	8	Open, semiopen, move
Connecticut	11	6	Move, open
North Carolina	11	8	Runoff, open, threshold
New Mexico	11	4	Open, top 2, runoff, RCV
Alabama	10	6	Close, top 2, runoff
Alaska	10	7	Blanket, top 2, RCV
Kentucky	10	7	Runoff, open, move
Michigan	10	7	Move, open

Source: Author's data, from National Conference of State Legislatures.

primary still experience efforts to do away with it; legislation was introduced in Indiana and Rhode Island (two states that did not use primaries at all for nearly half of the past century) to abolish the primary. In Rhode Island the proposed bill would have done away with it entirely, while in Indiana the bill would have abolished primaries for governor and senate. Oregon, as well, has had legislation introduced in multiple election cycles to abolish primaries. For the most part, however, the unusual reform proposals were offered in states that already have unusual primary systems and were aimed at establishing more typical laws. Connecticut, which uses a challenge primary, considered abolishing challenge primaries and simply using a mandatory direct primary. Legislation was also introduced in Utah, a state that uses a convention to winnow ballot access, to do away with the party convention. Virginia, another state that does not always use primaries, has had a range of different legislative proposals to expand the number of offices using primaries, increase ballot access, or otherwise remove the ability of parties and incumbent officeholders to determine whether to have primaries. On the flip side of this, Washington, a state that now uses a top two primary, had legislation introduced in the sessions before it adopted the top two primary that would have required parties to pay for their primaries.

Many of the miscellaneous pieces of legislation were also more tentative steps in the direction of broader changes, such as establishing research committees to explore different primary systems (proposed in New Mexico and Hawaii) or eliminating primaries in special circumstances such as special elections (proposed in Oregon and South Carolina). In several states legislation was also introduced requiring parties to use the same voter participation rules—that is, taking the choice to have a closed or open primary away from the parties. Almost all of the successful miscellaneous proposals were such tentative efforts.

The discussion above provides a general overview of the types of ideas that have been present in legislative discussions of primaries for the past decade and a half. It indicates that even though successful legislation altering primary laws is infrequent, efforts to change primaries are common. We should not assume that the period since 2000 has been atypical in this regard. The data in Table 8.2 suggest, however, that just as was the case during much of the twentieth century, those who introduce legislation are driven by beliefs about the consequences of primary law changes. Either there is a liberal or conservative component to attitudes toward primaries, or legislators have beliefs about which party will be advantaged by particular types of laws. The next section of this chapter will seek to disentangle these two approaches.

Primary Law Changes and Partisan Advantage in a Polarized Age

We turn finally to the question of whether majority and minority parties propose different types of changes or changes in party strength (as measured by seat share in the legislature) are related to proposed changes. Here again, there is substantial noise; in many instances, legislators with a particular interest in primaries may (and do) introduce legislation across several legislative sessions regardless of the fortunes of their party. We should not, in addition, assume that simply because a legislator of a given party has proposed a bill, that bill has support from the party leadership, or for that matter from anyone in the party other than the legislator himself or herself. With these major caveats, however, we can still address some patterns in the introduction of various types of changes.

The period from 2011 to 2020 was one in which Republicans made substantial gains in state legislatures. In thirteen states, Republicans gained majority status in at least one chamber of the state legislature in 2011, and in eight states Republicans gained control of both chambers. In total during that election cycle, Republicans flipped control of twenty-five different chambers. Democrats reacquired control of eight of these in 2013, while Republicans acquired majorities in three others. Republicans gained control of eleven more state legislatures in 2015 and had no net gains in 2017. Despite the magnitude of their midterm victories in congressional and state legislative elections in 2018, Democrats were only able to flip control of six chambers. Following Democrats' acquisition of power in both chambers of the Virginia legislature in 2019, the decade ended with Republicans in control of fifty-nine of ninety-nine state legislative chambers.

We have already seen that Republicans show a preference for more restrictive primary rules and Democrats for less restrictive ones. We can use these five election cycles to explore whether this is a function of ideology or of efforts by the parties to protect or enhance legislative majorities. Throughout the twentieth century, we have seen that rhetoric about opening primaries was often accompanied by claims about increasing the number of people with a voice—appeals that seem consistent with the claims of contemporary liberal or Progressive activists within the Democratic Party about voting, campaign finance, and other aspects of elections. Presumably, however, a state legislative majority party with self-interested, partisan aims would have an incentive either to maintain the status quo or to close primaries. Tables 8.4 and 8.5 show two efforts to distinguish between ideology and partisanship. These tables consider the relationship between partisan goals and majority or minority status in the chamber where the bill was introduced.[3]

Table 8.4 and Figure 8.3 compare the two parties using the basic expansive/restrictive dichotomous categorical variable discussed above. Table 8.4 suggests that majority status has little to do with interest in reforms; Democrats prefer expansive changes whether they are in the majority or not. Republicans propose a mixture of expansive and restrictive changes, but the balance does not appear to be affected by legislative control. Republicans are, however, more active in proposing legislation in chambers where they hold majorities. Figure 8.3 shows changes in these tendencies over the course of the decade. There was an increase in restrictive proposals among Republicans in the years immediately

Table 8.4 Legislative Introductions by Direction, Party of Sponsor, and Majority Status of Sponsor, 2011–2020

	Majority	Minority	Independent	Total
Democratic bills				
Expansive	46	39		85
Restrictive	8	7		15
Total	54	46		100
Republican bills				
Expansive	29	16		45
Restrictive	30	10		40
Total	59	26		85
Independent or bipartisan bills				
Expansive			7	7
Restrictive			1	1
Total			8	8
Total N expansive bills	75	55	7	137
Total N restrictive bills	38	17	1	56
Total bills	113	72	8	193

Source: Author's data, from National Conference of State Legislatures.
Note: Bills coded as neutral are excluded.

after the 2010 election, but Republicans became somewhat less enamored of restrictive proposals and more supportive of expansive ones as the decade wore on. Democrats, on the other hand, became steadily more enthusiastic about open primaries throughout the decades, but in particular after they gained seats in 2018.

Table 8.5, however, shows that when we further distinguish between types of bills introduced, there are noteworthy differences between how Republicans behave when in the majority and when in the minority. Twenty-three of the twenty-six Republican proposals for closed primaries occurred in states where Republicans hold majorities. Other types of primary proposals were more evenly split; for instance, only twelve of the twenty Republican efforts to switch to open primaries were made in states where Republicans held majorities. Thus, while partisanship seems to be more important than majority status in shaping beliefs about primaries, there appears, as well, to be a stronger interest on the

Table 8.5 Legislative Introductions by Bill Type, Party of Sponsor, and Majority Status of Sponsor, 2011–2020

	Democrats			Republicans			
	Majority	Minority	Total	Majority	Minority	Total	Combined Total
Closed	4	5	9	23	3	26	35
Open	18	15	33	12	8	20	53
Top 2	12	15	27	8	5	13	40
Semiclosed	0	1	1	0	0	0	
Semiopen	8	2	10	3	0	3	13
RCV	3	5	8	3	0	3	11
Runoff	7	6	13	8	1	9	22
Threshold	0	0	0	1	3	4	4
Move	24	4	28	17	10	27	55
Uncontested	1	0	1	1	2	3	4
Miscellaneous	13	6	19	10	6	16	35
Total	90	59	149	86	38	124	273

Source: Author's data, from National Conference of State Legislatures.
Note: Independent or bipartisan proposals are excluded.

part of majority Republicans in enacting changes that presumably are believed to advantage the party or factions of it. Closing primaries seems to fit both with arguments about restricting voting and with efforts in Republican-led states to protect incumbent Republican legislators. This accords with many journalistic accounts of such proposals—and again, it shows that conventional wisdom about what "closed" and "open" primary elections mean may be more important than the actual effects of legislation.

Republicans, however, gained seats in most legislatures in the 2010 election, so it is difficult to draw conclusions about the effects of changes in seat share apart from drawing a distinction between majority and minority parties. It is noteworthy that in the two election cycles immediately following the 2010 Republican wave, six of the nine Republican proposals to close primaries and one of the Republican proposals to open primaries occurred in legislatures where Republicans already were in the majority prior to 2010. Republicans in conservative states such as South Carolina or Idaho were not, then, trying to lock in newly won majorities. If they were seeking partisan advantage, it was either to

CONTEMPORARY PRIMARY REFORM EFFORTS 223

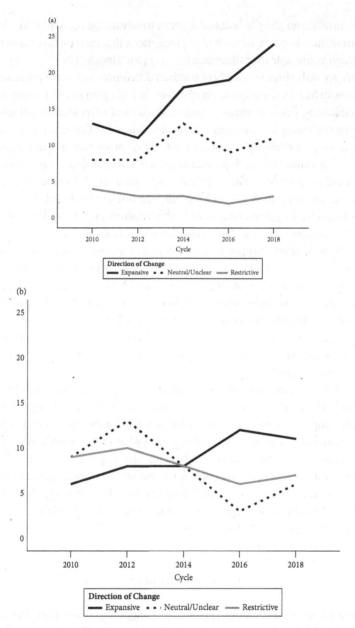

Figure 8.3. Direction of legislative introductions by sponsor party and cycle, 2010–2020
Note: The first graph shows direction of change for the Democrats, and second for the Republicans. Numbers on the y-axis represent the number of legislative introductions.
Source: Author's data, from National Conference of State Legislatures.

further insulate an already successful party, to advantage particular ideological factions within the party, or to combat perceptions that their primary laws might leave them vulnerable to malfeasance (see, e.g., McKissick 2020).

There are only three states where partisan differences in reform proposals appear to be driven by the acquisition of power. In Michigan in 2014, a Republican bill establishing a closed primary was introduced and a Democratic bill allowing for crossover voting in primaries was also introduced (Michigan is currently an open primary state without crossover voting; both proposals were unsuccessful). In New Hampshire, where Republicans gained a majority in the state House in 2010, a bill establishing a closed primary was introduced. Democrats regained the House majority in 2012, and the bill was not reintroduced. In Alabama, where Republicans gained control of both chambers in 2010 and held them in 2012, closed primary legislation was introduced in both sessions.

The effects of other changes in power are more ambiguous, suggesting perhaps that Democrats also sought advantage following the loss of legislative majorities. Democrats in Arkansas, Colorado, Indiana, and Mississippi proposed changes further opening primaries after the 2010 election. Democrats also introduced legislation creating top two primaries in two states, Minnesota and Maine, where they gained majorities in 2012, and a Republican in Montana also introduced top two legislation. None of these efforts were successful, although the Montana proposal came close.[4]

We cannot, again, rule out the idiosyncrasy of individual legislators in explaining these changes, nor can we conclusively determine how popular any of these proposals were (apart from the scant instances of success). There is also, as noted above, little evidence that primary law changes work the way their proponents might expect them to. The data here suggest, however, that both ideology and partisan gain are goals for those who introduce primary legislation. Democrats have sought to further open primaries, while Republicans have sought to close them, but Republican efforts are more clearly related to partisan gain than are Democratic efforts.

Conclusions

This chapter shows the enduring appeal of changes to primary laws. This appeal persists regardless of the actual consequences of such changes. In contrast to the historical work in Chapters 2 through 7 on successful changes between 1928 and 1968, however, the data here on proposed changes show the strongly partisan nature of the proposed reforms. Today, party ideology may be more important than partisan advantage. It is debatable whether a more open primary process corresponds to contemporary liberalism or that closed primaries have anything to do with conservatism, but the parties appear to have sorted themselves on this issue.

Given the failure of most of these proposals, one might ask whether cataloging state legislative proposals is merely a bit of esoterica. I maintain, however, that the data presented in this chapter help to fill three gaps in literature on election law in the United States.

First, the findings here echo those of other literatures on elections. Political scientists tend to emphasize the quest for partisan or factional power and to downplay the role that ideas can take on independent of their partisan implications. This is not always an accurate reflection of politicians' motives. Surveying several decades of changes to party finance law in Europe, Piccio and van Biezen (2015) note that partisan advantage cannot explain the growing trend toward more inclusive and more generous systems of public financing of elections. This trend, they argue, reflects the triumph of a philosophical argument that public funding should be readily available. The United States is hardly at this point regarding campaign finance or primary laws. Yet the growing popularity among Democrats of open primaries, top two primaries, and other such reforms seems to represent a belief in how elections should be conducted, even in instances where this conduct might disadvantage Democrats. Republican proposals here seem more oriented toward the preservation of post-2010 legislative majorities, but some also appear to stem from ideological convictions about who should have the right to vote in primaries that are separate from election-oriented concerns. The data here suggest that recent proposals for change accord with findings on other types of election law reforms.

Second, not only is the evidence of a quest for partisan advantage unspectacular, so (perhaps more so) is the evidence for regional effects. When one studies prior changes to primaries, it is necessary to first consider regional differences; one could conclude from Chapter 7, for instance, that the Southern party system was different and hence runoffs made sense in the South but not elsewhere. Similarly, one could conclude from Chapter 3 that states with a strong Progressive movement and weak party organizations tended to tinker with their primaries more frequently, Northern states with strong parties tended toward more restrictive primary laws, and so forth. These differences are not particularly obvious today. There is a substantial literature noting the decline of distinctive regional political cultures (e.g., Hopkins 2018). While there still are some experiments that are clearly a legacy of unique regional factors (most obviously, the appeal of the top two primary in California and the subsequent interest in neighboring states), for the most part differences between the two parties now are more salient than differences across regions or other state types.

Third, the sheer amount of proposed reform suggests that American primary laws and practices are far from settled. It has become commonplace for national campaign efforts—presidential races, most obviously, but also the efforts of national interest groups in choosing among congressional races to become active in—to take note of oddities in state election laws. These laws, however, are always at least potentially in flux. Attention to proposed changes can thus lead us to investigate why these changes are proposed. That is, who is interested in changing primary laws? Studies of the California primary law changes (discussed above) generally conclude that the groups behind the adoption of the blanket primary, and subsequently the top two primary, were predominantly liberal, although some pragmatic centrist Republicans saw potential in these changes. Groups that have championed voter referendums on ranked choice voting in Alaska, Maine, Massachusetts, and Nevada also could be categorized as being left-leaning, and all of the five states that passed laws prohibiting ranked choice voting are controlled by Republicans.[5] We know little, however, about the origins of Republican efforts to close primaries—that is, whether the legislators who have introduced these proposals have been acting on their own initiative or there is a nascent conservative movement to change primary laws. It is certainly possible that Republican concerns following the 2020 election about voter fraud may yet yield a new set of proposals regarding primary voting laws. This chapter does not answer these questions, but it might serve as a starting point for exploring them.

No area of American election law is ever settled. The growth of political polarization and the stresses we have seen in recent years within both parties' coalitions suggest that American state legislatures will continue to examine how to improve their primaries. A century of experimentation suggests that the states would do so anyway, even without these catalyzing events, and it also should make us pessimistic that changes are likely to solve primary problems. But it is certainly possible that the American public will have cause to think more about whether our current primary laws produce the types of nominees we want. This chapter has sought to provide baseline information that might be useful in such considerations. In the next chapter I explore why these reforms are perhaps even more likely to end in disappointment than were the reforms of the twentieth century.

9
Why Primary Reforms Rarely Work

In Chapter 8 we considered two different characteristics of contemporary primary election reforms. First, I showed that contemporary political scientists have concluded that primary reforms have few measurable consequences. Primary election laws cannot easily be changed in a way that would influence voter turnout or the level or nature of electoral competition. There also does not appear to be any clear way to change primary election laws in ways that would advantage one party or the other, or that would benefit ideologically moderate candidates. Second, however, the chapter demonstrated that while it is clear that proposals to change primary laws abound today, there are clear partisan differences in the types of laws that are pursued in state legislatures. One could infer that politicians think changes to primaries will help them or their parties, even if the evidence for this is scant.

Why do these apparently futile efforts persist? And are today's efforts at reform any different than the primary election reforms of the early and middle years of the twentieth century? Recall that in Chapter 1 of this book I commented on the resurgence of interest in primaries; many early twentieth-century political scientists explored the consequences of the direct primary, but there was very little scholarly consideration of primaries between 1928 and the early twentieth century. When students of American politics again turned their attention toward the consequences of the direct primary, they did so in a very different political climate. Twenty-first-century studies of primary elections, including my own, have been motivated by questions about whether election laws are culpable for the political polarization and ideological extremism that characterize contemporary American politics. Most reform efforts seek to reduce polarization and extremism, while also boosting turnout or improving the fit between legislators and the districts they represent. It is natural to expect such connections, and the palette of primary election reforms described in this book is a logical place to start.

In this chapter I explore what I see as the two major reasons that contemporary reforms are doomed to fail. The first has to do with a faulty but common assumption: the frequent assertion that primary electorates are more ideologically extreme than general election electorates. Many reformers have contended that placing greater restrictions on voting in primaries will render the primary electorate even more ideologically extreme, or that removing restrictions will make the electorate less extreme. As I will document, primary electorates are not much different from general election electorates, or at least they are not sufficiently different to be responsible for polarization. The second reason has to do with our ability to observe changes. The consequences of election reforms are frequently swamped by other, larger political trends. Primary election turnout and competition have far more to do with citizens' attitudes toward the president, for instance, than they do with the sorts of state-specific tweaks to primary rules documented in the early chapters of this book. In supporting these claims, I focus here on the U.S. Congress because congressional primaries have been with us for the duration of the time covered in this book and are susceptible to all of the changes discussed here, but the lessons here can be applied to any nonpresidential primaries.

I do not intend to argue here that primary election rule changes are all meaningless. They may marginally improve the process, they may be justifiable in themselves on purely normative grounds, or they may influence (and be designed to influence) one particular election. Yet as I will explain more fully in the conclusion to this book, primary election laws are, like voter eligibility rules, campaign finance laws, and other so-called process reforms, caught in a sort of vice. To inspire any sort of reform movement, reform advocates must promise results. Yet when results do not materialize, their supporters may well become disillusioned. On the other hand, unless they wish to pursue change through direct democracy or even more radical means, reformers must also promise skeptical lawmakers that reforms will not be that disruptive to the status quo. Rallying the public behind minimal changes is a recipe for failure.

I will explore the broader implications of this claim more fully in the next chapter. For now, however, consider one more empirical question raised by this claim. How big must a change be to be considered meaningful? Determining whether, for instance, the ideological difference between primary and general election voters is meaningful requires us to be able to tell a story about whether this difference should drive policy change, whether it suggests that primaries are more important as a source of polarization than many of the other alleged culprits, or whether changes that would erase these differences are worth the cost (economic and political) of pursuing them. A similar story could be told for the discussion in this chapter of partisan swings and competitiveness—even if we can prove in an experimental setting that a particular change to voting rules might have a measurable, but small, impact on voter turnout or on the types of voters who turn out, it is not at all clear that we would see these changes unless we were to have an election cycle (or, for that matter, a series of election cycles) that was considerably more placid and devoid of major national issues than those we have seen for at least the past couple of decades. Such an occurrence seems neither plausible nor necessarily desirable.

Are Primary Voters Extremists?

There is little dispute that the U.S. Congress has reached an unprecedented level of partisan and ideological polarization (see, e.g., Mann and Ornstein 2012). Several types of electoral rules have been investigated as potential causes of polarization, including campaign finance laws (Mann and Corrado 2014), which certainly have changed dramatically over the past fifteen years; redistricting practices, which have changed not so much because of changes in law but because of advances in technology (Mann and Cain 2005); and changes in primary elections. Primary elections have, as we have seen, been a feature of most congressional elections for a century, so using them to tell a story about contemporary changes is difficult, yet there are still compelling arguments that primary elections have been a greater source of ideological extremism in recent years than they were in previous decades.

It is commonplace to see arguments that primaries foster extremism, and such arguments make sense given our standard views about party coalitions and about voter turnout in primaries. In stylized accounts of ideological competition, if one party is to the left of the other, a primary within the left party will produce a candidate to the left of the general electorate median and the primary within the right party will produce a candidate to the right of the median. If candidates are unwilling (out of fear of retribution in the next election's primary) or unable (because they have precommitted themselves to a set of noncentrist positions) to move to the center, then polarization will result. If, furthermore, primary voters are more ideological than general election voters, the candidates chosen will be more extreme even than those who vote for them in the general election would prefer: Democratic primary voters may be more liberal than Democratic general election voters, and vice versa for Republicans. Given that primary turnout is often quite low (official estimates for 2014, for instance, are that less than 15 percent of the electorate voted in that year's primaries), this seems like a plausible assumption.

Despite the compelling theoretical logic here, there is surprisingly little evidence that congressional primary electorates are, in fact, more ideological than general election voters. We lack evidence to back up this story in part because it is difficult to study such electorates. Surveys of congressional primary voters are nearly nonexistent, and exit polling in congressional primaries has been infrequent. In addition, given differences in the competitiveness of primaries, in the drivers of turnout in primaries (i.e., some state primaries feature statewide candidates for governor or senate, some do not, and some are conducted at the same time as presidential primaries), and in state laws regulating who can vote in primaries, it is difficult to make generalizations about the role of voter ideology in congressional primaries. For much of the period discussed in this book, we have instead often relied on what McCarty, Poole, and Rosenthal (2006) describe as a set of indirect claims instead of proof.

Over the past decade it has become easier to look at primary voters' views. In the following pages I compare the ideological positions of all voters in each state's primaries for governor, senator, and U.S. House, using one such study, the 2010 Cooperative Congressional Election Study (CCES). I use 2010 because it represents, I contend, an extreme case. This election, often cast as one in which conservative candidates and their ideas were ascendant, seems to me more likely to feature a polarized primary electorate than others. As I show here, not only is there little evidence of polarization among primary voters at the national level, there is almost no evidence of polarization within any of the states, regardless of the type of primary election system, the competitiveness of the primary, the particular office for which the election was being held, or the characteristics of the candidates themselves. Of course, with any large selection of elections there will be some outliers. The paucity of such outliers, however, suggests that the very premise of so many arguments about primaries—that they feature overly ideological voters—should be re-examined. The same pattern holds in other midterm elections of the past decade.

What We Know about the Ideology of Congressional Primary Voters

Claims about the ideological extremism of primary voters are almost too numerous to mention. In popular and academic literature on American politics, primaries are often listed as one of the sources of dysfunction and conflict in today's Congress.[1] In their 2006 book, McCarty, Poole, and Rosenthal summarize what was, in their view, a weak causal story about the relationship between primary elections and polarization. In their telling, claims about extremist primary voters rest on five indirect claims:

- Participation in primaries has fallen.
- Partisans are more likely to participate in general elections.
- So they are more likely to participate in primaries.
- Partisan identifiers have become more ideological.
- Therefore, the primary electorate has become more ideological.

None of these claims are unreasonable, but, the authors conclude, this sequence does not constitute direct proof. Moreover, I contend, the implicit claim in almost all discussions of primaries is not merely that primary voters have become more ideological; it is that they have become more ideological than general election voters.

McCarty and his colleagues are not quite fair here to the literature as it stood at the time. As we have seen in the earlier chapters of this book, primaries have always had the capacity to feature ideologically extreme electorates, but for much of the twentieth century they did not. Primary elections were sufficiently novel and exciting for voters in the century's early years that primary turnout often was quite high, in some cases exceeding general election turnout. In addition, many states were so dominated by one party (even outside of the South) that the primary was more important than the general election, and there was as a result a diversity of types of candidates and types of voters in the dominant party's primary. According to Alan Ware (2002), the rise of candidate-centered elections, the increase in two-party competition, and the growth in ideological sorting in the electorate—all of which did not begin to happen until the late 1950s and arguably persisted for decades after—should have been expected to contribute to the alleged ideological extremism of primary voters.

In addition, there has been a substantial body of research on the characteristics of presidential primary voters. The same sorts of claims discussed here about congressional primary voters have been made with regard to presidential primaries, often in an effort to compare open and closed primaries or to describe presidential primary electorates. Ranney (1968, 1972) and Ranney and Epstein (1966) study Wisconsin and New Hampshire, finding few issue differences between primary and general election voters but some differences in level of political engagement. Southwell (1986) also finds few differences between presidential primary and general election voters nationally over the period from 1968 to 1984, concluding that where differences did exist they may have been a consequence of the entry of a third-party candidate in the general election. Norrander (1989) uses the 1980 American National Election Study to compare presidential primary voters in 1980 to general election voters who did not vote in the primary, finding no differences in ideology, some slight differences in issue positions (but no obvious pattern that would correlate with ideology), and some slight differences in political sophistication. Using a survey of Super Tuesday voters, Norrander (1991) also finds some differences across states in turnout and in characteristics of the voters, but these differences do not seem to predict extremism; they largely have to do with the presence of other races on the ballot or the history of voter turnout in the state. Norrander, Stephens, and Wendland (2013) study presidential primaries in 2004 and 2008 using exit polls and find few differences in ideology according to primary type, but speculate that nonpresidential primaries held separately in presidential election years may have more ideologically extreme electorates, depending on primary type, candidate characteristics, or state political culture.

As Norrander (1986, 1989, 1991), along with Southwell (1986) and Hedlund (1977), note, characteristics of presidential primary voters are not necessarily similar to those of congressional primary voters. Presidential primaries in early primary states can have higher turnout than later ones, and the competitiveness of primaries varies substantially from one year to the next, both within states and overall. Presidential primaries can also drive turnout in states holding other primaries at the same time (there were twenty such states in 2012), so a finding in such a state in a presidential year of any differences between primary and election voters would not necessarily say anything about the tendencies of congressional primary voters. Collectively, these studies show a lack of extremism among presidential primary voters, a lack of differences according to primary systems, and substantial variation in some attributes of the electorate from one election to the next. They suggest that we should be cautious about making claims about the unrepresentativeness of the electorate, at least in ideological terms; that we should be skeptical of claims that rules matter; and that we should be sensitive to candidate effects.

McCarty and his colleagues are correct, however, about the need in literature up to that time to make imputations about the characteristics of primary voters. Such imputations have tended to be made based on three types of observable characteristics: the type of primary system in use, the level of turnout in primaries, and the ideology of primary nominees. The relationship between these factors varies across studies; some seek a relationship between primary type and the candidates elected, while others seek a relationship between primary type and turnout. For instance, Kenney (1986) looks at turnout in Senate primaries, concluding that open primaries have higher turnout, but declines to speculate on the ideological characteristics of voters in higher and lower turnout primaries; he concludes that this is more a matter of state political culture and the level of interparty competition than of any systemic ideological pattern. Kanthak and Morton (2003; see also Calcagno and Westley 2008) show that open primaries correlate with increased turnout for Republicans, but not for Democrats. Gerber and Morton (1998) study the relationship between primary type and candidate ideology, using ideology estimates for House members elected from 1982 through 1990, controlling for district ideology, region, and the presence or absence of runoff elections. They conclude that primary type does have an effect on ideology, although not in a particularly obvious way. Candidates elected in semiclosed primaries are actually the most moderate. Burden (2001), however, concludes that the occurrence of a contested primary, regardless of its type, pulls candidates of both parties away from the median. My own work on primary challenges to House incumbents also concludes that primary type does not predict the occurrence of challenges to House incumbents after 1990, although it did have an effect in the 1970s and 1980s (Boatright 2013, 90–91).

All of these studies suggest that primaries have an effect on politicians, but they do not necessarily suggest that characteristics of the primary electorate are driving whatever this effect is. If primaries are expected to be competitive or at a minimum to be unpredictable in terms of their turnout, legislators have an incentive to make all sorts of changes they would not necessarily make if they expected to have no competition. One can expect similar effects for nonincumbent candidates, although they would be harder to measure. There is a large literature on the effects of divisiveness on incumbent and nonincumbent candidates' positions (Johnson and Gibson 1974; Born 1981; Kenney and Rice 1984; Kenney 1988; Miller, Jewell, and Sigelman 1988; Berry and Canon 1993, Lazarus 2005), and there are even some pieces on divisiveness that use primary type or voter characteristics to predict divisiveness (e.g., Herrnson and Gimpel 1995). None of these findings, however, directly implicate the voters. Voters may show up if they are mobilized by a particular primary candidate, but there is no reason to expect candidates at the ideological extremes to have a monopoly on such mobilization.

Since the mid-2000s, however, several studies have sought to provide more direct measures of extremism among congressional primary voters. Masket and Shor (2013) compare state legislative candidates chosen in primaries to candidates selected by vacancy committees. In this variant on the sort of work done by Gerber and Morton, Masket and Shor find, again, no substantial differences in candidates' ideological views. Norrander and Stephens (2012) use California exit poll data from 2000 through 2008 to compare primary and general election voters. They again find no differences, but caution that this result may say more about California than about primary rules.

Most consequentially, three recent studies have also used the same survey I use here, the 2010 CCES, and have reached similar conclusions, although they have not focused on differences within individual states. Jacobson (2012) uses a variety of issue scales to measure the positions of primary voters, general election voters who did not vote in the primary, and nonvoters. He concludes that on a variety of issue indexes and a variety of individual issues, primary constituencies tend to be more extreme than general election constituencies, especially on the Republican side. Similarly, Hill (2015) constructs a hierarchical model estimating the conservatism of each congressional district and finds, again, that the characteristics of primary electorates indicate greater ideological extremism in primary electorates than in general electorates. Sides et al. (2018) compare validated and unvalidated responses for the aggregate primary electorate, showing that differences between self-reported primary voters and general election voters are greater than those for validated responses. Furthermore, Sides and colleagues look at data from 2008, 2012, and 2014 in this article and reach similar conclusions.

Each of these recent studies, along with earlier work by Norrander (1986), has noted some of the difficulties in making empirical claims about congressional primary electorates. While we can predict characteristics of the general electorate, particularly in presidential election years, with substantial accuracy from one election to the next, primary electorates may be composed in part of people drawn to vote because of one of the candidates. That is, if a particularly charismatic, ideologically extreme candidate cultivates a loyal following, that candidate's campaign may make the primary electorate in his or her district different than it would otherwise be. Low turnout elections (which primaries usually are, particularly in instances where there is no competitive national or statewide primary race on the ballot) yield variable electorates from one year to the next. Voter turnout can be a cause of victory or defeat for ideologically extreme candidates; however, the presence of such candidates can also be a determinant of voter turnout.

Norrander and Wendland (2016) study the effect of primary type on primary voters' distance from the general election median. They find that primary type does have a slight effect on ideology, but that in 2010 this effect was different depending on the party, often in counterintuitive ways. Their study suggests that laws that encourage people to join a party for the purposes of primary voting can have an effect on the overall composition of the primary electorate, but that the magnitude of this effect is swamped by the effects of respondent characteristics. They also show that the extremism of the primary electorate is shaped by whether a party holds a comfortable majority in a state (in which case, they argue, a wider range of ideological viewpoints will be represented within the party).

To summarize, political scientists, practitioners, and journalists have long held that primary electorates are more extreme than general electorates or the public at large. Until recently, there has been little direct proof of this, and the evidence we have accumulated over the past three decades has suggested that there is in fact little or no difference.

Measuring Voter Ideology

The CCES (renamed the CES, or Cooperative Election Study, in 2021) is the only major public opinion survey conducted in nonpresidential election years that asks respondents whether they voted in that year's primary election. The CCES is an internet-based survey with over fifty-five thousand respondents; this ensures that the survey's state samples are large enough that one can study the behavior of electorates in particular states with at least some level of statistical confidence. State samples vary according to the size of the state; there are over five thousand respondents from California and just under one hundred from each of the two smallest states, Vermont and Wyoming. The margin of error thus ranges from 1 percent to 10 percent according to the size of the state subsample.

Most of my analysis in this chapter is based on the 2010 CCES, although I do compare it with results from the 2014 and 2018 CCES. One must be cautious about generalizing from this study. Surely no individual congressional election year is typical, but 2010 was particularly unusual. As is the norm in midterm elections, the party holding the presidency lost seats, but the magnitude of the backlash against President Barack Obama and the Democratic Party was particularly severe. The Republican Party picked up sixty-four seats in the House of Representatives (enough to win a majority within that body), along with six seats in the Senate and six governorships. The 2010 election year will be remembered both for the development of the Tea Party, which mobilized many conservatives who had not always been politically active, and for the Supreme Court's decision in *Citizens United v. FEC* (558 U.S. 310 (2010)), which substantially expanded the ability of nonparty organizations to spend money advocating the election or defeat of particular candidates. These factors may mean that voters in the 2010 primaries—and in particular, the Republican primaries—were atypical.

In a way, however, the very atypicality of the 2010 election makes it an excellent place to look for extremism. The extensive mobilization among conservatives and the high general election turnover suggest that the 2010 primaries, or at least the Republican primaries, were in fact more likely to tilt to the right than might be the case in other years. Punditry about extremism in the Republican primary electorate has become far more common (or so it seems to me) since 2010 than was the case before. One might conclude, then, that if we do not see signs of ideological extremism in 2010, we are not particularly likely to see it in other, less chaotic years.

CCES respondents were asked to place themselves on a seven-point scale from "extremely liberal" (1) to "extremely conservative" (7), with a response of "4" indicating that one was neither liberal nor conservative. In measuring respondent ideology, I exclude respondents who were unable or unwilling to place themselves on this scale. I also briefly consider respondents' self-reported partisanship and respondents' answers to some of the issue questions, but given that Jacobson has covered these responses quite thoroughly, I do not discuss these answers in great detail.

The CCES includes many questions regarding voter demographics, and I discuss some of these here as well. The most consequential question in making statements about primary voters, however, is what the comparison group is. There is a logic to comparing primary voters to the electorate as a whole, to the electorate's median voter (as do Norrander and Wendland), or to self-identified Democrats and Republicans (as does Jacobson). It is a given that if the electorate is at all polarized or sorted, primary voters will diverge from the median voter; the question, again, is whether primary voters are different from general election voters of the same party. Just as survey researchers have raised questions about the ideology measures, however, so reports of partisanship can be criticized. If a respondent identifies as a Democrat yet voted for a Republican in, for instance, the 2010 gubernatorial election, it is debatable whether one should count that respondent as a Democratic general election voter. Perhaps that respondent does tend to support Democrats but was displeased with the party's nominee, or perhaps the respondent preferred a losing candidate in the Democratic primary. Such imputations, however, cannot be proven, and as we shall see, instances in which voters vote in one party's primary yet then abstain or vote for another party's nominee in the general election are vanishingly rare. For the purposes of the primary electorate/general electorate comparisons here, I compare each party's primary voters with three different sets of general election voters: those who voted for that party's House candidate, those who voted for that party's Senate candidate, and those who voted for that party's gubernatorial candidate.

Using these three comparisons helps us avoid problems brought up by imputations about partisanship. In addition, it enables us to focus on race types: in instances where the primary electorate did diverge from one or more of the general election comparison groups, what distinguishing features did the primary have? Was it competitive? What types of primary voting laws existed? Were the candidates unusual in some way? And similarly, what distinguishing features did the general election have? Was it competitive? Was there a competitive third-party candidate? Many deviations here can be explained by such distinctions.

In the analysis that follows, I supplement the measures provided in the CCES with measures of primary type and with various measures of election competition. General election competition is relevant for two reasons: a competitive general election will have higher turnout than an uncompetitive one, and if voters expect the general election to be competitive, they may take an interest in the election early and thus may be more inclined to vote in the primary. Given that 2010 was a midterm election year, there are some states in which there either were no statewide races at all or no competitive races. Turnout thus should have been shaped by the types of races being held. Characteristics of the primary election, however, are important too, and the role of primary competition has not yet been assessed for the 2010 study. Even if a general election is expected to be close, voters will not necessarily have reasons to show up if there are no choices on the primary ballot. It is thus important to measure whether there was a contested primary on the ballot for the three offices under consideration here (House, Senate, and governor) and to measure whether the primary was competitive. I define a race as being competitive if the victorious candidate received less than 60 percent of the vote.

To put a more technical gloss on a point made at the outset of the chapter, the magnitude of what constitutes "extremism" is in the eye of the beholder. In the state-by-state comparisons that follow, significance levels and sample sizes vary, but the differences are rarely large enough to reach conventional thresholds. As a rule of thumb, then, I select out races in which the raw difference between the mean party primary voter's ideology and the furthest-away mean for any of that party's general election nominees is .25 (i.e., hypothetically, the mean Democratic primary voter score is 3.0 and the mean score for those who voted for the Democratic senatorial candidate is 3.25 or higher, or 2.75 or lower). One could use alternate thresholds, but this comparison enables us to at least look at where the largest differences emerge.

Results

It should first be noted that primary voters and general election voters differ in many consequential ways. Table 9.1 shows important demographic differences between the primary electorate and the general electorate in 2010, without explicitly separating out either party's primary or general election voters. The 2010 primary electorate was older, whiter, wealthier, and better educated than the general electorate, the universe of registered voters, or the American population as a whole. That electorate was also more conservative and more supportive of Republicans. Had Obama run before only the 2010 primary electorate, he would have lost in a landslide. Some of this variation is certainly a consequence of swings between midterm and general elections, and some is also likely a consequence of the Republican surge in 2010. Conservatives were unhappy in 2010, and they voted in much larger numbers in the primary election and in the general election. The difference in composition reflects what we know about who votes in low-salience elections and who sits them out (Anzia 2014), what we know about partisan swings in midterm years (Campbell 1987), and what we have come to learn over the past few midterm elections about the nature of the contemporary Republican Party coalition.

What this table does not show, however, is whether there are differences within the parties' primary and general election voters. As Jacobson and others have noted, primary voters differ on many important issues from registered party members and those who self-identify with a party. There is no need here to reproduce the Jacobson findings in great detail, but comparisons between primary voters and *potential* general election supporters of a party are not the same as comparisons between those who do in fact vote in one party's primary and for the same party's nominees in the general election. Table 9.2 shows such comparisons. On the issue questions here—the top nine rows in the table—the differences between party primary voters and supporters of that party's general election nominees for House, Senate, and governor are minimal. Within the Republican Party the numbers are virtually identical; on each question, the Democratic

Table 9.1 Primary vs. General Election Voter Traits, 2010

	Primary Voters (%)	General Election Voters (%)	Registered Voters (%)	Full Sample (%)
Male	55.4	53.4	50.6	49.5
White	83.6	81.6	79.6	77.9
60 years old or older	50.5	54.8	40.9	36.3
30 years old or younger	2.4	3.5	6.0	9.5
Family income below $40,000	21.3	22.8	25.5	42.2
Family income above $80,000	35.2	33.7	29.2	22.5
College graduate (incl. 2-year)	54.8	53.6	50.6	50.6
Voted for Obama in 2008	40.1	44.4	46.4	49.1
Voted for McCain in 2008	55.6	52.3	50.2	46.4
Liberal*	28.7	30.1	30.3	27.3
Middle of the road*	13.3	15.7	17.6	24.4
Conservative*	57.4	53.2	50.3	42.4
Registered Democrat	36.3	37.0	37.8	37.5
Registered Republican	45.7	39.8	37.0	31.0
Describes self as Democrat**	32.0	33.0	34.3	34.7
Describes self as Republican**	37.5	33.2	31.1	27.1
Describes self as Independent**	25.7	29.0	29.1	30.0
Voted in primary	—	63.5	53.7	40.0
Voted in general election	96.9	—	80.2	61.0
Registered	—	—	—	73.9
Valid percentage of total sample (N)	40.0 (22,152)	61.0 (33,798)	73.9 (40,965)	100.0 (55,400)

Source: Cooperative Congressional Election Study 2010 (Ansolabehere 2012).
Notes: All voter types are validated.
* Ideology measurements created by conflating self-placements on seven-point scale; 1–3 = liberal, 4 = middle of the road, 5–7 = conservative.
** Partisan descriptions taken from pre-election survey.

primary electorate is actually less liberal than voters who chose Democrats in the general election. Republican primary voters are very slightly more conservative on average than Republican general election voters, but not significantly so, and Democratic primary voters are actually more conservative than Democratic

Table 9.2 Primary vs. General Election Voters' Preferences, within Parties

	Democrat				Republican			
	Primary	General: House	General: Senate	General: Governor	Primary	General: House	General: Senate	General: Governor
Economy has gotten better*	43.4%	45.8%	46.3%	44.9%	4.3%	3.3%	3.0%	3.1%
Iraq was a mistake	85.2%	89.0%	89.7%	88.1%	17.6%	17.3%	16.9%	17.1%
Afghanistan was a mistake	43.3%	43.8%	44.3%	43.4%	16.0%	16.2%	16.3%	16.2%
Stricter gun control laws	68.5%	72.4%	73.2%	71.5%	11.7%	11.3%	11.3%	11.7%
Climate change is taking place*	85.8%	91.0%	91.9%	89.9%	12.6%	11.9%	11.7%	12.5%
Legal status to immigrants	63.5%	67.6%	67.9%	66.9%	14.0%	14.0%	13.9%	13.7%
Abortion a matter of choice	71.3%	73.5%	74.4%	73.3%	19.3%	19.3%	19.1%	19.9%
Legalize same sex marriage	81.5%	84.9%	85.8%	84.4%	32.6%	32.4%	31.9%	32.4%
Supports affirmative action*	62.1%	65.0%	67.5%	63.5%	6.2%	5.7%	5.6%	5.9%
Mean partisanship	1.83	1.84	1.77	1.93	6.03	5.87	5.90	5.87
Mean ideology**	2.97	2.82	2.78	2.87	5.99	5.95	5.95	5.93

Source: Cooperative Congressional Election Study 2010 (Ansolabehere 2012).
Notes: All voter types are validated.
* Conflates two categories.
** All standard errors for the partisanship and ideology variables are .02 or less.

general election voters. The standard error for the full Republican primary vote sample is .01, and the standard error for Democrats is .017. All of this might be a function of unique circumstances of the 2010 election, but it suggests that though differences are significant, they are hardly as substantial as some might expect.

It would be easy to stop our analysis here, but doing so would defy the spirit of the state-centered approach pursued so far in this book. Looking at national numbers conflates many types of primaries and many political cultures. When we break down the sample by state, however, it is apparent that the number of states where there is an obvious difference between the two electorates is still tiny. In fact, the number of states where primary voters are more extreme than that party's general election voters is smaller than the number where primary voters are in fact less extreme than general election voters. The appendix to this chapter provides state-by-state placement means, and Table 9.3 lists the small number of states where there are differences of note, using the .25 threshold discussed above.

As noted earlier, there is plenty of room for error in the state data; the sample sizes vary from 1,284 in the California Democratic primary to just 4 respondents in the Democratic primaries in the Republican bastions of Mississippi and Idaho. Not all states had contested or competitive primaries within both parties, and in some congressional districts and even some states parties did not produce nominees at all. The tally of states here, then, errs on the side of overstating differences. Unsurprisingly, small states (i.e., states with fewer respondents) are overrepresented among the states that did show a difference. To take an extreme example, the Mississippi Democratic primary electorate reported itself to be more conservative than the Republican primary electorate, but this is likely due to the small numbers. Out-parties in overwhelmingly partisan states comprise a large number of the states with primary electorates more extreme than their general election voters.

Another way to consider these data is to consider the variation within larger states. Not a single state with more than ten House members (there were twelve such states in 2010, excluding Virginia and Washington) had a primary electorate more extreme than the general electorate; five states with ten or more members (Ohio, Pennsylvania, Florida, Massachusetts, and North Carolina) had a primary electorate—or more precisely, a Democratic primary electorate—more centrist than the party's general election voters. And only one state (Vermont, a state with a small sample size and no competitive primaries) had two primary electorates that were more extreme than the general election voters.

One can make many inferences about particular states; for instance, someone knowledgeable about the peculiar history of the Rhode Island Democratic Party might be unsurprised to find that Rhode Island Democratic primary voters are

Table 9.3 State Primary Electorate Ideology Variation Summarized

No Variation	Primary Electorate More Extreme	Primary Electorate Less Extreme	Third-Party Candidate?
AL (D, R)			
	AK (D)	AK (R)	Center
AZ (D, R)			
AR (R)	AR (D)		
CA (D, R)			
CO (D)	CO (R)		Right
CT (D, R)			
DE (R)	DE (D)		
FL (R)		FL (D)	Center
GA (D, R)			
HI (R)		HI (D)	
ID (R)	ID (D)		
IL (D, R)			
IN (R)		IN (D)	
IA (D)	IA (R)		
KS (D)		KS (R)	
KY (R)		KY (R)	
ME (D, R)			Center
MA (R)		MA (D)	
MD (D)	MD (R)		
MI (D, R)			
	MN (R)	MN (D)	
MS (R)		MS (D)	
MO (D, R)			
MT (D, R)			
NE (R)		NE (D)	
NV (D, R)			
NH (R)	NH (D)		
NJ (D, R)			

(*continued*)

Table 9.3 Continued

No Variation	Primary Electorate More Extreme	Primary Electorate Less Extreme	Third-Party Candidate?
NM (R)		NM (D)	
NY (D, R)			
NC (R)		NC (D)	
ND (D, R)			
OH (R)		OH (D)	
OK (D, R)			
OR (D, R)			
PA (R)		PA (D)	
RI (R)		RI (D)	Left
SC (R)	SC (D)		
SD (D, R)			
TN (D, R)			
TX (D, R)			
UT (R)		UT (D)	
	VT (D, R)		
WV (R)		WV (D)	
WI (D, R)			
WY (R)	WY (D)		
Total			
63 (24D, 39R)	13 (8D, 5R)	17 (14D, 3R)	

more conservative than general election Democratic voters (see, e.g., Moakley and Cornwell 2001). The most evident feature specific to these elections, however, is noted in the final column of Table 9.3. I have identified instances in which an independent or third-party candidate for governor or senate attracted more than 25 percent of the vote.[2] In each case, these candidates received enough votes that the ideological self-placement of those who voted for them clearly influenced the comparisons between primary and general election voters. Four of these five states had primary electorates that diverged from the voters in the general election race in question, and in one instance (Alaska) the independent candidate appears to have drawn voters from both parties' primary electorates, skewing the comparison for both. The only unambiguous finding in this table is that the presence of a competitive third-party candidate in the general election can siphon off some voters, thereby rendering primary electorates more extreme than a party's voters in the general election. This says nothing about the primary electorate, however; rather, it indicates that defectors in these instances came predominantly from one party. In short, the primary-general comparisons accord with much of what political observers had to say about these races, except that they show little evidence of extremism within the primary electorate.

Are there, however, hidden patterns in the state data? There are many reasons to expect some states' primary voters to be more extreme than others. The type of primary system has been alleged by some to foster extremism; as discussed earlier. One might also contend that the competitiveness of the primary, the competitiveness of the general election, or the partisanship of the state might influence the ideology of primary voters. As Table 9.4 shows, there is some evidence that this is the case, yet the differences are not particularly dramatic. The ideological self-placement of voters within each party is different across different primary types; for instance, Democrats in open primary states are more liberal than Democrats in closed primary states. This is more a reflection of political culture (i.e., Wisconsin Democrats appear to be more liberal than Pennsylvania Democrats) than of characteristics of the primary system itself. What matters here is the differences one sees as one reads across the primary types. As in Table 9.2, Democratic general election voters are slightly more liberal than Democratic primary voters regardless of primary type, and Republican voters are substantially the same. It does appear that electorates in open primaries more closely resemble general electorates; within the Republican Party, in addition, it is the voters in closed primaries who are most conservative—relative to the state electorate's overall leanings—in comparison to general election voters. The second set of rows in the table shows that variation in the competitiveness of statewide primaries also has small effects. Voters in competitive Democratic primaries are slightly more moderate than those who voted in uncompetitive races; the same is true for Republicans.

In 2010 conservative voters turned out in force. While it is always possible that this skewed the composition of the Republican general electorate (perhaps making it more like the primary electorate), the relative centrism of the Democratic primary electorate renders such claims suspect. Surely some states, or some races, should have shown the sort of extremism that many expect. However, 2010 also featured a number of unusual primaries, races in which one party's primary produced a surprising upset or some other unusual feature might have been expected to heighten the contrast between primary and general election voters. A few of these races, then, deserve further explanation. Specifically, there was a trio of Republican Senate primaries in which moderates

Table 9.4 Primary vs. General Election Voter Ideology, by State/Primary Type

	Democrat				Republican			
	Primary (SE)	General: House	General: Senate	General: Governor	Primary (SE)	General: House	General: Senate	General: Governor
Closed primary	3.04 (.03)	2.84	2.82	2.86	6.01 (02)	5.93	5.97	5.91
Semiclosed Primary	2.79 (.03)	2.68	2.64	2.75	5.93 (.02)	5.88	5.88	5.86
Semiopen Primary	3.16 (.04)	3.06	2.96	3.15	6.05 (.02)	6.07	5.98	6.05
Open primary	2.84 (.05)	2.83	2.84	2.79	5.90 (.03)	5.97	5.96	5.92
Competitive Senate primary	3.06 (.03)	2.87	2.76	2.95	5.94 (.02)	5.92	5.91	5.86
Uncompetitive Senate primary	2.89 (.03)	2.80	2.79	2.82	6.03 (.02)	5.96	5.99	5.98
Competitive governor primary	2.95 (.03)	2.84	2.75	2.85	5.96 (.02)	5.93	5.95	5.92
Uncompetitive governor primary	2.91 (.02)	2.78	2.75	2.88	6.00 (.02)	5.95	5.90	5.94
All	2.97 (.01)	2.83	2.78	2.87	5.99 (.01)	5.94	5.95	5.93

Source: Cooperative Congressional Election Study 2010 (Ansolabehere 2012).
Note: Numbers represent mean voter ideology scores, calculated on a seven-point scale where 1 = most liberal, 7 = most conservative. Standard errors for primary electorates are shown in parentheses. Standard errors for the various general electorates are all smaller than those for the corresponding primary electorate.

alleged that Tea Party nominees effectively sabotaged the party's chance of winning these states' general elections. In Colorado, Tea Party favorite Ken Buck defeated moderate Ann Norton; in Nevada, Tea Party candidate Sharron Angle bested the more conventional conservative Sue Lowden; and in Delaware, political neophyte Christine O'Donnell upset moderate Republican Mike Castle. In each case, Republican general election voters were narrowly more conservative than primary voters, but the difference is small and statistically insignificant. We cannot disprove the notion that some disgruntled primary voters stayed home, or that some centrists swung over to another party's nominee in the general election, but the similarity between the mean position for general election voters in those races and general election voters in other races in those states suggests that candidate effects here are minimal. For the full CCES sample, 14.1 percent of Democratic primary voters voted for a Republican general election candidate, and 7.9 percent of Republican primary voters voted for a Democratic general election candidate. These numbers raise the possibility that Republican general election candidates peeled off some of the more centrist Democratic primary voters; these voters were substantially more moderate than those who voted a straight party ticket.[3] The number of defectors in these three states, however, was no higher than in other states with less controversial nominees.

Although space precludes offering a full state-by-state analysis, Tables 9.5, 9.6, and 9.7 replicate for 2014 and 2018 some of the considerations of 2010 using CCES data.[4] The 2014 midterms are often considered a more conventional election, in which the opposition party gained a small number of seats, and the 2018 election featured record-high turnout and a Democratic "blue wave" that yielded a Democratic House majority and was widely seen as a repudiation of President Donald Trump. Despite the differences between these elections and 2010, however, the comparisons between the primary electorate, the actual and potential general electorate, and the full sample are similar to what we saw for 2010. Table 9.5 shows that, again, the primary electorate is older, wealthier, better educated, and more partisan than the general electorate. Tables 9.6 and 9.7 show, however, that it is difficult to translate this into statements on ideology. Democratic primary voters are in fact slightly more conservative in terms of their self-placement than Democratic general election voters, although their issue positions are nearly identical. Republican primary voters are slightly more conservative than Republican general election voters. Primary type does not appear to make much of a difference.

There is one difference between these two midterm elections that bears consideration as we move on in the next section to considering year-to-year variation in primary results. In 2014, Republican primary voters consistently took more conservative positions on six of the seven issue questions considered than did Republican general election voters. In 2018, although Republican primary

Table 9.5 Primary vs. General Election Voter Traits, 2014 and 2018

	Primary Voters (%)	General Election Voters (%)	Registered Voters (%)	Full Sample (%)
2014				
Male	50.7	49.3	48.0	48.2
White	82.6	81.9	78.1	74.0
60 years old or older	50.1	41.6	35.7	29.5
30 years old or younger	6.9	11.0	16.1	23.4
Family income below $40,000	28.2	29.7	33.6	35.9
Family income above $80,000	27.1	25.8	23.5	21.5
College graduate (incl. 2-year)	45.1	43.0	39.5	35.8
Voted for Obama in 2012	44.8	46.1	48.1	49.2
Voted for Romney in 2012	51.7	49.5	47.2	45.9
Liberal*	28.7	27.6	26.9	25.8
Middle of the road*	18.1	21.1	23.2	25.8
Conservative*	51.4	48.8	46.4	43.0
Describes self as Democrat	35.8	34.5	35.6	34.6
Describes self as Republican	35.5	32.5	30.1	27.7
Describes self as Independent	26.1	29.8	29.9	30.5
Valid percentage of total sample (N)	25.3 (14,200)	48.2 (28,170)	64.2 (35,972)	100.0 (56,200)
2018				
Male	50.5	49.3	48.2	48.5
White	79.0	76.6	73.6	70.1
60 years old or older	49.2	41.2	35.6	30.2
30 years old or younger	9.7	13.5	17.2	23.2
Family income below $40,000	27.4	29.7	33.5	36.0
Family income above $80,000	29.1	28.0	25.2	23.1
College graduate (incl. 2-year)	49.8	47.0	43.2	40.4
Voted for Clinton in 2016	46.2	47.2	47.2	47.5
Voted for Trump in 2016	49.0	46.6	46.4	45.8
Liberal*	35.2	35.6	33.4	31.8

Table 9.5 Continued

	Primary Voters (%)	General Election Voters (%)	Registered Voters (%)	Full Sample (%)
Middle of the road*	13.6	17.5	20.0	21.9
Conservative*	50.0	45.1	43.2	40.4
Describes self as Democrat	38.3	38.2	37.6	35.6
Describes self as Republican	36.1	36.2	31.1	28.8
Describes self as Independent	20.8	24.0	24.6	26.2
Valid percentage of total sample (N)	14.5 (7,535)	53.3 (27,610)	71.5 (37,050)	100.0 (51,808)

Source: Cooperative Congressional Election Study 2014 and 2018, (Schaffner et al 2015, 2019).
Notes: All voter types are validated.
* Ideology measurements created by conflating self-placements on seven-point scale; 1–3 = liberal, 4 = middle of the road, 5–7 = conservative.

voters still saw themselves as being slightly more conservative, on average, than Republican general election voters, they were only consistently more conservative than Republican general election voters on one of the seven policy items (abortion). It is important to remember that primary electorates are not the same from one election to the next; in this, the first post-Trump midterm election, it could well be that some conservatives fled the party, or that some new Republican voters, attracted by Trump, may have seen themselves as symbolic conservatives yet held some policy views at odds with Republican orthodoxy.

In sum, however, these data suggest that for the most part primary voters look quite similar to general election voters in both parties. Democratic primary voters tend to be slightly more moderate than those who support Democrats in the general election, and Republican primary voters tend to be very slightly more extreme. The nature of the election year, the individual races, and the states' political cultures may play a role in establishing these differences. The comparison here between primary and general election voters is, I argue, a more accurate way to compare primary and general electorates than is a comparison between primary voters and registered voters or self-identified partisans. It compares two actions as opposed to one action and one form of belief or self-identification. It is possible that people change their minds about which party they prefer between the primary and the general election, or that primary outcomes can determine citizens' general election choices. In unusual races this may well happen, but there is little reason to expect this to shape the overall comparison.

Table 9.6 Primary vs. General Election Voters' Preferences, within Parties, 2014 and 2018

	Democrat				Republican			
	Primary	General: House	General: Senate	General: Governor	Primary	General: House	General: Senate	General: Governor
2014								
Ban assault rifles	85.0%	83.1%	82.3%	83.4%	34.9%	40.3%	37.9%	39.9%
Abortion a matter of choice	76.6%	77.5%	76.5%	78.3%	29.0%	35.3%	31.0%	36.0%
Legal status to immigrants	66.0%	67.4%	66.6%	67.7%	23.7%	26.6%	24.2%	25.1%
Extend Bush tax cuts	15.4%	16.3%	16.4%	17.1%	38.2%	36.8%	37.0%	37.4%
Repeal Affordable Care Act	21.5%	22.4%	21.0%	23.3%	86.3%	85.8%	88.5%	85.5%
Support same sex marriage	73.6%	76.1%	73.9%	76.7%	28.9%	34.4%	29.3%	35.0%
Strengthen EPA enforcement	73.1%	71.3%	71.3%	71.1%	15.9%	21.2%	17.9%	21.1%
Mean ideology	3.22	3.16	3.13	3.14	5.66	5.55	5.64	5.54
2018								
Ban assault rifles	90.4%	89.4%	88.4%	91.8%	32.9%	30.4%	36.2%	34.2%
Abortion a matter of choice	81.0%	86.2%	86.2%	86.4%	21.3%	21.8%	26.6%	24.2%
Build a border wall	9.8%	7.5%	8.0%	7.2%	86.7%	90.7%	85.9%	88.3%
Cut corporate income tax	19.0%	16.0%	16.3%	13.9%	83.5%	85.5%	77.4%	83.3%
Repeal Affordable Care Act	10.4%	8.7%	9.9%	7.7%	81.1%	83.5%	76.0%	79.6%
Support Kavanaugh appointment	9.7%	5.0%	5.7%	3.3%	91.2%	95.1%	88.0%	92.0%
Withdraw from Paris climate pact	8.7%	5.6%	5.6%	3.4%	85.1%	88.5%	81.7%	85.9%
Mean ideology	2.72	2.62	2.63	2.53	5.90	5.82	5.54	5.72

Source: Cooperative Congressional Election Study 2014, 2018 (Schaffner et al. 2015, 2019).
Note: All voter types are validated. Ideology scores calculated on a seven-point scale where 1 = most liberal, 7 = most conservative.

Table 9.7 Primary vs. General Election Voter Ideology, by State/Primary Type, 2014 and 2018

	Democrat				Republican			
	Primary	General: House	General: Senate	General: Governor	Primary	General: House	General: Senate	General: Governor
2014								
Closed primary	3.17	3.14	3.01	3.27	5.76	5.43	5.58	5.52
Semiclosed Primary	3.28	3.13	3.15	3.00	5.64	5.64	5.75	5.54
Semiopen Primary	3.09	3.16	3.07	3.03	5.58	5.55	5.52	5.43
Open primary	3.56	3.20	3.17	3.16	5.77	5.67	5.71	5.67
Top two	—	3.13	3.66	3.01	—	5.45	5.79	5.54
All	3.22	3.16	3.13	3.14	5.66	5.55	5.64	5.54
2018								
Closed primary	2.81	2.59	2.33	2.41	5.99	5.93	5.79	5.80
Semiclosed Primary	2.69	2.47	2.30	2.37	5.93	5.80	5.78	5.91
Semiopen Primary	2.62	2.74	2.78	2.65	5.83	5.65	5.22	5.58
Open primary	2.71	2.54	2.54	2.42	5.90	5.94	5.85	5.83
Top two	2.92	2.59	2.59	2.59	5.94	5.91	5.87	5.73
All	2.72	2.62	2.63	2.53	5.90	5.82	5.54	5.72

Source: Cooperative Congressional Election Study 2014, 2018 (Schaffner and Ansolabehere 2015; Schaffner, Ansolabehere, and Luks 2019).
Note: All voter types are validated. Numbers represent mean voter ideology scores, calculated on a seven-point scale where 1 = most liberal, 7 = most conservative.

The question here hinges, then, on what a significant difference is. This is not necessarily a statistical question; the standard errors here are small enough that very small differences between primary and general electorates attain conventional levels of statistical significance. The question is rather one of opinion. What does it mean that the mean for the Republican primary electorate was 5.99 and the mean for those who supported the Republican Senate candidate was 5.95? This could simply be a function of the fact that conservative Republican candidates, running in conservative states, received more votes. The small number of substantial differences within the states indicates that we cannot point to any large states where the primary electorate seems likely to have pulled the candidate away from the center. Or to contextualize the numerical difference here, a comparison of these two means drawn from a hypothetical one-hundred-person electorate would result in a primary electorate in which ninety-nine voters classified themselves as "conservative" and one voter classified himself or herself as "somewhat conservative," while in the general electorate, four additional voters called themselves "somewhat conservative," or an additional two called themselves "middle of the road." Put in these terms, the distinction, although it clearly exists, does not seem to say very much about primaries, nor does it seem to suggest that there is a "problem" that has not always existed.

Why Would We Get Extreme Candidates without Extreme Voters?

The idea that primary voters pull candidates to the extremes has a long history in political science. How are we to understand the prevalence of this idea among politicians and activists if it appears not to be true? One potential answer is that candidates have incentives to take positions that do not reflect the voters' views. Perhaps candidate beliefs might shape primary competition, even if those beliefs are wrong (see Broockman and Skovron 2018). If candidates believe that they must play to the extremes in primaries, then they will do so even if there is no obvious benefit to be had from doing so. There is nothing in these data to suggest that overly ideological candidates are punished by primary electorates. Primary electorates may reward ideological candidates for nonideological reasons—that is, they may admire candidates who take strong positions even if they do not share these positions. Some research has also suggested that ideologically extreme candidates excel at raising money (Johnson 2010) or that candidates adopt extreme positions in order to appeal to donors (Kujala 2019), and such concerns may pull candidates away from the center without being reflected in the electorate.

If primaries of one party or the other do tend to produce noncentrist candidates, these victories may also reflect the nature of competition. Even if candidates are taking vote-maximizing positions, there is no guarantee that multicandidate competition will reward moderate candidates. There is no reason that it systematically should not, but if one party's primaries feature more candidates than the other party's, the likelihood of noncentrist candidates emerging increases. To put this in the framework of recent elections, Republican House and Senate primaries have featured more competition than Democratic primaries for six of the past seven election cycles (see Boatright and Albert 2021). Even if voters chose candidates strictly on the basis of ideological proximity (a dubious assumption), a candidate running uncontested would have incentives to move toward the general election median, and two candidates running against each other in a primary would seek the primary median. In a three- or-more-candidate race, however, there is no equilibrium. A party with a higher number of races with three or more candidates should thus produce more extreme candidates regardless of any differences between primary and general election voters.

The first two reasons given here assume that findings about extreme candidates emerging from primaries are, in fact, correct. It is important to note, however, that the few such studies that exist are many years old. To the extent that the claims of these articles are repeated today, however, it seems likely that the pundits making such claims are not referring to academic findings; more likely they have particular elections in mind. As we have seen, 2010 featured a few primaries that drew national attention because of the victories of apparently inferior general election candidates. Meanwhile, stories in which incumbents hold off challengers or run unopposed draw little scrutiny. It is also possible, then, that a small number of idiosyncratic races attract media attention and distort our understanding of what goes on in primaries.

Primary elections, like other low-salience elections—municipal elections (Hajnal 2009), midterm elections, or other such races—are dominated by the kinds of voters who vote out of habit. These people may be idiosyncratic in many ways; they are wealthier, they are older, they have lived in the same place for longer, and they know more about politics. Such voters are not, however, automatically the sorts of ideological insurgents that they are sometimes alleged to be. If primaries do produce extreme candidates, it is easy to blame the voters, but there are certainly other compelling stories that could be told: about the candidates, about the groups and individual donors who support the candidates, and perhaps about the media and the punditocracy. None of these stories leads directly, however, to reforms to the primary system.

Partisan Swing and Primary Competition

Just as it is common to blame primary voters for party polarization, so also has it become common to use particular election years' primary results to dramatize, or personify, polarization. Individual primary victories such as David Brat's defeat of House Majority leader Eric Cantor in 2014, or Alexandria Ocasio-Cortez's primary victory in 2018 over House Democratic Caucus chair Joseph Crowley in 2018, have been used as shorthand to describe those years' congressional elections.

More generally, election victories such as these raise the possibility that general election surges might be accompanied by increased unrest in the primaries as well. Some of the time series presented in this book—particularly the evidence of dramatic changes in party support during the 1930s throughout the United States—suggest that any effort to understand primary competition must reckon with broader partisan surges in the electorate. However, there is no established theory of patterns in congressional primary election competition over time. Our understanding of congressional general election competition has for decades been shaped by theories regarding partisan seat swing. Indeed, one could argue that the decisions of candidates and party leaders themselves rest on a small set of regular patterns: presidential coattails, midterm backlashes against the incumbent president, "waves" of party support, and so forth. This section of the chapter explores the relationship between such general election voting patterns and competition in congressional primaries. The evidence here shows that partisan surges explain far more of the change in competition in primaries over time than do changes in primary laws; furthermore, these variations are so substantial that they make it nearly impossible to identify any other causes of variation.

At first glance, it would seem that congressional primary competition should be immune to such patterns. After all, there are no partisan cues within primary elections, and there is little evidence that attitudes about the president or about party performance in Congress should have an obvious influence on primaries. Literature on congressional primaries has thus emphasized factors such as regional differences between the parties, voter eligibility rules for primaries, or other factors that may change over time but have no obvious relationship to individual election years.

In previous work (Boatright 2013, 89–91), I have documented the declining differences between regions of the country and party organizational strength in one type of primary, intraparty challenges to incumbents. This decline suggests that if ever parties had the ability to structure primary competition, they have lost that ability over the past forty years. However, challenges to incumbents appear to have been more common in years when there was a partisan surge. That is, Democratic incumbents were more likely to face challenges from the left in good Democratic years such as 1974 and 2006, and Republican incumbents were more likely to face challenges from the right in good Republican years such as 1994 and 2010. We can add to this observation the expectation drawn from literature on candidate emergence that challenger primaries (i.e., primaries whose nominee expects to face a sitting incumbent in the general election) and open seat primaries should be more crowded in a party that expects to pick up seats in a given election year. There may be some cases in which parties recruit strong candidates and/or take steps to stave off primary competition, but such efforts still seem unlikely to deter all interested candidates.[5] In short, we can develop an argument about partisan tides that speaks to competition in all different types of primaries.

The Insulation of Primaries from National Trends

As we have seen, variations in state primary laws make comparing primary elections across time difficult. Political scientists have solved this problem in three different ways.

The decline of competitiveness: First, Ansolabehere et al. (2006, 2007, 2010) show that competition in congressional primary elections was quite common in the 1920s but declined steadily thereafter, reaching a stable and low level by the 1980s. Variations in state primary rules are endogenous to the Ansolabehere et al. study—if states change their primary laws in order to reduce competition, the precise nature of the rules is less consequential for their argument than is the outcome of the rule changes. In addition, the lengthy period under consideration in these articles takes precedence over short-term variation. If primary competition is more common, for instance, in a high-turnover year such as 1992, this increase may look impressive in relationship to competition levels in 1988 or 1990 but relatively insignificant in comparison to the level of competition in the 1930s. Overall, however, the explanation Ansolabehere et al. provide for declining competitiveness suggests that this decline had little to do with overall changes in *general* election competitiveness. General elections, too, became less competitive over this period, but at a different rate and for different reasons. The Ansolabehere et al. findings also suggest that any analysis of a connection between primary and general election competition must either account for an overall decline in competition or be limited to the past three to four decades.

Primary rules: Most studies of primary rules (Kanthak and Morton 2001; Burden 2001; Gerber and Morton 1998; Telford 1965) have sought to assess the degree of moderation of eventual nominees; evidence is mixed as to whether primary rules have any effect at all. The adoption of a particular primary type, or a change in primary type, may be driven by partisan considerations and may be aimed at insulating the dominant party from partisan waves. It is thus not entirely exogenous to the state of national politics. Because primary rules are "sticky," however, it is arguably possible to separate out open and closed primary states for analysis and to avoid here a detailed consideration of the timing of the adoption of primary voting rule changes.

Primary divisiveness: A third approach to sorting out the relationship between primary and general election competition is to look at the divisiveness literature described earlier in this chapter. Studies of the divisiveness of congressional primaries have had mixed results. Hacker (1965) argued that they have no effect on general election outcomes; in a study of Senate primaries, Bernstein (1977) argued that they hurt the stronger party but not the weaker party; and in their study of Senate and gubernatorial races, Kenney and Rice (1984) found that the impact of divisiveness varies by party and office, and that these differential effects are conditioned by the degree of primary divisiveness experienced by the other party in that same election (see also Kenney and Rice 1987). A 1975 study of House races by Piereson and Smith found that divisive primaries hurt in competitive districts but not in uncompetitive ones.[6] Alvarez, Canon, and Sellers (1995) find that general election challengers benefit from competitive primaries while incumbents' general election fortunes are harmed by competitive primaries; these effects are magnified when primary dates are close to the general election. Ware (1979), finally, questions the methodology behind such studies, arguing that close races are not ipso facto more competitive than lopsided ones.

More recent studies of divisiveness have also criticized the methodology of these earlier studies. Jeffrey Lazarus (2005) summarizes the preponderant theme of the early literature—that divisive primaries help challengers and hurt incumbents (or help "outsider candidates" and harm "insider candidates") in the general election—and then argues that this literature has matters backward. Lazarus argues that more candidates will get into a race when their chance of winning the seat is greater, so the appropriate thing to look at is the number of candidates running, not necessarily the closeness of the race. The more candidates there are in a primary, and the more money is spent in the primary, the better the party does in the general election—not because multiple candidates have run or spent money, but because the emergence of multiple candidates and the high level of spending are a consequence of the likelihood that the primary nominee will win the general election. The effects here are stronger for the out-party, or nonincumbent party, than for the incumbent party. Johnson, Petersheim, and Wasson (2010) generally corroborate Lazarus's results but measure the effects of the primary date on general election outcomes; the authors contend that competitive late primaries yield better general election results for out-parties. The excitement generated by nonincumbent primaries, in this accounting, dissipates quickly but can have an effect on general elections if the primary and general elections are close enough.

This literature suggests, first, that there is a plausible reason for there to be a relationship between primary and general election competition, and second, that parties or candidates might act to encourage or discourage competition based on their expectations of what will happen in the general election. With the exception of the Ansolabehere et al. work, the literature relies on individual-level analyses, positing a relationship in a forward-looking manner, exploring the effects of primary divisiveness on candidates' and parties' fortunes come November. In the case of the Ansolabehere et al. work, primary competitiveness is observed but explained in a long-term, institutional manner: Why did primaries become less competitive across decades? In the other two types of literature, primaries serve as Independent variables: What sorts of nominees are produced by different primary types, or what sorts of general election results are the consequences of a particular level of primary competition? As Lazarus (2005) has pointed out, primary competition may well be a function of the expected outcome rather than the cause of the actual outcome, and hence we should look at the factors that create competition. All of these studies suggest that there are reasons candidates or parties might have taken steps to insulate primaries from national fluctuations in partisan support, but that such a relationship might still be expected to exist absent deliberate efforts to counteract it.

The Connection between Primaries and Partisan Waves

From the inception of primary elections, political elites had many expectations about how they might be influenced by general election concerns. For instance, one of the early objections to primary elections was that they stripped political parties of their traditional balancing function. Such balancing was generally seen as a matter of ensuring that different geographic constituencies had representation, or that officers alternated among different constituency groups (Hormell 1923). For some Progressives, balancing was a means of satisfying ethnic blocs at the expense of quality candidates, while in today's politics (in the United States and elsewhere) balancing a ticket to ensure representation by women or by minority racial groups is often a goal for liberals (Reynolds 2006, 187). In either instance, primary elections can be sensitive to ideological unrest among voters—even in instances where the candidates do not win, the presence of candidates with a particular viewpoint may be a sign of turmoil in the electorate. Absent the ability to placate such groups, parties have no choice but to watch such conflict play out in the electorate.

These sorts of concerns indicate that from the beginning some saw the potential for primary elections to be influenced by national events. The party system, however, was not sufficiently nationalized for this to be the case. That is, as documented in the earlier chapters of this book, many of the more systematic primary challenges (i.e., primary challenges that were not based solely on characteristics of individual candidates or officeholders) were decidedly regional in nature, as shown by unusual primaries in states such as California, Minnesota, and North Dakota. In such instances, qualitative researchers have drawn a clear link between economic disarray and primary competition. In each of these cases, however, the dominant party in the state (in these examples, the Republicans) was diverse enough that an intraparty challenge made more sense than a challenge from the opposition (Democratic) Party. By the late twentieth century, however, more states had competition between the two parties, and the two major parties had become more ideologically consistent. Primary competition was not necessarily a substitute for general election competition; instead, primary competition could be linked to expectations about the general election in ways that it could not in the early twentieth century. And yet, as we have seen most recently with the Tea Party, ideological factions that see themselves in opposition to the parties themselves still appear. Is there a way to discuss the appearance of these sorts of factions, not in terms of their consequences for the general election, but following Lazarus, as consequences themselves of the dynamics of general election competition?

To assess the relevance of national levels of competition to primary competition, let us turn to a consideration of the salient features of the literature on party surge and decline. Each election has its own partisan dynamic, and political scientists have developed several theories—some competing, some complementary—to understand these partisan rhythms. Campbell (1997) identifies an enduring presidential "pulse" to congressional elections, in which the party of the winning presidential nominee picks up seats in the House in presidential election years and then loses seats in the subsequent midterm election. Presidential year successes left the president's party overexposed in subsequent midterm elections, in which they were forced to defend seats that would be held by the opposing party under more "normal" circumstances (Oppenheimer, Stimson, and Waterman 1986). The "exposure thesis" builds on this explanation and sits at the nexus of explanations of party surge and decline that hinge on structural forces and those that treat midterms as referenda on the president's performance. In this account, the president's party's performance in the midterm is driven not only by the extent to which it is exposed in districts in which it has historically struggled, but also by the extent to which it is exposed in districts in which vulnerable incumbents have chosen to retire (Gaddie 1997).

Kernell (1977) proposes an alternative causal process in which voters motivated and mobilized by disappointment in the president's performance explain much of the loss of seats experienced by the president's party in midterm elections. Often this disappointment is operationalized in terms of economic growth and unemployment (Tufte 1975). More recently, Fiorina (1996) has argued that midterm voters who perceive the president's party as having moved too far to the right (in the case of Republicans) or left (in the case of Democrats) use midterm elections as an opportunity to "balance" or offset the presidential advantage by enlarging the ranks of his opponents in Congress. This work builds on Erikson's (1988) argument that the president's party is punished in midterms simply for holding the White House, what he dubbed the "presidential penalty" explanation of electoral decline in midterm elections.

All of these models and theories are less relevant here for their content than for the fact that they suggest the political class has a reasonably accurate means of predicting what will happen, and that these beliefs could plausibly shape candidate entry and competitiveness in primaries. In short, it is reasonable to assume that primary competition is shaped by relatively accurate expectations about general election competition, and that these effects may well swamp characteristics of the primary laws.

Expectations

Let us then consider the relationship between congressional primary competition, on the one hand, and general election competition between the parties on the other. We are not looking at the effect of the individual primary election on the nominee's general election performance; rather, we are concerned with the relationship between expectations about party advantage in an election year and the appearance of candidates of each party in primary elections. Candidate expectations can be difficult to quantify. First, there is certainly variation in the expected degree of turnover in a particular election cycle; we cannot, for instance, simply assume that all midterm elections will be similarly disastrous for the incumbent president's party. Second, candidates must file for the primary as early as ten months before the general election in some states (Ansolabehere and Gerber 1996), and candidates who are capable of raising significant amounts of money must often begin preparing for the election much earlier than that. Expectations are, therefore, fallible, subjective, and difficult to qualify. We can, however, use estimates of competitiveness in the general election (at the national level, again, as at least a proxy for expectations.

There are different ways to think about national patterns in elections, however. If we are keeping matters at the national level—that is, considering how prospective primary candidates are thinking about the election's broader context rather than about the characteristics of the district or the incumbent—we can think about partisanship or generally about the public's dissatisfaction with Congress. Some elections may be characterized by a hostility toward one party, as arguably was the case in 2010, while others may be characterized by a hostility toward incumbents and politicians more broadly, as may have been the case in 1992. It makes sense to look at partisan swing (the seat gain for one party) as well as overall turnover, as measured by the number of defeated incumbents of both parties. The national political context can also be assessed using other ex post measures, such as the number of seats won by less than a ten-point margin.

It is also important to consider the consequences of national partisan trends for different kinds of primaries. The most consequential distinction to make is between open seat primaries, primaries for the nomination to challenge an incumbent (challenger primaries), and primaries featuring an incumbent.

Open seat primaries occur for a variety of reasons, some of which are directly related to the departing incumbent's assessment of his or her chances in the general election (and, in rare instances, the primary). The number of incumbents who retire increases in election years expected to be difficult for the departing incumbent's party (Hibbing 1982a, 1982b, 1982c), but departures also occur because incumbents wish to seek higher office or simply because incumbents wish to leave politics. The number of open seats is somewhat correlated with partisan swing in the next general election—that is, there tend to be more retirements in the party that would go on to lose seats in the general election, although the differences are not as striking as one might expect at first glance. From 1970 to 2020, an average of 20.9 members of the party that went on to lose seats in the general election retired per cycle. The comparable number for members of the party that eventually picked up seats in November was 17.8. However, retirements have been shown to be a major factor in aggregate seat changes in the House (Gaddie 1997).

To summarize, because at least some incumbents who retire will have done so out of concern about the impending general election, open seat primaries should, on average, be less competitive within the party harmed by the national partisan swing than within the party advantaged by the swing. Furthermore, competition in open seat primaries should be higher in years marked by a higher overall level of turnover, irrespective of party.

Challenger primaries are perhaps the clearest case of primary elections whose competitiveness is dependent on the general election context. The more vulnerable incumbents of one party are, the more likely it is that candidates of the other party will line up to challenge them. Hence, challenger primaries in the party expected to gain seats should be more competitive than primaries in the party expected to lose seats. It is more difficult than in the open seat case to predict the effects of general election turnover without reference to partisanship, however. Since 1970, there have only been five elections (1976, 1988, 1990, 2000, and 2002) in which one party did not win more than 70 percent of the races in which incumbents were defeated. These were all election years in which a very small number of seats changed hands at all. There are, then, no election years in recent memory when the defeat of a large number of incumbents was not a rebuke of one party. Hence, we should also expect that heightened competition in challenger primaries in high turnover years will be limited to the party expected to gain seats in that year.

Finally, we have what might appear at first to be counterintuitive expectations about *incumbent primaries*. One would expect competition in incumbent primaries to follow a different logic according to party. For one thing, it is relatively rare for incumbents to face primary opposition at all. Some incumbents certainly face primary opponents for reasons unrelated to the incumbent's partisanship or ideological stance—that is, a percentage of primary challenges will simply be waged by ambitious challengers or by challengers unhappy about nonpolicy matters such as ethical wrongdoing by the incumbent. We have no reason to expect such challenges to cluster in one party or to be more prevalent in particular types of election years.[7]

However, at least some primary challenges to incumbents will be ideological in nature, as signified by Tea Party challenges to sitting Republican incumbents in recent elections. How can we understand the relationship of such races to partisanship? Consider two different scenarios.

First, primary challenges may be indicative of a party's difficulty in holding together a diverse coalition. Following the logic of theoretical models such as Riker's (1982) "minimum winning coalition" model and Alfred Hirschman's (1970) distinction between "exit and voice," some primary challenges may be a product of the same intraparty disagreements that may cause some other party members to flee the party altogether. Hence, incumbent primary challenges may be more common in a party that expects to lose seats in the upcoming election.

Second, however, partisan surges are often related to an overall increase in enthusiasm among those who hold strong ideological views. In 2010, for instance, some Tea Party activists channeled their dissatisfaction into supporting challenges to sitting Democrats, while other channeled their dissatisfaction into supporting challenges to Republicans they deemed insufficiently hostile toward the Democratic Party's agenda. The same might be said about Democratic activists in 2018. Incumbent primary challenges may, according to this logic, be more common in parties expecting to gain seats than in parties expecting to lose seats.

As we shall see later in the chapter the two parties differ in the relationship between challenges to incumbents and overall partisan trends. The Democratic

Party—arguably the party with the broader and more unwieldy coalition during much of the period considered here (see Freeman 1986 for a discussion)—follows the first logic more closely, while Republicans follow the second.

Measuring Primary Competition

The analyses below consider all major party elections for the House of Representatives from 1970 through 2010, excluding special election primaries and primaries in which two incumbents faced each other. Competitiveness is considered not as a determinant of general election outcomes but as a consequence of reasonably correct expectations about the national political context as it would be reflected in the general election results. While the partisan surge and decline literature suggests that there is a variety of complicated predictive variables we might use, for the sake of simplicity we can simply use the eventual results to reflect elite expectations about party fortunes in any given election. I thus use two general election measures: the total partisan swing, measured both as a raw number (the absolute value of the change in party representation) and as a positive or negative number for each party; and the total number of defeated incumbents, again in the aggregate and for each party. These two measures capture both the effects of partisan swings and the overall unrest in the electorate.

Competitiveness, the dependent variable of interest, is measured differently for the three election types. In the case of open seat and challenger primaries, I follow several recent studies (Canon 1978; Herrnson and Gimpel 1995; Hogan 2003; Brogan and Mendilow 2012) in employing a fractionalization index, which is operationalized as

$$F = 1 - \Sigma\left[(C_1)^2 + (C_2)^2 + (C_3)^2 + (C_4)^2 \ldots\right]$$

where F is the fractionalization index, C_1 is the percentage of the total vote received by the first candidate, C_2 is the percentage of the total vote received by the second candidate, and so on. This yields an index in which a one-candidate race has a fractionalization index of zero, and a race in which two candidates split the vote would have a fractionalization index of 0.5 (or $1 - (0.5^2 + 0.5^2)$). The larger the number of similarly competitive candidates, the closer the index is to 1; that is, a race with ten candidates who received 10 percent of the vote each would have an index of $1 - [(.1)^2 * 10]$, or 0.9. The intuition behind these indexes, in other words, is that an election in which one candidate gets most of the votes is not very fractionalized, even if there are multiple candidates; races with two candidates with similar vote share are split, and those with more than two equally competitive candidates are even more divided.

The fractionalization index is adept at capturing differences in competition in races in which competition between multiple candidates is the norm. For incumbent primaries, fractionalization is not necessarily the best indicator of competition. As noted previously, the vast majority of incumbents run without serious primary opposition. Thus, following my previous work (Boatright 2013), I distinguish here between incumbents who ran without a serious opponent and incumbents who were held to 75 percent or less of the primary vote. We thus have a binary measure: either incumbents faced a credible challenge or they did not. Because challenges to incumbents are so few, it is also easy to categorize primary challenges as being related to ideology or not. Again, open seat and challenger primary competition is always about the partisanship of the incumbent or departing incumbent—in the challenger party case, all challengers disagree with that incumbent's political views, while in open seat races the candidate of the party that does not hold the seat also disagrees. It is possible, and I argue, necessary, to separate out primary challenges to incumbents that have an ideological or policy component from those that do not. Here, as well, I follow the coding of my previous work (Boatright 2013, 65–72) to identify such races.

Results

Table 9.8 shows bivariate correlations between, on the one hand, various indicators of primary competition, and on the other, two indicators of general election competitiveness, the number of incumbents defeated in the general election (columns 1–3), and the seat swing (columns 4–6). The table shows these correlation coefficients in the aggregate and by party. Coefficients that the above hypotheses predict to be significant are shown in bold; for all, the predicted correlation should be positive.

Five of the six aggregate correlation coefficients (presented in columns 1 and 4) are significant, and all are positive. Correlations between challenger primary competition and general election turnover are the highest, but open seat correlations are all still significant as well. The hypotheses regarding incumbent primaries are somewhat more cautious, and perhaps justifiably so; incumbent primary challenges are highly and positively correlated with the number of incumbent defeats in the general election, but the correlation with seat swing is small and not significant.

Correlations within both parties between challenger primary competition and general election turnover are also highly significant, but none of the predicted open seat or incumbent primary coefficients is significant. For Republicans, open seat competition is related to the total number of seats changing from Democratic to Republican hands but not with the number of incumbent defeats—something

Table 9.8 Correlations between Level of Primary Competition and General Election Results

	Incumbents Defeated in General (Total)	Dem Incumbents Defeated in General	Rep Incumbents Defeated in General	Seat Swing (Total)	Seat Swing (D to R)	Seat Swing (R to D)
Open seat Fractionalization	.410*			.562**		
Dem open seat Fractionalization		.242	.268		.246	.171
Rep open seat Fractionalization		.140	-.188		.447*	-.285
Challenger Fractionalization	.527**			.555**		
Dem challenger Fractionalization		-.126	.567**		-.219	.276
Rep challenger Fractionalization		.581**	-.144		.636**	-.362
Incumbents challenged in primary	.408*			.195		
Dem incumbents challenged in primary		.499**	-.018		.258	-.047
Rep incumbents challenged in primary		.112	.033		.070	-.129

Source: Author's data.
Note: Coefficients in bold are those predicted to be significant in hypotheses. All cases except fractionalization index are sums for each category in individual election years. Fractionalization is as defined in text.
* $p < .05$; ** $p < .01$.

that may say more about the nature of the open seats in play than about partisan competition. Competition in Republican incumbent primaries is positively correlated with both measures of Republican gain in the general election, but the correlations are not significant. As noted later in the chapter, however, correlations for the period from 1970 through 2010 *are* significant, indicating, perhaps, that the nature of Republican primary challenges has changed in the past decade. And oddly, Democratic incumbent primary challenges are positively correlated with the number of *Democratic incumbents* defeated in the general election but not with the number of incumbent Republicans defeated in the general election, a result that clearly merits further investigation.

These correlations show that most of our expectations are borne out in the full time series, but they highlight neither unusual elections nor changes in the relationship between primary and general election competition over time. To explore this, let us turn now to a series of visual depictions of the trends from 1970 through 2018.

Open Seat Primaries

One might expect that open seat primaries would be the races that would most clearly show the influence of national trends, but as Table 9.8 showed, the results are decidedly mixed. Open seat primaries are more competitive in years when large numbers of incumbents lose and seat swings are high; when we disaggregate by party, we find that open seat primaries are more competitive in years when Republicans pick up seats, but there is no equivalent relationship for Democrats. Figure 9.1 shows fractionalization in Democratic and Republican open seat primaries, with lines inserted, for viewing convenience, in years generally considered to be surge years for one party. The time series here suggests three things: first, that all four of the high-turnover elections in the time series, 1974, 1994, 2010, and 2018, are associated with unusually high fractionalization within the party that benefited from the surge; second, that in two of these surge years *both* parties exhibited unusually high levels of fractionalization; and third, that the Democratic Party generally had higher fractionalization than the Republican Party before 1992 but had consistently lower levels of fractionalization from 1994 until 2018.

The patterns shown in this figure are similar when one separates out primaries by region of the country and according to the level of competitiveness of the general election.[8] As one might expect, there is more competition in races in which the nominee stands a better chance of winning the general election, but there is no obvious pattern across time. With the exception of 1974, the various surge years show heightened competition for open seat races regardless of the prospective nominees' general election prospects. The Democratic decline in fractionalization is somewhat driven by the party's decline in the South; Southern primaries are more competitive than other Democratic races before 1992 but less so afterward.[9] Our ability

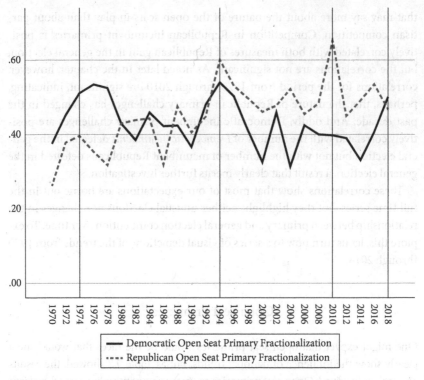

Figure 9.1. Open seat primary fractionalization by party, 1970–2018
Source: Author's data.

to make inferences based on region, however, is limited because the number of open seat races in the South is quite small in many years in this time series.

The time series here shows, then, that in most high turnover years, there is heightened primary competition. The low correlations overall between open seat primary fractionalization and seat swing suggest that the small number of open seat races, the trend toward greater competition in Republican primaries, and the changing role of the South in the Democratic coalition all make this relationship more complicated than it might be in other types of races.

Challenger Primaries

The relationship between primary and general election competition is much more straightforward for challenger primaries. There are more of them, so idiosyncrasies cause fewer variation when we look at patterns over time. As we saw in Table 9.5, the correlation coefficients are all significant and signed in the correct direction. Challenger primaries are most competitive when the party holding the primary expects to do well in the general election. Figure 9.2 shows this relationship across time, with lines again to mark surge years. Here, not only is there greater competition in surge years within the party that benefits from the surge, but there is also reduced competition within the party that is harmed by the surge. There are still some anomalies here, however; for instance, Democratic challenger primaries were unusually competitive in 1984 despite the party's lackluster showing in that year's general election. And in contrast to the pattern for open seats, both parties saw heightened competition in challenger primaries in 1992, the lone high turnover year for both parties in this period.

Further analysis (not shown) indicates that most of the heightened competition in challenger primaries takes place within districts where the nominee goes on to receive at least 40 percent of the general election vote.[10] That is, primary competition is clearly driven by the expectation that the nominee will have a chance of victory in November. Fractionalization in primaries for the challenger nomination in less competitive seats was relatively consistent through

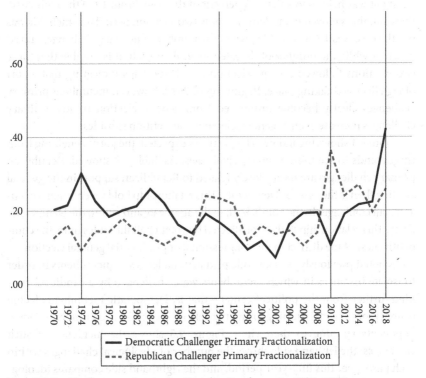

Figure 9.2. Challenger primary fractionalization by party, 1970–2018
Source: Author's data.

2008 but grew noticeably beginning in 2010. This growth initially occurred on the Republican side, but Democratic primaries also became much more competitive by the late 2010s. The growth in competitiveness in Republican primaries has also been driven by the party's growing support in the South; Southern challenger primaries, which tended to take place in the Republican Party during the 1970s and 1980s, were less competitive than primaries in other parts of the country during this time, but the regional difference disappeared after 1992. As is the case for open seats, there is no discernible pattern to the competitiveness of challenger primaries that relates to rules governing voter eligibility in primaries.

Incumbent Primaries

As noted earlier, competition in incumbent primaries is not the norm; therefore, we shall use a different measurement of competitiveness in looking at primary challenges to incumbents. Figure 9.3 shows the relationship between general election defeats of incumbents and primary challenges in which the incumbent was held to less than 75 percent of the vote. From 1970 through 2010, these numbers moved in tandem. The only two-election period in which this was not the case was 1976 and 1978, when the number of primary challenges stayed constant while the number of defeated incumbents fell. It is notable that these two elections followed a surge election (1974), perhaps indicating that a sort of lag effect was taking place. Beginning in 2012, however, incumbent primary challenges clearly become unmoored from general election trends. Primary challenges increase even as general election competition subsides.

Figure 9.4 shows breakdowns by party. As expected, the party benefiting from surges tends to see more primary challenges. As Table 9.3 showed, Republican primary challenges are more closely related to Republican support in the general election than is the case for Democrats. This relationship holds even when we separate out challenges in the South, both in the aggregate and within the Democratic Party. This relationship is also not affected by voter eligibility rules or by the competitiveness of the district in the congressional or presidential general election.

As noted previously, we can code primary challenges to incumbents in order to isolate instances in which incumbents were challenged by a candidate running further from the political center—that is, Democratic incumbents facing primary opponents running from the left or Republican incumbents facing opponents running to their right. Figure 9.5 shows the incidence of such challenges; the lefthand side shows the number of ideological challenges within each party over this fifty-year period, and the righthand side compares ideological challenges over time to other types of challenges.

This figure shows that there is a relationship between primary challenges to incumbents and general election competition, but this correlation has weakened

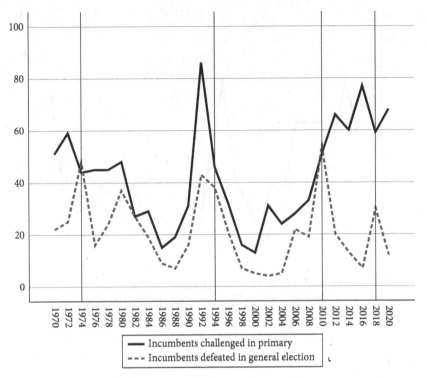

Figure 9.3. Primary challenges to incumbents and general election turnover, 1970–2020
Source: Author's data.

substantially over the past decade. During the time it has weakened, ideology has become a more common reason for challenges than was the case in the past. Through about 2010, good Democratic years featured a higher than usual number of primary challenges, and the same held for Republicans. The overall number of such challenges was small, however, and these challenges were concentrated in heavily partisan districts. The Republican surge in primary challenges in 2010 might have been expected, then, because of the strong Republican wave that year, and one might even have expected, based on the pattern in earlier decades, that this surge in challenges would continue in 2012 and 2014. Republican challenges remained high over the subsequent two election cycles, and Democratic challenges increased with the 2018 Democratic wave. Looked at in historical perspective, then, incumbent primaries have become somewhat unmoored from general election competition over the past decade, but it is too soon to tell whether this is an aberration caused by partisan waves or short-term changes in the party coalitions, or whether there has been a more enduring change in primary competition.

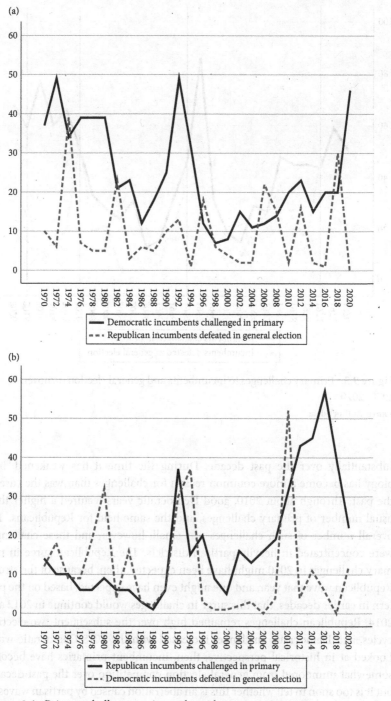

Figure 9.4. Primary challenges to incumbents by party, 1970–2020
Note: The first graph shows Democratic challenges, the second Republicans challenges. The numbers on the y-axis represent the number of candidates challenged.
Source: Author's data.

WHY PRIMARY REFORMS RARELY WORK 269

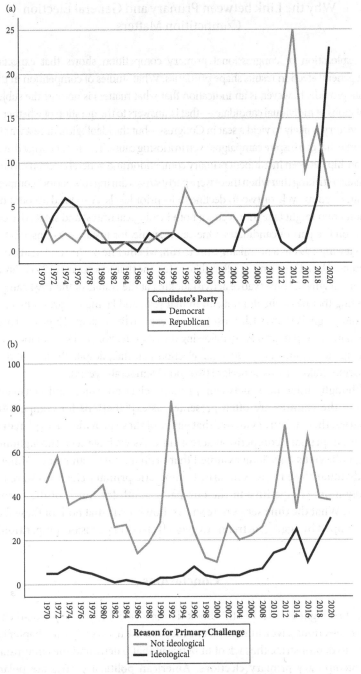

Figure 9.5. Ideological primary challenges to incumbents, 1970–2020
Note: The first graph compares Democratic and Republican primary challenges. The second graph compares ideological and all other types of challenges. The numbers on the y-axis represent the number of candidates challenged.
Source: Author's data.

Why the Link between Primary and General Election Competition Matters

This exploration of congressional primary competition shows that expectations about general election results shape primaries. What studies of competition in the aggregate provide, however, is an indication that what matters is not just the subjective calculations of individual candidates—that is, answers to the question of whether a primary victory is likely to yield a seat in Congress—but the ideological unrest within the electorate that can inspire campaigns even in a losing cause. This may be what drives the relationship between incumbent primary competition and general election turnover.

It is also striking that when there were party surges during this period, competition took an election cycle or two to decline to its prior levels. A stylized account of this phenomenon might take into account both ideological unrest and subjective expectations on the part of candidates. One can imagine, for instance, a conservative activist viewing 1994 as a promising time to run, whether he or she resided in a district represented by a Democrat or a Republican (or one that was open in 1994). Similarly, one can imagine a conservative activist looking at the results of the 1994 campaign, lamenting that he or she did not run in that year, and laying the groundwork for a 1996 campaign. Perhaps such considerations explain the sustained high level of competition in the Republican Party following the 2010 election, or Democratic primary challenges to incumbents in 2010 (an election year that, despite the blow it dealt to Democrats, followed on the heels of two good Democratic years).

Although differences between primary election rules and between regions of the country are often presented as explanations for competition in primaries, there is little evidence that either of these provides an explanation of changes in primary competition across time. As we have seen throughout this book, politicians have long assumed that primary rules can make a difference in individual close races. Similarly, Democratic primary elections were indisputably more competitive in the one-party South for much of the twentieth century. What the time series here shows, however, is that both of these factors are swamped by aggregate trends in general election partisan competition.

Conclusions

As the first eight chapters of this book demonstrated, those who would change primary elections have a limited palette they can use to do so. In this chapter I have sought to demonstrate the lack of fit between that palette and the circumstances of contemporary primary elections. American political parties are polarized today to an extent that would make them unrecognizable to the party reform proponents of the early twentieth century, or even the mid-twentieth century. That polarization is not, however, the fault of primaries. Using traditional tools to increase or restrict voter access to primaries would likely make little difference, because we have no evidence that primary voters are any different than the parties' general election voters. And any changes that we might make are nearly impossible for voters to notice given the dependence of primary election outcomes on the broader political climate. In short, we could make changes, but it's not at all clear that these changes would make a difference, and even if they did make a small difference, it is not at all clear that voters would notice.

In the next chapter I will explore the consequences of this claim: whether it means that we should worry less about primary elections (and perhaps spend more time thinking about other types of reforms) or the limited results throughout the century of primary reforms suggest that anyone dissatisfied with contemporary politics should consider more radical changes to our election system. How one evaluates these options depends in part on four questions that have been raised in this chapter.

First, what are our standards for determining whether any differences in primary laws are salient? To return to the data on primary and general election voters, there were some very slight differences in these data, in some circumstances, between the parties' primary and general election voters in some systems. Do these differences matter? What is the threshold for concluding that the consequences of any change in election systems are worth doing something?

Second, how should we interpret trends? In the data on primary and general election outcomes, there is some evidence that the primary elections of the past decade have been unusual. Is this an aberration, or an omen of future changes within the parties? If one sees the increased ideological conflict within the parties as harmful to democracy, what are the risks of waiting to find out whether or not they are temporary?

Third, where do primaries fall on the agenda of would-be reformers? It is common to see open primaries listed as one of a number of good government reforms, including changes to districting practices, alternative voting schemes, voter registration laws, and campaign finance reform practices. Are primary reforms complementary to any of these efforts, or are they a distraction from changes that might be of greater consequence?

And fourth, should our standard for identifying any reform as worthwhile be whether it yields clear results that a political scientist would be able to identify or that change is popular among voters? As this book has shown again and again, voters liked primaries initially, and when states sought to restrict primaries, the voters often rebelled. In a democracy there is certainly a case for doing things that the voters want, even if such things ultimately yield results that render them worse off. The primary laws enacted in the early twentieth century may be an example of this, and some of the reforms proposed in the states in recent years, by both conservatives and liberals, may similarly be ineffective yet popular.

None of these questions have definitive answers, and the evidence in this chapter suggests that we are unlikely to find definitive answers to them. The easy answers we are at times offered about "fixing" American primaries are inadequate. In the concluding chapter of this book, however, I will offer my own thoughts on how one might use the history presented in this book to make sense of the future of American primary elections.

Appendix

Table 9A.1 State-by-State Voter Ideology Means

	Primary Vote	Mean	N	House Vote	Mean	N	Senate Vote	Mean	N	Governor Vote	Mean	N
ALABAMA	Democrat	3.59	64	Democrat	3.40	60	Democrat	3.38	78	Democrat	3.64	97
	Republican	5.99	195	Republican	6.06	201	Republican	6.04	223	Republican	6.08	213
ALASKA	*Democrat*	*2.55*	*22*	*Democrat*	*2.54*	*26*	*Democrat*	*2.39*	*23*	*Democrat*	*2.94*	*33*
	Republican	*5.67*	*45*	*Republican*	*5.84*	*51*	*Republican*	*6.07*	*41*	*Republican*	*5.95*	*42*
							Other	4.40	15			
ARIZONA	Democrat	2.98	221	Democrat	2.75	328	Democrat	2.79	312	Democrat	2.83	351
	Republican	6.03	494	Republican	6.05	589	Republican	5.91	523	Republican	5.97	633
ARKANSAS	*Democrat*	*4.01*	*79*	*Democrat*	*3.08*	*89*	*Democrat*	*3.16*	*83*	*Democrat*	*3.99*	*154*
	Republican	6.10	82	Republican	6.02	180	Republican	6.00	190	Republican	6.11	139
CALIFORNIA	Democrat	2.72	1,284	Democrat	2.60	1,524	Democrat	2.59	1,682	Democrat	2.66	1,697
	Republican	5.92	1,280	Republican	5.88	1,526	Republican	5.87	1,677	Republican	5.83	1,552
COLORADO	Democrat	2.66	194	Democrat	2.73	277	Democrat	2.74	291	Democrat	2.85	309
	Republican	5.99	259	Republican	5.99	343	Republican	6.05	346	Republican	5.74	46
										Other	5.97	300

CONNECTICUT	Democrat	2.93	134	Democrat	2.94	243	Democrat	2.94	241	Democrat	2.86	219
	Republican	5.87	118	Republican	5.82	218	Republican	5.78	229	Republican	5.73	225
DELAWARE	Democrat	2.72	25	Democrat	2.91	65	Democrat	3.06	70			
	Republican	5.88	42	Republican	5.96	56	Republican	5.88	56			
FLORIDA	Democrat	2.97	666	Democrat	2.89	784	Democrat	2.67	503	Democrat	3.04	1,130
	Republican	6.01	1,078	Republican	5.88	1,421	Republican	6.02	1,397	Republican	6.00	1,284
							Other	3.45	646			
GEORGIA	Democrat	3.23	204	Democrat	3.29	285	Democrat	3.16	333	Democrat	3.31	398
	Republican	6.06	399	Republican	6.04	543	Republican	5.98	560	Republican	6.09	438
HAWAII	Democrat	3.26	70	Democrat	2.55	58	Democrat	3.00	67	Democrat	2.58	59
	Republican	5.94	31	Republican	5.65	49	Republican	6.00	38	Republican	5.72	53
IDAHO	Democrat	3.00	9	Democrat	3.62	55	Democrat	3.03	38	Democrat	3.34	50
	Republican	6.00	67	Republican	6.06	70	Republican	5.96	101	Republican	5.97	92
ILLINOIS	Democrat	2.92	430	Democrat	2.89	637	Democrat	2.74	592	Democrat	2.74	525
	Republican	5.93	496	Republican	5.86	669	Republican	5.82	665	Republican	5.84	690
INDIANA	Democrat	3.36	136	Democrat	3.17	175	Democrat	3.07	169			
	Republican	5.95	282	Republican	6.09	278	Republican	6.09	271			
IOWA	Democrat	2.73	60	Democrat	2.70	142	Democrat	2.63	135	Democrat	2.74	146
	Republican	6.10	135	Republican	6.00	219	Republican	5.79	242	Republican	5.89	206

(continued)

Table 9A.1 Continued

	Primary Vote	Mean	N	House Vote	Mean	N	Senate Vote	Mean	N	Governor Vote	Mean	N
KANSAS	Democrat	2.87	63	Democrat	2.81	138	Democrat	2.61	109	Democrat	2.86	139
	Republican	4.97	234	Republican	6.04	202	Republican	5.87	217	Republican	6.03	199
KENTUCKY	Democrat	3.83	168	Democrat	2.99	152	Democrat	3.05	171			
	Republican	6.04	157	Republican	6.04	241	Republican	6.02	236			
LOUISIANA				Democrat	3.34	65	Democrat	3.40	112			
				Republican	5.87	255	Republican	6.14	233			
MAINE	Democrat	3.03	67	Democrat	2.90	109				Democrat	2.87	68
	Republican	5.90	68	Republican	5.93	104				Republican	5.97	98
										Other	3.35	43
MARYLAND	Democrat	3.06	232	Democrat	3.01	316	Democrat	3.00	326	Democrat	2.89	297
	Republican	5.98	160	Republican	5.95	247	Republican	5.91	258	Republican	5.72	298
MASSACHUSETTS	Democrat	2.67	214	Democrat	2.48	310				Democrat	2.37	293
	Republican	5.74	165	Republican	5.73	263				Republican	5.67	290
MICHIGAN	Democrat	2.80	294	Democrat	2.85	447				Democrat	2.71	393
	Republican	5.83	453	Republican	5.96	542				Republican	5.80	603
MINNESOTA	Democrat	2.80	214	Democrat	2.63	279				Democrat	2.53	270
	Republican	6.32	95	Republican	6.05	273				Republican	6.14	250

MISSISSIPPI	*Democrat*	6.50	*4*	*Democrat*	3.54	72				
	Republican	6.22	36	Republican	6.18	114				
MISSOURI	Democrat	3.08	179	Democrat	3.13	264	Democrat	2.95	299	
	Republican	6.04	325	Republican	6.12	359	Republican	6.14	364	
MONTANA	Democrat	3.00	29	Democrat	2.95	37				
	Republican	5.89	37	Republican	5.87	47				
NEBRASKA	*Democrat*	*3.40*	*15*	*Democrat*	2.96	26				Democrat	3.04	23
	Republican	5.66	29	Republican	5.85	52				Republican	5.61	59
NEVADA	Democrat	2.98	93	Democrat	2.81	146	Democrat	2.87	157	Democrat	2.81	133
	Republican	5.95	165	Republican	5.90	239	Republican	6.00	227	Republican	5.80	253
NEW HAMPSHIRE	**Democrat**	**2.55**	**47**	**Democrat**	**2.93**	**95**	**Democrat**	**2.79**	**86**	**Democrat**	**3.32**	**119**
	Republican	5.61	108	Republican	5.71	121	Republican	5.73	122	Republican	5.71	105
NEW JERSEY	Democrat	2.74	68	Democrat	2.69	299					
	Republican	5.90	214	Republican	5.82	410					
NEW MEXICO	*Democrat*	*2.79*	*61*	*Democrat*	2.46	115				*Democrat*	2.39	*107*
	Republican	5.96	82	Republican	5.92	141				Republican	5.80	*152*
NEW YORK	Democrat	2.84	310	Democrat	2.70	750	Democrat	2.78	840	Democrat	2.78	*804*
	Republican	5.81	275	Republican	5.76	694	Republican	5.85	679	Republican	5.82	*574*

(continued)

Table 9A.1 Continued

	Primary Vote	Mean	N	House Vote	Mean	N	Senate Vote	Mean	N	Governor Vote	Mean	N
NORTH CAROLINA	Democrat	3.16	178	Democrat	3.04	320	Democrat	2.87	319			
	Republican	6.15	224	Republican	6.08	451	Republican	6.07	468			
NORTH DAKOTA	Democrat	3.23	22	Democrat	3.24	34	Democrat	3.15	26			
	Republican	6.00	25	Republican	6.09	45	Republican	5.78	55			
OHIO	Democrat	3.04	446	Democrat	2.80	628	Democrat	2.69	581	Democrat	2.93	695
	Republican	6.08	544	Republican	5.87	852	Republican	5.87	894	Republican	5.93	833
OKLAHOMA	Democrat	3.19	81	Democrat	3.31	48	Democrat	2.77	92	Democrat	3.19	115
	Republican	6.27	148	Republican	6.17	217	Republican	6.19	221	Republican	6.14	204
OREGON	Democrat	2.43	199	Democrat	2.42	262	Democrat	2.55	282	Democrat	2.34	255
	Republican	6.04	195	Republican	5.93	269	Republican	6.01	240	Republican	5.89	284
PENNSYLVANIA	Democrat	3.11	593	Democrat	2.86	627	Democrat	2.77	696	Democrat	2.80	673
	Republican	6.07	570	Republican	5.93	806	Republican	5.98	866	Republican	5.94	866
RHODE ISLAND	Democrat	3.43	47	Democrat	2.61	46				Democrat	3.48	25
	Republican	5.79	14	Republican	5.76	50				Republican	5.65	34
										Other	3.14	42

SOUTH CAROLINA	Democrat	2.88	58	Democrat	3.02	125	Democrat	2.90	40	Democrat	3.25	148
	Republican	5.92	183	Republican	6.02	203	Republican	5.98	225	Republican	6.10	188
SOUTH DAKOTA	Democrat	2.75	4	Democrat	3.11	35	(No Democrat)			Democrat	2.90	30
	Republican	5.79	42	Republican	5.95	59	Republican	5.71	66	Republican	5.76	62
TENNESSEE	Democrat	3.11	94	Democrat	2.90	133				Democrat	2.88	130
	Republican	6.04	277	Republican	6.19	308				Republican	6.05	339
TEXAS	Democrat	3.19	352	Democrat	2.99	497				Democrat	3.21	770
	Republican	6.14	881	Republican	6.13	1,225				Republican	6.16	1,190
UTAH	*Democrat*	*3.24*	*21*	*Democrat*	*3.12*	*65*	*Democrat*	*2.78*	*69*	*Democrat*	*3.03*	*78*
	Republican	6.11	75	Republican	6.07	109	Republican	6.17	105	Republican	6.15	104
VERMONT	Democrat	2.20	20	Democrat	2.57	37	Democrat	2.50	38	Democrat	2.59	32
	Republican	5.00	7	Republican	5.27	11	Republican	5.17	12	Republican	4.63	19
VIRGINIA												
WASHINGTON				Democrat	2.54	437	Democrat	2.56	458			
				Republican	5.95	388	Republican	5.91	440			
WEST VIRGINIA	*Democrat*	3.82	77	*Democrat*	3.23	70	*Democrat*	3.43	88			
	Republican	6.06	35	Republican	5.92	106	Republican	6.09	96			

(*continued*)

Table 9A.1 Continued

		Primary Vote	Mean	N	House Vote	Mean	N	Senate Vote	Mean	N	Governor Vote	Mean	N
WISCONSIN		Democrat	2.71	148	Democrat	2.73	275	Democrat	2.81	309	Democrat	2.80	292
		Republican	5.80	302	Republican	5.90	365	Republican	5.94	375	Republican	5.90	371
WYOMING		*Democrat*	2.30	10	*Democrat*	2.75	20				*Democrat*	2.55	20
		Republican	5.97	33	Republican	6.48	29				Republican	5.90	29
TOTAL		Democrat	2.97	8,006	Democrat	2.82	12,027	Democrat	2.78	9,715	Democrat	2.87	11,077
		Republican	5.99	11,092	Republican	5.95	16,210	Republican	5.95	12,958	Republican	5.93	13,017
		Other party	4.68	366	Third candidate	4.25	169	Third candidate	3.66	812	Third candidate	5.05	763
		Do not recall	4.56	346	Fourth candidate	3.30	10	Other	4.76	351	Fourth candidate	3.08	26
		Total	4.72	19,810	Other	4.21	620	I'm not sure	4.29	1,671	Other	5.03	457
					I'm not sure	4.31	3,113	No one	4.27	551	I'm not sure	4.45	1,576
					No one	3.97	1,009	Total	4.54	26,058	No one	4.56	679
					Total	4.56	33,158				Total	4.54	27,595

Source: Cooperative Congressional Election Study 2010 (Ansolabehere 2012).

Notes: Virginia is excluded because it had no statewide primary; Louisiana and Washington are excluded because they held nonpartisan primaries in 2010. Statewide independent and third-party candidates are included in instances in which these candidates received greater than 25 percent of the vote. State party primaries in **bold** are races in which the primary electorate mean was .25 or more ideologically extreme than the mean for one or more of the general election races; those in *italics* were .25 or more less extreme, and those in ***bold italics*** were .25 or more extreme than one general election race and .25 less extreme than another.

10
The Future of the Direct Primary

Much scholarly attention has been paid to the development of the direct primary in the first two decades of the twentieth century, but there has been little systematic consideration of how primary laws changed in subsequent years. Perhaps because of growing political polarization and party conflict in the twenty-first century, a number of scholars have again discovered the early twentieth-century literature on primaries and have undertaken their own analyses of what ails today's primaries. We need, however, to consider today's primaries with a full appreciation of the limits inherent in previous efforts to reform them.

Primaries are probably not going anywhere. They are unlikely to go away, and they are also not likely to evolve in any particular direction. Political parties and partisans have tinkered with them throughout the past century, and they will continue to do so. It is possible to identify ideological goals in this tinkering—notions, for instance, of making elections more democratic, of offering meaningful choices, of limiting the power of unelected elites, or of simply making elections work better. Yet it is often difficult to separate these goals from the imperatives of short-term political advantage. As is the case for many types of democratic reforms, politicians propose changes for idiosyncratic reasons, then dress up their proposals with rhetoric about democracy. Perhaps we should stop doing this, but this book offers little hope that we will.

Five Major Developments since 2020

In the immediate aftermath of Donald Trump's 2020 general election defeat, there were several noteworthy developments in the national discussion of primary elections. None of these would have any impact on presidential elections or on the fortunes of any Trump-esque presidential candidates, yet all can arguably be seen as responses to the challenges raised by Trump's presidency.

First, in the 2020 election, Alaska voters passed, by a 51–49 percent margin, an initiative establishing a nonpartisan "top four" primary, to be followed by ranked choice voting (RCV) in a general election contest between the four primary victors. The initiative was a novel combination, in that other states have used top two primaries, but no state or municipality currently uses a top four primary, and in that it combined this primary process with a ranked choice general election. Only one state, Maine, currently uses a ranked choice method in its general elections. Although most of Alaska's leading politicians opposed the measure, supporters of the initiative outspent opponents by a more than eleven-to-one margin. A large percentage of the $6.9 million spent on advocacy for the initiative came from 501(c) groups based in Texas, Colorado, and Massachusetts (Ballotpedia 2020a; OpenSecrets 2020). Advocates of the initiative spoke of giving more of a voice to the large number of Alaska voters who have chosen not to join one of the two major parties, while opponents, including former Democratic senator Mark Begich and former Republican governor Sean Parnell, referred to the chaos the initiative would create and its violation of the rights of political parties (McGuire 2020). At the time of the initiative's adoption, some observers speculated that the biggest beneficiary of the new law would be current senator Lisa Murkowski (Sabato 2021b). Murkowski, one of the more moderate Republicans in the Senate, lost her 2010 primary but won the general election as a write-in candidate. Murkowski has also been among Donald Trump's more persistent Republican critics, and she voted for his second impeachment. In a state where Democrats are heavily outnumbered, a top four primary would guarantee Murkowski a spot on the general election ballot, where she would likely pick up a number of second-choice votes from Democratic voters. In addition, Alaska's lone U.S. representative passed away in March 2022, and more than forty people had announced their candidacy for his seat by early summer, providing a very different test for the new election law.

Murkowski did indeed win the 2022 election, although she placed first in the primary balloting as well, so she might have won in a regular party primary. The big surprise in Alaska's 2022 election, however, was the victory of Democrat Mary Peltola in the special election for the state's lone House seat, and again in the regular 2022 election. In both elections, Peltola received a plurality of the first-round votes, but her two strongest Republican opponents cumulatively received a majority. Peltola's two Republican opponents were Nick Begich III, the grandson of a former congressman and the nephew of a former senator, and former governor and vice presidential nominee Sarah Palin. Begich and Palin feuded throughout the campaign; Begich presented himself as a more traditional Alaska Republican, while Palin allied herself with Donald Trump. Despite efforts by the Alaska Republican Party to persuade voters to "rank the red"—to give both Republicans their first-choice and second-choice votes—enough of Begich's supporters ranked Peltola second to provide Peltola with a victory over Palin. Peltola became the state's first Democratic representative since 1972 and the state's first Native American representative. For RCV supporters, Peltola's victory was a stirring example of how the system is supposed to work: she sought to downplay partisanship, to emphasize her ability to provide benefits to the state and to the state's marginalized communities, and to avoid attacking her opponents. RCV opponents, however, noted that most of the first-place votes had gone to Republicans, and that one of the nation's most Republican states had sent a Democrat to Washington.

Second, on January 13, 2021, the House of Representatives voted to impeach President Trump a second time, as a result of the January 6 attack on the Capitol. Ten Republicans voted for the impeachment; most prominent among these Republicans was the House Republican conference chair (its third-most powerful member), Wyoming representative Elizabeth Cheney. Wyoming is a solidly Republican state, but Cheney has occasionally faced opposition in her primary campaigns. In the months that followed, several prominent Wyoming Republicans expressed interest in challenging Cheney. While some surveys conducted during the summer of 2021 suggested that a majority of the state's Republican voters did not want to vote for Cheney again, the split field raised the prospect that Cheney could be renominated despite receiving less than half of the votes (Mutnick 2021). A bill to create a runoff primary in Wyoming was introduced in March, and the bill was defeated by only one vote (Erickson 2021a, 2021b). Donald Trump Jr., son of the former president, announced his support for establishing a runoff, as did the leadership of the Wyoming Republican Party. While Trump made it clear that his major concern was retribution against Cheney, state Republican leaders spoke instead about ensuring that the nominee had the support of the majority, and some Republican leaders also noted that the state's current governor received only one-third of the vote in his initial primary campaign. Cheney ultimately lost the primary by 36 percentage points.

Third, on May 10, 2021, Virginia Republicans met at a convention to cast ranked choice votes for their gubernatorial candidate. The party held four separate votes on the format for the convention, with some supporters of President Trump seeking to ensure that candidate selection would be done through a plurality winner scheme (Epstein 2021). Virginia's political parties have greater leeway than any other state's parties in selecting nominees, and many of the state's votes have had extremely low turnout; for instance, one of the state's 2020 House primaries (in which the incumbent lost) was conducted as a "drive-in" primary, in which only 2,537 votes were cast (Ballotpedia 2020b). In the state's 2021 gubernatorial primary, approximately 30,000 votes were cast, and wealthy CEO and political novice Glenn Youngkin edged out two more experienced candidates (Gabriel 2021). Veteran Virginia political analyst Larry Sabato (2021a) frames this result as the best possible outcome for Virginia Republicans; Youngkin did not present himself as a foe of Donald Trump, but he avoided discussing Trump during the campaign and lacked the direct ties to Trump that the other two Republicans candidates had shown. Youngkin's subsequent general election victory was a bright spot for Republicans in 2021, yet Youngkin might well have lost the nomination had the state not used the ranked choice convention system.

Fourth, New York City held its Democratic mayoral primary on June 22, 2021. With nearly one million votes cast, this was the largest use yet of RCV in a primary. Primary victor Eric Adams criticized the RCV system, and his supporters criticized the efforts of two other candidates to form an alliance in the week preceding the election (Rubinstein 2021).[1] Media accounts noted that Adams, who is Black, ran somewhat to the right of other Democrats, touting his law enforcement background, his support among Republicans, and his support among working-class voters. The second-place and third-place candidates, in contrast, were women who courted progressive voters (Goldberg 2021). Adams's opposition to RCV, combined with very public ballot counting errors, left some proponents of the new law on the defensive (Glueck 2021). Some progressives, including third-place finisher Maya Wiley (2021), wrote after the election that the law had worked as intended, but some Republicans (including former President Trump) sought to link the uncertainties of the New York vote count to Trump's larger claims about fraud in the 2020 presidential race (Goldiner 2021).

And fifth, the 2022 election defied the traditional pattern of midterm elections. Despite lukewarm public approval for President Biden, Democrats gained a seat in the Senate and only lost nine seats in the House of Representatives. A projected "red wave" ultimately became merely a "red ripple." One oft-cited reason for Republicans' poor performance was the difficulty Republican elites had in selecting competitive candidates in battleground states. One could argue that Republicans lost Senate races in New Hampshire, Arizona, and Pennsylvania; governorships in Maryland, Massachusetts, Pennsylvania, Arizona, and Illinois; and several House races as well because primary voters had chosen more politically extreme and less experienced candidates than party insiders would have preferred. In New Hampshire, for instance, retired general and political neophyte Don Bolduc, a Trump-endorsed candidate who alleged the 2020 election had been stolen and expressed sympathy for the jailed January 6 rioters, easily defeated State Senate president Chuck Morse in the primary, then went on to lose the general election by 10 percentage points. Similar stories unfolded elsewhere. Many of the underperforming candidates had been endorsed by Donald Trump; one postelection study estimated that Trump-endorsed candidates received an average of 7 percent fewer votes than candidates in the same states or districts would have been expected to had Trump not offered endorsements (Wallach 2022). The 2022 elections were a vivid example of the problems Donald Trump has caused for the Republican Party, but they were also an example of the problems that have developed in Republican primaries. The party is far less able, or willing, than is the Democratic Party to converge in the primary around its preferred general election candidates.

All of these primary election results or election law changes show the relationship between normative claims about democratic elections and the practical concerns of politicians. They are not by any means unique; a summary of primary legislation published by the National Conference of State Legislatures (2021) described primary changes as the year's "hot trend" and noted that there were differences in which reforms were proposed by members of the two major parties. As is the case for the data considered in Chapter 8 of this book, the NCSL study found that top two or RCV systems and open primary procedures were proposed by Democrats, and efforts to close primaries or tighten restriction requirements for primaries were being proposed by Republicans, in some of the same Republican-leaning states that had explored other voting restrictions following the 2020 election. The circumstances in these states suggest, however, that even while partisan gain may be the motivating factor for these changes, those who would analyze these changes should not see them only as partisan exercises. Runoff elections may benefit Elizabeth Cheney's opponents in Wyoming, but they are not necessarily a reform that aids conservatives; RCV is popular at the moment among voters on the left, but it may well have helped Republicans in Virginia. It is debatable whether any of these changes can yield lessons applicable beyond the elections in which they were used, and to the extent that many of these problems have a particular impact on the Republican Party, it is difficult to argue that primary reforms are the answer for a party that has changed so radically during the years since Donald Trump became its leader.

Four Paths Forward for Primary Reformers

After a century of experimentation with primary elections, there really is no way to argue that there is a progressive approach, a populist approach, a conservative approach, or a liberal approach to primary elections. Most reforms have been situational—they have been a response to imbalances of power or to the perception that those who have achieved power have not done so in as democratically legitimate a way as they could have. It is clear today, as well, that political polarization is reflected in primary elections, but primaries are probably not the cause of polarization.

What principles might we use, then, in evaluating contemporary discussions of primaries? Rather than offering a grand ideological perspective on primaries, in this concluding chapter I frame what I see as the major choices before us with a note of caution, drawn from the work of Bruce Cain. In his 2015 book *Democracy More or Less*, Cain argues that the history of primaries, as well as many other types of electoral and governmental process reforms, has been characterized by waves of what he calls "reform populism." Reform populism, not to be confused with the sort of populism attributed to a Viktor Orban or a Donald Trump, is characterized by the reasonable goals of improving citizens' ability to monitor government and increasing democratic control over elections and policy. In practice, however, reform populism feeds on itself; reforms create demands for further reform. They also create a demand for purity of motive, which can be at odds with the sort of short-term partisan calculations that characterize most legislator-initiated efforts. Transparency reforms, for instance, lead to an increase in perceptions of corruption, which lead in turn to further efforts to expose and prohibit corruption and to an expansion in the definition of what "corruption" is.

As applied to primaries, reform populism has led to a diminution of the role of party elites or gatekeepers and a rejection of efforts to compromise or deliberate. Efforts by parties or party elites to winnow the field or to use whatever powers they have to confer advantage on particular types of candidates are suspect, even though the incentives of parties often involve deliberation over what is best for the party and concern over selecting candidates who have the ability to speak to and for different party constituencies or to seek compromise while in office. Reducing the role of these elites leads to polarization and to policy outcomes that leave citizens feeling less represented. And while citizen-initiated changes, often enacted through referendum or voter initiative, can look pure, Cain joins a large field of scholars who have argued that direct democracy has long been manipulated by special interests in the United States.

One does not need to subscribe to Cain's perspective in its entirety to extract some principles for reform. While some level of accountability is still necessary, we should, following Cain, prioritize democratic outcomes over ensuring that all procedures that get us there are as democratic as possible. We should, furthermore, be wary of the consequences of reform cycles. Any popular movement to change government will confront twin paradoxes: those who support it must hope for clear results, while those threatened the most by it will need reassurance that they will not lose power entirely. Political reform movements must oversell their effects to supporters while underselling them to opponents. When reform movements achieve ambiguous results, they can be debilitating to both constituencies. The response may either be disillusionment or a call for further reforms.

Cain's "reform pluralist" approach is not tantamount to an argument against all reforms, then—it is an argument to be cautious about reform movements and reform cycles. Reform efforts also must be understood as part of an ecosystem. Some recent studies broadly sympathetic to Cain's perspectives have shown this to be the case for primary reforms. For instance, Hill (2022) shows that the establishment of the top two primary in California changed the political contribution strategies of interest groups who expected to be disadvantaged by the law. One might conclude from this that reforms should be thoroughly tested before being applied so that we know as many of the potential consequences as possible. One lesson from the history of primaries is that untested reforms can be difficult to fix or undo once established.

At the same time, it is important to separate the practical effects of any reform from the political ones, especially because political success or failure can have an impact on future reform efforts. The New York RCV experiment illustrates this clearly. RCV in New York may have been a success according to the metrics of RCV proponents, but if voters are convinced that it was a failure, then future RCV efforts may suffer as a result. Another recent article on the top two primary by Crosson (2020) raises this question directly; he shows that the top two primary has succeeded in helping to elect more moderate legislators in predominantly one-party districts but notes that the overall level of polarization in Congress may mean that these changes are likely to go unnoticed by voters. If a reform has an effect and nobody notices, does it really have an effect? Or conversely, as again may be the case for primaries over the course of the twentieth century, if a reform does not have an effect but is believed by citizens to have been salutary, can one really say it has not had an effect?

Cain's perspective seems to me to largely fit the stories told throughout this book, as well as the skepticism about reform noted in the closing chapters of the Hassell (2018) and Hirano and Snyder (2019) books on primaries. Cain's perspective advises us to be cautious about grand claims about the effects of reform, while at the same time being open to very real concerns about polarization and extremism. It suggests that we should seek to understand the secondary effects of reforms and the adaptations the political system can make over long periods of time, and to separate out political consequences and practical consequences. And this perspective preserves a role for deliberation, compromise, and coalition building as goals to be balanced against representation and direct accountability. We can use it, as well, to distill the options for the direct primary into four categories. These categories do not coincide neatly with the four post-2020 changes described earlier, but those four changes can all be discussed with reference to these categories. These categories are also not mutually exclusive, and the language politicians and activists use to talk about them is at times inconsistent enough that it is not evident which category best fits them. For instance, some of those who call for a national open primary also are sympathetic to having a national top two, four, or five primary; some of those who call for a national solution support state-level changes as well, and calls for abolishing primaries are often ambiguous about what would replace them. Most notably, almost all of the changes to the direct primary can be subsumed within the first of the following categories.

Accept Continual Tinkering with Primary Laws

It is not at all evident that there is anything wrong with the complicated national history told in this book. Many state-level changes have been justified with reference to the political culture or circumstances of those states. To take just the most obvious example, Wisconsin Progressives of the early twentieth century presented the state's open primary as a reflection of the state's values, and their descendants fought to defend the open primary decades later, in the 1970s, with similar arguments (Wekkin 1984). The struggles of New Mexico's parties, documented in Chapters 5 and 6, to develop primary laws that fit the demographics of the state seem similarly to make the case that primary rules should be a matter of state or local concern. Under the principle of federalism, many areas of national policy delegate to the states the responsibility of adapting laws to fit them; why should primary laws be any different? Such a federalist approach is of course easiest to square with existing Supreme Court jurisprudence on the primary, and it would redirect any agitation for changes to the primary exclusively toward the state level or suggest that we should abandon any effort to develop big stories about what sorts of primary election rules are "best."

Quirks in state primary laws might, of course, be abused or manipulated at times. In recent years, there have been instances when nonparty groups spent heavily. The aforementioned Virginia House primary, which was moved and organized on very short notice due in part to the coronavirus pandemic, is one such example. States such as Utah and Massachusetts, which hold party conventions at which candidates must meet a vote threshold in order to appear on the primary ballot, give outside interests the opportunity to shape primary competition well before the public begins to pay attention. Muddling through need not require accepting any and all instances in which questionable primary election procedures take place, but it would mean that these would be treated as a matter of state politics, not the target of any national reform effort. They could be tinkered with in the same way that the "bad laws" discussed in Chapter 5 were.

A federalist argument might incorporate two features of the recent reforms noted above. First, it might recognize the important role of state parties. The Virginia gubernatorial race provides one instance in which state political elites searched for ways to limit the influence of Donald Trump in candidate selection without formally rebuking the former president. The Iowa Republican Party's primary rules, which allow parties to choose the nominee if no candidate gets 35 percent of the vote or more, are another. The party's rules drew some attention in 2010 when party leaders chose a congressional district primary's third-place finisher as their nominee; that candidate, arguably the least conservative of the candidates, went on to win the general election in a competitive district. In other races in which the convention process has been used, however, Iowa's rules have generated controversy within the state (Obradovich 2018).

Second, we might think about legislator-initiated and citizen-initiated reforms differently. Throughout the history of primary elections, citizen initiatives have served as a tool for re-establishing primaries when states have sought to limit or do away with them. Some of the more consequential recent reform efforts, such as Maine's RCV law, California's top two primary, and the new Alaska law, were established by initiative, not by legislators. Although the same laws have been proposed by legislators in many states, such bills have often been introduced by members of the minority party and not with any real hope of passage. As the Alaska example has shown, voter initiatives create the possibility of a reform dialogue that is not strictly a matter of party conflict. This does not mean a patchwork of state initiatives is better than a patchwork of legislation, only that it can be a more authentic way for reform groups in the states to tailor their proposals and their rhetoric to the political culture of their states.

The strongest argument for muddling through, however, is simply an argument about priorities. If there is no obvious way for primaries to be reformed in a way that reduces polarization or otherwise improves democracy, reformers might be better off turning their attention to other matters. I can report from my own experience studying primaries that foundation money and reform groups' attention shifted, during the Trump administration, away from primary reform and toward efforts to combat voter suppression and to change districting practices, and toward other types of research that may yield less ambiguous results than has primary election research.

Abolish the Direct Primary

This book began with quotes from Bernard Freyd's 1926 book *Repeal the Direct Primary*. While Freyd's rhetoric was somewhat over the top, even for the time, he was not alone in arguing against the direct primary. The argument was within the bounds of legitimate democratic conversation; well-respected political scientists such as Henry Jones Ford (1909) and former presidents such as William Howard Taft (1922) could get a respectful hearing arguing against it. Today, some arguments against the direct primary are decidedly out of the mainstream, offered in jest or as provocation. It does seem, however, that they have become more common in recent years and have become somewhat more serious. Political writers such as the Brookings Institution's Jonathan Rauch (2015) have argued that primaries should be abandoned and that we should explore ways to encourage some sort of a modern return to the proverbial backroom deals or smoke-filled rooms that preceded the introduction of primaries. Nick Troiano (2021), the executive director of the 501c group Unite America, penned a piece in the *Atlantic Monthly* arguing for the abolition of primaries. And political scientists Benjamin Page and Martin Gilens (2017, 222–223) have argued that doing away with primaries would be a step toward more equitable social outcomes. It is noteworthy that Page and Gilens take up Cain's basic mantra: the only way to make a political case for abandoning primaries would be to link their abolition to more democratic policy outcomes.

The easiest argument against abolishing primaries is a practical one. It is not at all clear how one would go about doing it. When states have done away with primaries, they have eventually returned. Primaries appear democratic to most voters. The argument for abolishing primaries also requires a claim about next steps. One possibility is that we could revert to the nineteenth-century status quo ante: the proverbial smoke-filled room. Had we never abandoned the practice of party nominations in the first place, and had we instead embarked on other sorts of party reforms, this might be practical. But, apart from the fact that no one smokes any more, we would have difficulty returning to such practices because political parties are not what they once were. They are not necessarily able to handle the prospect of choosing nominees, and they might wind up just delegating this responsibility back to the people. In countries without a mandatory primary, such as Mexico, parties often find it advantageous to hold primaries in order to avoid choosing sides or to see how their candidates do in open competition (Bruhn 2018).

Political parties are also more ideologically extreme in many states than is the electorate. For every case in which party elites play a moderating role in choosing electable candidates, there is another state where the party organization poses a threat to officeholders. A state such as Arizona, where the state party censures its own governor for accepting President Biden's victory, seems unlikely to be able to choose candidates more wisely than the voters. The Arizona experience, and the movement in some states since the 2020 election to reject Electoral College results or to limit the vote-counting abilities of elected secretaries of state, suggest that any call to abandon primaries would be seen as a nakedly partisan and antidemocratic move.

Abolishing primaries does not necessarily mean restoring parties' ability to choose candidates, however. Some reform advocates, like Troiano, still favor nonpartisan primaries, while leaving it unclear whether they in fact are against primaries or only against partisan ones. In his 2020 book *Breaking the Two-Party Doom Loop*, Lee Drutman argues for replacing primaries with a single-round RCV system: single-winner RCV in the Senate and multiwinner RCV in the House. This is, to be clear, not the same as the primary election RCV system discussed earlier, but rather a multicandidate, multiparty election that would replace the primary and the general election. Drutman harbors no expectation that such a change is imminent, but he sees this change as something that would severely weaken the power of the two major parties and lead to the creation of a system with four or so competitive parties. Such a change would certainly have to develop at the local level and gradually gain popularity as voters observed the results. In short, any call for abolishing primaries needs first to clarify what a primary is, how it would be abolished, and what would replace it.

Open Primaries

There have been several calls for a national law mandating open primaries. Although the For the People Act, the Democratic Party's omnibus election reform bill of 2019 and 2021, does not address primary rules, some progressive activists argued for including them in the bill. Advocacy groups such as Open Primaries and Unite America have called for a national open primary law. The 501(c) group Open Primaries argues that the Democratic National Committee and the Republican National Committee could require states to use this procedure in order to have presidential convention delegates seated, and that Congress also has the ability to require states to permit any registered voter to vote in a primary (Opdycke 2018). It is not at all clear that congressional legislation would be upheld by the Supreme Court, but the Democratic Party's experience with presidential primaries suggests that the parties could try to require this, and might have some success, but they would also face some opposition.

The case for open primaries is as clear as was the Progressive case for primaries in the early twentieth century. The Open Primaries website begins by claiming that "no American should be required to join a political party to exercise their right to vote" (Open Primaries 2023). The case against creating a national open primary is also simple: it is not necessarily feasible, but it is also not clear how much of a difference it would make. More people would have the right to vote, but given that most Americans already live in states with open or semiopen primaries, even that result might not be particularly evident.

Radical Reforms: Ranked Choice Voting, Top 4 or 5 Primaries, and a National Primary Day

A final approach might be to accept that there is no silver bullet lurking among the various primary law changes explored in this book and to turn to more radical measures. By "radical" I do not mean to suggest reforms that would yield nominees far outside the bounds of the American political mainstream, but rather to note that there are some proposed reforms that have not been implemented in the United States since the advent of the direct primary, and thus we cannot use the historical record to say anything about their effectiveness or ineffectiveness. RCV, proportional representation, or multimember districts, for instance, fall into this category, as does Alaska's new top four primary law. They are not entirely novel, but in order to get clues to how they would work we need to look at other countries or at short-lived local experiments, rather than at enduring practices at the state or national levels.

Advocates for such changes have offered grand claims about their consequences. One political problem, however, is that we don't know how long it would take the political system to adjust. The track record of RCV, for instance, is disputed, and most of the American municipal RCV or proportional representation laws were repealed within a decade or two of their passage (Barber 2000; Santucci 2022). In many ways, those who would advocate radical reform today find themselves in the same position Progressives were in when direct primary laws were enacted: even in places where these laws are passed, they might find it difficult to defend them after their passage.

I argue that the most promising of the untried proposals is one that has received far less attention than any of the others considered here: the proposal for a National Primary Day. A Bipartisan Policy Center (BPC) Commission on Political Reform (2014) report offered this idea among a number of other governmental reforms, and primary elections expert Elaine Kamarck (2014) also endorsed the idea. Although the BPC report suggested a late June date, the research I have discussed in this book suggests that it doesn't necessarily matter when the date is. It may be difficult for the federal government to require such a law, but it seems possible that states could agree to gradually move toward this or to precommit themselves to this change if some sort of threshold of involvement is met, as is the case for the Electoral College Compact. The BPC and Kamarck have spoken of the effect a National Primary Day would have on voter turnout: everyone would know when their primary is, and citizens would likely be exposed to more media coverage of the primary. Doing this might also allow for a more accurate media narrative about what has happened in the primaries and make emerging ideas and factions within the parties more evident. State autonomy in setting primary rules would be preserved while at the same time making primaries more of a national event. This change would also be easy for states to undo should it yield unexpected consequences. It is in many ways a smaller reform than many of those discussed, but it is one of the few truly untried ideas that might yield short-term results that would be visible to citizens.

Perhaps the Direct Primary Was a Mistake, but We're Stuck with It

It may seem odd to end a book with a rather lukewarm endorsement of reform at a moment when American democracy is facing such profound challenges. One reason I undertook this project was a relatively apolitical one: the history of the direct primary in the twentieth century has not really been told, and it does provide, I think, a unique way to look at party development over the course of the century. There is, however, a story about contemporary reform priorities to be taken away from this book: primary elections are not necessarily the reason for the state of American politics today, and even if they were, there is not much we could do about them at this point.

I certainly would not judge primaries an abject failure, in part because of course we do not know how the twentieth century would have played out without them and in part because we do not necessarily have the metrics we can use to measure success or failure. If we just look at popularity, they have probably on balance been a success. If we want to measure our primary elections by the politicians we have chosen, any partisan will find some cases in which primaries yielded great candidates and disastrous ones. It is difficult to pass any similar judgment on the people who did not win or did not even run. More sophisticated metrics, such as those presented in the Hirano and Snyder (2019) work, also have found much to like about primaries. The important questions about primary elections have to do with their variants and the alternatives.

Although he thought the direct primary was a bad idea, William Howard Taft understood its appeal. He noted in 1922 that it was clear why Americans were hostile toward the political parties. Partisanship, he said, divided the country and privileged factional interests over the common interest. We need, he said, "great" parties that are able to separate themselves from factional interests and can offer strong, patriotic candidates. Efforts to reform the political system are doomed to fail because they do not reform individuals. The main goal, he argued, should be to educate individuals better in the principles of democracy. In other words, if we want to change our political institutions, we must first consider whether the problem really has to do with our institutions or with ourselves.

Notes

Chapter 2

1. There are different approaches to determining when to conclude that a state has implemented the direct primary; many states established primaries for some offices and gradually expanded the number of offices covered by the primary. For discussions of the sequence in which states established primaries, see Merriam and Overacker (1928, 61–64), Galderisi and Ezra (2001, 17), Ware (2002, 123–124), and Lawrence, Donovan, and Bowler (2013).
2. Three other states had platform-writing conventions in advance of the primary, but South Dakota's was by far the most elaborate (Merriam and Overacker 1928, 83–91).
3. This is a common contention in literature on the South, as shown in Key (1949) and Kousser (1974).
4. Utah established a primary in the late nineteenth century, but although it was widely used, the primary was not mandatory until 1947.
5. Kang (2011; see also Burden, Jones, and Kang 2014) has compiled a list of sore loser laws, many of which were enacted during this period. Although Kang's findings are clearly relevant to this project, I do not draw on his list because doing so would potentially bias the results here, as Kang is only looking for one type of primary law change, and this would thus overrepresent changes of a particular type. In addition, Kang's listing of changes lists only the final enactment of sore loser laws, while the intent here is to look at all passages of laws related to primaries during this period.
6. For discussion see Kaufmann, Gimpel, and Hoffman (2003) and Green and Herrnson (2002).
7. This coding decision ensures that we have a conservative measure of primary election change. In the case of runoff elections, for instance (discussed in Chapter 7), many contemporary arguments suggest that runoffs do, in fact, provide parties with a greater ability to ensure that their preferred candidate wins. Because the literature on this is not unanimous, however, I have not presented this as a restrictive change. The same logic goes for other "no effect" categorizations. Because the individual states and adoption dates are listed in Table 2.1, readers with knowledge of these states can draw their own conclusions about the effects of changes in these states. See Lamis (1984b) and Bullock and Smith (1990).
8. See, for instance, Kurlowski (2014) and Sinclair and O'Grady (2018). These studies are useful in assessing the magnitude of reforms, but one can only use them to explore results; they do not provide a means of scaling the intended results of reforms.
9. These states are (in order of adoption of the initiative) South Dakota, Utah, Oregon, Montana, Maine, Michigan, Missouri, Arkansas, Colorado, Arizona, California,

Idaho, Nebraska, Nevada, Ohio, Washington, Wyoming, Minnesota, Mississippi, North Dakota, and Massachusetts.

10. Minnesota had a nonpartisan legislature from 1914 to 1950. Nebraska had a nonpartisan legislature beginning in 1936, and Alaska and Hawaii did not become states until 1959.
11. This, then, leaves Maryland and New Jersey as the only states with primary laws that do not fall into any of these groups. Both of these states passed relatively minor laws restricting primaries; Maryland abolished primaries for some offices in 1928, and New Jersey passed a party affiliation law in 1928. The remaining states that made no changes to their primary laws and that do not fall into any of the three categories are the Southern states Louisiana, South Carolina, Tennessee, and West Virginia, and the Northern states Delaware, New Hampshire, Pennsylvania, and Vermont.
12. There are few state-specific sources that discuss Colorado's decisions; however, Progressives never controlled the state, and the state's governor, "Big Ed" Johnson, took many steps designed to isolate Colorado from neighboring states' political movements, including closing the New Mexico border and campaigning against the New Deal (Cronin and Loevy 2012, 23, 70).
13. Massachusetts Democrats returned to having a preprimary convention in 1982, and Republicans followed suit in 1986 (Natsios 1990).
14. Any conclusions drawn from such observations would, however, be subject to the same criticism I raised earlier about Ware's and Merriam and Overacker's claims about repeal attempts: it is debatable whether unsuccessful legislation aimed at changing primary rules is indicative of any pattern or movement.

Chapter 3

1. I take up the case of Mississippi, and of Southern Progressivism more generally, in Chapter 7.
2. For early commentary on the Cleveland reforms, see National Conference on the Practical Reform of Primary Elections (1898, 92).
3. Lockard (1959b, 191) makes reference to the failure of Democrats to overcome Republican opposition to a variety of initiatives during the time they held the governorship in the 1930s. Although he does not provide details of the circumstances surrounding the passage of the direct primary legislation, it is evident from the growth in party representation in the legislature (shown in the figures in Chapter 2) and Governor Pastore's emphasis on the direct primary law in his inaugural address to the legislature that both he and the party's new majority made the law a priority.
4. This happened most recently to incumbent Republican senator Robert Bennett in 2010.

Chapter 4

1. For details on the CCF, see Lipset (1971) and Whitehorn (1992).
2. The Lindbergh name is best known today for the aviation feats of the congressman's son; those would not happen until the 1920s, so Lindbergh (the elder) was known for his tenure in Congress, not for his son's exploits.
3. Toward the end of his first term, Langer was convicted of forcing state employees to contribute to the NPL. He was removed from office, but the conviction was overturned in 1935, and Langer ran successfully for office again in 1936 (Vogel 2004).

Chapter 5

1. For a full summary of Alaska primary changes, see the "Alaska's Primary History" timeline at http://www.elections.alaska.gov/doc/forms/H42.pdf.
2. The full text of the law is available at https://www.loc.gov/item/19016058/.
3. To make matters more complicated, however, the two slates were organized such that the majority slate was listed first, ensuring that more politically aware voters did know which slate had received more convention support.

Chapter 6

1. See McCarty et al. 2015.
2. I use Lawrence, Donovan, and Bowler's (2009) list of states that adopted the citizen initiative between 1898 and 1918, as described in Chapters 2 and 3. These states are (in order of adoption of the initiative) South Dakota, Utah, Oregon, Montana, Maine, Michigan, Missouri, Arkansas, Colorado, Arizona, California, Idaho, Nebraska, Nevada, Ohio, Washington, Wyoming, Minnesota, Mississippi, North Dakota, and Massachusetts.
3. These states are Alabama, Arkansas, Florida, Georgia, Kentucky, Louisiana, Mississippi, Missouri, North Carolina, Oklahoma, South Carolina, Tennessee, Texas, Virginia, and West Virginia. The anomalous expansive rule change shown in Table 6.2 is Missouri's open primary law, enacted in 1946.
4. The Supreme Court's redistricting decisions of the early 1960s requiring districts of equal population may be partially responsible for the anomaly in Senate representation.

Chapter 7

1. See, for example, Bass and DeVries (1976), Black and Black (2002), Craig and Austin (2008), Davidson (1990), Echols and Ranney (1976), Havard (1972), and Lamis (1984a).
2. For a chronological table of restrictions, see Aldrich and Griffin (2018, 104).
3. See Kousser (1974, 45–48) for examples.
4. See Caughey (2018, ch. 5), Davidson (1990, 24), Grynaviski (2004), Hirano and Snyder (2019, ch. 3), and Key (1949, 384).
5. For a discussion of different classification schemes for defining the South, see Springer (2019).
6. For full histories of the cases leading up to *Smith*, see Weeks (1948) and Zeldin (2004).
7. For examples of such claims regarding Arkansas, see Blair and Barth (2005), Key (1949, ch. 20), and Bullock and Johnson (1992, 93–109).
8. For a state-by-state discussion of recent Southern elections, see Ray and Whitlock (2019).
9. The Louisiana "jungle primary"—a multicandidate race held on the date of the general election, followed by a two-candidate runoff in December if no candidate receives a majority—was adopted in 1975, for idiosyncratic reasons that differ from the race-based motivations of other southern states discussed here. For discussion see Parent (2004, 36–45).
10. This was a response to arguments by contemporary African American politicians such as Jesse Jackson (see Lamis 1984b; Bullock and Smith 1990). For an even more recent presentation of this claim, see Clyburn 2020.
11. Bullock and Johnson (1992, 106) conclude that runoff turnout averages 90 percent of primary turnout, and that in 25 to 40 percent of cases it exceeds primary turnout.
12. Klarman (2014, 388–389) contends that the 1950 primary defeats of two white southern liberal incumbents gave the impression that the runoff could have this effect, but that on closer examination their defeats had more to do with liberal stances on other issues than with their racial views.
13. Mississippi senator Thad Cochran has been said to have done this in his 2014 primary runoff (Cohn and Willis 2014).
14. Bullock and Johnson (1992, 168) tested this and found there was no effect.
15. See, for example, Kousser's (1974, 239) table listing eight categories of restrictive suffrage laws and Klarman's (2004) history of Supreme Court decisions on civil rights.

Chapter 8

1. See the Electoral Reform Research Group website, https://www.newamerica.org/political-reform/errg/, for a compendium of recent research papers on RCV; for a full description of the expected results of RCV on elections, see Amy (2002).

2. The cycles listed on the x axis are marked by the election preceding the cycle; for instance, the 2000 cycle consists of the two years following the 2000 election. For ease of display I allocated bills from New Jersey and Virginia, the two states that hold elections in odd-numbered years, into these cycles based on the year of introduction. In other words, bills introduced in Virginia in 2003 and 2004 are listed as part of the 2002 cycle even though Virginia had an election in November 2003.
3. In a small number of instances neither party had a majority in the chamber; here, I define the majority party according to which party held the tie-breaking vote or comprised a majority of coalition members. Unlike in Figure 8.1, I do adjust the Virginia and New Jersey reforms to reflect any changes in party control following these states' odd-year elections.
4. The Montana Senate passed a bill in 2023 that would establish a top two primary for 2024 only, and only for the state's U.S. Senate race. This strongly suggests that the intention of Republicans was to prevent Libertarian or other third-party candidates from draining votes from the Republican candidate. Democratic incumbent Jon Tester had won re-election in 2018 with only 50.3 percent of the vote, while a Libertarian candidate had received 2.9 percent (see Kimbel-Sannit 2023).
5. For a summary of prohibitions on ranked choice voting, see the ongoing list maintained by Ballotpedia at https://ballotpedia.org/Ranked-choice_voting_(RCV).

Chapter 9

1. For a review of such claims see Boatright (2013, ch. 1).
2. These were Lisa Murkowski, write-in candidate for Alaska Senate; Tom Tancredo, third-party candidate for Colorado governor; Charlie Crist, independent candidate for Florida governor; Elliot Cutler, independent candidate for Maine governor; and Lincoln Chafee, independent candidate for Rhode Island governor. Chafee and Murkowski won, and the other three placed second, ahead of one of the major party nominees.
3. Among Democratic primary voters who were able to place themselves on the ideology scale, those who voted exclusively for Democrats in the general election had a mean ideology of 2.65 as compared to a mean of 4.87 for Democratic primary voters who voted for at least one Republican general election candidate; the corresponding numbers for Republican primary voters are 6.12 and 4.46.
4. Briefly, the analysis here is hampered because the questions are slightly different. In both years, respondents were not asked directly about their primary voting choices; instead, Catalist data are used to identify Democratic and Republican primary voters. This procedure yields a smaller set of primary voters for both years.
5. In fact, in postmortems of the 2014 midterms, several journalists linked Republican successes to efforts by the Republican establishment—including party leaders in both chambers as well as outside groups like the U.S. Chamber of Commerce—to "avoid the kinds of disastrous candidates . . . whose extreme positions and outré comments

hampered the GOP up and down the ballot in 2012 and 2010 (Altman 2014; see also Peters and Hulse 2014; Jaffe and Kamisar 2014).
6. For other studies of divisiveness, see Kenney (1988); Born (1981); Johnson and Gibson (1974); Kenney and Rice (1987); Miller, Jewell, and Sigelman (1988); and Berry and Canon (1993).
7. Or perhaps more accurately, there is no reason to expect such challenges to change across time absent unusual external stimuli. Studies of the 1992 election have attributed the extremely high number of competitive primaries, of retirements, and of competitive general election races to a combination of partisan factors, changes in redistricting practices, the presence of a major scandal that affected many incumbents, and a change in House rules that affected the ability of retiring incumbents to convert their campaign treasuries to personal use (Groseclose and Krehbiel 1994). This is, to say the least, an unusual set of circumstances.
8. I do not show these breakdowns here; for graphs showing this relationship see Boatright and Moscardelli (2018).
9. For discussion of changes in Southern primary turnout and competitiveness over this period, see Hill and Tausanovitch (2017).
10. Again, see Boatright and Moscardelli (2018) for graphs showing this pattern.

Chapter 10

1. One of the salutary consequences RCV supporters have predicted is that candidates will refrain from campaigning against each other and will even encourage giving their supporters advice on which candidates to rank second. In New York, candidates Kathryn Garcia (the eventual second-place finisher) and Andrew Yang campaigned together in late June 2021; Garcia encouraged her supporters to rank Yang second, and Yang reciprocated.

Bibliography

Abramowitz, Alan I. 2012. "Grand Old Tea Party: Partisan Polarization and the Rise of the Tea Party Movement." In *Steep: The Precipitous Rise of the Tea Party*, ed. Lawrence Rosenthal and Christine Trost, 195–211. Berkeley: University of California Press.

Abrams, Richard M. 1964. *Conservatism in a Progressive Era: Massachusetts Politics, 1900–1912*. Cambridge, MA: Harvard University Press.

Aldrich, John E., and John D. Griffin. 2018. *Why Parties Matter: Political Competition and Democracy in the American South*. Chicago: University of Chicago Press.

Altman, Alex. 2014. "How the Republican Establishment Got Its Groove Back." *Time*, November 5. wp.me/p5HMd-eVGw.

Alvarez, R. Michael, David T. Canon, and Patrick Sellers. 1995. "The Impact of Primaries on General Election Outcomes in the U. S. House and Senate." Unpublished manuscript, California Institute of Technology.

Alvarez, R. Michael, and Jonathan Nagler. 1998. "Analysis of Crossover and Strategic Voting." Unpublished manuscript, California Institute of Technology.

Alvarez, R. Michael, and J. Andrew Sinclair. 2014. *Nonpartisan Primary Election Reform: Mitigating Mischief*. New York: Cambridge University Press.

American Political Science Association, Committee on Political Parties. 1950. "Toward a More Responsible Two-Party System." *American Political Science Review* 44 (3): pt. 2 (Supplement): 1–99.

Amy, Douglas J. 2002. *Real Choices, New Voices*. 2nd ed. New York: Columbia University Press.

Anderson, Frank Maloy. 1902. "The Test of the Minnesota Primary Election System." *Annals of the American Academy of Political and Social Sciences* 20: 142–152.

Ansolabehere, Stephen. 2012. "CCES Common Content, 2010." Harvard Dataverse, V3. doi.org/10.7910/DVN/VKKRWA.

Ansolabehere, Stephen, and Alan Gerber. 1996. "The Effects of Filing Fees and Petition Requirements on U.S. House Elections." *Legislative Studies Quarterly* 21 (2): 249–264.

Ansolabehere, Stephen, John Mark Hansen, Shigeo Hirano, and James M. Snyder Jr. 2006. "The Decline of Competition in US Primary Elections, 1908–2004." In *The Marketplace of Democracy: Electoral Competition and American Politics*, ed. Michael P. McDonald and John Samples, 74–101. Washington, DC: Brookings Institution and Cato Institute.

Ansolabehere, Stephen, John Mark Hansen, Shigeo Hirano, and James M. Snyder Jr. 2007. "The Incumbency Advantage in U.S. Primary Elections." *Electoral Studies* 26 (3): 660–668.

Ansolabehere, Stephen, John Mark Hansen, Shigeo Hirano, and James M. Snyder Jr. 2010. "More Democracy: The Direct Primary and Competition in U.S. House Elections." *Studies in American Political Development* 24 (2): 190–205.

Anzia, Sarah. 2014. *Timing and Turnout: How Off-Cycle Elections Favor Organized Groups*. Chicago: University of Chicago Press.

Argersinger, Peter H. 1995. *The Limits of Agrarian Radicalism: Western Populism and American Politics*. Lawrence: University Press of Kansas.

Bacon, Jerry D. 1918. "Townleyism Unmasked! Now Stands before the World in Its True Light as Radical Socialism!" Nonpartisan League Collection, MS 51, Box 1, Folder 27. Institute for Regional Studies, North Dakota State University, Fargo.

Bacon, Jerry D. 1919. "Carry the Truth to the People: A.fter C.ash Townley Smoked Out; A Companion Volume to 'The Farmer and Townleyism.' Being the second volume of an expose and inside story of the methods, personnel and menace of the most remarkable phenomenon in fifty years of American political history; House bill 44 explained." Nonpartisan League Collection, MS 51, Box 1, Folder 27. Institute for Regional Studies, North Dakota State University, Fargo.

Bagashka, Tanya, and Jennifer H. Clark. 2016. "Electoral Rules and Legislative Particularism: Evidence from U.S. State Legislatures." *American Political Science Review* 110 (3): 441–456.

Baker, Paula. 2012. *Curbing Campaign Cash: Henry Ford, Truman Newberry, and the Politics of Progressive Reform*. Lawrence: University of Kansas Press.

Ballotpedia. 2020a. "Alaska Ballot Measure 2, Alaska Top-Four Ranked-Choice Voting and Campaign Finance Laws Initiative (2020)." Ballotpedia, December 1, 2020. ballotpedia.org/Alaska_Ballot_Measure_2,_Top-Four_Ranked-Choice_Voting_and_Campaign_Finance_Laws_Initiative_(2020).

Ballotpedia. 2020b. "Virginia's 5th Congressional District election, 2020" (June 13 Republican convention). Ballotpedia, November 3, 2020. ballotpedia.org/Virginia%27s_5th_Congressional_District_election,_2020_(June_13_Republican_convention).

Barber, Kathleen L. 2000. *A Right to Representation: Proportional Election Systems for the Twenty-First Century*. Columbus: Ohio State University Press.

Barnett, James D. 1912. "Forestalling the Direct Primary in Oregon." *Political Science Quarterly* 27 (4): 648–668.

Bass, Jack, and Walter DeVries. 1976. *The Transformation of Southern Politics: Social Change and Political Consequence since 1945*. New York: Basic Books.

Bateman, David A., Ira Katznelson, and John Lapinski. 2018. *Southern Nation: Congress and White Supremacy after Reconstruction*. Princeton, NJ: Princeton University Press.

Beard, Charles A. 1910. "The Direct Primary in New York." *Proceedings of the American Political Science Association* 7: 187–198.

Bell, Jonathan. 2012. *California Crucible: The Forging of Modern American Liberalism*. Philadelphia: University of Pennsylvania Press.

Beman, Lamar T., ed. 1926. *The Direct Primary*. New York: H. W. Wilson Company.

Berdahl, Clarence A. 1923. "The Operation of the Richards Primary." *Annals of the American Academy of Political and Social Science* 106: 158–171.

Berdahl, Clarence A. 1942. "Party Membership in the United States, II." *American Political Science Review* 36 (2): 241–262.

Bernstein, Robert A. 1977. "Divisive Primaries Do Hurt: US Senate Races, 1956-1972." *American Political Science Review* 71 (2): 540–545.

Berry, Jeffrey M., Kent E. Portney, and Robert Joseph. 2014. "The Tea Party in Local Politics." Paper presented at the Annual Meeting of the American Political Science Association, Washington, DC.

Berry, William D., and Bradley C. Canon. 1993. "Explaining the Competitiveness of Gubernatorial Primaries." *Journal of Politics* 55 (2): 454–471.

Bipartisan Policy Center Commission on Political Reform. 2014. *Governing in a Polarized America: A Bipartisan Blueprint to Strengthen our Democracy*. Washington,

DC: Bipartisan Policy Center. bipartisanpolicy.org/report/governing-polarized-america-bipartisan-blueprint-strengthen-our-democracy/.
Birch, Sarah. 2011. *Electoral Practice*. London: Oxford University Press.
Black, Earl, and Merle Black. 2002. *The Rise of Southern Republicans*. Cambridge, MA: Harvard University Press.
Blackorby, Edward C. 1963. *Prairie Rebel: The Public Life of William Lemke*. Lincoln: University of Nebraska Press.
Blair, Diane D., and Jay Barth. 2005. *Arkansas Politics and Government*. 2nd ed. Lincoln: University of Nebraska Press.
Boatright, Robert G. 2013. *Getting Primaried: The Changing Politics of Congressional Primary Challenges*. Ann Arbor: University of Michigan Press.
Boatright, Robert G. 2014. *Congressional Primary Elections*. New York: Routledge.
Boatright, Robert G., ed. 2018. *Handbook of Primary Elections*. New York: Routledge.
Boatright, Robert G. 2019. "Retrenchment or Reform? Changes in Primary Election Laws, 1928–1970." *Polity* 51 (1): 126–160.
Boatright, Robert G., and Zachary Albert. 2021. "Factional Conflict and Independent Expenditures in the 2018 Democratic House Primaries." *Congress and the Presidency* 48 (1): 50–77.
Boatright, Robert G., and Vincent G. Moscardelli. 2018. "Is There a Link between Primary Election Competition and General Election Results?" In *Handbook of Primary Elections*, ed. Robert G. Boatright, 188–212. New York: Routledge.
Boatright, Robert G., Vincent G. Moscardelli, and Clifford Vickrey. 2017. "The Consequences of Primary Timing." Paper presented at the Annual Meeting of the Midwest Political Science Association, Chicago, IL.
Boatright, Robert G., Vincent G. Moscardelli, and Clifford Vickrey. 2020. "Primary Election Timing and Voter Turnout." *Election Law Journal* 19 (4): 472–485.
Boots, Ralph S. 1922. "The Trend of the Direct Primary." *American Political Science Review* 16 (3): 412–431.
Born, Richard. 1981. "The Influence of House Primary Election Divisiveness on General Election Margins, 1962–1976." *Journal of Politics* 43 (3): 640–661.
Brogan, Michael J., and Jonathan Mendilow. 2012. "Public Party Funding and Intraparty Competition: Clean Elections in Maine and Arizona." *International Journal of Humanities and Social Science* 2 (6): 120–132.
Broockman, David E., and Christopher Skovron. 2018. "Bias in Perceptions of Public Opinion among Political Elites." *American Political Science Review* 112 (3): 542–563.
Bruce, Andrew A. 1921. *Non-partisan League*. New York: Macmillan.
Bruhn, Kathleen. 2018. "Party Primaries as a Strategic Choice: The Costs and Benefits of Democratic Candidate Selection." In *Routledge Handbook of Primary Elections*, ed. Robert G. Boatright, 354–368. New York: Routledge.
Buenker, John D. 1973. *Urban Liberalism and Progressive Reform*. New York: Charles Scribner's Sons.
Bullock, Charles S., and A. Brock Smith. 1990. "Black Success in Local Runoff Elections." *Journal of Politics* 52 (4): 1205–1220.
Bullock, Charles S., and Loch K. Johnson. 1992. *Runoff Elections in the United States*. Chapel Hill: University of North Carolina Press.
Bullock, Charles S., Susan A. MacManus, Jeremy D. Mayer, and Mark J. Rozell. 2019. *The South and the Transformation of U.S. Politics*. New York: Oxford University Press.

Bullock, Charles S., III. 2010. *Redistricting: The Most Political Activity in America*. Lanham, MD: Rowman and Littlefield.

Burden, Barry C. 2001. "The Polarizing Effects of Congressional Primaries." In *Congressional Primaries and the Politics of Representation*, ed. Peter F. Galderisi, Marni Ezra, and Michael Lyons, 95–115. Lanham, MD: Rowman and Littlefield.

Burden, Barry C., Bradley Jones, and Michael S. Kang. 2014. "Sore Loser Laws and Congressional Polarization." *Legislative Studies Quarterly* 39 (2): 299–325.

Burdick, Usher. 1944. *History of the Farmers Political Action in ND*. Baltimore, MD: Wirth Bros.

Cain, Bruce E. 2015. *Democracy More or Less: America's Political Reform Quandary*. New York: Cambridge University Press.

Calcagno, Peter T., and Christopher Westley. 2008. "An Institutional Analysis of Voter Turnout: The Role of Primary Type and the Expressive and Instrumental Voting Hypotheses." *Constitutional Political Economy* 19 (2): 94–110.

Campbell, James E. 1987. "The Revised Theory of Surge and Decline." *American Journal of Political Science* 31 (4): 965–979.

Campbell, James E. 1997. "The Presidential Pulse and the 1994 Midterm Congressional Election." *Journal of Politics* 59 (3): 830–857.

Canon, Bradley. 1978. "Factionalism in the South: A Test of Theory and a Revisitation of V. O. Key." *American Journal of Political Science* 22 (3): 833–848.

Carson, Jamie L., and Jason M. Roberts. 2013. *Ambition, Competition, and Electoral Reform: The Politics of Congressional Elections across Time*. Ann Arbor: University of Michigan Press.

Casdorph, Paul D. 1981. *Republicans, Negroes, and Progressives in the South, 1912–1916*. Tuscaloosa: University of Alabama Press.

Caughey, Devin. 2018. *The Unsolid South: Mass Politics and National Representation in a One-Party Enclave*. Princeton, NJ: Princeton University Press.

Chamberlain, John. 1932. *Farewell to Reform: The Rise, Life, and Decay of the Progressive Mind in America*. New York: John Day Company.

Cheeseman, Nic, and Brian Klaas. 2018. *How to Rig an Election*. New Haven, CT: Yale University Press.

Chrislock, Carl H. 1971. *The Progressive Era in Minnesota, 1899–1918*. St. Paul: Minnesota Historical Society.

Clyburn, James. 2020. "Runoff Elections Suppress Black Representation: Relegate Them to the Past." *Washington Post*, December 23.

Cohen, Martin. 2012. "The Future of the Tea Party: Scoring an Invitation to the Republican Party." In *Steep: The Precipitous Rise of the Tea Party*, ed. Lawrence Rosenthal and Christine Trost, 212–241. Berkeley: University of California Press.

Cohen, Michael D., James G. March, and Johan P. Olson. 1972. "A Garbage Can Model of Organizational Choice." *Administrative Science Quarterly* 17 (1): 1–25.

Cohn, Nate, and Derek Willis. 2014. "More Evidence That Thad Cochran Owes Runoff Win to Black Voters." *New York Times*, July 15.

Council of State Governments. 1936–1970. *The Book of the States*. Lexington, KY: Council of State Governments.

Courier-News (Fargo). 1917. "Washington Bureau: Baer Surprises East by Work as Artist-Writer: He's Making Good." November 7. John Miller Baer Cartoon Collection, Photo Folio 108, Institute for Regional Studies, North Dakota State University, Fargo.

Craig, Stephen C., and Roger Austin. 2008. "Elections and Partisan Change in Florida." In *Government and Politics in Florida*, 3rd ed., ed. J. Edwin Benton, 48–89. Gainesville: University Press of Florida.

Crespin, Michael H. 2004. "Direct Primaries and the Openness of the Two Party System, 1904–1920." Unpublished manuscript, Michigan State University.

Croly, Herbert. 1909. *The Promise of American Life*. New York: Macmillan.

Croly, Herbert. 1915. *Progressive Democracy*. New York: Macmillan.

Cronin, Thomas E., and Robert D. Loevy. 2012. *Colorado Politics and Government: Governing a Purple State*. Lincoln: University of Nebraska Press.

Crosson, Jesse M. 2021. "Extreme Districts, Moderate Winners: Same-Party Challengers and Deterrence in Top-Two Primaries?" *Political Science Research and Methods* 9 (3): 532–548.

Dallinger, Frederick. 1897. *Nominations for Elective Office*. Cambridge, MA: Harvard University Press.

Dalton, Russell J. 2004. *Democratic Challenges, Democratic Choices*. New York: Oxford University Press.

Davidson, Chandler. 1990. *Race and Class in Texas Politics*. Princeton, NJ: Princeton University Press.

Davies-Roberts, Avery, and David J. Carroll. 2014. "Assessing Elections." In *Advancing Electoral Integrity*, ed. Pippa Norris, Richard W. Frank, and Ferran Martinez I Coma, 18–33. New York: Oxford University Press.

Davis, James W. 1980. *Presidential Primaries: Road to the White House*. Westport, CT: Greenwood Press.

Dawes, Charles. 1926. "Speech to the PA Club of New York, December 18, 1926: Reprinted at the Request of Senator Johnson." Charles G. Dawes Archive, Box 154, Folder 14. Charles Deering McCormick Library of Special Collections, Northwestern University.

DeBonis, Mike, and Paul Kane. 2021. "McCarthy Moves to Keep Splintering GOP Intact, with Protection for Both Cheney and Greene." *Washington Post*, February 3.

Delmatier, Royce D., Clarence F. McIntosh, and Earl G. Waters. 1970. *The Rumble of California Politics, 1848–1970*. New York: John Wiley and Sons.

Democratic Party of New Mexico. 2018. "Rules of the Democratic Party of the State of New Mexico." nmdemocrats.org/wp-content/uploads/2019/02/392001909-DPNM-Rules-as-of-10-13-18.pdf.

Denver Express. 1917. "Three Million Western Farmers Ready to Join North Dakota Movement." National Nonpartisan League Collection, Roll 2. Minnesota Historical Society, St. Paul.

Diemer, Tom. 1994. "Ohio in Washington: The Congressional Delegation." In *Ohio Politics*, ed. Alexander P. Lamis, 196–232. Kent, OH: Kent State University Press.

Dobson, Richard. 1956. Interview with A. C. Townley. Nonpartisan League Collection, MS 51, Box 1, Folder 33. Institute for Regional Studies, North Dakota State University, Fargo.

Dominguez, Casey B. K. 2013. "Before the Primary: How Party Elites and Ambitious Candidates Respond to Anticipated General Election Competitiveness." Paper presented at the Annual Meeting of the Midwest Political Science Association, Chicago, IL.

Donovan, Todd. 2012. "The Top Two Primary: What Can California Learn from Washington?" *California Journal of Politics and Policy* 4 (1): 1–22.

Dorr, Harold M. 1937. "Tightening the Direct Primary in Michigan: First Applications of the Filing Fee." *American Political Science Review* 31 (1): 56–65.

Dovre, Paul John. 1963. "A Study of Nonpartisan League Persuasion, 1915–1920." PhD diss., Northwestern University.

Drutman, Lee. 2019. *Breaking the Two-Party Doom Loop*. New York: Oxford University Press.

Dubin, Michael J. 2007. *Party Affiliation in the State Legislatures: A Year by Year Summary, 1789–2006*. Jefferson, NC: McFarland.

Eaves, Lucas. 2013. "Montana to Vote on Adding Nonpartisan Top Two Primary to 2014 Ballot." Independent Voter Network. ivn.us/2013/04/19/montananscould-adopt-a-nonpartisan-top-two-primary-in-2014/.

Echols, Margaret Thompson, and Austin Ranney. 1976. "The Impact of Interparty Competition Reconsidered: The Case of Florida." *Journal of Politics* 38 (1): 142–152.

Elazar, Daniel J. 1972. *American Federalism: A View from the States*. 2nd ed. New York: Thomas Y. Crowell.

Elazar, Daniel J. 1999. *Minnesota Politics and Government*. Lincoln: University of Nebraska Press.

Engstrom, Erik J., and Jason M. Roberts. 2020. *The Politics of Ballot Design*. New York: Cambridge University Press.

Epstein, Leon D. 1958. *Politics in Wisconsin*. Madison: University of Wisconsin Press.

Epstein, Reid J. 2021. "The Virginia G.O.P. Voted on Its Future: The Losers Reject the Results." *New York Times*, February 19.

Erickson, Camille. 2021a. "Donald Trump Jr. Lobbies for Wyoming Election Runoff Bill." *Casper Star-Tribune*, March 9.

Erickson, Camille. 2021b. "Bid to Change Primary Election Process in Wyoming Fails." *Casper Star-Tribune*, March 24.

Erikson, Robert S. 1988. "The Puzzle of Midterm Loss." *Journal of Politics* 50 (4): 1011–1029.

Ewing, Cortez. 1953. *Primary Elections in the South: A Study in Uniparty Politics*. Norman: University of Oklahoma Press.

Fanning, C. E. 1905. *Selected Articles on Direct Primaries*. Minneapolis, MN: H. W. Wilson.

Farrell, David M. 2011. *Electoral Systems: A Comparative Introduction*. 2nd ed. New York: Palgrave Macmillan.

Feldman, H. 1917. "The Direct Primary in New York State." *American Political Science Review* 11 (3): 494–518.

Flower, Walter C. 1898. "Address of Hon. Walter C. Flower." Presented at National Conference on Practical Reform of Primary Elections, Held at the Room of the New York Board of Trade and Transportation, New York, January 20–21.

Forcey, Charles. 1961. *The Crossroads of Liberalism: Croly, Weyl, Lippmann, and the Progressive Era, 1900–1925*. New York: Oxford University Press.

Ford, Henry Jones. 1909. "The Direct Primary." *North American Review* 190 (644): 1–14.

Fortenberry, Charles N., and F. Glenn Abney. 1972. "Mississippi: Unreconstructed and Unredeemed." In *The Changing Politics of the South*, ed. William C. Havard, 472–524. Baton Rouge: University of Louisiana Press.

Fossum, Paul Robert. 1925. *The Agrarian Movement in North Dakota*. Baltimore, MD: Johns Hopkins University Press.

Freeman, Jo. 1986. "The Political Culture of the Democratic and Republican Parties." *Political Science Quarterly* 101 (3): 327–356.

Frei, Matthew D., J. Quin Monson, Leah Murray, and Kelly D. Patterson. 2012. "Tea for Only Two: The Ousting of Utah Senator Robert Bennett." In *Tea Party Effects on 2010 U.S. Senate Elections: Stuck in the Middle to Lose*, ed. William J. Miller and Jeremy D. Walling, 105-119. Lanham, MD: Lexington Books.

Freyd, Bernard. 1926. *Repeal the Direct Primary*. Seattle: McKay Printing Company.

Frier, Ted, and Larry Overton. 1992. *Time for a Change: The Return of the Republican Party in Massachusetts*. Boston: Lafayette Graphics/Davis Press.

Gabriel, Trip. 2021. "Glenn Youngkin Wins G.O.P. Nomination for Virginia Governor." *New York Times*, May 10.

Gaddie, Ronald Keith. 1997. "Congressional Seat Swings: Revisiting Exposure in House Elections." *Political Research Quarterly* 50 (3): 699-710.

Gaines, Brian J., and Wendy K. Tam Cho. 2002. "Crossover Voting before the Blanket." In *Voting at the Political Fault Line: California's Experiment with the Blanket Primary*, ed. Bruce E. Cain and Elisabeth R. Gerber, 12-35. Berkeley: University of California Press.

Galderisi, Peter F., and Marni Ezra. 2001. "Congressional Primaries in Historical and Theoretical Context." In *Congressional Primaries and the Politics of Representation*, ed. Peter F. Galderisi, Marni Ezra, and Michael Lyons, 11-28. Lanham, MD: Rowman and Littlefield.

Galderisi, Peter S., and Benjamin Ginsberg. 1986. "Primary Elections and the Evanescence of Third Party Activity in the United States." In *Do Elections Matter?*, ed. Benjamin Ginsberg and Alan Stone, 115-130. Armonk, NY: M. E. Sharpe.

Gardner, Amy. 2010. "Tea Party Wins Victory in Utah as Incumbent GOP Senator Loses Bid for Nomination." *Washington Post*, May 9.

Gaston, Herbert E. 1920. *The Nonpartisan League*. New York: Harcourt, Brace, and Howe.

Geiser, Karl F. 1923. "Defects in the Direct Primary." *Annals of the American Academy of Political and Social Sciences* 106: 31-39.

Geras, Matthew J., and Michael H. Crespin. 2018. "The Effect of Open and Closed Primaries on Voter Turnout." In *Routledge Handbook of Primary Elections*, ed. Robert G. Boatright, 133-146. New York: Routledge.

Gerber, Elizabeth R. 2001. "California's Experience with the Blanket Primary." In *Congressional Primaries and the Politics of Representation*, ed. Peter F. Galderisi, Marni Ezra, and Michael Lyons, 143-160. Lanham, MD: Rowman and Littlefield,.

Gerber, Elizabeth R., and Rebecca B. Morton. 1998. "Primary Election Systems and Representation." *Journal of Law, Economics, and Organization* 14 (2): 304-324.

Gieske, Millard L. 1979. *Minnesota Farmer-Laborism: The Third-Party Alternative*. Minneapolis: University of Minnesota Press.

Glaab, Charles Nelson. 1981. "John Burke and the Progressive Revolt." In *The North Dakota Political Tradition*, ed. Charles Nelson Glaab and Thomas William Howard, 40-65. Ames: Iowa State University Press.

Glueck, Katie. 2021. "New York Mayor's Race in Chaos after Elections Board Counts 135,000 Test Ballots." *New York Times*, June 29.

Goble, Danney. 1980. *Progressive Oklahoma*. Norman: University of Oklahoma Press.

Goldberg, Michelle. 2021. "Eric Adams Is Awful: I'm Putting Him on My Ballot." *New York Times*, June 18.

Goldberg, Ray Allan. 1955. *The Nonpartisan League in North Dakota: A Case Study of Political Action in America*. Fargo, ND: Midwest Publishing.

Goldiner, Dave. 2021. "Trump: 'Nobody Will Ever Know Who Really Won' NYC Mayoral Vote—Just Like Presidential Election, He Says." *New York Daily News*, June 30.

Gould, Lewis L. 1974. *The Progressive Era*. Syracuse, NY: Syracuse University Press.
Graham, Otis L. 1967. *An Encore for Reform: The Old Progressives and the New Deal*. New York: Oxford University Press.
Grantham, Dewey W. 1983. *Southern Progressivism: The Reconciliation of Progress and Tradition*. Knoxville: University of Tennessee Press.
Grantham, Dewey W. 1988. *The Life and Death of the Solid South*. Lexington: University of Kentucky Press.
Grantham, Dewey W. 1994. *The South in Modern America: A Region at Odds*. New York: HarperCollins.
Green, John C., and Paul S. Herrnson, 2002. "Party Development in the Twentieth Century: Laying the Foundations for Responsible Party Government?" In *Responsible Partisanship: The Evolution of American Political Parties since 1950*, ed. John C. Green and Paul S. Herrnson, 37–60. Lawrence: University Press of Kansas.
Greene, Lee S., and Jack E. Holmes. 1972. "Tennessee: A Politics of Peaceful Change." In *The Changing Politics of the South*, ed. William C. Havard, 165–200. Baton Rouge: University of Louisiana Press,.
Grose, Christian R. 2020. "Reducing Legislative Polarization: Top-Two and Open Primaries Are Associated with More Moderate Legislators." *Journal of Political Institutions and Political Economy* 1: 267–287.
Groseclose, Timothy, and Keith Krehbiel. 1994. "Golden Parachutes, Rubber Checks, and Strategic Retirements from the 102nd Congress." *American Journal of Political Science* 38 (1): 75–99.
Grynaviski, Jeffrey D. 2004. "The Impact of Electoral Rules on Factional Competition in the Democratic South, 1919–48." *Party Politics* 10 (5): 499–519.
Guild, Frederic H. 1923. "The Operations of the Direct Primary in Indiana." *Annals of the American Academy of Political and Social Sciences* 106: 172–180.
Hacker, Andrew. 1965. "Does a 'Divisive' Primary Harm a Candidate's Chances?" *American Political Science Review* 59 (1): 105–110.
Hackney, Sheldon. 1969. *Populism to Progressivism in Alabama*. Princeton, NJ: Princeton University Press.
Hain, Paul L., and Jose Z. Garcia. 1994. "Voting, Elections, and Parties." In *New Mexico Government*, 3rd ed., ed. Paul L. Hain, F. Chris Garcia, and Gilbert K. St. Clair, 233–250. Albuquerque: University of New Mexico Press.
Hajnal, Zoltan L. 2009. *America's Uneven Democracy: Race, Turnout, and Representation in City Politics*. New York: Cambridge University Press.
Hall, Arnold Bennett. 1923. "The Direct Primary and Party Responsibility in Wisconsin." *Annals of the American Academy of Political and Social Sciences* 106: 40–54.
Hansen, John Mark, Shigeo Hirano, and James M. Snyder. 2017. "Parties within Parties: Parties, Factions, and Coordinated Politics, 1900–1980." In *Governing in a Polarized Age: Elections, Parties and Political Representation in America*, ed. Alan S. Gerber and Eric Schickler, 143–190. New York: Cambridge University Press.
Hasen, Richard L. 2012. *The Voting Wars*. New Haven, CT: Yale University Press.
Hassell, Hans J. G. 2013. "The Non-existent Primary-Ideology Link, or Do Open Primaries Actually Limit Party Influence in Primary Elections?" Paper presented at the Annual State Politics and Policy Conference, Iowa City, IA.
Hassell, Hans J. G. 2018. *The Party's Primary: Control of Congressional Nominations*. New York: Cambridge University Press.

Havard, William C., ed. 1972. *The Changing Politics of the South*. Baton Rouge: University of Louisiana Press.

Heard, Alexander. 1952. *A Two Party South?* Chapel Hill: University of North Carolina Press.

Hedlund, Ronald. D. 1977. "Cross-Over Voting in a 1976 Open Presidential Primary." *Public Opinion Quarterly* 41 (4): 498–514.

Heersink, Boris, and Jeffery A. Jenkins. 2020. "Whiteness and the Emergence of the Republican Party in the Early Twentieth-Century South." *Studies in American Political Development* 34 (1): 71–90.

Herrnson, Paul S. 1998. "Party Organizations at the Century's End." In *The Parties Respond: Changes in the American Party System*, 3rd ed., ed. L. Sandy Maisel, 50–82. Boulder, CO: Westview Press.

Herrnson, Paul S., and James G. Gimpel. 1995. "District Conditions and Primary Divisiveness in Congressional Elections." *Political Research Quarterly* 48 (1): 117–134.

Hibbing, John R. 1982a. "Voluntary Retirements from the House in the Twentieth Century." *Journal of Politics* 44 (4): 1020–1034.

Hibbing, John R. 1982b. "Voluntary Retirement from the U.S. House: The Costs of Congressional Service." *Legislative Studies Quarterly* 7 (1): 57–74.

Hibbing, John R. 1982c. "Voluntary Retirement from the U.S. House of Representatives: Who Quits?" *American Journal of Political Science* 26 (3): 467–484.

Hill, Seth J. 2015. "Institution of Nomination and the Policy Ideology of Primary Electorates." *Quarterly Journal of Political Science* 10 (2): 461–487.

Hill, Seth J. 2022. "Sidestepping Primary Reform: Political Action in Response to Institutional Change." *Political Science Research and Methods* 10 (2): 391–407.

Hill, Seth J., and Chris Tausanovitch. 2017. "Southern Realignment, Party Sorting, and the Polarization of American Primary Electorates, 1958–2012." Unpublished manuscript, University of California, San Diego.

Hirano, Shigeo, and James M. Snyder Jr. 2019. *Primary Elections in the United States*. New York: Cambridge University Press.

Hirschman, Albert O. 1970. *Exit, Voice, and Loyalty*. Cambridge, MA: Harvard University Press.

Hofstadter, Richard. 1955. *The Age of Reform*. New York: Vintage Books.

Hogan, Robert E. 2003. "Competition in State Legislative Primary Elections." *Legislative Studies Quarterly* 28 (1): 103–126.

Holbrook, Thomas M., and Emily Van Dunk. 1993. "Electoral Competition in the American States." *American Political Science Review* 87 (4): 955–62.

Holland, Lynwood M. 1949. *The Direct Primary in Georgia*. Champaign: University of Illinois Press.

Holmes, Jack E. 1967. *Politics in New Mexico*. Albuquerque: University of New Mexico Press.

Hopkins, Daniel J. 2018. *The Increasingly United States: How and Why American Political Behavior Nationalized*. Chicago: University of Chicago Press

Horack, Frank E. 1923. "The Workings of the Direct Primary in Iowa, 1908–1922." *Annals of the American Academy of Political and Social Sciences* 106: 148–157.

Hormell, Orren Chalmer. 1923. "The Direct Primary Law in Maine and How It Worked." *Annals of the American Academy of Political and Social Science* 106: 128–141.

Huthmacher, J. Joseph. 1959. *Massachusetts People and Politics, 1919–1933*. Cambridge, MA: Harvard University Press.

Issacharoff, Samuel, and Richard H. Pildes. 1998. "Politics as Markets: Partisan Lockups of the Democratic Process." *Stanford Law Review* 50 (3): 643–717.

Jacobs, Lawrence. 2022. *Democracy under Fire*. New York: Oxford University Press.

Jacobson, Gary C. 2012. "The Electoral Origins of Polarized Politics: Evidence from the 2010 Cooperative Congressional Election Study." *American Behavioral Scientist* 56 (12): 1612–1630.

Jacobson, Gary C. 2013. *The Politics of Congressional Elections*. 8th ed. New York: Longman.

Jaffe, Alexandra, and Ben Kamisar. 2014. "Has the Tea Party Been Tamed?" *The Hill*. November 6. thehill.com/blogs/ballot-box/223278-after-victories-tea-party-wont-back-down.

Jewell, Malcolm E., and David Breaux. 1988. "The Effect of Incumbency on State Legislative Elections." *Legislative Studies Quarterly* 13 (4): 495–514.

Jewell, Malcolm E., and Everett W. Cunningham. 1968. *Kentucky Politics*. Lexington: University of Kentucky Press.

Jewell, Malcolm E., and David M. Olson. 1988. *Political Parties and Elections in American States*. 3rd ed. Chicago: Dorsey Press.

Johnson, Bertram. 2010. "Individual Contributions: A Fundraising Advantage for the Ideologically Extreme?" *American Politics Research* 38 (5): 890–908.

Johnson, Donald Bruce, and James R. Gibson. 1974. "The Divisive Primary Revisited: Party Activists in Iowa." *American Political Science Review* 68 (1): 67–77.

Johnson, Gregg B., Meredith-Joy Petersheim, and Jesse T. Wasson. 2010. "Divisive Primaries and Incumbent General Election Performance: Prospects and Costs in U. S. House Races." *American Politics Research* 38 (5): 931–955.

Johnson, Hiram, 1926a. "Response to Vice President Dawes, December 20, 1926." Hiram Johnson Papers, BANC MSS C-B 581l Part III, carton 2. The Bancroft Library, University of California, Berkeley.

Johnson, Hiram. 1926b. "Senator Johnson, Floor Remarks, 69th Cong., 2nd sess." Hiram Johnson Papers, BANC MSS C-B 581l Part III, box 42. Berkeley: The Bancroft Library, University of California.

Judah, Charles B. 1957. *Aspects of the Nominating Systems of New Mexico*. Albuquerque: Department of Research, Department of Government, University of New Mexico.

Kamarck, Elaine. 2014. "Increasing Turnout in Congressional Primaries." Brookings Institution, Center for Effective Public Management, July. www.brookings.edu/research/increasing-turnout-in-congressional-primaries/.

Kang, Michael S. 2011. "Sore Loser Laws and Democratic Contestation." *Georgetown Law Review* 99: 1013–1075.

Kanthak, Kristen, and Eric Loepp. 2018. "Strategic Candidate Entry: Primary Type and Candidate Divergence." In *Routledge Handbook of Primary Elections*, ed. Robert G. Boatright, 147–158. New York: Routledge.

Kanthak, Kristin, and Rebecca B. Morton. 2001. "The Effects of Electoral Rules on Congressional Primaries." In *Congressional Primaries and the Politics of Representation*, ed. Peter F. Galderisi, Marni Ezra, and Michael Lyons, 116–131. Lanham, MD: Rowman and Littlefield.

Kanthak, Kristin, and Rebecca B. Morton. 2003. "Primaries and Turnout." Unpublished manuscript, New York University.

Katz, Richard S., and Peter Mair. 1995. "Changing Models of Party Organization and Party Democracy: The Emergence of the Cartel Party." *Party Politics* 1 (1): 5–28.

Katz, Richard S., and Peter Mair. 2009. "The Cartel Party Thesis: A Restatement." *Perspectives on Politics* 7 (4): 753–766.

Kaufmann, Karen M., James G. Gimpel, and Adam H. Hoffman. 2003. "A Promise Fulfilled? Open Primaries and Representation." *Journal of Politics* 65 (2): 457–476.

Kenney, Patrick J. 1986. "Explaining Primary Turnout: The Senatorial Case." *Legislative Studies Quarterly* 11 (1): 65–73.

Kenney, Patrick J., 1988. "Sorting Out the Effects of Primary Divisiveness in Congressional and Senatorial Elections." *Western Political Quarterly* 41 (4): 765–777.

Kenney, Patrick J., and Tom W. Rice. 1984. "The Effect of Primary Divisiveness in Gubernatorial and Senatorial Elections." *Journal of Politics* 46 (3): 904–915.

Kenney, Patrick J., and Tom W. Rice. 1987. "The Relationship between Divisive Primaries and General Election Outcomes." *American Journal of Political Science* 31 (1): 31–44.

Kernell, Samuel. 1977. "Presidential Popularity and Negative Voting: An Alternative Explanation of the Midterm Congressional Decline of the President's Party." *American Political Science Review* 71 (1): 44–66.

Kettleborough, Charles. 1923a. "Direct Primaries." *Annals of the American Academy of Political and Social Sciences* 106: 11–17.

Kettleborough, Charles. 1923b. "Digest of Primary Election Laws." *Annals of the American Academy of Political and Social Sciences* 106: 181–273.

Key, V. O. (1949) 1984. *Southern Politics in State and Nation*. Knoxville: University of Tennessee Press.

Key, V. O. 1956. *American State Politics: An Introduction*. New York: Knopf.

Kimbell-Sanitt, Arren. 2023. "Attempt to Revive Controversial Top-Two Primary Proposal Stalls in Senate Committee." *Montana Free Press*, April 24. montanafreepress.org/2023/04/24/attempt-to-revive-controversial-top-two-primary-proposal-stalls-in-montana-senate-committee/.

King, Judson, to Henry G. Teigan. 1917a. March 12. National Nonpartisan League Collection, Roll 2. Minnesota Historical Society, St. Paul.

King, Judson, to Henry G. Teigan. 1917b. April 21. National Nonpartisan League Collection, Roll 2. Minnesota Historical Society, St. Paul.

Kirby, Jack Temple. 1972. *Darkness at the Dawning: Race and Reform in the Progressive South*. Philadelphia, PA: J. B. Lippincott.

Kirwan, Albert. 1951. *Revolt of the Rednecks: Mississippi Politics, 1876-1925*. Lexington: University of Kentucky Press.

Klarman, Michael J. 2014. *From Jim Crow to Civil Rights: The Supreme Court and the Struggle for Racial Equality*. New York: Oxford University Press.

Klarner, Carl. 2013. "Other Scholars' Competitiveness Measures." Dataverse Network [Distributor] V1 [Version]. hdl.handle.net/1902.1/22519; UNF:5: we2ixYigyI3GVaDGKsU58A== Harvard.

Knepper, George W. 1994. "Ohio Politics: A Historical Perspective." In *Ohio Politics*, ed. Alexander P. Lamis, 1–17. Kent, OH: Kent State University Press.

Kousser, J. Morgan. 1974. *The Shaping of Southern Politics: Suffrage Restriction and the Establishment of the One-Party South, 1880-1910*. New Haven, CT: Yale University Press.

Kousser, J. Morgan. 1984. "Origins of the Runoff Primary." *The Black Scholar* 15 (5): 23–26.

Kousser, Thad, Justin H. Phillips, and Boris Shor. 2018. "Reform and Representation: Assessing California's Top-Two Primary and Redistricting Commission." *Political Science Research and Methods* 6 (3): 809–827.

Kujala, Jordan. 2019. "Donors, Primary Elections, and Polarization in the United States." *American Journal of Political Science* 64 (93): 587–602.

Kurlowski, Drew A. 2014. "Selection before Election: The Direct Primary and Responsible Party Nomination." PhD diss., University of Missouri.

La Raja, Raymond J. 2008. *Small Change: Money, Political Parties, and Campaign Finance Reform*. Ann Arbor: University of Michigan Press.

Lamis, Alexander P. 1984a. *The Two-Party South*. New York: Oxford University Press.

Lamis, Alexander P. 1984b. "The Runoff Primary Controversy: Implications for Southern Politics." *PS: Political Science and Politics* 17 (4): 782–787.

Lansing, Michael J. 2018. *Insurgent Democracy: The Nonpartisan League in North American Politics*. Chicago: University of Chicago Press.

Larsen, William. 1965. *Montague of Virginia: The Making of a Southern Progressive*. Baton Rouge: Louisiana State University Press.

Lawrence, Eric, Todd Donovan, and Shaun Bowler. 2009. "Adopting Direct Democracy: Tests of Competing Explanations of Institutional Change." *American Politics Research* 37 (6): 1024–1047.

Lawrence, Eric, Todd Donovan, and Shaun Bowler. 2013. "The Adoption of Direct Primaries in the United States." *Party Politics* 19 (1): 3–18.

Lawson, Steven F. 1976. *Black Ballots: Voting Rights in the South, 1944–1969*. New York: Columbia University Press.

Lazarus, Jeffrey. 2005. "Unintended Consequences: Anticipation of General Election Outcomes and Primary Election Divisiveness." *Legislative Studies Quarterly* 30 (3): 435–61.

LeSeuer, Arthur. 1919. "Unclogging the Channels of Trade." Address Given at the Reconstruction Conference of the National Popular Government League, Washington, DC, January 9–11.

Levy, David W. 1985. *Herbert Croly of the New Republic*. Princeton, NJ: Princeton University Press.

Link, Arthur S. 1959. "What Happened to the Progressive Movement in the 1920s?" *American Historical Review* 64 (4): 633–651.

Link, William A. 1992. *The Paradox of Southern Progressivism, 1880–1930*. Chapel Hill: University of North Carolina Press.

Lippmann, Walter. (1921) 1965. *Public Opinion*. New York: Free Press.

Lippmann, Walter. (1925) 1993. *The Phantom Public*. New Brunswick, NJ: Transaction.

Lipset, Seymour Martin. 1971. *Agrarian Socialism: The Cooperative Commonwealth Federation in Saskatchewan*. Berkeley: University of California Press.

Literary Digest. 1919. "Topics of the Day: North Dakota's 'Revolution.'" 60 (1510): 11–15. National Nonpartisan League Papers, Minnesota Historical Society.

Lo, Clarence Y. H. 2012. "Astroturf vs. Grass Roots: Scenes from Early Tea Party Mobilization." In *Steep: The Precipitous Rise of the Tea Party*, ed. Lawrence Rosenthal and Christine Trost, 98–130. Berkeley: University of California Press.

Lockard, Duane. 1959a. *Connecticut's Challenge Primary: A Study in Legislative Politics*. New York: Henry Holt.

Lockard, Duane. 1959b. *New England Politics*. Princeton, NJ: Princeton University Press.

Loeb, Isidor. 1910. "Direct Primaries in Missouri." *Proceedings of the American Political Science Association* 7: 163–174.

Lovejoy, Allen Fraser. 1941. *La Follette and the Establishment of the Direct Primary in Wisconsin, 1890–1904*. New Haven, CT: Yale University Press.

Lower, Richard Coke. 1993. *A Bloc of One: The Political Career of Hiram W. Johnson*. Stanford, CA: Stanford University Press.

Lowitt, Richard. 1992. *Bronson M. Cutting, Progressive Politician*. Albuquerque: University of New Mexico Press.

Lublin, David. 2004. *The Republican South*. Princeton, NJ: Princeton University Press.

MacNeil, Neil, and Richard A. Baker. 2013. *The American Senate: An Insider's History*. New York: Oxford University Press.

Mann, Thomas E., and Bruce E. Cain, eds. 2005. *Party Lines: Competition, Partisanship, and Congressional Redistricting*. Washington, DC: Brookings Institution.

Mann, Thomas E., and Anthony Corrado. 2014. *Party Polarization and Campaign Finance*. Washington, DC: Brookings Institution.

Mann, Thomas E., and Norman J. Ornstein. 2012. *It's Even Worse Than It Looks*. Washington, DC: Brookings Institution.

Margulies, Herbert F. 1968. *The Decline of the Progressive Movement in Wisconsin, 1890–1920*. Madison: State Historical Society of Wisconsin.

Marini, John, and Ken Masugi, eds. 2005. *The Progressive Revolution in Politics and Political Science: Transforming the American Regime*. Lanham, MD: Rowman and Littlefield.

Martin, William. 2013. *Rich People's Movements: Grassroots Campaigns to Untax the One Percent*. New York: Oxford University Press.

Masket, Seth E. 2013. "Polarization Interrupted? California's Experiment with the Top-Two Primary." In *Governing California: Politics, Government, and Public Policy in the Golden State*, 3rd ed., ed. Ethan Rarick, 175–192. Berkeley, CA: Institute for Government Studies.

Masket, Seth E. 2016. *The Inevitable Party*. New York: Oxford University Press.

Masket, Seth E. 2019. "What Is, and Isn't, Causing Polarization in Modern State Legislatures." *PS: Political Science and Politics* 52 (1): 430–435.

Masket, Seth E., and Boris Shor. 2013. "Primary Electorates vs. Party Elites: Who Are the Polarizers?" Paper presented at the Annual Meeting of the Midwest Political Science Association, Chicago, IL.

Mayhew, David R. 1974. *Congress: The Electoral Connection*. New Haven, CT: Yale University Press.

McBeath, Gerald A., and Thomas A. Morehouse. 1994. *Alaska Politics and Government*. Lincoln: University of Nebraska Press.

McCarty, Nolan Keith T. Poole, and Howard Rosenthal. 2006. *Polarized America: The Dance of Ideology and Unequal Riches*. Cambridge, MA: MIT Press.

McCarty, Nolan, Jonathan Rodden, Boris Shor, Christopher N. Tausanovitch, and Chris Warshaw. 2015. "Geography, Uncertainty, and Polarization." Unpublished manuscript, Princeton University. papers.ssrn.com/sol3/papers.cfm?abstract_id=2477157.

McCraw, Thomas K. 1974. "The Progressive Legacy." In *The Progressive Era*, ed. Lewis L. Gould, 181–201. Syracuse, NY: Syracuse University Press.

McGhee, Eric, Seth Masket, Boris Shor, Steven Rogers, and Nolan McCarty. 2014. "A Primary Cause of Partisanship? Nomination Systems and Legislator Ideology." *American Journal of Political Science* 58 (2): 337–351.

McGhee, Eric, and Boris Shor. 2017. "Has the Top Two Primary Elected More Moderates?" *Perspectives on Politics* 15 (4): 1053–1066.

McGuire, Brendan. 2020. "The Top-Four Primary and Alaska Ballot Measure 2." *Alaska Law Review* 37 (2): 309–314.

McKissick, Drew. 2020. "Why SC Should Abolish Open Primaries." *Charleston Post & Courier*, June 2.

McNitt, Andrew D. 1980. "The Effect of Preprimary Endorsement on Competition for Nominations: An Examination of Different Nominating Systems." *Journal of Politics* 42 (1): 257–266.

McWilliams, Carey. 1949. *California: The Great Exception*. New York: Current Books.

Mechem, Floyd. 1905. "Constitutional Limitations on Primary Election Legislation." *Michigan Law Review* 3 (5): 364–386.

Melendy, H. Brett. 1964. "California's Cross-Filing Nightmare: The 1918 Gubernatorial Election." *Pacific Historical Review* 33 (3): 317–330.

Memo to Governor Johnson. 1916. Hiram Johnson Papers, BANC MSS C-B 581l Part II, box 42. The Bancroft Library, University of California, Berkeley.

Menefee-Libbey, David. 2000. *The Triumph of Campaign-Centered Politics*. Chatham, NJ: Chatham House.

Merriam, Charles. 1908. *Primary Elections*. Chicago: University of Chicago Press.

Merriam, Charles, and Louise Overacker. 1928. *Primary Elections*. Chicago: University of Chicago Press.

Meyer, Ernst Christopher. 1902. *Nominating Systems*. Madison, WI: Self-published.

Mickey, Robert. 2015. *Paths Out of Dixie*. Princeton, NJ: Princeton University Press.

Mileur, Jerome. 1999. "Progressive Government, Regressive Politics." In *Progressivism and the New Democracy*, ed. Sidnley M. Milkis and Jerome M. Mileur, 259–288. Amherst: University of Massachusetts Press.

Milkis, Sidney M., and Jerome M. Mileur, eds. 1999. *Progressivism and the New Democracy*. Amherst: University of Massachusetts Press.

Miller, Penny M., Malcolm F. Jewell, and Lee Sigelman. 1988. "Divisive Primaries and Party Activists: Kentucky, 1979 and 1983." *Journal of Politics* 50 (2): 459–70.

Millspaugh, Arthur C. 1916. "The Operation of the Direct Primary in Michigan." *American Political Science Review* 10 (4): 710–726.

Moakley, Maureen, and Elmer Cornwell. 2001. *Rhode Island Politics and Government*. Lincoln: University of Nebraska Press.

Moncrief, Gary. 2012. "BSU's Moncrief: Idaho GOP Closed Primary Failed to Stop Crossover Voting, If It Was Occurring at All." *Idaho Statesman Blogs*, May 8. voices.idahostatesman.com/2012/05/18/idahopolitics/bsus_moncrief_idaho_gop_closed_primary_failed_stop_crossover_vot.

Moore, R. Lawrence. 1974. "Directions of Thought in Progressive America." In *The Progressive Era*, ed. Lewis L. Gould, 35–53. Syracuse, NY: Syracuse University Press.

Morlan, Robert L. 1955. *Political Prairie Fire: The Nonpartisan League, 1915–1922*. Minneapolis: University of Minnesota Press.

Mowry, George E. 1951. *The California Progressives*. Berkeley: University of California Press.

Mowry, George E. 1958. *The Progressive Era, 1900–20: The Reform Persuasion*. Washington, DC: American Historical Association.

Mummolo, Jonathan, 2013. "Nimble Giants: How National Groups Harnessed Tea Party Enthusiasm." In *Interest Groups Unleashed*, ed. Paul. S. Herrnson, Christopher J. Deering, and Clyde Wilcox, 193–212. Washington, DC: Congressional Quarterly Press.

Munro, William Bennett, 1926. "Has the Direct Primary Failed?" In *The Direct Primary*, ed. Lamar T. Beman, 73–79. New York: H. W. Wilson.

Mutnick, Ally. 2021. "Cheney Faces the Boot in Washington: Wyoming Isn't Looking Much Better." *Politico*, May 6. www.politico.com/news/2021/05/06/cheney-wyoming-2022-primary-485508

National Conference of State Legislatures. 2021. "Primary Changes: The Hot Trend of 2021?" *The Canvass*, March. www.ncsl.org/research/elections-and-campaigns/the-canvass-march-2021.aspx.

National Conference on the Practical Reform of Primary Elections. 1898. *Proceedings of the National Conference on Practical Reform of Primary Elections, January 20 and 21, 1898*. Chicago: National Conference on the Practical Reform of Primary Elections.

National Municipal League. 1951. *A Model Direct Primary Election System: Report of the Committee on the Direct Primary*. New York: National Municipal League.

Natsios, Andrew. 1990. "On Being a Republican in Massachusetts: Notes of a Party Chairman." *New England Journal of Public Policy* 6 (2): article 5.

Norrander, Barbara. 1986. "Measuring Primary Turnout in Aggregate Analysis." *Political Behavior* 8 (4): 356–373.

Norrander, Barbara. 1989. "Ideological Representativeness of Presidential Primary Voters." *American Journal of Political Science* 33 (3): 570–587.

Norrander, Barbara. 1991. "Explaining Individual Participation in Presidential Primaries." *Western Political Quarterly* 44 (3): 640–655.

Norrander, Barbara. 2018. "The Nature of Crossover Voters." In *Routledge Handbook of Primary Elections*, ed. Robert G. Boatright, 119–132. New York: Routledge.

Norrander, Barbara, and Kerri Stephens. 2012. "Primary Type and Polarization of State Electorates." Paper presented at the Annual State Politics and Policy Conference, Houston, TX.

Norrander, Barbara, Kerri Stephens, and Jay L. Wendland. 2013. "Primary Type, Polarization of State Electorates, and the Ideological Composition of Primary Electorates." Paper presented at the Annual Meeting of the Midwest Political Science Association, Chicago, IL.

Norrander, Barbara, and Jay L. Wendland. 2016. "Open Versus Closed Primaries and the Ideological Composition of Presidential Primary Electorates." *Electoral Studies* 42 (2): 229–236.

Norris, Pippa. 2004. *Electoral Engineering*. New York: Cambridge University Press.

Norris, Pippa. 2014. *Why Electoral Integrity Matters*. New York: Cambridge University Press.

Norris, Pippa, Sarah Cameron, and Thomas Wynter, eds. 2018. *Electoral Integrity in America: Securing Democracy*. New York: Oxford University Press.

Norris, Pippa, Jorgen Elklit, and Andrew Reynolds. 2014. "Methods and Evidence." In *Advancing Electoral Integrity*, ed. Pippa Norris, Richard W. Frank, and Ferran Martinez I Coma, 34–50. New York: Oxford University Press.

Nye, Russel B. 1951. *Midwestern Progressive Politics: A Historical Study of Its Origins and Development, 1870–1950*. East Lansing: Michigan State College Press.

Obradovich, Kathie. 2018. "It's Time to Remove the Convention Hurdle for Iowa Primary Winners." *Des Moines Register*, June 7.

Omdahl, Lloyd. 1961. *Insurgents: The Switch of the NPL to the Democratic Column*. Brainerd, MN: Lakeland Color Press.

Opdycke, John. 2018. "A 50-State Open Primary in 2020 is Within our Reach." *The Hill*, December 14. thehill.com/opinion/campaign/421399-a-50-state-open-primary-in-2020-is-within-our-reach.

Open Primaries. 2023. "Our Mission." Open Primaries. Accessed November 15, 2023. www.openprimaries.org/mission/.

OpenSecrets. 2020. "Measure 002: Open Primary, Ranked-Choice Voting, and Campaign Finance Disclosure Initiative." OpenSecrets. Accessed November 15, 2023. www.followthemoney.org/entity-details?eid=50171505.

Oppenheimer, Bruce I., James A. Stimson, and Richard W. Waterman 1986. "Interpreting U. S. Congressional Elections: The Exposure Thesis." *Legislative Studies Quarterly* 20 (2): 227–248.

Ostrogorski, Moisei. (1902) 1982. *Democracy and the Organization of Political Parties.* New Brunswick, NJ: Transaction Books.

Otto, Kathryn. 1979. *The Richard Olsen Richards Papers at the South Dakota Historical Resource Center.* Pierre: South Dakota State Historical Society.

Overacker, Louise. 1923. "The Operation of the State-Wide Direct Primary in New York State." *Annals of the American Academy of Political and Social Science* 106: 142–147.

Overacker, Louise. 1928. "Direct Primary Legislation in 1926–27." *American Political Science Review* 22 (2): 353–361.

Overacker, Louise. 1930. "Direct Primary Legislation in 1928–29." *American Political Science Review* 24 (2): 370–380.

Overacker, Louise. 1932. "Direct Primary Legislation in 1930–31." *American Political Science Review* 26 (2): 294–300.

Overacker, Louise. 1934. "Direct Primary Legislation in 1932–33." *American Political Science Review* 28 (2): 265–270.

Overacker, Louise. 1936. "Direct Primary Legislation in 1934–35." *American Political Science Review* 30 (2): 279–85.

Overacker, Louise. 1940. "Direct Primary Legislation, 1936–1939." *American Political Science Review* 34 (3): 499–506.

Page, Benjamin I., and Martin Gilens. 2017. *Democracy in America? What Has Gone Wrong and What We Can Do about It.* Chicago: University of Chicago Press.

Parent, Wayne. 2004. *Inside the Carnival: Unmasking Louisiana Politics.* Baton Rouge: Louisiana State University Press.

Pastore, John. 1945. "State of the State Address." *House Journal*, January 2.
Pastore, John. 1946. "State of the State Address." *House Journal*, January 1.
Pastore, John. 1947. "State of the State Address." *House Journal*, January 7.
Pastore, John. 1949. "State of the State Address." *House Journal*, January 4.

Peters, Jeremy W., and Carl Hulse. 2014. "Republicans' First Step Was to Handle Extremists in Party." *New York Times*, November 5. nyti.ms/1wwm0mR.

Phillip, Emanuel L. (1910) 1973. *Political Reform in Wisconsin.* Ed. Stanley P. Caine and Roger E. Wyman. Madison: State Historical Society of Wisconsin.

Piccio, Daniel R., and Ingrid van Biezen. 2016. "More, and More Inclusive, Regulation: The Legal Parameters of Public Funding in Europe." In *The Deregulatory Moment? A Comparative Perspective on Changing Campaign Finance Laws*, ed. Robert G. Boatright, 200–219. Ann Arbor: University of Michigan Press.

Pickett, John E. 1918. "A Prairie Fire." *The Country Gentleman* 83 (20): 3–31.

Piereson, James E., and Terry B. Smith. 1975. "Primary Divisiveness and General Election Success: A Re-Examination." *Journal of Politics* 37 (2): 555–562.

Pollock, James K. 1943. *The Direct Primary in Michigan.* Ann Arbor: University of Michigan Press.

Powell, G. Bingham, Jr. 2000. *Elections as Instruments of Democracy*. New Haven, CT: Yale University Press.

Pratt, Richard C., and Zachary Smith. 2000. *Hawai'i Politics and Government: An American State in a Pacific World*. Lincoln: University of Nebraska Press.

Ramiro, Luis. 2016. "Effects of Party Primaries on Electoral Performance: The Spanish Socialist Primaries in Local Elections." *Party Politics* 22 (1): 125–136.

Ranney, Austin. 1965. "Parties in State Politics." In *Politics in the American States: A Comparative Analysis*, ed. Herbert Jacobs and Kenneth N. Vines, 45–88. Boston: Little, Brown.

Ranney, Austin. 1968. "The Representativeness of Primary Electorates." *Midwest Journal of Political Science* 12 (2): 224–238.

Ranney, Austin. 1972. "Turnout and Representation in Presidential Primary Elections." *American Political Science Review* 66 (1): 21–37.

Ranney, Austin, and Leon D. Epstein. 1966. "The Two Electorates: Voters and Non-voters in a Wisconsin Primary." *Journal of Politics* 28 (3): 598–616.

Ranney, Joseph A. 2019. *A Legal History of Mississippi: Race, Class, and the Struggle for Opportunity*. Jackson: University Press of Mississippi.

Rasmussen, Scott, and Douglas Schoen. 2010. *Mad as Hell: How the Tea Party Movement is Fundamentally Remaking our Two-Party System*. New York: HarperCollins.

Rauch, Jonathan. 2015. *Political Realism: How Hacks, Machines, Big Money, and Back-Room Deals Can Strengthen American Democracy*. Washington, DC: Brookings Institution Press.

Ray, P. Orman. 1919. "Recent Primary and Election Laws." *American Political Science Review* 13 (2): 264–274.

Ray, P. Orman. 1926. "Objections to the Direct Primary."?" In *The Direct Primary*, ed. Lamar T. Beman, 51–53. New York: H. W. Wilson.

Ray, Rashawn, and Mark Whitlock. 2019. "Setting the Record Straight on Black Voter Turnout." Washington, DC: Brookings Institution. www.brookings.edu/blog/how-we-rise/2019/09/12/setting-the-record-straight-on-black-voter-turnout/.

Reid, Bill G. 1977. "John Miller Baer: Nonpartisan League Cartoonist and Congressman." *North Dakota History* 44 (1): 4–13.

Remele, Larry R. 1981. "Power to the People: The Nonpartisan League." In *The North Dakota Political Tradition*, ed. Charles Nelson Glaab and Thomas William Howard, 66–92. Ames: Iowa State University Press.

Remele, Larry R. 1988. *The Lost Years of A. C. Townley (After the Nonpartisan League)*. Bismarck: North Dakota Humanities Council.

Reynolds, John F. 2006. *The Demise of the American Convention System, 1880–1911*. New York: Cambridge University Press.

Riker, William. 1982. *Liberalism against Populism*. Prospect Heights, IL: Waveland Press.

Rogowski, Jon C., and Stephanie Langella. 2015. "Primary Systems and Candidate Ideology: Evidence From Federal and State Legislative Elections." *American Politics Research* 43 (4): 846–871.

Rohde, David. 1991. *Parties and Leaders in the Postreform House*. Chicago: University of Chicago Press.

Rosenblum, Nancy L. 2008. *On the Side of the Angels: An Appreciation of Parties and Partisanship*. Princeton, NJ: Princeton University Press.

Rubinstein, Dana. 2021. "Candidates Make a Last Dash for Votes, and Battle over Alliances." *New York Times*, June 22.

Rylance, Dan. 1981. "Fred G. Aandahl and the ROC Movement." In *The North Dakota Political Tradition*, ed. Charles Nelson Glaab and Thomas William Howard, 151–182. Ames: Iowa State University Press.

Sabato, Larry. 1977. *The Democratic Party Primary in Virginia*. Charlottesville: University of Virginia Press.

Sabato, Larry. 2021a. "Youngkin Captures Virginia GOP Nomination." *Sabato's Crystal Ball*, May 11. centerforpolitics.org/crystalball/articles/notes-on-the-state-of-politics-may-11-2021/.

Sabato, Larry. 2021b. "Murkowski Faces Weakness on her Right Flank." *Sabato's Crystal Ball*. July 14. centerforpolitics.org/crystalball/articles/notes-on-the-state-of-politics-july-14-2021/.

Sabella, Jonathan D. 2009. "Primary Rules: Institutional Effects on U.S. House Primary Elections." PhD diss., University of Rochester.

Saloutos, Theodore. 1964. *Farmer Movements in the South, 1865–1933*. Lincoln: University of Nebraska Press.

Sanders, Elizabeth. 1999. *Roots of Reform: Farmers, Workers, and the American State 1877–1917*. Chicago: University of Chicago Press.

Santucci, Jack. 2022. *More Parties or No Parties?* New York: Oxford University Press.

Scarrow, Susan E. 2004. "Explaining Party Finance Reforms: Competition and Context." *Party Politics* 10 (6): 653–675.

Scarrow, Susan E. 2006. "Party Subsidies and the Freezing of Party Competition: Do Cartel Mechanisms Work?" *West European Politics* 29 (4): 619–639.

Schaffer, Frederic Charles. 2008. *The Hidden Costs of Clean Election Reform*. Ithaca, NY: Cornell University Press.

Schaffner, Brian, and Stephen Ansolabehere. 2015. "CCES Common Content, 2014." https://doi.org/10.7910/DVN/XFXJVY, Harvard Dataverse, V5, UNF:6:WvvlTX+E+iNraxwbaWNVdg== [fileUNF].

Schaffner, Brian, Stephen Ansolabehere, and Sam Luks. 2019. "CCES Common Content, 2018." https://doi.org/10.7910/DVN/ZSBZ7K, Harvard Dataverse, V6, UNF:6: hFVU8vQ/SLTMUXPgmUw3JQ== [fileUNF].

Schedler, Andreas. 2002. "Elections Without Democracy: The Menu of Manipulation." *Journal of Democracy* 13 (2): 36–50.

Schmitt, Carly A. 2013. "Congressional Primaries and Legislative Behavior." PhD diss., University of Illinois.

Schwartz, Mildred. 2006. *Party Movements in the United States and Canada: Strategies of Persistence*. Lanham, MD: Rowman and Littlefield.

Selden, Charles. 1920. "Terrorism and Fraud in the NPL." *New York Times*, January 4.

Sides, John, Chris Tausanovitch, Lynn Vavreck, and Christopher Warshaw. 2018. "On the Representativeness of Primary Electorates." *British Journal of Political Science* 50 (3): 677–685.

Simpser, Alberto. 2013. *Why Governments and Parties Manipulate Elections*. New York: Cambridge University Press.

Sinclair, J. Andrew, and Ian O'Grady. 2018. "Beyond Open and Closed: Complexity in American Primary Election Reform." In *Routledge Handbook of Primary Elections*, edited by Robert G. Boatright, 427–455. New York: Routledge.

Smith, Glenn H. 1981. "William Langer and the Art of Personal Politics." In *The North Dakota Political Tradition*, ed. Charles Nelson Glaab and Thomas William Howard, 123–150. Ames: Iowa State University Press.

South Dakota Legislative Research Council. 2005. *Direct Primaries and the Democratization of the Party Nominating Process*. Pierre: South Dakota Legislative Research Council, Issue Memorandum 96-02.

Southwell, Patricia. 1986. "The Politics of Disgruntlement: Nonvoting and Defection among Supporters of Nomination Losers, 1968-1984." *Political Behavior* 8 (1): 81-95.

Springer, Melanie J. 2019. "Where Is 'the South'? Assessing the Meaning of Geography in Politics." *American Politics Research* 47 (5): 1100-1134.

Taft, William Howard. 1922. *Liberty under Law*. New Haven, CT: Yale University Press.

Teigan, Henry G., to Arthur Stonehouse. 1917a. September 25. National Nonpartisan League Collection, Roll 3. Minnesota Historical Society, St. Paul.

Teigan, Henry G., to Kate Barnard. 1917b. July 3. National Nonpartisan League Collection, Roll 3. Minnesota Historical Society, St. Paul.

Teigan, Henry G., to T. P. Quinn. 1917c. August 1. National Nonpartisan League Collection, Roll 3. Minnesota Historical Society, St. Paul.

Teigan, Henry G., to O. J. Arness. 1918. October 3. National Nonpartisan League Collection, Roll 4. Minnesota Historical Society, St. Paul.

Telford, Ira Ralph. 1965. "Types of Primary and Party Responsibility." *American Political Science Review* 59 (1): 117-118.

Thayer, George. 1973. *Who Shakes the Money Tree? American Campaign Financing Practices from 1789 to the Present*. New York: Simon and Schuster.

Theriault, Sean. 2008. *Party Polarization in Congress*. New York: Cambridge University Press.

Thompson, Dennis F. 2013. "Two Concepts of Corruption." Cambridge, MA: Edward J. Safra Research Lab Working Paper #16, Harvard University.

Tindall, George Brown. 1967. *The Emergence of the New South, 1913-1945*. Baton Rouge: Louisiana State University Press.

Townley, Arthur C. 1917. Address to the Thirty-Seventh Annual Convention of the American Federation of Labor, Buffalo, NY, November 16. A. C. Townley Speeches and Related Materials Collection, A.C. Townley Speeches and Related Materials. OGLMC 1572, Box 1, Folder 1, Item 4. Elwyn B. Robinson Department of Special Collections, Chester Fritz Library, University of North Dakota.

Troiano, Nick. 2021. "Party Primaries Must Go." *The Atlantic*, March 30.

Tufte, Edward R. 1975. "Determinants of the Outcomes of Midterm Congressional Elections." *American Political Science Review* 69 (3): 812-826.

Turner, Julius. 1953. "Primary Elections as the Alternative to Party Competition in 'Safe' Districts." *Journal of Politics* 15 (2): 197-210.

Tweton, D. Jerome. 1981. "The Anti-League Movement: The IVA." In *The North Dakota Political Tradition*, ed. Charles Nelson Glaab and Thomas William Howard, 93-122. Ames: Iowa State University Press.

Unger, Nancy C. 2000. *Fighting Bob La Follette: The Righteous Reformer*. Chapel Hill: University of North Carolina Press.

Valelly, Richard M. 2004. *The Two Reconstructions*. Chicago: University of Chicago Press.

Vogel, Robert. 2004. *Unequal Contest: Bill Langer and His Political Enemies*. Mandan, ND: Crain Grosinger Publishing.

Wallace, Schuyler C. 1923. "Pre-Primary Conventions." *Annals of the American Academy of Political and Social Sciences* 106: 97-104.

Wallach, Philip. 2022. "We Can Now Quantify Trump's Sabotage of the GOP's House Dreams." *Washington Post*, November 15. www.washingtonpost.com/opinions/2022/11/15/data-trump-weighed-down-republican-candidates/.

Walter, Amy. 2015. "Bring Back the Smoke Filled Rooms." *Cook Political Report*, May 1.

Ware, Alan. 1979. "'Divisive' Primaries: The Important Questions." *British Journal of Political Science* 9 (3): 381–384.

Ware, Alan. 2002. *The American Direct Primary: Party Institutionalization and Transformation in the North*. New York: Cambridge University Press.

Ware, Alan. 2006. *The Democratic Party Heads North, 1877–1962*. New York: Oxford University Press.

Warner, Hoyt Landon. 1964. *Progressivism in Ohio, 1897–1917*. Columbus: Ohio State University Press.

Warren, Mark E. 2006. "Political Corruption as Duplicitous Exclusion." *PS: Political Science and Politics* 37 (4): 803–807.

Watson, Bradley C. S. 2009. *Living Constitution, Dying Faith: Progressivism and the New Science of Jurisprudence*. Wilmington, DE: Intercollegiate Studies Institute.

Weeks, O. Douglas. 1948. "The White Primary: 1944–1948." *American Political Science Review* 42 (3): 500–510.

Wekkin, Gary D. 1984. *Democrat versus Democrat: The National Party's Campaign to Close the Wisconsin Primary*. Columbia: University of Missouri Press.

Wekkin, Gary D. 1988. "The Conceptualization and Measurement of Crossover Voting." *Western Political Quarterly* 41 (1): 105–114.

Wekkin, Gary D. 1991. "Why Crossover Voters Are Not 'Mischievous Voters': The Segmented Partisanship Hypothesis." *American Politics Quarterly* 19 (2): 229–247.

West, Victor J. 1923. "The California Direct Primary." *Annals of the American Academy of Political and Social Sciences* 106: 116–127.

Weyl, Walter. 1912. *The New Democracy: An Essay on Certain Political and Economic Tendencies in the United States*. New York: Macmillan.

White, John Kenneth. 1983. *The Fractured Electorate: Political Parties and Social Change in Southern New England*. Hanover, NH: University Press of New England.

White, William Allen. 1910. *The Old Order Changeth*. New York: Macmillan.

Whitehorn, Alan. 1992. *Canadian Socialism: Essays on the CCF-NDP*. Toronto: Oxford University Press.

Wiebe, Robert H. 1967. *The Search for Order, 1877–1920*. Westport, CT: Greenwood Press.

Wiley, Maya. 2021. "I Lost the NYC Mayoral Race, but Women and Minorities Win with Ranked-Choice Voting." *Washington Post*, July 11.

Wilkins, Robert P. 1981. "Alexander McKenzie and the Politics of Bossism." In *The North Dakota Political Tradition*, edited by Charles Nelson Glaab and Thomas William Howard, 3–39. Ames: Iowa State University Press.

Wilson, Andrew. 2005. *Virtual Politics: Faking Democracy in the Post-Soviet World*. New Haven, CT: Yale University Press.

Winger, Richard. 2013. "South Carolina Republican Party Withdraws from Its Own Lawsuit against Open Primary." *Ballot Access News*, June 13.

Wolf, Michael R., and Andrew Downs. 2007. "The Missing 3,847 Voters: Strategic Voting in a Congressional Primary." *Indiana Journal of Political Science* 10: 10–22.

Woodward, C. Vann. 1971. *Origins of the New South, 1877–1913*. Baton Rouge: Louisiana State University Press.

Zeldin, Charles L. 2004. *The Battle for the Black Ballot: Smith v. Allwright and the Defeat of the Texas All-White Primary*. Lawrence: University Press of Kansas.

Zernike, Kate. 2010. *Boiling Mad: Inside Tea Party America*. New York: Times Books.

Zimmerman, Joseph P. 2008. *The Government and Politics of New York State*. 2nd ed. Albany: State University of New York Press.

Index

For the benefit of digital users, indexed terms that span two pages (e.g., 52–53) may, on occasion, appear on only one of those pages.

Tables and figures are indicated by *t* and *f* following the page number

Abrams, Richard, 72–73
Adams, Eric, 282
Affordable Care Act of 2010, 14–15
Aldrich, John E., 176–77
Alvarez, R. Michael, 254
American Direct Primary, The (Ware), 11, 27
American National Election Study, 231
American Political Science Association, 9
American Political Science Association Committee on Political Parties, 136
American Political Science Review, 2
Ames, Butler, 62
Annals of the American Academy of Political and Social Sciences, 2
Ansolabehere, Stephen, 12, 253, 255
Anti-Socialist Union, 93
Argersinger, Peter H., 51–52, 110–11
Arness, O. J., 99
authoritarianism, 96, 176–77
Aycock, Charles B., 181, 194

Bacon, Jerry, 92–93
Baer, John Miller, 88–89, 92–93
Bagashka, Tanya, 206–7
Baker, Paula, 67–68
Baker, Richard A., 67–68
Baker v. Carr (1962), 9–10
Barber, Kathleen, 210–11
Bateman, David A., 199–200
Begich, Mark, 280–81
Bennett, Robert, 106
Berdahl, Clarence, 140–41
Berger, Victor, 88–89
Bernstein, Robert A., 254
Beveridge, Albert, 137
Biden, Joe, 282, 288
Bilbo, Theodore, 188–89
Bipartisan Policy Center (BPC), 290
Birch, Sarah, 112–13, 115, 128
Black, Earl, 178
Black, Merle, 178

Black voters
 Democratic Party and, 181, 186, 192, 199–200
 disenfranchisement and exclusion of, 176, 181–82, 195–96, 197, 198, 199–200
 in Progressive Democratic Party, 191
 Progressive movement and, 181, 191
 runoff elections and, 197, 198
 Smith v. Allwright and, 186, 187, 192
 Southern primary law changes and, 174–75, 177–78, 181–82, 186, 187, 194
blanket primary, 207–8, 284
Bolduc, Don, 282
Book of States, 33, 34–38, 54, 152, 183–84
Borah, William, 30–31, 90–91, 97
Bowler, Shaun, 27–28, 40, 48, 56, 71
BPC. *See* Bipartisan Policy Center
Brat, David, 252
Buenker, John D., 62, 67–68, 77
Bull Moose Party, 143
Bullock, Charles S., 198
Bullock v. Carter (1972), 180
Burden, Barry C., 232
Burdick, Quentin, 97–98
Burdick, Usher, 88–89, 97
Burke, Edmund, 4–5
Burke, John, 84–85
Burtniss, Olger, 96–97

Cain, Bruce E., 62, 283–84, 285, 287–88
California Democratic Party v. Jones (2000), 130, 207, 213–15
Campbell, James E., 256
candidate-centered elections, 9–10, 97, 231
Canon, David T., 254
Cantor, Eric, 252
Carroll, David J., 113
Carson, Jamie L., 8
cartel party thesis, 146, 147–48
Cooperative Election Study (CES), *see* Cooperative Congressional Election Study

CCF. *See* Cooperative Commonwealth Federation
challenger primaries, 258–59, 264–66, 265f
Chamberlain, John, 70
Chandler, Happy, 171–72
Cheney, Elizabeth, 281, 282–83
Chesterton, G. K., 4
CIO. *See* Congress of Industrial Organizations
Citizens for a Direct Primary, 79
Citizens United v. FEC (2010), 235
civil rights movement, 187
Clark, Jennifer H., 206–7
closed primaries, 28–29, 78–79, 117–19, 124, 133, 139–40, 224
  open primaries and, 26, 206–7, 231, 243, 253–54
Cohen, Michael D., 109–10
Cold War, 9–10
comparative politics, 14–15, 132, 136–37, 146–47
Congress of Industrial Organizations (CIO), 79
Coolidge, Calvin, 69–70
Cooperative Commonwealth Federation (CCF), 89–90
Cooperative Congressional Election Study (CCES), 230, 233, 234–36, 243–45
Coughlin, Charles, 96–97
COVID-19, 212–13
Crane, Murray, 72–73
Crespin, Michael H., 51–52, 173
Croly, Herbert, 61, 63–64, 65, 66–67, 68, 70, 81–82
Cronin, Thomas E., 162
Crosson, Jesse M., 285
crossover voting, 75, 129–32, 199–200, 206–7, 224
cross-party coalitions, 152
Crowley, Joseph, 252
cultural modernization theory, 114–15
Cutting, Bronson, 133

Davies-Roberts, Avery, 113
Davis, James W., 28
Davis, Jeff, 188–89
Dawes, Charles, 170–71
Demise of the American Convention System, The (Reynolds), 11, 27
Democratic-Farmer-Labor Party, 97–98
Democratic Party and Democratic primaries
  in Alaska and Hawaii Lower Chambers, 131f
  Black voters and, 181, 186, 192, 199–200
  in California, 144–45, 151–52, 161–62, 240
  in Colorado, 163
  in Connecticut, 162
  incumbent primaries, 266–67, 268f, 269f
  in Indiana, 137–38, 138f
  in Massachusetts, 162
  McGovern Fraser Commission and reforms, 7–8, 23–24, 28–29, 33
  in Michigan, 126, 127f
  in Mississippi, 240
  in New Mexico, 133, 134f, 162–63
  in North Dakota, 151, 152
  NPL and, 96, 97–98, 151
  in Oklahoma, 190
  open seat, 263–64, 264f
  in open *versus* closed primary states, 243
  primary electorates *versus* general electorates, 237–45, 239t, 241t, 244t, 246t, 247, 248t, 249t
  primary reform proposals, after 2011, 215–16, 216t, 220–21, 221t, 222t, 224
  on primary rule changes, 156, 156t, 160
  Progressives in, 69–70, 73–74
  Republican Party, crossover voting and, 129–32
  in Rhode Island, 151–52, 161–62, 240–43
  runoff elections and, 194
  in the South, 153–54, 156, 176–78, 180–81, 183, 186, 198, 200, 210
  Southern primaries and, 174, 175–76, 179, 180, 183, 192, 194–95
  standardization of rules, 174
  superdelegates in, 10
  surge of candidates in 1930s, 125–26
  in 2014, 245
  two-party competition and, 32
direct primary, abolition of, 287–88
direct primary elections, decline of, hypotheses on, 27–56
direct primary movement, 25–33, 126, 128
Dodd, Thomas, 171–72
Donovan, Todd, 27–28, 40, 48, 56, 71
Dorr, Harold M., 126–28, 161–62
Drutman, Lee, 211, 288
Dubin, Michael J., 42, 153
DuPont, Pierre, 104–5

Edwards, Edwin, 171–72
Elazar, Daniel, 115–16, 208, 209–10
electoral engineering, 114–15
electoral integrity, 111, 113, 114–15, 116–20
electoral malpractice and mispractice, 112–13, 125–28, 129–32
Elklit, Jorgen, 114
Elmore v. Rice (1947), 186

Engstrom, Erik, 11, 13
Epstein, Leon D., 231
Erikson, Robert S., 257
Eu v. San Francisco County Democratic Central Committee (1989), 136
Ewing, Cortez, 173, 193, 197–98
Ezra, Marni, 173, 208–9

Farmer-Labor Party, 90
federalism, 285–86
Feldman, H., 31, 138–39
Flower, Walter, 83
Ford, Henry Jones, 135, 287–88
For the People Act of 2021, 289
Fourteenth Amendment, 180
Frazier, Lynn, 51, 88, 93–94, 96–97
Freedom Democrats, 192
Freyd, Bernard, 4, 5, 83, 107, 287–88
frivolous candidacies, 108, 125–26, 128

Galderisi, Peter S., 76–77, 173, 208–9
garbage can theory of organizational choice, 109–10
Gaston, Herbert E., 86, 89
Geiser, Karl F., 76–77, 208
Gerber, Elizabeth R., 206–8, 232, 233
Gilens, Martin, 287–88
Gimpel, James G., 28–29, 208–9
Ginsberg, Benjamin, 76–77
Glaab, Charles Nelson, 84–85
Goble, Danney, 190
Goldberg, Michelle, 97
Graham, Otis L., 69
Grantham, Dewey, 177–78, 179, 188
Great Depression, 9–10, 29, 31–32, 96, 100, 126, 153–54
Griffin, John D., 176–77
Grose, Christian R., 207–8
group capture, 190–92
Guild, Frederick, 137

Hacker, Andrew, 254
Hackney, Sheldon, 189
Hanna, Louis, 84–85
Hansen, John Mark, 12, 75–76
Harding, Warren, 99–100
Harding, Warren G., 69–70
Hassell, Hans, 11–12, 59, 285
Havard, William C., 173, 192
Heard, Alexander, 195
Hedlund, Ronald, 231–32
Herrnson, Paul S., 209–10
Hickel, Walter, 130

Hill, Seth J., 233, 284
Hirano, Shigeo, 11, 12, 58, 75–76, 285, 291
Hirschman, Alfred, 259
Hoffman, Adam H., 28–29, 208–9
Hofstadter, Richard, 29, 68, 69
Holbrook, Thomas M., 154
Holmes, Jack E., 54–55, 133, 134–35, 162–63
hostile takeover attempts, in primaries, 102–6, 107
Hughes, Charles Evans, 138–40, 143
Huthmacher, J. Joseph, 73–74

incumbent primaries, 259–60, 261–63, 266–67, 267f, 268f, 269f
Independent Voters Association (IVA), 51, 93–94
interest group endorsements, in primaries, 104–5
IVA. *See* Independent Voters Association

Jacobson, Gary C., 233, 235–36, 237–40
January 6 attack on the Capitol, 281
Jewell, Malcolm E., 28–29
Johnson, Gregg B., 208–9, 254–55
Johnson, Hiram, 25, 143–44, 167–70, 171–72
Johnson, Loch K., 198
Johnson, Tom, 62, 76–77
Jones Ford, Henry, 3–4
Judah, Charles, 134–35

Kamarck, Elaine, 290
Kang, Michael, 100–1, 293n.5
Kanthak, Kristin, 206–7, 232
Katz, Richard, 147–48
Katznelson, Ira, 199–200
Kaufmann, Karen M., 28–29, 208–9
Kenney, Patrick J., 232, 254
Kernell, Samuel, 257
Key, V. O., 2–3, 7, 10–11, 28–29, 32–33, 95, 173, 175–76, 178–79, 180, 190–91, 194, 198
King, Judson, 89, 99–100
Kirwan, Albert, 189
Klarman, Michael J., 199, 296n.12
Kousser, J. Morgan, 176–77

La Follette, Robert, 25, 40, 62, 68, 69–70, 71, 74–75, 77, 84–85, 139–40
La Follette, Robert, Jr., 75
Lamis, Alexander P., 178
Langer, William, 30–31, 91–92, 93–94, 96–98, 100–1
Lansing, Michael J., 90–91, 141
Lapinski, John, 199–200

Lawrence, Eric, 27–28, 40, 48, 56, 71
Lazarus, Jeffrey, 254–55, 256
Lee, Mike, 106
Legislative Voters Association, 138–39
Lehman, Herbert, 171–72
Lemke, William, 51, 91–92, 96–97
LeSeuer, Arthur, 89
Lincoln Republican League, 93
Lincoln-Roosevelt League, 143, 145
Lindbergh, Charles A., 90
Link, William, 188
Lippmann, Walter, 70, 81–82
Lockard, Duane, 7, 58, 79–80, 135–36, 151, 294n.3
Lodge, Henry Cabot, 73
Loepp, Eric, 206–7
Loevy, Robert D., 162
Long, Huey, 96–97
Lublin, David, 175–76
Luce, Robert, 62, 73

MacNeil, Neil, 67–68
Mair, Peter, 147–48
March, James G., 109–10
Masket, Seth E., 75, 233
Mayhew, David, 109–10
McAskill, D. A., 182
McBeath, Gerald A., 130, 206
McCarthy, Joseph, 75–76, 171–72
McCarty, Nolan, 229–31, 232
McGovern Fraser Commission and reforms, 7–8, 23–24, 28–29, 33
McGrath, Howard, 78–79
McKaig, Ray, 89
McNitt, Andrew D., 102–3
McWilliams, Carey, 144
Melendy, H. Brett, 169–70
Merriam, Charles, 3, 7, 11, 23–24, 26–28, 29–30, 33, 42–44, 57, 66–67, 70, 77–78, 173, 208
Mickey, Robert, 176–77, 180, 187
Mileur, Jerome, 69
Miller, Nathan, 139
Montesquieu, 114–15
Morehouse, Thomas A., 130, 206
Morlan, Robert L., 85–86, 91–92, 95
Morton, Rebecca B., 206–7, 232, 233
Mowry, George E., 69
Munro, William Bennett, 3–4
Murkowski, Lisa, 279–81
Mussolini, Benito, 170–71

National Association for the Advancement of Colored People (NAACP), 181–82, 187, 191
National Conference of State Legislatures (NCSL), 204–5, 212, 282–83
National Municipal League, 136
National Primary Day, 290
NCSL. *See* National Conference of State Legislatures
New, Harry S., 137
Newberry v. United States (1921), 6–7
New Deal, 9–10
New Democracy, The (Weyl), 63, 64
New Democratic Party, 89–90
New England Politics (Lockard), 7
Nonpartisan Leader, 86, 87, 88, 92–93, 94–95
Nonpartisan League (NPL), 13–14, 15–16, 80
  candidate selection by, 102–3
  Democratic Party and, 96, 97–98, 151
  fate of, 96–98
  IVA against, 93–94
  in Minnesota, 49–51, 90, 94–95, 102–3
  in Montana, 90–91, 95, 99
  in North Dakota, 49–51, 57, 83–87, 88–91, 92–93, 94–95, 97–98, 99, 100–1, 104–5, 106, 171–72
  in Oklahoma, 190–91
  origins of, 84–87
  preprimary conventions and, 102–3
  primary elections and, 98–102
  reactions to, 91–95
  Republican Party and, 14, 30, 87–91, 93, 94–95, 96–98, 100, 103, 107, 141
  Southern primaries and, 174, 190–91
  in state changes to primary laws, 30–31, 40–41, 41t, 49–52, 49f, 50t, 57, 100–1, 123
  subsequent hostile takeover attempts and, 102–3, 104–6, 107
  Tea Party and, 105–6
nonpartisan primaries, 48, 121–22, 168–69, 196–97, 207–8, 209–10, 288
Norrander, Barbara, 206–7, 231–32, 233–34, 235–36
Norris, Pippa, 111, 113, 114–15, 116
North Dakota Good Government League, 93
North Dakota Republican Party, 30
NPL. *See* Nonpartisan League
Nugent, John, 90–91

Oakeshott, Michael, 4–5
Obama, Barack, 235, 237
Ocasio-Cortez, Alexandria, 252
Old Order Changeth, The (White), 63, 65
Olson, David M., 28–29
Olson, Johan P., 109–10
Omdahl, Lloyd, 97–98

one-partyism, 32–33, 174, 175–76, 179, 198
open primaries, 28–29, 40, 49–51, 59, 75, 84–85, 121–22, 130, 161–62, 213–15, 220–24, 232, 289
  closed primaries and, 26, 206–7, 231, 243, 253–54
Open Primaries (nonprofit organization), 289
open seat primaries, 258, 263–64, 264f
optional primaries, 66–67, 80, 121–22
Orban, Viktor, 283–84
Ostrogorski, Moisei, 3–4
Overacker, Louise, 7, 11, 23–24, 26–27, 28, 29–30, 33, 34–38, 42–44, 54, 70, 139, 141, 152, 183–84

Packard, Frank, 104–5
Page, Benjamin, 287–88
Palin, Sarah, 280–81
Parnell, Sean, 279–80
partisan advantage
  in California, 151–52, 153
  changes in party strength, measuring, 152–54
  in Connecticut, 151, 152, 154
  in North Dakota, 151, 152
  polarization and, 219–24
  primary law changes and, 15, 17, 57, 145–46, 148–61, 149f, 157t, 167–68, 172, 193–95, 219–24, 225
  in Rhode Island, 151–52, 153
  Southern primary law changes and, 193–95
  theories of, 146–48
partisanship, 144–45, 154–61, 157t, 169–70, 236, 253–54
  in abolition of primaries, 288
  corruption and, 171
  primaries, partisan waves and, 255–57, 259
  Taft on, 291
partisan swing, primary competition and, 252–70
party factions, 102–4, 147–48, 162–63, 169–70, 225
Party's Primary, The (Hassell), 11–12
Pastore, John, 78–79
Peltola, Mary, 280–81
Percy, LeRoy, 180
personality, politics of, 167–72, 175
Petersheim, Meredith-Joy, 208–9, 254–55
Phillip, Emmanuel, 74–75
Piccio, Daniel R., 225
Piereson, James E., 254
Pingree, Hazen, 126
polarization, 219–24, 229, 252, 283, 285
Politics of Ballot Design, The (Engstrom and Roberts), 11, 13

Pollock, James K., 126–27, 128
Poole, Keith T., 229–31, 232
Populist movement, 84–85, 110–11, 191
preprimary conventions, 29, 47–48, 54–55, 72, 73–74, 94–95, 121–22
  endorsements and, 209–10
  in Massachusetts, 162
  in New Mexico, 132–36
  NPL and, 102–3
preprimary endorsements, 102–4, 209–10
primary competition
  in challenger primaries, 258–59, 264–66, 265f
  expectations and, 257–60
  general election competition and, 252–55, 256, 257–60, 261–67, 262t, 270
  in incumbent primaries, 259–60, 261–63, 266–67, 267f, 268f
  measuring, 260–63
  in open seat primaries and, 258, 263–64, 264f
  partisan swing and, 252–70
  partisan waves and, 255–57
primary divisiveness, 254–55
Primary Elections (Merriam and Overacker), 7, 26–27, 33, 70
Primary Elections in the United States (Hirano and Snyder), 11, 12
primary electorates, 227–28
  extremists and, 229–51
  general electorates in 2010 *versus*, 237–47, 238t, 239t, 241t, 244t, 246t, 248t, 249t, 251, 252
  ideology of, 230–37
primary laws. *See also* Southern primaries
  California, 32–33, 54, 144
  consequences of changes, 14–15
  decline of competitiveness and, 253
  decline of primaries and, 25
  explanations for changes to, 24–25
  in insulation of primaries from national trends, 253–55
  in New Mexico, 54–55
  New York, 31–32
  NPL and, 98–102
  partisan competition and, 15
  partisanship and, 253–54
  South Dakota, 26, 28, 47–48, 54
  state differences in, 5–7, 26
  state repeal efforts, 1920s, 28
  Tea Party and, 106
  two-party competition and, 32–33, 42, 55–56
  Wisconsin, 25–26

primary laws, bad/defective, 142, 286
   in Alaska and Hawaii, 121–22, 124, 129–32
   categorizing, 120–22, 122t
   classification scheme for, 119–20, 119t
   corruption and, 136–42
   fixing, 123–42
   in Indiana, 137
   Michigan, 108, 125–28, 141–42
   New Mexico, 132–36, 141–42
   in New York, 137, 138–39, 141
   preprimary convention and, 132–36
   in South Dakota, 137, 139–41
   Southern primaries and, 192–93
   state changes to, 52–55, 52f, 53t, 123–42
   states with, 43t, 52–55, 52f, 53t, 108–9, 116–17, 118t, 120–22, 125–28
   studying, 109–16
primary laws, changes/reforms to, 34–45, 35t, 39t, 58–59, 203–5, 224–26. *See also* Southern primary laws, changes to
   in Alaska, 130–31, 131f, 279–81
   alternative voting methods, 210–11
   ballot access, 31–32, 33, 34–38, 35t, 46t, 48, 74, 77, 101, 138–39, 179–80, 183, 186, 213, 215–16, 217–19
   blanket primary, 207–8
   in California, 145–46, 168
   competitiveness and, 154–56, 156t, 157–61, 158f, 159t
   in Connecticut, 79–80
   consequences of, 205–11
   consolidated ballot, 35t, 46t, 50t
   cross-filing and, 32, 35t, 46t, 53t, 144–45, 151–52, 161–62, 168
   election timing and, 208–9
   mandatory primary, 35t, 46t, 50t, 53t, 54, 121–22, 183–84, 184t, 196t
   in Michigan, 80, 123–24, 161–62
   in New York, 124, 282, 285
   NPL and, 30–31, 40–41, 41t, 49–52, 49f, 50t, 57, 100–2, 123
   open and closed primaries, 206–7, 220–22, 224
   partisan advantage and, 15, 17, 57, 145–46, 148–61, 149f, 157t, 167–68, 172, 219–24, 225
   party affiliation test, 35t, 46t, 50t, 53t, 128, 161–62, 184t
   paths forward for, 283–90
   politics of personality in, 167–72
   preprimary endorsements and conventions, 209–10
   Progressive movement decline and, 60, 71–80

   Progressive movement reforms and, 45–48, 45f, 46t, 54, 55, 57, 60–61, 123
   Progressive reforms in late adopter states, 78–80
   Progressive reforms in Massachusetts, 72–76, 77–78
   Progressive reforms in Ohio, 76–78
   Progressive reforms in Wisconsin, 74–76, 77–78
   radical, 289–90
   reform proposals since 2000, 212–19, 213t, 214f, 216t, 217f, 218t, 223f
   in Rhode Island, 78–79
   runoff elections, 35t, 46t, 50t, 53t, 210, 281
   signature thresholds, 35t, 46t, 50t, 53t, 79
   since 2020, 279–83
   sore loser laws, 35t, 46t, 48, 49–51, 50t, 53t, 100–1, 167–68, 293n.5
   state-specific accounts of, 148, 149f, 160–67, 164f
   in states with defective primary laws, 52–55, 52f, 53t, 123
   two-party competition and, 55–56
   in Utah, 80
   write-in candidacies, 35t, 46t, 48, 50t, 184t, 186
   in Wyoming, 281
   by year and direction, 42–44, 44f
primary timing, 208–9
Progressive Democracy (Croly), 63–64
Progressive Democratic Party, 191
Progressive Era, 5, 7–8, 60–61, 68, 72, 78–79, 81–82, 110–11, 143–44, 183–84, 189–90
Progressive intellectuals, direct primary and, 63–66
Progressive movement, 1–5, 10, 13–14, 15–16
   Black voters and, 181, 191
   in California, 143–44, 169–70
   decline of, 29, 40, 60, 68–80, 109
   on direct primaries, 27, 29–30, 31–32, 40, 61–68, 80–81
   Johnson, H., in, 143–44, 167–68
   in New York, 138–39
   NPL and, 91, 95, 99–100
   in Oklahoma, 190
   Open Primaries and, 289
   on political corruption, 62, 64
   primary reforms, 45f, 45–48, 46t, 54, 55, 57, 60–61, 78–80, 123
   primary reforms in Massachusetts, 72–76, 77–78
   primary reforms in Ohio, 76–78
   primary reforms in Wisconsin, 74–76, 77–78

INDEX   325

Progressive Party, 40, 69
Progressivism, 29, 56, 60, 61, 63, 65, 66, 80–82
   context of, 66–68
   decline of, 68–80
   late adopters and, 78–80
   in North Dakota, 84–85
   Southern primaries and, 188–90, 191
Prohibition and prohibitionism, 68, 73–74, 88, 105
Promise of American Life, The (Croly), 63, 64

QAnon conspiracy theory, 1

Ramiro, Luis, 208–9
ranked choice voting (RCV), 210–11, 213–15, 225–26, 279–83, 285, 288, 289–90
Rankin, Jeanette, 90–91
Ranney, Austin, 153, 154–55, 231
rational choice individualism (RCI), 114–15
Rauch, Jonathan, 287–88
Ray, P. Orman, 3–4
RCI. *See* rational choice individualism
RCV. *See* ranked choice voting
Reconstruction Era, 181
Red Flame, 92–93
reform populism, 283–84
Remele, Larry R., 91
Repeal the Direct Primary (Freyd), 4
Republican Party and Republican primaries
   in California, 143–45, 151, 169–70, 171–72
   Citizens United v. FEC and, 235
   in Colorado, 162, 163–67
   in Connecticut, 151
   Democratic Party, crossover voting and, 129–32
   incumbent, 266–67, 268*f*, 269*f*
   Iowa rules, 286
   Lincoln-Roosevelt League and, 143
   in Maine, 135–36
   in Michigan, primary laws and, 126, 161–62
   in New Mexico, 133–34
   in North Dakota, 30, 151, 152
   NPL and, 14, 30, 87–91, 93, 94–95, 96–98, 100, 103, 107, 141
   open seat, 263, 264*f*, 264
   on party control over primary law reforms, 204–5
   primary electorates *versus* general electorates, 237–40, 239*t*, 241*t*, 243–50, 244*t*, 246*t*, 248*t*, 249*t*
   primary reform proposals, from 2011-2020, 215–16, 216*t*, 220–24, 221*t*, 222*t*
   Progressives in, 69–70, 73, 74, 143–44, 189–90
   in Rhode Island, 79
   in the South, 176–77, 178, 194–95, 198, 199
   Southern primary law changes and, 194–95
   Tea Party and, 14, 24, 83, 105–6, 235, 243–45, 259
   in 2014, 245–47, 297–98n.5
   in 2010, 234–35, 237–40, 243–45
   in 2022 midterms, 282
   two-party competition and, 32
   Wisconsin candidate endorsements, 75–76
Republican Party of Connecticut v. Tashjian (1986), 79
Reynolds, Andrew, 114
Reynolds, John, 11, 27, 51–52, 66–67
Ribicoff, Abraham, 79
Rice, Tom W., 254
Richards, R. O., 26, 139–40, 141
Richards primary, in South Dakota, 26, 28, 47–48, 121, 139–41
Riker, William, 259
Roberts, Jason M., 8, 11, 13
Rolph, James, Jr., 169–70
Roosevelt, Franklin Delano, 29, 69–70, 133
Roosevelt, Theodore, 40, 63, 71, 72–73, 99–100, 138–39, 143, 144–45
Roraback, J. Henry, 79, 151, 154
Rosenblum, Nancy L., 61
Rosenthal, Howard, 229–31, 232
runoff elections, 32, 180, 281
   in primary law reforms, 35*t*, 46*t*, 50*t*, 53*t*, 210, 281
   in Southern primaries, 173–74, 183, 184*t*, 186, 187, 192, 193, 194, 196–99, 196*t*, 210

Sabato, Larry, 194, 281
Sabella, Jonathan D., 209–10
Scarrow, Susan, 148
Schaffer, Frederic Charles, 110–11, 115
Schedler, Andreas, 113
Schwartz, Mildred, 89–90
second primary. *See* runoff elections
Sellers, Patrick, 254
semiclosed primary, 130, 206–7, 215–16, 232
semiopen primaries, 206–7
Seventeenth Amendment, 179
Shor, Boris, 233
Sides, John, 233
Simpser, Alberto, 113, 115
Sinclair, Upton, 103–4
Smith, Al, 171–72
Smith, Terry B., 254
Smith v. Allwright (1944), 174, 186, 187, 192, 196–97

Snyder, James M., Jr., 11, 12, 58, 75–76, 285, 291
Southern Farmers' Alliance, 191
Southern Politics in State and Nation (Key), 7, 175
Southern primaries, 7, 8–9, 15–16, 146–47
    bad primary laws and, 192–93
    Black voters and, 176, 195–96
    Democratic Party and, 174, 175–76, 179, 180, 183, 192, 194–95
    group capture and, 190–92
    Northern primaries and, 173–74, 177, 182–83, 184–86, 188, 189, 191, 199–200
    NPL and, 174, 190–91
    one-party system and, 175–76
    runoff elections in, 173–74, 183, 184t, 186, 187, 192, 193, 194, 196–99, 196t, 210
    Smith v. Allwright and, 174, 196–97
    suffrage restrictions and, 199–200
    theories about, 175–79, 188–95
    unique features of, 195–99
    Voting Rights Act of 1965 and, 174
    white primary in, 182
Southern primary laws, changes to, 184t, 185f
    in Alabama, 179, 186
    in Arkansas, 186, 193
    Black voters and, 174–75, 177–78, 181–82, 186, 187, 194
    in Georgia, 179, 187
    history of reforms, 179–87
    in Mississippi, 179–80, 181–82, 193
    in North Carolina, 180, 181
    in Oklahoma, 183–84, 186
    party advantage and, 193–95
    Republican Party and, 194–95
    Smith v. Allwright and, 186, 187
    in South Carolina, 179, 186, 187
    in Texas, 186
Southwell, Patricia, 231–32
Sparkman, John, 192
Stennis, John, 178
Stephens, Kerri, 231, 233
Stephens, William Dennison, 169–70
suffrage restrictions, 199–200

Taft, William Howard, 99–100, 135, 170, 287–88, 291
Talmadge, Herman, 178
Tashjian v. Republican Party of Connecticut (1986), 131–32
Taylor Greene, Marjorie, 1
Tea Party, 14, 24, 83, 105–6, 235, 243–45, 256, 259

Teigan, Henry, 89, 91, 99–100, 101
Tennessee Voters Council, 192
Terry v. Adams (1953), 103–4, 186
Thurmond, Strom, 178
ticket balancing, 132–33, 135–36
Tingley, Clyde, 54–55, 133, 162–63, 171–72
top four primary, 211, 279–80, 289
top two primary. *See* blanket primary
Townley, Arthur C., 86, 87–88, 89, 91, 92–93, 94–95, 96, 97, 98–99, 100, 104–5
Troiano, Nick, 287–88
Trump, Donald, 1, 245, 279, 280–82, 283–84, 286, 287
Trump, Donald, Jr., 281
Turner, Julius, 173
two-party competition, 32–33, 42, 55–56

uncontested primaries, 213t, 216t
U'Ren, William, 69

Valelly, Richard M., 181
van Biezen, Ingrid, 225
Van Dunk, Emily, 154
Vardaman, James, 180, 188–89
Voting Rights Act of 1965, 174, 187

Wallace, George, 192
Wallace, Henry, 69
Wallace, Schuyler C., 209
Walsh, David, 73–74
Walton, Jack, 190–91
Ware, Alan, 3, 11, 27–28, 30–31, 38–39, 57, 66–67, 147, 173, 203–4, 231, 254
Warren, Mark, 136–37
Wasson, Jesse T., 208–9, 254–55
Wekkin, Gary D., 74–76
Wendland, Jay L., 206–7, 231, 234, 235–36
Western Tax Council, 104–5
Weyl, Walter, 61, 63, 64–65, 66–67, 68, 70
White, William Allen, 61, 63, 65–66, 67, 80–81, 82, 189
white primary, 182, 186, 197
Whitman, Charles Seymour, 139
Wiley, Maya, 282
Wilson, Andrew, 115–16, 119
Wilson, Woodrow, 67, 143, 180
Woodward, C. Vann, 177–78, 189
World War I, 29, 68, 69–70, 91–93
World War II, 8, 42–44

Yarborough, Ralph, 175–76
Youngkin, Glenn, 281